Banting

A Biography

Banting

A Biography

Michael Bliss

McClelland and Stewart

Financial assistance of the Ontario Arts Council toward the
publication of this book is gratefully acknowledged.

McClelland and Stewart Limited
The Canadian Publishers
25 Hollinger Road
Toronto, Ontario
M4B 3G2

Canadian Cataloguing in Publication Data
Bliss, Michael, 1941–
   Banting : a biography

Bibliography: p.
Includes index.
ISBN 7710-1573-9

1. Banting, Frederick Grant, Sir, 1891–1941.
2. Medical research – Canada – Biography.
3. Diabetes – Research – Canada – Biography. I. Title.

R464.B3B54 1984   616.4′62027′0924   C83-099208-1

Printed and bound in Canada

Contents

Writing about Banting

Sir Frederick Banting died in an airplane crash in 1941, during his fiftieth year. At the time of his death he was world-famous for his role in the discovery of insulin some twenty years earlier. He was also the commanding figure organizing medical research in his native land, Canada. He was killed while on a secret mission to Great Britain regarding wartime scientific research.

Banting's close associates, who mourned him deeply, were surprised to learn that there were more dimensions to the medical researcher than they had realized. Intimate personal diaries were found, literally beside his body. His young widow, Henrietta, Lady Banting, showed to the scientists he had been working with at the National Research Council other diaries, as well as a two-hundred-page manuscript he had written only a year earlier describing the discovery of insulin. She possessed more notebooks and papers he had accumulated over the years. Some of Banting's pen portraits were very impressive, their quality equal to the sketches and paintings he did in oils.

The president of the National Research Council, C.J. Mackenzie, considered publishing a little book of Banting's writings, organized around the insulin manuscript. Then Mackenzie and his co-workers at the NRC realized that some events in Banting's life were too controversial for publication, particularly in the form that Banting treated them in his writings: bluntly, honestly, passionately, pulling no punches. This "problem" with Banting's life and writing was as true of the insulin period – in many ways a bad time in Banting's career which his friends did not think should be written about in isolation – as it was of his last years, when he was a more mature man but just as fierce a hater. Nor were his likes and dislikes constant. As Mackenzie described the problem to General Andrew McNaughton, "Many of those whom he despised and hated twenty years ago have become his closest, most intimate and loyal friends today and some of those who were closest to him then became incompatible throughout the years." He was referring particularly to J.B. Collip and Charles H. Best, the surviving co-discoverers of insulin.

To cap the issue, almost all of Banting's war work was being kept secret at the time of his death. Neither the details of Banting's last mission nor the report on the crash of his plane would be released during the war. Some of his war work, such as his involvement in biological warfare, would remain classified for many years. Mackenzie, who acted as one of Henrietta Banting's unofficial advisers, concluded that neither a book of Sir Frederick's writings nor a full-scale biography could be published for the time being. But eventually it should come to pass. "Some day his complete life with all its strengths and weaknesses should be written for posterity."[1]

This book is Banting's complete life, insofar as it can be known from all his surviving diaries and papers, and from interviews with people who knew him. It is not the first biography of Banting. It proved impossible and undesirable to prevent his life story being told soon after his death. Two biographies were published in 1946, both based on extensive interviews, both utilizing passages from some of his diaries and letters. Neither *Banting's Miracle*, by an American physician, Seale Harris, nor *Sir Frederick Banting*, by Lloyd Stevenson, a young medical graduate from the University of Western Ontario, was a bad book for the time. In fact both contained accurate general portraits of Banting. Stevenson's biography, which became the standard, contained many thousands of words taken from his travel diaries, as well as many Banting anecdotes and appraisals related to Stevenson by his friends. Both books have been drawn upon at times as primary sources for this biography.

But the earlier biographies were seriously incomplete. Without access to the vital documents relating to the discovery of insulin, which were under lock and key in archives from Toronto to Stockholm, neither Harris nor Stevenson could present a clear, authoritative account of the most controversial and most important event in Banting's life. Neither author had access to Banting's uncensored diaries and correspondence. They did not know many of the details of his personal life; writing almost forty years ago, when most of the *dramatis personae* were alive, they may have chosen not to publish some of the details they did know. Consequently these first Banting biographies did not probe very far into the depths of Banting's motivation, his problems in research and in human relations, his real feelings about the people he lived and worked with. Because they were written so close to his death, and in a less frank generation, they could not present what Banting himself once asked for in the story of a life: "the true picture of the struggling human soul, with weakness, strength, ideals, shortcomings, imperfections." Banting hoped such a book would be "absolutely honest."[2]

This book is almost absolutely honest. I had unrestricted access to Banting's papers, which are owned by the University of Toronto, and spent hundreds of hours interviewing everyone I could find who knew Banting. I used many other collections of personal and public papers. Because most of Banting's friends and associates are dead, I have been able to write far more freely about his life than any previous biographer. His war correspondence has all been declassified. Still, I have withheld two or three pieces of information the publication of which would deeply hurt living people without significantly altering the portrait of Banting. They may someday be added to a revised edition.

This book has been about three and a half years in preparation. My attitude towards Banting went through several stages as the work developed. I first became involved with him only as part of a desire to satisfy my curiosity about how a great and controversial event, the discovery of insulin, had happened in Toronto. Banting's life after insulin did not seem of much interest, for from the point of view of scientific achievement it was little more than a long anticlimax.

One night early in the insulin research, I found myself taking detailed notes as the widow of the co-respondent in Banting's sensational 1932 divorce told me the inside history she had heard from her husband. I was seeing her reluctantly, really only as a favour to a distinguished Toronto medical man who was being helpful about insulin. He had not seemed to understand that my interest in Banting stopped about the time the Nobel Prize was awarded in 1923. If anything, my insulin research was causing the interest to diminish, for I had soon realized that Banting was neither the sole discoverer of insulin nor a great or even a very good scientist.

As I listened to the outrageous, almost ridiculous story of the Banting divorce, which is presented, following much more research, in Chapter Nine, I began to realize that it was also a sad and revealing episode, and one which the earlier biographers had avoided. Perhaps it was grist for a Banting biography yet to be written. For the first time I began reading Banting's post-insulin writings carefully, particularly the more than fifteen hundred pages of diary he had compiled in the last eighteen months of his life. This reading revealed that Banting was much more interesting as a man than as a scientist. He grew upon a reader of his diaries because he appeared to be an honest, unpretentious son of rural Ontario, wrestling with a reputation and position he had never expected to have, dealing with people and responsibilities that constantly threatened to overwhelm him. He was not without strengths: native shrewdness, intense determination, a wry sense of humour, an impressive achievement in self-education as a writer and painter. He also touched the life of his time at many points, starting with insulin, but also as a friend of the Group of Seven (which dominated Canadian art between the wars), as a sympathizer with Russian communism, as a divorced man tangled in the thickets of his generation's moral dilemmas, and as the central figure launching Canada's medical research effort in Hitler's war.

The book I was working on, *The Discovery of Insulin* (published in 1982), was going to diminish whatever reputation Banting had as a scientist. That did not seem either inappropriate or unfair; when I interviewed C.J. Mackenzie and asked him whether he believed Banting was a great scientist, he had replied simply: "No. Neither did Banting." But perhaps it might be possible, appropriate and fair to lower Banting's scientific stature in one book, and then write a second book about the life of an engaging and important human being.

This biography is necessarily a study in the problems of being a hero. Insulin catapulted Banting into fame and adulation that were with him for the rest of his life. Banting's seemed to be a kind of Horatio Alger story of Canadian science, the raw, untrained genius who had started with nothing but an idea and faith, and then conquered all obstacles on the way to achieving brilliant triumph. Five years after the discovery of insulin the world saw another example of such heroism in Charles Lindbergh's solo flight across the Atlantic. Banting and Lindbergh had much in common. Both were indeed raw and unequipped to handle either everyday prominence or the public's expectation of future triumph upon triumph. Both were shy at first and then increasingly hostile when faced with the unrelenting glare of publicity, particularly in the news media. The press's obsession with the details of their personal lives, centring in Lindbergh's case on the kidnapping and murder of his first son, and in Banting's on his divorce, helped create in both men a deep distrust of North American democracy. Then they went different ways, with Lindbergh appearing to flirt with fascist ideas, while Banting wholly approved of the treatment of the press and other aspects of life in Communist Russia. At bottom, of course, both men were intense patriots and proved it in wartime. In an odd twist of history, Banting went to his death in 1941 as he was about to become one of the first handful of men to fly the North Atlantic in winter.

A popular hero's life after his achievement is often an anticlimax. The later years are unhappy, as the memory of the achievement, the challenge to repeat it, and the failures to meet expectations, begin to weigh heavily. In *The Great Gatsby*, F. Scott Fitzgerald refers to the "acute limited excellence" of a star college football player and his wistful lifelong search for "the dramatic turbulence of some irrecoverable football game."[3] In Banting's case the burden of his fame was increased by the huge question mark hanging over the achievement itself: not just the gossip that Banting had been lucky to be in on the discovery of insulin, which was bad enough, but the stories, largely true, that he could never have got to insulin at all without the skills of his collaborators, Macleod and Collip, men whom he heartily despised during the discovery period. For Banting, insulin was not a clear-cut personal triumph, not an unambiguous demonstration of even limited excellence. He was not Babe Ruth in 1927, perhaps not even Roger Maris in 1961. Was he really worthy of the honours he had won, the stature most others automatically accorded him? The conflicting desires to prove himself unequivocally and yet to lead a normal, quiet life caused Banting nearly endless turmoil and unhappiness. His difficulties handling his fame were magnified by his failure to marry a woman who could cater to his unusual needs. In this area of life Charles Lindbergh was incomparably more fortunate.

Books about the problems of men attempting to live with fame almost always appear to be debunking. Referring to his friend

11

Lindbergh, the novelist John P. Marquand once told George S. Kaufman, "George, you've got to remember that all heroes are horses' asses."[4] To many readers for whom Banting has only been the name of a famous Canadian discoverer, this biography will seem to diminish him as a man and a scientist. At times, Fred Banting's capacity for being a horse's ass seemed almost unlimited.

Most people who knew Banting knew this. A fair number of them, ranging from scientists who wrote him off as an inconsequential bumbler, through friends of his first wife who found his cruelty and boorishness unforgivable, had no regard for Banting. Readers who understand this situation will find, I hope, that Banting is more human and engaging than they had expected. At the least, he is a man for whom all of us who recognize our own limitations ought to have a certain sympathy. As a biographer I found Banting sometimes to be silly, childish and pathetic; I also found him extraordinarily complicated, refreshingly honest and deeply moving as he struggled to cope with pressures and situations that continually threatened to overwhelm him.

In the context of his country and his times, Banting seems to fit the novelist Joan Didion's definition of a "great literary character" as "a character so ambiguous and driven and revealing of his time and place that his gravestone might well contain only his name and nationality."[5] Banting's life reveals his time and place in several ways. He was a farm boy, brought up in a traditional rural culture, who was thrust into big city life. He was trained to be an ordinary physician and surgeon, yet found himself at the head of a world-class medical research facility. His upbringing was based on the traditional Christian beliefs of his community; he found himself wondering whether there was anything to cling to in the wreckage of them after the Great War. He was brought up to be a manly man and treat women the way his father had treated his mother, only to find out that women and many men had changed; he could not find his mother, or be exactly like his father.

An unsophisticated man who had won a Nobel Prize, Banting was caught between generations, between North American ways of life. He is a product of old traditions, who is fated to be modern. Throughout his life we will see him try to get out of this predicament, try to escape, usually through a journey, first from London, Ontario, to Toronto, then anywhere to get out of Toronto. No novelist could have invented a more appropriate end to a life than the way Banting's concluded in Newfoundland in 1941. While he was alive, the closest Banting came to peace of mind was sometimes on his trips to Quebec with A.Y. Jackson, where they made modern sketches in oil of traditional subjects.

Banting's was a North American life. In most ways the border means as little in his biography as it does in the history of insulin or medical research or apple pie. But readers who have some familiarity with Canadian culture – the place and the people who have been written about by Stephen Leacock and Donald Jack and Hugh Hood, among others – will recognize Banting as particularly located in the Canada of his time. His nationality goes with his name on his gravestone, and the several references in this book to the writers who have helped me understand the dimensions of Banting's nationality are not casual.

The details of Fred Banting's life after insulin will tempt many readers to become armchair psychologists. As a biographer I have been wary of presenting anything like a psycho-biography of my subject. There are several reasons for caution. First, many generalizations about individual psychology still rest on shaky and controversial theoretical foundations. Second, even though the sources for many chapters in this book are unusually rich and revealing, there is so much that we do not and cannot know about key areas of Banting's life – his relations with his parents and his siblings, for example, or his sexual impulses, or the affair with his first fiancée – that too confident generalization would be both unhistorical and unfair to Banting. Third, for all his veneer of down-home simplicity, Banting was an extraordinarily complex man, very difficult to categorize easily. We see a little of this complexity in pictures of him, I think, for his face is so expressive that it reveals a different Fred Banting almost every time the camera clicks.

A biographer's job is not to write a case history anyway. It is to re-create a life. The biographer tries to do what Walt Whitman requires of the poet. He "drags the dead out of their coffins and stands them again on their feet. . . . He says to the past, Rise and walk before me that I may realize you."[6] This book is an attempt to stand Fred Banting again on his feet.

CHAPTER ONE

"A White Boy, a Right Boy"

F red Banting was born in the downstairs bedroom of his family's clapboard farmhouse on November 14, 1891. The Banting farm was on the third concession line of Essa Township, Simcoe County, in the province of Ontario, about two miles from the town of Alliston. It is rich, slightly rolling countryside, Canadian heartland, some forty miles north of Toronto.

His earliest memories were of being bathed on his mother's knee before the kitchen stove, the warmth of the fire, his mother's kisses, and the rhyme on his toes,

This little pig went to market
This little pig stayed home . . .

She would tuck him into bed with the prayer, "Now I lay me down to sleep," blow out the lamp, and leave him to rest. At first he was afraid. Someone, probably one of his big brothers, had told him there were bears under his bed. "Tho' scared and timid I talked gently to myself & bear & since he did not bite my face I became bolder. I finally crawled under the bed & felt all around. The next time I heard of bears being under beds I proudly denounced the idea."[1]

The big clock on the shelf at the head of the kitchen table set the times of his day. Time to get up. Meal time. Church time. Later on, time to study lessons. Bed time. The family Bible rested on the shelf beside the clock; it was taken down every morning after breakfast for family prayers. Every Saturday night Fred's father opened the painted glass door – palm trees and a faded moon – of the clock. The clock smelled old inside. Mother kept the little bottle of rat poison there. Only the right-hand weight, controlling the ticking,

15

needed winding; the old clock would never strike the hour. Fred could not figure out why because he could make the clock strike by pressing down the little rod below the face. Someone told him the clock only struck on its own to foretell a death in the family.

The best time of the day, he remembered, was after the supper dishes and evening chores. The family would sit around the kitchen stove. His father would read aloud while his mother mended or knitted or did fancy work. "Father was very sympathetic and if the hero of a romance was good or to be pitied his eyes would fill with tears until he could not see. He would clear his eyes with the back of his strong firm hand but the reading would go slower & slower until mother, impatient to hear the exciting part, would say 'Will I read a while now father?', and gently take the book and read till the touching part was over and then father would read the dry descriptions."

On winter evenings when town company came everyone sat in the parlour. It was usually a cold room, full of stiff-backed chairs, an old melodeon, sea-shells under the table, a what-not in the corner, and all sorts of trinkets, including a disc of polished olive wood all the way from Jerusalem. Fred's father would get a fire going in the big box-stove with the nickel trimmings and the mica window. As the hardwood blocks blazed, the stove would glow dull red. By bedtime the room would be boiling hot. Mother would bring out a dish of butternuts or popcorn or Northern Spy apples and then Fred would be ordered to make the cold trek upstairs to bed.

The Bantings were of British descent, having been in Canada since 1842 when Fred's grandfather, John Banting, had come out from Ballyfrim, Northern Ireland. John Banting's fifth son, William Thompson Banting, was born near the Simcoe County hamlet of Bond Head in 1849. Like his father and other Bantings before them, William Thompson Banting became a farmer, working land in Tecumseh township. In 1879 he took as his wife twenty-five-year-old Margaret Grant, daughter of the mill manager in the nearby village of Alliston. Of Scottish descent, the Grants had been in Canada since at least the 1830s. William and Margaret Banting had six children: Nelson (1881), Thompson (1882), Kenneth (1884), Alfred (who died of whooping cough as a baby in 1886), Esther (1887), and, just after buying the farm near Alliston in 1891, Frederick Grant. He was always called Fred or Freddie.

William and Maggie Banting were hard-working, God-fearing

folk, the salt of the earth. William was a taciturn, somewhat dour man, a pillar of Alliston's Wesley Methodist Church, one of the best and most progressive farmers in the community. He made his one-hundred-acre farm bear fruit, grains and vegetables, cattle, sheep and hogs. As turn-of-the-century farm families went, the Bantings were well-to-do, members of the upper ranks of their agricultural community.

"Father was one of the most tolerant men I have ever known," Fred remembered. "As a consequence neighbours who were mean to him, who were dishonest and tried to put things over were the first to turn to him to seek his help in times of trouble. When neighbours quarrelled they often came to him instead of going to law. When there was sickness in their homes they wanted him to visit. When they had difficulties and wanted to borrow they came to him and he was usually able to help them. He was respected and loved but also criticized and beaten in a deal. People even blamed him for their failures when he was more successful than they. But he was always very tolerant." William Banting tended to be a very private man, and declined repeated invitations to serve on local municipal councils.

Fred thought his father's even disposition explained the special relationship he seemed to have with the farm animals. "The dog would lie at his feet when we as kids wanted to play. The cat would follow him as he went about the work of the farm. . . . Every animal of the farm knew him & did not shrink from him. Cows, horses, sheep, pigs, the cat, the dog – all trusted him."

Maggie was William's helpmate, a typical farm wife who worked at least as long and hard as the head of the family, her husband. She loved her husband, loved her children, gloried in hard work, especially in keeping her home neat and clean, and, with William, enjoyed reading in the evenings. She was a very traditional wife, who kept her place, taking pride in her husband's and her children's achievements. Perhaps all these farm women were downtrodden by our standards; but William Banting was solicitous enough of his household that he enlarged and bricked the house in 1903, and installed indoor plumbing in 1907, at that time an almost unheard-of luxury on Simcoe County's concession lines. On Sunday evenings Maggie and William liked to walk arm-in-arm down the lane the full length of their farm, watching the crops grow, taking pride in their accomplishment.

None of Fred's reminiscences suggest that he was particularly close to or influenced by any other Grants or Bantings. To be sure, his mother passed on her family's lore, usually stories with an obvious moral. Grandmother Grant, for instance, as a girl used to have an iron collar placed around her neck if she was bad in school and she once carried a sick child twenty miles from Bolton to Toronto to have it seen by a doctor and then carried it home. A great-uncle was stabbed in the back at a dance because he danced with another fellow's girl, developed a progressive paralysis, and died at the age of thirty-four. Great-uncle Sam, whose funeral Fred attended, was a runt all his life because one day when he was about 14 and left alone in the house he got into the cellar with a bowl of sugar and a mug to experiment with the barrel of whiskey. The oily old rye knocked him out for four days and he never grew again.

Uncle Sam and Aunt Mary Jane had three adopted children. Mary Jane had had one child of her own, who was born dead. The mother fainted during birth and when she revived was told that the baby had been buried. It was thought to be bad luck for a mother to see a stillborn babe – she might never have another child. No matter what the consequences, Mary Jane was determined to see her baby. Three days later she slipped out of the house and dug up the grave. "Maggie, I have seen hundreds of new born babies but I never saw a finer and more perfect one in my life. I looked him over every inch. I held him on my knee and cuddled him. Then I was satisfied."

So there were elements of Hardy in the Bantings' rural background. Years later, Fred learned of his distant Dickensian relative, William Banting, a London cabinet-maker who in 1864 published his method of reducing corpulence by avoiding fats, starch and sugar. "Banting" entered the language – it can be found in the Oxford English Dictionary – as a description of what was later called dieting. The verb was to bant, and you could bantingize or practise bantingism.

Back in Canada, Fred Banting's boyhood was in most ways an amalgam of Norman Rockwell, Tom Sawyer and Stephen Leacock's Mariposa (the model for that town, Orillia, was not many miles away from Alliston). Fred was born into a stable family and a stable rural community in a relatively stable and prosperous time for his country. We have a farm boy of the eighteen-nineties and early nineteen-hundreds, usually barefoot and overalled: riding old Sue as his father ploughed; helping mother gather eggs and feed the chickens; bringing in the cows; picking huckleberries and thimble-berries on an outing to the Pine Plains; throwing stones at old Tom McKnight's yellow-eyed mongrel; walking past the cemetery on a dark night and being scared by a cow; skinning the skunk he caught in the chicken coop and selling its oil as a rheumatism cure; helping at soap-making and maple-sugaring; skating and playing shinny on the Boyne River in winter, swimming in the summer; building doghouses for Jap, or Collie, or Kruger; watching the circus parade and getting a free pass in reward for some hard trench-digging; playing tag at the church social and stepping on Mrs. Martindale's violin, hiding in terror in the Banting democrat, trying to get out of next Sunday's Sunday School, and then the relief of seeing Mrs. Martindale and her violin whole.

In those years most North American farm boys learned quite a bit about the people who had been there before, the Indians. Fred's parents told him many stories of the Indians who used to live in the Alliston area – his mother had actually been the first white child born in the settlement – and he always kept an eye out for arrow- and spear-heads in the fields. The area right around the Banting farm had been an Indian camping place; the plough would still turn up ashes from their fires. When Fred saw his first Indian, an old man who wore white man's clothes and sold baskets, he found the image confusing. This was not the savage, noble redskin he had heard so much about.

Fred remembered much of his growing up fondly. His farm boyhood was the stuff of good nostalgia. But all his life Banting had a passion for honesty, and sometimes in his late night reflections wondered if he, or anyone else, could write a really true auto-biography. When he looked back frankly, he remembered that he had actually been a lonely child on the farm. He was four years younger than his sister, seven years younger than his next oldest brother. "My older brothers could not be bothered with me for the most part." There seem to have been no other playmates on neigh-bouring farms, and he was drawn to the farm animals and his pets for lack of human company.

When he started school, at about the age of seven (kindergartens existed only in a few big city schools), Fred Banting was a shy, skittish boy, who found the long walk between home and Alliston monotonous and tiring. It was worse still being at the school in town – being a country boy at the town school, having to eat a cold lunch in a hallway or the basement while the town kids went home for dinner. Being left alone there to be picked on by the bigger farm boys who found it was easy to make little Freddie cry.

I developed a horror for this hour and a half at noon and the cold lunch. Many times I threw my lunch into the river or more frequently gave it to the Maybury's dog to save carrying it. During the first couple of years at school . . . I used to take my lunch and go down by the old fair grounds & sit alone by the side of the road & eat it. . . . Those lovely lonely lunches stick deep in my memory as unhappy times. I remember on one birthday, Nov. 14 (and by this time it is cold weather) that it was firmly fixed in my mind that what one did on ones birthday happened every day in the year . . . and on this birthday, the 6th or 7th, I did my best not to cry the whole day. I went at lunch time off to the fair grounds to fill in the time until afternoon school. I was alone and tried so hard not to cry that despite myself I started – which naturally meant that I would cry every day in the year. This thought made me cry all the more. I could hardly get over it in time to get back to school. I had been taught that if I cried to be quiet about it so whereas I never howled the least thing made me cry both at school and at home. Crying tends to separate a child from other children for even children dislike a cry baby and I had no friends in the world.

School hours were not much better than lunch hour. "I lived in constant terror of being asked a question in class. Even if I knew the answer I was never able to tell it before the class. I liked composition and geography but of all the things in this world that contributed to my unhappyness it was spelling. I simply could not spell. Every word seemed to have about three ways of spelling. It was a guess and I invariably guessed wrong." He covered hundreds of scribbler pages writing words out five, ten, a hundred times. All his other grades suffered because on every exam he lost all possible marks off for spelling mistakes.

In later life Banting thought these early experiences either created or were the product of an inferiority complex. Whether or not this was an exaggeration, he was certainly an uncommunicative and unsocial lad. The earliest second-party account of his relations with other people came to me from a ninety-year-old distant cousin, Marion Walwyn, who first met Fred one day in 1901 when they were both ten years old. "We sat together in the swing in our yard. In an hour he didn't say one word."

He tended to turn to the farm, his animals, and his mother for solace and refuge. He became something of a mother's boy, though no amount of time they spent on his spelling seemed to help very much.* His father was more distant, getting on with a farmer's work while leaving problems like these to the boy and his mother. Fred seems to have respected, obeyed and later admired his father. There is no evidence of any serious disobedience or father-son conflict.

Fred was just beginning to grow up when he suffered the ordeal of the button boots. When he was about twelve, he needed a new pair of boots for school. His Scotch mother handed down to him a pair of almost new high-button boots that sister Essie had found too small for her embarrassingly large feet. To mother they were excellent quality boots, perfectly useful. To Fred they were girls' boots, with small high heels and buttons coming up each side halfway to the knee. He didn't dare wear them to school.

Every day he would take the back way through the fields to the Scotch Line bridge over the Boyne, take off the boots, hide them under the bridge, and go on to school barefoot. "Each day I hated those boots more bitterly. I kicked every stone or stick I came across in order to ware them out. I wet them each morning in the river so they would rot. I tried to grind thro' the soles with a rough stone but they were made of the best of leather. As the weather grew colder all the other boys put on their shoes & stockings and I found myself the last one in bare feet. This was a bad perdicament."

By the last week of October it was a desperate predicament, and came to a climax the morning when there was snow on the ground. He had to wear his button boots to school.

He got to school by the back fields and back streets, waited outside the yard till the bell rang, then dashed for his desk. He was surprised – and, he recollected wryly, a little disappointed – when no one noticed the boots. All through the lesson, keeping his feet up under his desk, he wondered what he would do at recess. As he bolted for the back door the worst possible thing happened: he ran

---

*It did not seem necessary to reprint every spelling oddity in Banting's unpublished writings, so I only allow the occasional error to stand in quotations, as a reminder of his problem.

into "Smack" Godden, the class bully, a smoker and swearer and renowned fighter, given to extorting candy from the little kids. Smack chased Fred Banting into the yard, taunting him – "sissie", "little girl", "wearing mother's boots." At that last taunt, Fred started fighting back (at least he did in memory, writing about this incident in 1931). "Fight! fight!" they all cried. It was a famous fight, with everyone crowding around, and Fred holding on desperately until Smack's smoker's constitution gave out. "Finally breathless & overcome with rage & blood he burst into tears & covering his face in the sleeve of his blouse he lay down a pitiable ruined supremacy. The bell rang & we all rushed to our places. I was the hero of the hour. It was the first time we had ever seen this bully & tyrant in tears. The button boots had done it. I almost liked them."

He could wear the boots to school now, but a few days later when he had to walk down Victoria Street with his mother he crowded close to her long skirts to hide the boots from adult view. When she asked what he was doing, he confessed. "My dear child, why didn't you tell your mother? Come right in and I'll buy you a pair of boys' boots."

Fred replied to an unfriendly, frightening world with stubborn, passive resistance. The four or five lickings he got during his school days were all for stubbornness, he remembered. Later in the year of the button boots a teacher gave him a tongue-lashing before the class for being unable to answer a question. He said nothing, but at noon picked up his books and went home. He told his mother he was never going to school again as long as he lived. "She explained to me that it was a terrible thing to say & that I must go back, but I was determined. While we were still talking, father came along & mother explained that I would not go to school – My father simply said – 'Why that's fine. We'll be needing an extra man and there is plenty of work – It is too bad you can never be anything more useful in the world than a labourer but a good honest worker is alright. Think it over & in the meantime put on your overalls and clean out the hen house.'"

Cleaning the hen house was the most unpleasant of all farm chores, worse than shovelling manure. "Not another word was said but the next morning I started off to school as usual." To drive the lesson home, William Banting made cleaning the hen house Fred's Saturday morning job.

Every farm boy had to decide by his teens how long he would stick it out in school. Most never finished the eighth grade, dropping out before taking the entrance examinations to high school. A few carried on a year or two more; a very few took the final matriculation examinations at the end of the twelfth grade. Ontario farm boys who could handle high school sometimes went on to spend a year or two at the Ontario Agricultural College at Guelph (this was John Kenneth Galbraith's educational path, for example). Rural high school graduates who went on to university were a distinct elite, no more than one or two out of every hundred from the gang that started school. The graduation rate was little different in the city. This should be kept in mind as we consider Banting's struggles with his higher education. The fact that he seldom achieved very good grades does not mean that he was intellectually mediocre. The examinations he had to endure were far harder than today's equivalent; so was the marking. In both his educational aspirations and his achievements, Fred Banting was far superior to most of the young men bred on Ontario farms in the early years of the century.

His aspirations were unusually high. Partly they were a reaction to the drudgery of cleaning hen houses and other farm chores. Partly they were passed on by his family, who believed in reading, writing and getting ahead in life. Fred's grandfather, John Banting, had urged his sons to pursue their education; William, who was needed on the farm to help support his older brothers' aspirations, was the only one who did not get substantial schooling ("and yet by the time of his death in 1929, at the age of 80 years my father was one of the most highly educated men I have ever met," Fred wrote). The standing offer William made to his sons was a gift of $1,500, a horse, harness and a buggy, when they turned twenty-one. They could use the money any way they wanted. Nelson, Thompson and Kenneth spent their portions helping to establish themselves as farmers. Fred spent his on higher education.

His boyhood and his parents – perhaps also his lessons in the Methodist Sunday school – taught him what was possible with hard work. All anyone had to do in these farm communities was walk down a concession road and look at the fences, the crops, the houses and barns, to see how work and thrift paid off for some farmers, sloth and sloppiness held others back. A neighbour, Tom McKnight, was a frequent visitor to the Banting farm. Lazy and mean himself, old Tom was always predicting that William Banting could never make his land pay. The Bantings prospered. One morning old Tom was found hanging from a rafter in his house. He was little better than the tramps who wandered the countryside, sometimes begging meals or bedding down in the barn, always worrying the farm women. A roving lumberman once spent a night in the Banting hayloft, was taken in for breakfast, and gave the good lady the only suitable possession he had, a mug stolen from a bar. It became baby Fred's mug.

William Banting used to make his sons responsible for their own animals: "That lamb may live if it is nursed. If you look after it and it lives it is yours." According to Fred, "We always had a share in things, responsibilities and profits. We made or thought we were making our own money and it gave a feeling of independence, responsibility and interest." When Fred was still a young boy his father bought him a $1.50 pocket watch from the city. William Banting told Fred not to wind it too tightly; if he took good care of it he'd get a gold watch when he was older. Unlike most of his chums with watches, Fred never tried to take his apart. It worked for ten years until the mainspring broke. Then William Banting gave Fred the gold watch he kept for the rest of his life.

The Bantings spent a lot of time at church activities, and it was said by friends and relatives that William and Maggie hoped Fred would enter the Methodist ministry. A dutiful son, he did not rebel against his upbringing, and according to people who knew him he certainly memorized a lot of verses from scripture in Sunday school. He learned to take life seriously and purposefully, to try to live by a moral code and to expect others to do the same. His first secretary remembered how earnestly he could lecture her on the need to ask herself what she had done each day to make the world a better place. There is no evidence in any of his autobiographical writings, however, that Fred was deeply religious or spiritual. The farm, his animals, his horrible experiences at school, were all more real, or more memorable, to him than anything that happened at church. In the one fragment of recollection that mentions church life, Banting writes of the "strenuousness" of the week-to-week activities and then dwells on the pleasures of church sleigh-rides, Sunday school picnics, and lawn socials.

By his late teens little Freddie Banting had developed into a tall, wiry, tough young man. He was big-boned, and almost a six footer. He began to find himself in school sports, playing on his school's football and baseball teams, sometimes playing on a makeshift

Alliston town team. The great competitions were at picnics and on holidays, especially the big spring holiday, May 24th, Queen Victoria's birthday. The high point of Banting's youth was the 24th at Beeton when he played two football matches, three baseball games, competed in base running and ball throwing, and after covering all his expenses brought home $8 as his share of the prize money. We used to see superb H.T. Webster cartoons of a country boy after a day like this – he looked a little bit like Fred actually – entitled "The Thrill That Comes Once In a Lifetime." The Fred Banting whose photograph was taken with Wes Dugey in ball uniform about 1910 is a happy young fellow, his smile stretching from first to third, ready for anything.

Including young women. His first girlfriend was Isabel Knight, whose father ran a private bank in Alliston and whose cousin married Thompson Banting. Fred was still shy, but he seemed to think deeply about things, and Isabel liked his quiet, chuckling sense of humour. He was turning into a great kidder.[2] A big fellow to admire on horseback, when he rode old Betsy to high school, and maybe would give a girl a ride on the way home. Of course he was doing a man's work on the farm now (a farm boy's inheritance at twenty-one included a lot of back wages). At the end of a hard day's work with the Clydesdales in the fields, Fred would hitch up his mother's pony, Mollie, to the light buggy, get himself spruced up and then go out driving with his girl. On Saturday nights the young farmers liked to show off their horseflesh on that good stretch of gravel east of town. Fred could hardly hold Mollie back when she got in a racing mood. The hired hands and the townies rode around on their bicycles.

The country boys had a few things to learn though; they were a little hayseed, a little bumpkin. One year the captain of the Alliston volunteer militia promised to make Fred a corporal if he persuaded enough of his friends to join up. He did so and was given his corporal's two stripes. The day the men gathered in their new bright red uniforms to leave for training camp Corporal Banting made his appearance with a stripe sewn on each arm.[3]

A lot of Fred Banting's deep thinking was about his subjects at school. In July 1908, after two years at high school, he took his junior matriculation examinations. The passing grade was 33 out of 100. Fred's marks were: English Composition, 30; English Literature, 39; English Grammar, 26; British and Canadian History, 46;

Ancient History, 42; Algebra, 40; Geometry, 41; Arithmetic and Mensuration, 40; Physics, 24; Chemistry, 52. His Physics and Chemistry averaged out to a pass, but he had to repeat his English Composition paper and pick up French and Latin to matriculate. The next July, 1909, he squeaked through in Latin, failed his French, and failed his English "Comp" again. He considered giving up, had a long talk with his principal, and decided to stick with it. "We would not have picked him for one on whom fame should settle," Principal Davidson said later. But Fred kept trying. "He was a white boy, a right boy."[4]

It is not clear what Fred was intending to do if he ever got through school. There was his parents' hope that he would be a minister. His own preference, as he stated on his application to university, was to become a teacher. He may have also had medicine on his mind. He later wrote down a story about stopping on the way home from school one day to watch two men shingling a roof. As he watched, their scaffold broke, they both fell, and were badly hurt. Fred ran for the doctor. "I watched every movement of those skillful hands as he examined the injured men & tended to cuts, bruises and broken bones. Both men recovered. In those tense minutes I thought that the greatest service in life is that of the Medical profession. From that day it was my greatest ambition to be a doctor." The ambition may have been helped along by the time he spent hanging around Hipwell's drug store in town, run by an uncle. His cousin, Fred Hipwell, was, and always would be, his greatest chum.

Fred Banting's own health had always been excellent. Once he had almost cut off his thumb trying to make a dog house for Kruger and fainted when his mother cleaned the wound with turpentine. Another time he had had a bad reaction to vaccination; he later wrote that mosquito bites caused him to revaccinate himself from head to heel. During the worst of the reaction he sat burning with fever in church while the minister preached on St. Paul's text, "I must see Rome." He went to bed right after the service and had a terrible nightmare in which Paul was chasing him all around his room to take him to Rome. "I finally escaped from the room & rushing down stairs ran into mother's arms to escape Paul."

He escaped from English Composition and French by finally passing his papers in July 1910. Perhaps as a reward, his father bought him a round-trip train ticket to see the Canadian West. He went as far as Winnipeg with Fred Hipwell, who was to work on a relative's farm that summer, and then kept going on his own. He pulled into Calgary at five one morning and had a job digging rose trenches at Terrill's florists by seven. A week of 15-cent meals at one of the local Chinese restaurants did him in, though, and he had to quit. He went on to Edmonton and took a room at the cheapest hotel he could find, 50 cents a night. He remembered it as a two-storey frame tavern with a verandah and hitching rail across the front. Above the verandah was a balcony, "and here were congregated four or five girls which I took to be waitresses or chamber maids. They talked, giggled & gossiped." Banting's reminiscences break off as he is describing a conversation with a shifty-eyed stranger over supper that night, and nothing more is known about his stay at the cheap "hotel" in Edmonton. Perhaps it was an event there – or one that happened some time in the next thirty years – that caused him to scribble in one of his little notebooks, probably in the 1930s, "I once called at a Lady House. I'll never call there again."[5]

From Edmonton he drifted back to Saskatoon where he spent the rest of the summer stooking wheat and riding the binder on the farm of a former Allistonian. The images that stayed in his mind were of the huge meals he ate and of seeing his first coyote.[6]

CHAPTER TWO

Becoming a Man

B ack from the West in September 1910, Fred Banting enrolled in the General Arts course at Victoria College of the University of Toronto. It was logical that he would attend the nearby provincial university, which was also the largest and best in both Ontario and Canada, and it was logical that he would enroll in its Methodist college, Victoria, which had become affiliated with the University several decades earlier. His local Methodist minister, the Reverend Peter Addison, went with him on his first day to register. It would not have been easy for a country boy to find his way around either the University or the bustling metropolis of almost half a million people.

Little is known about Banting's first year in university. He apparently roomed with his cousin, Fred Hipwell, sang in the college glee club and worked hard. His grades are on record. The passing mark was 40 out of 100. Banting obtained 40 in Latin, 40 in English, 50 in Mathematics, 43 in Biology, 53 in Greek and Roman History, 35 in German, and 25 in French. He was required to write supplemental examinations in German and French in September. He passed his German with a 40, but failed French with 34. Having failed to complete his first year course, Banting was not allowed to enter second year.

He was back at "Vic" for the 1911-12 session, presumably repeating first year. By now, if not before, he had decided that he wanted to become a doctor. To be admitted to the Faculty of Medicine he had to have passed first year, which at that time in Ontario was the equivalent of senior matriculation. Learning that the University's Senate would, in special cases, grant a student matriculation into medicine, Banting petitioned in February 1912 to be allowed to enter medicine. His petition was granted, apparently on condition that he pick up the missing arts course during his medical studies.

The decision to abandon arts for medicine was not taken lightly. Banting was a confused young man, who must also have been wondering whether to give it all up and settle down to farming. One of his classmates remembered a weekend at Alliston where there were long discussions and "prayerful review" of Fred's options. He also talked the situation over with Rev. Addison, who told him that he ought to follow his own rather than his parents' desires. When Addison offered to tell William Banting of the decision to change course, Fred said, "Thanks, but I can speak to him myself. He'll understand." One version of William's understanding was that he said he'd go along with anything so long as the boy made up his mind. After all, Fred had turned twenty-one now, was a man, and was still trying to figure out what to make of himself.[1]

Having cleared the way to enter medicine the next September, Fred dropped out of Victoria College and spent the spring and summer of 1912 working on the farm. His earnings and his father's gift would cover the cost of his education. He must have been sensitive about his relatively advanced age, for in applying to the Faculty of Medicine he lied about it, giving his birth year as 1892 instead of 1891 (on his Arts application he had left a blank). It made him appear closer in age to Fred Hipwell, who was also enrolling in medicine that fall, having stuck out second year at Victoria only to fail the final examinations. It is not clear whether Banting had influenced Hipwell to choose medicine or vice versa.

Falsifying his birth date was the kind of innocent lie that Fred's new girlfriend, Edith Roach, would not have approved of. They had met in the summer of 1911 when Edith's family moved to Alliston where her father took up duties as Methodist minister on the West Essa circuit. Edith was a quiet, intelligent, willowy, Browningesque girl, appropriately but not offensively strait-laced. Her first dates with Fred were probably assignations to attend church together. Then there were church picnics, boating outings on the Boyne, sleigh-rides and skating and parties in the winter.

If there was dancing at some of these parties, even square-dancing, Methodists like Fred and Edith would be somewhat perplexed, for their church and probably their parents still frowned on dancing as intrinsic or prospective sin. The Bantings do not seem to have been as rigid as some Methodist folk, so Fred probably made up his own mind about dancing. He decided that he did not much care for it. He may have had as much Methodism in his feet as in his soul – the dancing steps just did not come naturally to Methodist boys or farm boys. There is no evidence that Fred had as yet developed any taste for liquor either, which was more strictly tabooed in Methodist circles. Acquaintances' recollections are unclear as to whether he was still a non-smoker – yet another habit banned for upstanding Methodists, but in fact being taken up by almost all normal young men. For all his seriousness and adherence to Methodist mores, Fred was a normal young man. Along with whatever minor vices he had adopted, he liked to tease Edith about boys' and girls' things. She sometimes felt he was going too far with it, and made clear her displeasure.[2]

In September 1912 Fred came down from Alliston to enter the first year of the University of Toronto's five-year course in medicine. For an earnest youth, brought up to believe in doing good and serving his fellow man, medicine was not a bad alternative to the ministry. By the second decade of the twentieth century, doctors and most things medical ranked high in public esteem. The bad old days of the early nineteenth century, when ignorant lanceteers bled their patients to death or poisoned them with mercury and arsenic, were long gone. Even the helpless days of more recent times, when good doctors knew that about the best they could advise was to let nature take its course, were passing away. Doctors were now much closer to understanding and being able to treat sickness.

The great nineteenth-century researchers, such as Pasteur and Koch, had uncovered the mysteries of infectious disease. Now vaccines and antitoxins and sanitary reforms were starting to reduce the death toll from typhoid, diphtheria and even tuberculosis, building on progress already made against smallpox and cholera. Lister's introduction of aseptic and antiseptic techniques, following closely on the adoption of effective anesthetics, had revolutionized surgery and childbirth, as well as hospital procedures. Instead of being death houses for the poor, hospitals were starting to become institutions where even well-off people went to have operations and babies and advanced medical care. Many of the well-to-do were starting to give money to build hospitals, to build universities in which more good doctors could be trained, and to build facilities for medical researchers whose work would lead to still more triumphs of modern medicine.

Consider only one example. It was not talked about in genteel company, but what a magnificent achievement of applied research had come out of Germany in 1908 when Paul Ehrlich's endlessly painstaking experiments led to the development of Salvarsan as a specific treatment for syphilis. It was a discovery that would save hundreds of thousands of lives, a great gift to frail, sinful humanity. Ehrlich was one of the early winners of those magnificent prizes that Alfred Nobel, the Swedish dynamite titan, had established in his will, to further research and discovery. The very existence of a Nobel Prize in physiology or medicine, first awarded in 1901, was a symbol of the public's fascination with and support for medical research.

The researchers and the surgeons were certainly impressive, but no medical star shone brighter than that of the great physician, Canada's own Sir William Osler. First at McGill University, then at Johns Hopkins in Baltimore, and finally as Regius Professor at Oxford, Osler personified the physician as teacher, inquirer and gentleman. In his teaching, in his classic textbook and in his devotion to professional associations and his fellow physicians, Osler symbolized medicine's elevation from a trade to a calling, a way of life. Through his writings and his personal example, Osler inspired at least two generations of medical students and is still almost a cult-figure among classically inclined physicians. Osler was in England when Banting entered medicine and the two never met. But Banting would have known that Osler, who had attended a predecessor to the University's medical school, had opened Toronto's new Medical Building in 1903 with one of his famous addresses, "The Master-Word in Medicine." The master-word was "work," suitable advice to Canadian medical students from one of their own. Osler had been born in Bond Head, Simcoe County, the same hamlet as William Banting, and in the same year, 1849. They had been baptized by the same parson, William Osler's minister father.

The new Medical Building that Osler had helped dedicate at the University of Toronto was tangible evidence of the enthusiasm the University, the city and the province of Ontario evinced for keeping abreast – or, better still, moving into the first ranks – of modern medicine. A movement to modernize the whole university in the early 1900s put special emphasis on reforming medical education, particularly by creating a great teaching hospital for medical students and university researchers. Generous private citizens and governments poured money and equipment into the University, outstanding new people were hired (Osler turned down the presidency of the University of Toronto, but the man who took the job, Robert Falconer, did superlatively well; he was particularly committed to the furtherance of research and graduate studies). When the completely rebuilt, relocated Toronto General Hospital opened its doors in June 1913, the city and the University possessed one of the world's finest hospital facilities. Toronto did not yet have McGill's international reputation in medicine, but in the early twentieth century it was one of the largest, best-equipped, and best-staffed medical schools in North America.[3]

Why, then, was it incredibly easy by today's standards for Banting, a failing arts student, to be admitted to medicine? There were many reasons, but most of them boiled down to the limited number of applicants for medical training. The pool of literate young men and women was still small, and its currents were mostly classical. The material rewards of medical practice were not yet large. The hours were long, the vacations short. After the wars it would be hard to get into medicine, and some schools had quotas on Jewish students, but as late as 1960 almost anyone who applied and met the minimal entrance qualification was automatically admitted at most Canadian medical schools.

As a medical student at Toronto, Fred Banting was just another face in his class. He did not stand out in any way, except perhaps as a good inter-faculty rugby player. He roomed with another Simcoe County farm boy, Sam Graham, at the Gloucester Street residence of an Irish family, the O'Neals, not far from the University, paying $5 a week for room and board. Fred Hipwell stayed in the same house. Graham remembered Fred Banting as being particularly hard-working, studying long into the night after Graham, a math student, had gone to bed. For relaxation the boys would go skating or out for a walk. Fred's walks were often down Church Street to the Clarks, where their niece, Edith Roach, might be visiting from Alliston. Later she lived with the Clarks while she studied modern languages at Victoria. Fred learned much of his medicine on long evenings spent at their home studying with Edith.[4]

Fred's marks improved in medicine, possibly because of Edith's influence, possibly because he was rid of English and other difficult languages. His grades now ranged from bare passes to decent A's, averaging about a middle B. He was apparently slightly above average in his class. He had more difficulty picking up that last damned arts course to complete the first year requirements. Giving up on French, he tried Mechanics and Physics, failed it on his first attempt in 1912-13, then finally scraped through with a 41 the next year.

Fred worked on the farm in the summers. During the winter he wrote his mother every Sunday, a habit which he continued for the rest of his life. Once or twice a term he would take the train up home for a weekend. His sister would meet him at the station, and they would walk over to where the horses were waiting in the church shed. "I would call out − 'Where are you Mollie?', and a whinnying would answer me half way down the row. A white head would turn to me & an excited greeting await me as I hugged her neck & patted her. She knew my voice and I knew her whinny. She could almost talk. I shall always remember the conversations that we had on those nights when I returned from college & hugged her all over & how she talked back."[5]

Other times Edith might be with him, and what a stir Fred and his girl would make when they showed up in church together: the handsome local boy studying to be a doctor and the good-looking minister's daughter who people were starting to say was going to be his wife. There were other Sunday nights in the city when he was alone or with Graham or Hipwell, and they would drift over to the 25-cent Sunday supper put on by the Philathea Bible Class of St. James Square Presbyterian Church. You could eat a huge meal there and sleep it off during the service afterwards. Another pleasant way to spend a Sunday evening in a city with so many churches to choose from was to take young ladies to church. One time when he and Sam Graham were taking Edith and Mabel Clark to a Baptist service, Fred suggested they wear their cadet uniforms. They were amused when the minister asked the Lord's blessing on the men in uniform in the congregation.

There was good reason for that blessing if it came after the British Empire's declaration of war against Germany. Most Canadian men in uniform would sooner or later be sent over there to the Western Front. Intensely patriotic all his life, Fred Banting wanted to go to war. He tried to join the army on August 5, 1914, the day after Canada's war started, and again in October, but both times was rejected because of his eyesight (by now he wore glasses). After the next school year, his third in medicine, he tried to enlist again and this time was taken as a private, soon promoted to sergeant, in the Canadian Army Medical Service. He spent the summer of 1915 in training camp at Niagara Falls before returning to Toronto on furlough for his fourth year. During most of that winter he lived in an army hospital for returned soldiers, doing night duty while attending classes in the day. To speed up the education of doctors, the University condensed the fifth year for Banting's class, offering it in a special summer session in 1916.

Banting later wrote that his medical training was "very deficient." Much of the deficiency came from the shortening of the fifth year, during which he accumulated, he remembered, only five pages of lecture notes.[6] The lecture notes he kept from some of his third and fourth year courses show that his teachers were giving him a good grounding in academic medicine as it was taught in the early years of the century. His third year notes in anatomy and physiology are detailed and highly technical. The surgery lectures started mundanely with inflammations and swellings, for which were recommended such old-fashioned treatments as blood-letting (including the use of leeches to take blood from difficult places, such as around the eyes), along with the use of counter-irritants such as mustard plasters and blistering. But they went on through a wide range of surgical procedures, giving much attention to gangrene and shock, and discussing such advanced techniques as blood transfusion.

Banting kept a particularly complete set of lecture notes from the therapeutics course he took in fourth year from a Toronto practitioner, Dr. G.W. Ross, who was one of the part-time professors in the faculty. The course was vintage advice for a would-be general practitioner, encompassing recommendations to use up-to-date drugs such as aspirin for headaches and arthritis, practical tips (obesity: "patients are enthusiastic at first but they don't want to help. Tell them they have fatty hearts & they must do as you tell them." Syphilis: "tell him what your fees will be & collect them first"), and discussions of some of the most advanced therapies. In this last regard, virtually a full lecture was devoted to the recently published Allen treatment of what Banting spelled "diabetus." Based on his experience with patients at the Rockefeller Institute in New York, Dr. Frederick M. Allen was recommending that diabetic patients, whose disease meant that they were unable fully to metabolize their food, be allowed to consume only as much food as they could metabolize. Diabetics should be put on a starvation diet until the tell-tale sugar in their urine disappeared, then given carefully measured, increasing amounts of food until their tolerance levels – just below the point at which they would show sugar – were found. Banting's notes on the diabetes lecture contain sample diets, with special reference to the thrice-cooked vegetables Allen recommended to provide nearly carbohydrate-free bulk, comments on the value of exercise, and recommendations that patients learn to do their own urine tests. "Chief point in Allen's treatment," Banting noted, " – not dangerous to starve patients – not always best for them to maintain their own weight."

The lecture made little impression on Banting in 1916. He had no particular interest in diabetes. Stories told after his death about his having been profoundly affected by the death of a diabetic chum in Alliston have no foundation. None of the patients he examined during his fourth year clinical work in medicine at Toronto General Hospital was diabetic. "I remember seeing one patient only on the wards of the Toronto General Hospital. I heard of people mostly well on in life dying in coma and believed there was nothing one could do. I was never interested and knew nothing of diabetic diets. There was no such thing as a diabetic on any ward in my surgical experience."

It was surgical experience that the young medical student was most interested in obtaining. By 1915 he had made up his mind that surgery would be his specialty. He may have been influenced by his own physical handiness. He may have been influenced by the glamour surgeons enjoyed in those years – they were the medical men who could really repair the body. His experiences at Niagara in the summer of 1915 seem also to have been important: he was inspired by one of the officers there to think about surgery, and one of the nurses told him that if he ever got the opportunity he should work under Dr. Clarence L. Starr, the chief surgeon at Toronto's Hospital for Sick Children.

The next winter, while working in the soldiers' convalescent hospital and taking his fourth year lectures, Banting performed his first operation. A soldier with a large abscess or quinsy on his throat needed it opened and drained so he could go overseas with his battalion. Banting was the only medical person around and the orderly officer did not bother to ask whether he was actually qualified to wield a scalpel. Banting thought he could do the operation as well as anyone; just to make sure, he was still reading up on it in a textbook when it was time to start. He lanced the quinsy, breathed a sigh of relief when the pus welled out, and then didn't know what to do when the tired soldier fell into a sound sleep. Banting finally woke the patient up to see if he was alright. "I watched him all night for fear that he might have a haemorrhage. In 48 hours he rejoined his battalion as they moved out of barracks for overseas."[8] That summer Banting took his fifth year hospital training as an undergraduate house surgeon under C.L. Starr at Sick Children's.

Little is known about Banting's personal development during his college years. He was a rural boy at a big university in the big city. It was a big jump from country ways to city sophistication. Banting does not seem to have made more than a token leap. He was a solid, conservative, farmer's son. Proud of it, too. He was not interested in being a fancy dresser, a slick talker, or an airy-fairy intellectual. The thing to do was get on with the work, graduate, do your duty in the war, and then go on and do some good as a doctor.

The class of 1917 ("1T7" or "onety-seven" in Varsity parlance) finished its final examinations in October 1916 and graduated on December 9. Banting received the then first degree in medicine, a baccalaureate or bachelor's degree, making him Frederick Banting, M.B. Passing fairly routine examinations set by the College of Physicians and Surgeons of Ontario gave him the right to practise medicine and be informally called "doctor." These exams were held at a special session before Christmas because most of the newly minted doctors were about to leave for action: on December 10 every able-bodied member of Meds 1T7, Banting included, had reported for military duty.

He was promoted to lieutenant, spent several months working at a base hospital in Toronto, was sent to Campbelltown, New Brunswick, for a month, and finally sailed from Halifax for Britain and the war on March 26, 1917. Before leaving he had become engaged to Edith Roach, sealing their pledge with the gift of a diamond ring. Studying the old Clark family snapshot of Fred and Edith reclining in the grass at Alliston in 1915 – printed here in the picture section – takes us back to the idyll of innocence at the start of the Great War. The other couple in that 1915 snapshot, Sam Graham and Ella Knight, were still alive in 1981 to reminisce about Fred and Edith and growing up Methodist in Alliston before the Great War.

Banting's work as a student at Sick Children's had evidently impressed C.L. Starr. Starr, a specialist in orthopedic surgery, had also enlisted in 1916 and was posted abroad to the Granville Canadian Special Hospital (Orthopedic) at Ramsgate, Kent, just across the Channel from the battlefields in France. According to Banting, Starr requested that the young doctor be assigned to assist him. On May 2, 1917, Banting took up his duties in the English resort hotels which had been converted into the Granville Hospital.

Starr was doing pioneering work in nerve suturing, the effects of which might not be evident for years. He asked Banting to compile special case records for follow-up later. Fred's earliest surviving letter was written on May 6, 1917, to his former girlfriend, Isabel Knight (we will see later why his fiancée, Edith, eventually destroyed all his letters):

> You will be a little surprised to hear from me, but this is for your father and mother too and not all for yourself. You know Edith might not like it if it was.
>
> Well after many tribulations I have landed a posting at this hospital, and am now very happy under Lt-Col Starr. He is absolutely the finest man both as a gentleman and Surgeon that I have met, and it pleases me that fortune was so good as to allow me to come and work under such a man.
>
> . . .On a clear day on the eastern horizon France can be seen and when the wind is from that direction the heavy guns can be heard. The Granville overlooks the sea from a 70 foot rock and boats of all kinds are always to be seen in the Channel. Air raids are always interesting of course, but do but little harm. Such things make one forget the war but those patients with arms & legs off always recall it very quickly.
>
> My work is entirely Surgical and Col. Starr has given me a very interesting task of collecting nerve cases that have had the nerves sown together. I may also do some experimental work for him. I am glad to get some useful work again, for the last two months have been very long, but I think time will go much faster now. I may add that it cannot go too fast till I get back to Canada again. I will be glad to hear from you anytime.[9]

Banting stayed with Starr at the Granville Hospital for thirteen months. In January 1918 he wrote Isabel from the hospital's new location in Buxton, Derbyshire, that he was looking after 125 patients, assisting at operations three mornings a week, and being "doctor" to about a dozen families of Canadian servicemen. He didn't charge for these extra services, he wrote, for "it gives me a certain amount of pleasure to be able to help them which repays me in a way that money never could. I was at a home last night that I wish you could have seen. A sick mother, two children already (and another soon), not many comforts, no money. But such things teach us what good we can do and I came home quite happy myself tho with a feeling of pity. Isabel I think you had better train for nursing and let music and art go for some things more real."[10]

He still had plenty of extra time on his hands ("I found there was more wasted time in the army than in almost any occupation or profession in the world"), so Banting decided to try to upgrade his professional credentials by qualifying for membership in some of the colleges of physicians and surgeons in Britain. He began studying every night to take the examinations. "I do not know what I would do if I were not busy," he wrote Isabel, "for one gets the habit of being 'on the go' and as well as getting something done one keeps out of trouble, and the latter is inclined to present itself too often over here."[11]

The reference to trouble may be a vague allusion to an incident known through the oral history of the Starr family. Despite his engagement to Edith, Fred is said to have fallen in love with one or more English girls and fallen into the habit of bringing back expensive presents which the girl[s] would not accept. Dr. Starr's daughter, a nurse in the unit, wound up returning them.[12] The story reinforces an image, which seems to be accurate, of a moonstruck Canadian farm boy abroad, Banting as Bartholomew Bandy (they had a distinct physical resemblance), a young innocent who needs help, especially advice from older and wiser women.

His first examination towards Royal College certification was in obstetrics and gynecology. Banting thought he had passed the written paper. "But an old examiner named Stevens took the oral. He had written a book on the subject which I had never heard of let alone read. His third question was a definition from his book. I was plucked." Angrily he burned all his notes and gave away his books. In a memoir he claimed this was part of an experiment to prove the unfairness of the British examining system. With no further preparation he repeated the exams three months later, got a decent oral examiner, and passed. He eventually got his other exams, and was starting to study toward the difficult examinations for fellowship in the Royal College of Surgeons of England when he was suddenly transferred for service in France. "I gave up all hope of a try at further examinations and wrote to my mother and told her that I would sooner win the Military Cross than an F.R.C.S."[13]

Captain F.G. Banting went to France late in June 1918, where he was posted to No. 3 Canadian General Hospital and then to No. 13 Canadian Field Ambulance in the Amiens-Arras sector. He was used as a relief officer, filling in wherever he was needed.

Having fought off Germany's desperate offensive in the spring, the Allied armies were beginning to mount what became their final triumphant attacks. Banting got his first taste of close medical support duty on August 8 — what Ludendorff called "the black day of the German army" — when Canadian forces attacked east of Amiens. He worked in dressing stations and casualty clearing stations, receiving the wounded who had been sent back after first aid at the advanced posts. His job was to clean, close and dress their wounds, then send the men further back to base hospitals. After several days' frantic work "clearing" the wounded (it was a matter of professional pride to clear a battle's casualties as quickly as possible), the battle tapered off and there was time for sight-seeing and souvenir-hunting. Banting was anxious for action, and briefly hoped he could go on from France to serve with the Canadian forces being sent to Siberia. In spare time between battles he continued to study anatomy: on August 16 his war diary records, "Started on the thirteen day campaign to read anatomy fifty pages per day." That campaign was cut short on the 26th when he was posted as medical officer to the 44th Battalion, 4th Canadian Division, which was on its way north to join the fighting around Arras.

As a battalion medical officer he was in the front lines, serving as a kind of general practitioner to the thousand men in the unit, commanding the stretcher-bearers, and being the first to treat the wounded in action. On September 2 the 44th joined the attack. Banting described the day in his war diary:

The barrages were terrific on both sides. I went over the top with the battalion. we passed through heavy shell-fire and gas valley [*sic*]. I dressed a few in a sunken road west of Dury then went on to Dury. . . . By this time the battalion was out of sight. Sniping and shells prevented further progress so I returned to the south-west corner of Dury to the quarries and established R[egimental] A[id] P[ost] in Hun Dressing Station using their dressings and Red Cross Flag. . . . The wounded poured in and I kept eighteen bearers and twenty to thirty Huns carrying out. A couple of nice Heinies worked around all day. One said, "La guerre est fini pour moi". From about 11 a.m. till 10 p.m. I got a little sleep during the night but had to wear a gas mask for about four hours.

The next day he caught up with his battalion and stayed with them, establishing new aid posts in bombed-out cellars as they moved forward, working under steady shelling. He was withdrawn for a few days' rest, and then became involved in preparations for the assault on Cambrai. It began with "an absolutely wonderful" barrage on September 27.

Banting saw a lot of war in those days and weeks. Once (according to notes he later made about a certain "Captain Grant") his wounded had not been cleared when the Germans counterattacked. He stayed with his patients, and had his life saved when a sergeant whose foot he had just amputated shot down a German in the door of the aid post. Another time Banting and his batman, Kells, were forced to take shelter in a German trench. Picking their way around mutilated corpses on the trench floor, one of the Canadians trampled on the bowels of a live German. The dying soldier was in agony, apparently gesturing for relief. "Will I shoot him?" Kells asked. Banting walked on, four steps, before he heard the pistol shot.[14]

While reconnoitring locations for aid posts before the Cambrai show, Banting and his superior, Major L.C. Palmer, suddenly heard shells coming in. Banting dove into a ditch full of the putrefied remains of a mule. When he came out, "plastered with dead mule and smelling like a glue factory," Palmer laughed and laughed – until the next shell drove them both for cover.[15]

A few days later Palmer marvelled at Banting's stamina and courage. When the attack started on the 27th, Fred worked all day clearing casualties for the 44th Battalion, then went over to the 50th Battalion's aid post to work all night. Learning that the medical officer of the 46th Battalion, which had taken over the assault, had been hit, Banting determined to get forward to help with their wounded. Taking a party of stretcher-bearers with him, he headed toward the front. The Canadians were making a difficult, bloody attack across open terrain in the teeth of continuing German shelling and resistance from machine-gun nests. When several of the men with him were wounded, Banting stopped to attend to them, and became pinned down in a stretch of sunken road.

While trying to figure out what to do next, Banting saw one of the rare sights of the Great War, a mass of cavalry galloping to the attack. They soon turned and retreated in the face of German fire. Banting watched as their leader, now riding behind his men, was thrown headlong from his horse by a shell that seemed to explode directly under them. The horse got to its feet, started galloping away, then stopped and returned to its rider. "The horse stood perfectly still while he slowly climbed into the saddle. When he grasped the rein the horse galloped off. I stood and watched him go . . . hurdling shell holes, ditches, and the debris of war." He always remembered and was fascinated by the intelligence and discipline the animal had shown.[16]

About an hour later, apparently as he was making a dash for the battalion's advanced dressing station, Banting was hit in the arm by a piece of shrapnel from an exploding shell. He wanted to stay at the front; but Palmer, who was at the post after a day's harrowing experiences of his own, insisted on taking him "out" to get his wound properly treated. This was the end of Banting's front-line duty. Palmer later recommended that Banting be decorated for his valour. He was awarded the Military Cross. "His energy and pluck were of a very high order," the official citation concluded.[17]

The war experiences were Banting's final rites of passage into manhood. The lonely little boy, crying by a ditch in the Alliston fairground, had become a veteran medical officer, risking his life to save other men's lives on some of history's most bloody battlefields. He had proved his manhood, his toughness, his courage, his guts, in action. He proved the worth of his training as a doctor, and found it exhilarating to know that he was literally saving men's lives as he tended their wounds. Captain Banting was a quiet fellow, and, in his spare time, surprisingly studious. He was starting to lose his shyness as he became one of several brotherhoods: the class of 1T7 who had taken their medical training together, and the brotherhood of Canadian men who had served their country in battle. Banting's experiences abroad were not making him more sophisticated exactly; rather, he was becoming more manly. He liked to drink and smoke and swap stories with his medical or his army buddies, enjoying the bonds of male fellowship later caricatured in a million

41

beer commercials. In fact it was a way of belonging that filled an intense need in Banting and countless men of his and most other generations. A little frightened of the complexities of life, not at all sure how to behave in the presence of women, a little lonely, you found security and acceptance and could come out of your shell when you got together with the fellows, the boys, the old gang.

An L-shaped piece of shrapnel had entered Banting's right fore-arm between the bones. By late evening on the 28th he had reached the casualty clearing station where a surgeon gave him a smooth anesthetic and took out the shrapnel. There was no fracture, but some damage to the ulna and its nerves. The arm was painful, but next day Banting was able to travel across France in an ambulance train, scribbling a left-handed letter to his mother: ". . . NOW PLEASE DON'T WORRY. I AM THE LUCKIST BOY IN FRANCE." Within two days he was in England in a general hospital in Manchester, able to write right-handed again. The surgeon had said the wound would be six weeks' healing, but Fred estimated he would be back in France in two. One of the senior surgeons from Sick Children's and the Granville Hospital, Dr. W.E. Gallie, came to see him and also thought there would be no problem.[18]

The prognosis was incorrect. Banting spent the next nine weeks in hospital. The stories he later told about his wound were not always consistent or credible,[19] but it seems that the moderate infec-tion Gallie had noted in the wound became much worse. Or, perhaps, there was continual hemorrhaging. Banting later said, many times as the boys sat up late at night reminiscing about the war, that at one point the doctors were considering amputation, but he refused and took charge of his treatment himself. The truth in this could range from somebody saying "If the arm becomes too much worse it'll have to come off," to a carefully considered decision, influenced by a patient's wishes, to take the risk that a gangrenous infection would not spread to the rest of the system. No doubt Banting bossed his nurses, telling them what to do when the regular doctors were not around.

He was released on December 4, 1918, three weeks after the war had ended. He spent his sick leave in Scotland, introducing himself to a number of the medical people in Edinburgh, who were very hospitable to a wounded medical man from Canada. On Christmas Eve he was invited to dinner at the home of A.H.F. Barbour, who had written a famous text in gynecology with one of Banting's former Toronto professors, B.P. Watson. After dinner there was memorable doctor-to-doctor story-telling about the medical life. Fred was thinking about the possibility of doing graduate work in Edinburgh, he wrote Isabel Knight, "But alas the two great enemies 'time' & 'poverty' prevent."[20]

Banting resumed his duties at the Granville Hospital, and was back at his studies for a fellowship in surgery, when he was recalled to Canada in late February, 1919. He had a rough winter passage home aboard the *Belgic*, working as a medical officer the whole time. A brother officer on that passage remembered Banting as a tolerant doctor who would bend the rules for an honest soldier. Detecting a case of venereal disease at "short-arm parade" one day, Banting extracted a pledge to follow instructions and let the poor fellow go back to civilian life.

The ship landed at Halifax in early March. Banting was anxious to get back to civilian life, but was first posted to Christie Street Hospital in Toronto for another six months of helping mend and straighten and manipulate the broken bones of soldiers.

CHAPTER THREE

Getting out of Town

B anting was discharged from the army in the summer of
1919. To complete his training as a surgeon he decided to
spend a year at Toronto's Hospital for Sick Children. C.L.
Starr, by now a medical father-figure to him, had returned there,
and was surrounded by a cluster of bright young surgeons, some of
whom Banting had already worked with or under, including W.E.
Gallie, L.Bruce Robertson, and D.E. Robertson. Banting hoped to
join this group of rising surgical stars. He would practise surgery in
Toronto with his main staff appointment at Sick Children's.[1]

The decision to take another year of apprenticeship could not
have been made without considerable thought. The war had taken
almost three years of Banting's life after graduation. He was now in
his late twenties, and did not have much money. During the year at
Sick Children's he would have no more than a token income. Edith
had been waiting for him since their engagement in 1916. She had
graduated from Victoria College, winning the gold medal in Modern Languages in 1918, and was now beginning to make a living
teaching high school. When would they get married?

Why not now, with Edith supporting Fred while he was finishing
his training and getting on his feet as a practising surgeon? Fred
would have found the prospect humiliating. In most of his attitudes
to women and marriage he was intensely conservative, reflecting his
own family's traditions and values. In Canada in the 1920s a self-
respecting young man did not get married until he could support
his bride. If she was working herself, it was only until marriage;
then she would immediately retire to make a home for her husband
and bear and raise his children. Fred and Edith would simply have

44

to wait until Fred's training was over and he became established in his own right.

Perhaps they were not unhappy at the prospect of waiting a bit longer. Soon after Fred's return from the wars, he and Edith began to wonder if theirs was truly the heaven-made match every couple dreamed of. No reliable details of how and why and exactly when things started to go wrong can be found. Acquaintances' sixty-year-old memories of Fred and Edith's relationship are partisan and contradictory. The stories add up, though, to a picture of two young people beginning to question the uncritical image each had had of the other.

By everyone's testimony, Edith found some of Fred's habits disturbing, such as his readiness to swear and take a drink, and possibly the heavy smoking habit he had brought back. Oh, the boys were never the same after the war. Or perhaps the trouble was that Fred was too much the same, still a country boy who was not going to turn into the perfect gentleman after all. (This could be deceptive, for Fred could be a perfect gentleman with women when he wanted to be; Edith was finding out that he simply would not be on his best behaviour all the time.) After a few years and in a different light those manly traits were not quite as attractive as they might have seemed in the student days. Nor were the uncertainties about the future. Was Fred really growing up? When was he going to mature, settle down, stop hero-worshipping people like Dr. Starr, start becoming financially secure?

Edith, on the other hand, appears to have matured into a successful young woman, earning her own way in the world, having a mind of her own. Stories about her having developed other "interests" while Fred was away are true in the sense that she had realized there was more to life than doggedly waiting for her man to marry her. She was not going to be the docile, obliging helpmate that Fred's mother was to his father. She was a much more modern woman.

These changes, or persistences, in the couple's personalities led to the beginning of a troubled time in their relationship. What form did the troubles take? There is only one specific story: Fred once tried to get Edith to slip onto a streetcar through the exit doors with him so they wouldn't have to pay. She objected. We have to imagine the molehill swelling into a mountain, causing a profound personality clash, discussions of ultimate morality, days and weeks of strain and silence. As someone has said, the trouble with Methodists was that they had a tendency to stand always at attention morally. During the war Fred had learned to stand at ease occasionally.

Through the autumn of 1919 and into 1920 young Dr. Banting carried out his duties as a senior house surgeon and registrar at the highly regarded Hospital for Sick Children. He kept a record of his surgical experiences – a daily list of the operations he gave the anesthetic for, assisted at, or did himself. Much of the work was general surgery, ranging from routine removal of tonsils and adenoids through appendectomies, the setting of fractures and the removal of swallowed safety pins. Starr, Gallie and the others did a lot of orthopedic work, on which Banting would assist, correcting cleft palates and hare lips, lengthening tendons, attacking bone deformities. Banting was involved with twenty to thirty surgical cases a week. By the end of February 1920 he had assisted at 232 operations, done 101 on his own (mostly "t & a"s), and given 106 anesthetics.

He often participated, first as an assistant and then on his own, in a blood transfusion procedure being pioneered in the hospital as a result of Dr. L. Bruce Robertson's war work. Robertson had decided that a substantial number of severe infant maladies could be combatted by a change of blood. Babies would be ex-sanguinated by the insertion of a needle into the fontanelle or soft spot on top of the head, with new blood being injected into a vein. Twenty years after his Sick Children's internship, Banting recalled doing one of these blood replacements on a baby suffering from a bad scalding:

> The child suffered from severe shock and it was found that about one-sixth of the body surface of the child had been scalded with boiling water. The Surgeon looked at the child and said that there was little hope. I asked him if I might draw off blood and then give a transfusion. He did not think it worth while but said 'Go ahead and do anything you can, but the child will likely die.' This was all I could ask for. The child was so young that the fontanelle had not closed so I got Dr. Roy Simpson to draw off blood. Dr. Robert Janes drew blood from the father and when Simpson had bled the baby until it was white I started to inject new blood. In all we drew off 280 cc. and injected 350 cc. The child stood it well. Next morning the child's temperature was nearly normal and the child seemed fine. We were delighted but

46

in another 24 hours the temperature had gone back up to 105F and the child was again very dangerously ill. The ex-sanguination was repeated with again a favourable result. After a third transfusion the child completely recovered.

Banting's memory for events like this was never very precise – few people's are – and it was typical of his tendency to highlight, embellish and forget, that he claimed it was the first case of ex-sanguination "of which I had ever heard."[2]

He made this claim in a passage in his "Story of Insulin" manuscript aimed at refuting stories about his never having done medical research. He instanced the wartime work with Starr compiling the case records of the nerve sutures, as another piece of research. (Back in Toronto, he remembered, he tried to follow up these cases, "but although some of the results were remarkably good, others were disappointing and many of the cases could not be traced.") During his period at Christie Street Hospital in 1919, he remembered, he became interested in seeing whether cartilage could be transplanted in the same way that some of his colleagues were working with bone. "I applied to the Committee on Research of the University and obtained a grant," he wrote in 1940. "Dr. R.I. Harris and I carried out many experiments in the old Pathology building." His papers contain a special "Cartlage" notebook from April 1919 which contains a few pages of notes he took from articles in a leading journal. There is no record of experiments, no published report, no reference in the University's records of research being supported at that time. The cartilage research was more impressive in memory and retelling than it was at the time. Banting was stronger at having ideas and planning projects than he was at executing them.

To be sure, Banting was more interested than the average doctor in advanced surgical techniques. He wanted to become a pioneering surgeon, like Starr, Gallie and the others, working out new procedures and operations, contributing to the onward march of medical research. It must have been a considerable disappointment to him when he learned that he would not be able to stay on at Sick Children's. The only explanation for this is his own brief comment in 1940: "Surgeons were very plentiful in Toronto. It was my greatest ambition to obtain a place on the staff of the hospital, but this was not forthcoming."

Banting seems to have been popular with his patients, the children at the hospital. Perhaps the appointment was not forthcoming because he had a run-in with a colleague: a remark in his memoir that he and Alan Brown, the autocratic physician-in-chief of the hospital, disliked each other, may explain a lot. Or there simply may have been no staff positions available. Possibly Banting was judged not good enough to be worth the trouble of making one available. It was natural in later years for friends to remember Banting as a skilful surgeon. Perhaps he was – he appears to have had skilful fingers. But perhaps as surgeons went he was only ordinary, even a bit less careful and painstaking – patience was never his strong suit – than many. The documents, including his own fragments of autobiography, do not reveal any noteworthy surgical achievements by Banting. He quickly abandons his specialty a few years and a few chapters from now.

Banting left the Hospital for Sick Children in June 1920, fully intending to practise as a physician and surgeon. On July 1 he commenced the practice of medicine in the city of London, Ontario, a prosperous inland community of about 60,000 people located 110 miles west of Toronto. London was the largest city in the rich southwestern Ontario peninsula. It was the home of Western University, which housed a small faculty of medicine with ambitious plans for expansion. Edith was teaching secondary school a few miles away in the town of Ingersoll. Assuming that Toronto was full of surgeons, London was a good place for Banting to choose to practise. Starr may have been influential in advising the move. William Banting and Thompson apparently lent Fred the money he needed to purchase the big brick corner house at 442 Adelaide Street in London from a local shoe merchant, Rowland Hill. The total purchase price was $7,800, with Fred putting up $2,000 and the Hills taking back a mortgage for the balance. Fred had no objection to letting the Hills continue to live in the house for a few months while their new home was being built – he wouldn't need all that space until Edith moved in as his bride – so he only occupied part of the house for his office and a bedroom. He took a few days off at the end of June to visit Sam Graham in Sarnia, obliging his former room-mate by doing a kitchen table hernia repair (they thought there would be less danger of infection than in the Sarnia hospital), and then opened for business in London.[3]

It ought not to have surprised Banting that patients were a long time coming. He was not following the custom of starting out with an older doctor or buying an established practice. He had no professional friends in the city who could refer patients to him and the summer months were not a good time to begin developing contacts. Advertising was prohibited by doctors' professional organizations. How would anyone find their way to Banting's office except as a drop-in who noticed the nameplate on his lawn? No sensible doctor trying to start a practice this way would have expected instant success or solvency. For at least the first year he would be bound to have a lot of time on his hands and not much money coming in.

It is not evident that Banting went to London with any sensible or clear expectations about his practice. Perhaps he did, and later magnified his disappointment for effect. More likely, he had just not given the matter of where the patients would come from very much thought. You hung out your shingle, kept your office hours, and the patients came. Banting duly hung out his shingle, kept his office hours, and nobody came. No patients. None. Day after day.

Banting had nothing to do. A hard worker all his life – there was never an end of things to do on the farm – he found the enforced idleness intensely frustrating and worrying. Here Banting's memory is accurate: his account book confirms that his first customer did not arrive for four weeks, until July 29. Then the stories conflict again: In the "Story of Insulin" Banting wrote that the patient was an old soldier who wanted a liquor prescription. (During this prohibition period in Ontario doctors could still prescribe alcohol for medicinal purposes. They and the druggists did a booming business. "It is necessary to go into a drug store," Stephen Leacock wrote, "and lean up against the counter and make a gurgling sound like apoplexy. One often sees these apoplexy cases lined up four deep.") But in telling the story of insulin to his cronies he used to say that his first patient needed to be treated for syphilis. In fact, on July 29 he recorded in his account book a $2 fee from one Carruthers for "baby-feeding."

Dr. Banting's July income from the practice of medicine was $4. In August it rose to $37, then to $48 in September and $66 in October.* By the fall he was developing professional contacts, for he was starting to do the occasional anesthetic and supplement his general practice with a few orthopedic cases, such as club feet and hare lips. (He was always proud of one of his first orthopedic cases, a

_____
*The easiest way to translate these figures into modern, devalued dollars is to multiply them by a factor of ten.

little boy born without a foot, for whom he constructed a wooden foot and brace. "I shall always remember the look on the boy's face when he stood up in his new outfit. He walked − then he ran − then he jumped on it and he could not take his eyes off it. Instead of tucking it under the chair, he put it out for everyone to see. The whole thing only cost me a few dollars and I was more pleased than the boy."[4]) To fill more of his time he got a job as a demonstrator in surgery and anatomy at Western, receiving $2 an hour. He also introduced himself to F.R. Miller, Western's Professor of Physiology, volunteered to help Miller with his research, and was soon spending hours helping Miller with interesting neurological experiments on cats.

By reasonable standards his practice was developing satisfactorily, but Banting did not see it that way. His expenses still exceeded his costs. He continued to endure whole days when there were no patients. He worried about the lack of business: were the physicians and surgeons of London conspiring to drive a competitor out of town? He worried about the location of his office: would he have been better off downtown, where his friend and classmate Billy Tew had started a practice in obstetrics late that summer? He worried about his debts, money, and the whole idea of being a practising doctor. Would he be better off somewhere else or in some other branch of medicine? Banting and Tew spent many evenings together comparing notes, damning London and wondering if they shouldn't have chosen some other line of work.

Fred also worried about Edith and their future. There she was in Ingersoll, a respected professional woman with a secure income. When would they be able to marry? Did she still want to marry? Who was to blame that everything was not what it should have been between them? Again, we do not know any details. Anyone who has ever been in love or read a good romance can imagine the confusion, the emotions and the frustration. For a healthy male, who knew a little bit about the world and the body, a considerable amount of that frustration would have been sexual, increasing the tensions in an unchaperoned, adult relationship with a minister's daughter.

He used up some of his excess energy building a garage for the old car he had bought. It was a beat-up fourth- or fifth-hand vehicle that went less than 250 miles and quit. Banting killed more time taking the car apart to see if he could get it going. He did, but "every mile was insecure and filled with trouble" − a fair description, too, of the driver's mood that season. Banting finally gave up and took the streetcar or walked. The realization that he had been gypped in the car purchase must have added to his sense of failure. At least in memory, he was now virtually poverty-stricken, cooking meals on the bunsen burner in his office, cutting out even the movies to reduce expenses. Eventually he arranged to take his meals with the Hill family.[5]

He developed a new pastime the day in July he was attracted to the window of a little store displaying pictures. It doesn't matter whether Banting's recollections are accurate in every detail here. They make a good story:

> I looked at one little print for a long time. It was called 'The Landing'. It showed men tugging on a rope, pulling a boat up onto skids out of the water. The thought occurred to me that I might paint such a picture. I went into the store, bought the picture for seventy-five cents and looking at it, asked the girl for red, blue, green, white and yellow colours. These she took out of little boxes and then I asked her for a brush. I knew absolutely nothing about painting and had never seen an artist at work. Apparently the girl knew little more for she sold me oil colours and a watercolour brush. I did not know the difference until some months later, when I met an artist. When I got home I took a cardboard that had come from the laundry in a shirt and commenced work. I found the paint too thick for my camel's hair brush and it said on the box "oil paints". I had not bought oil so I used castor oil from the dispensary. My happiest hours of this period were spent thus trying to copy pictures mostly from old magazines or books. I was very proud of some of them. On one occasion when I was particularly hard up I took some of the best to a dealer and tried to sell them. He passed some scathing remarks and laughed at my best efforts. I felt disappointed and offended.[6]

On Monday, November 1, 1920, Banting was scheduled to give a talk to one of his classes at Western on the subject of the pancreas. Edith spent the day with him on Saturday, October 30. He spent Sunday boning up from his textbooks on the anatomical features of the pancreas and its role in metabolism.

No one was quite sure what the pancreas's complete role was. The long, flat, blobbish piece of tissue, located below and behind the stomach, seemed to have more than a single function. It was clear enough that the main body of cells in the pancreas secreted digestive enzymes or pancreatic juice, which travelled out through the pancreatic ducts into the duodenum. That was the *external* secretion of the pancreas. But the organ seemed to do another job, for when it was removed from animals experimentally, their bodies immediately lost the ability to metabolize carbohydrates. Excess sugar built up in their systems, circulating at abnormally high levels in the blood, spilling into their urine. They began urinating frequently, and drinking and eating excessively. In short, depancreatized animals (researchers almost always used dogs, tough animals whose pancreas is much like that in humans) developed all of the symptoms of diabetes mellitus, "sugar diabetes," the metabolic disorder whose name comes from the Greek word for "siphon" or "pipe-like."

Ever since this relationship between the pancreas and diabetes had been discovered, by Minkowski and von Mering in 1889, scientists had postulated that the pancreas must emit some kind of *internal* secretion, some chemical substance that somehow normalizes the body's capacity to burn carbohydrates. Studies of the pancreas had shown that it contains separate clusters of cells, known after their discoverer as the islets of Langerhans, and these were probably where the internal secretion was produced. But no one had actually discovered or isolated the hypothetical internal secretion, so it was still just an academic hypothesis, leaving the pancreas as something of a mystery organ.

His talk prepared on that Sunday night, Banting went to bed, taking the November issue of a leading surgical journal, *Surgery, Gynecology and Obstetrics*, to read himself to sleep. His attention was naturally drawn to the first article, "The Relation of the Islets of Langerhans to Diabetes with Special Reference to Cases of Pancreatic Lithiasis," by Moses Barron, M.D. It was an unpretentious survey of the literature on pancreatic degeneration, built around Barron's study of a rare case of the formation of a pancreatic stone which had then blocked the main pancreatic duct. The blockage caused the pancreas to shrivel, or atrophy, Barron reported, particularly the acinar cells, which produce the external secretion of the pancreas. By contrast, the islets of Langerhans did not seem to atrophy, but remained relatively healthy. Barron had read of similar observations in cases where the pancreatic ducts had been deliberately blocked by being ligated or tied. The fact that diabetes did not develop in such cases of blockage and degeneration, unless or until the islet cells were damaged, seemed to reinforce the hypothesis, advanced by many others, that some secretion of the islet cells was critical in the prevention of diabetes. Barron's was an interesting article for a practitioner to read, good background for Banting's talk the next day, but nothing special as far as diabetes or pancreatic research was concerned.

Banting put down the journal and tried to get to sleep. Sleep did not come. Perhaps something had gone wrong with Edith the day before. Perhaps it was a touch of the restlessness from lack of physical exercise that would come to bother him chronically in later years. His mind continued to work and mull over what he had just read. In 1940 he remembered that night this way:

> It was one of those nights when I was disturbed and could not sleep. I thought about the lecture and about the article and I thought about my miseries and how I would like to get out of debt and away from worry.
>
> Finally about two in the morning after the lecture and the article had been chasing each other through my mind for some time, the idea occurred to me that by the experimental ligation of the duct and the subsequent degeneration of a portion of the pancreas, that one might obtain the internal secretion free from the external secretion. I got up and wrote down the idea and spent most of the night thinking about it.

Banting's notebook is preserved in the Academy of Medicine in Toronto. He wrote down a date, October 30. Then he changed the 0 to a 1.[7] Then he wrote:

Diabetus
   Ligate pancreatic ducts of dogs. Keep dogs alive till acini degenerate leaving Islets.
   Try to isolate the internal secretion of these to relieve glycosurea.*

It was a deceptively simple idea. The Barron article claimed that blocking the ducts destroyed the cells producing the external secre-

---

*In later descriptions of his inspiration Banting never checked his notebook; he always gave a different, inaccurate version of his idea, one which contained the word "extract." The difference is important.

tion of the pancreas, but did not destroy the cells that were supposed to produce the internal secretion. What if the reason why no one had ever found the internal secretion was that the external secretion, a powerful digestive juice, was somehow neutralizing or destroying or cancelling out the internal secretion in any pancreatic tissue being used in experiments? Well, if you ligated the ducts and let the pancreas atrophy, would the result be surviving tissue that did not contain the external secretion? Theoretically, it seemed as if it would contain only the internal secretion. If you got the internal secretion, and proved you had it by showing its ability to relieve glycosuria (sugar in the urine, the most easily measured effect of the disease), then perhaps you would have conquered diabetes.

Banting remembered mentioning the idea to Professor Miller later that morning. He may have wondered whether it was possible to give the idea a try right away at Western. It was not. Miller had no facilities for major animal experimentation (he had to use his own office as quarters for the cats he was working on), and in any case had no expertise in this field. He suggested that Banting consult a real expert close at hand, Professor J.J.R. Macleod at the University of Toronto. In the next few days Banting mentioned the idea to several other people in London, including Billy Tew. He was still excited by it that weekend when he was scheduled to be in Toronto for the wedding of a Starr daughter. Perhaps he should drop everything and start the research. Before leaving London for Toronto he told Rowland Hill a little about his inspiration. "Dr. Banting . . . is very much discouraged as he has so little to do," Hill wrote in his diary. "He is taking up further studies and has his mind on some other plans which may lead him to sell the place."[8] At the festivities in Toronto, Fred told his surgical friends about the idea. They were skeptical. But Banting stayed in Toronto on Monday, November 8, to see what Professor Macleod would think.

When he went into the Professor of Physiology's office in the Medical Building, Fred saw a small, well-dressed, middle-aged scholar who would have addressed him formally as Dr. Banting. John James Rickard Macleod was a native of Aberdeen, Scotland, born in 1876, educated locally and then in Germany and England, who had emigrated to America to teach at the Western Reserve University in Cleveland, Ohio, in 1903. A hard-working professional scientist, Macleod had gradually won an international reputation for himself in the field of carbohydrate metabolism through extensive publication. He was a productive researcher, specializing in studies of the behaviour of sugar in the blood, as well as a talented writer and popularizer who had issued both a well-received textbook in physiology and a monograph on diabetes. In 1918 he had come to the University of Toronto as the Professor of Physiology and Associate Dean of the Faculty of Medicine. At the peak of his career in 1920, a popular and talented lecturer as well as a world-class scholar and researcher, Macleod was one of the ornaments of the Toronto faculty. Banting had graduated before Macleod came to Toronto, so he had not been taught by the Scotsman and does not seem to have had any contact with him before this meeting. Like any conscientious professor, Macleod would have been pleased to meet with a young doctor and University of Toronto graduate to discuss a research idea. It happens all the time.

The meeting did not go as well as Banting had hoped. He was not a good talker in formal situations at any time in his life. In this situation, he would have been specially ill at ease because of the aura of wisdom and sophistication that a distinguished professor like Macleod commanded. He was not well prepared either, knowing next to nothing about diabetes or the pancreas – a disease and an organ that had already generated thousands of publications and consumed the best efforts of scores of specialists, including Macleod. Banting's presentation of his idea must have been halting and uncertain.[9]

Macleod soon realized that his visitor did not know very much about the pancreas or diabetes or how to go about the kind of research he was discussing. At one point early in the interview Macleod began reading some of the letters on his desk, a sometimes unconscious and common gesture, bound to offend a sensitive visitor to anyone's office. Macleod's first comments on Banting's presentation, delivered in a tone that could only seem formal and patronizing (Macleod was chillingly formal to most strangers because he was a shy man) were to the effect that this kind of research was a serious matter. Dr. Banting would have to realize that many eminent scientists had spent many years of their lives in some of the world's best-equipped laboratories trying to isolate the internal secretion of the pancreas. None had succeeded. Any serious research on the pancreas would require a researcher's full time for several months. Are you sure you are prepared to undertake this, Dr. Banting?

Banting did not back off. He was not the kind of man to back off. He earnestly repeated himself. We do not know exactly what he said, exactly what he wanted from Macleod, or even exactly what his research plan was. We know that he wanted to try an experiment involving ligating the ducts of the pancreas in living animals in the hope of producing tissue that might contain the internal secretion. Macleod was not at that time engaged in advanced research on the pancreas, but he knew the literature very well. As he thought about Banting's proposal, he realized that it might be an interesting approach after all.

Many other researchers had experimented with ligation of the pancreatic ducts, studying the physiological results. But it was not clear that any of them had carried out careful tests to see if the atrophied pancreas resulting from ligation contained the internal secretion. One American researcher, E.L. Scott, had hoped to do this in 1911, but found it too difficult to do duct-ligation surgery on living animals. Banting was a surgeon, and could presumably handle the fairly tricky operation. More interestingly, Banting the surgeon may have been proposing to Macleod that the surgical technique of grafting or transplanting be used as the main way of testing the duct-ligated pancreas to see if it contained the internal secretion. Grafting had been suggested by several experts as a promising direction in which pancreas research should move. The idea of grafting would have occurred naturally to Banting, a surgeon who knew about bone grafts and had been interested in grafting cartilage. Macleod would have found a proposal to do tissue grafts, coming from a surgeon with the ability to do them, a credible research project. Finally, Macleod may have realized that the new techniques now available for determining levels of blood sugar, which permitted more, and more precise, measurements during research than the old sugar in the urine tests, were a good reason for someone in his lab taking another stab at finding the internal secretion of the pancreas.

Macleod told Banting that his idea was worth trying. But, doing his duty as an experienced professor facing an inexperienced enthusiast, Macleod warned that success was unlikely. After all, there was that thirty-year record of failure in the search for the internal secretion. It was such a record of failure – as many as four hundred attempts – that many scientists, including Macleod, were beginning to wonder if the internal secretion could ever be found. Perhaps it didn't really exist. Still, any unexplored avenue of attack on the problem should be investigated. Negative results would be of value, Macleod told Banting. So, if Banting was prepared to make the substantial commitment necessary to carry out the research, Macleod would make facilities and animals available to him.

Banting was sobered by Macleod's warnings. Was it worth giving up his practice and his university appointments in London to produce valuable negative results? He told the professor that he would consider the situation carefully. That was the end of their interview.

Banting then saw C.L. Starr to ask his advice. The question was whether he should leave London right away and come to Toronto to do the work. After talking with Macleod, Starr wrote that he and Macleod felt the proposition was too "problematical" to leap into. Banting should stick with his promising situation in London. If he did want to pursue the idea, and it was a most interesting idea, Macleod had suggested that he might wait until the summer and then come to Toronto to put in a month or two's work. Banting accepted Starr's advice to stick with his London jobs for the time being.[10]

Life seemed to be looking up from a professional point of view. Banting's practice was gradually increasing. In January he took in over $200, and in February over $500 (including his demonstrator's fees). He was starting to do more surgical work – a tendon fixation brought in $75 – and at Western the experiments with Miller on cerebral and cerebellar localization were becoming quite interesting and more of a partnership as Miller found out how useful Banting's surgical skill could be. Banting later talked and wrote about how much time he spent studying the pancreas and carbohydrate metabolism during this winter. The evidence from his notebook suggests that Banting actually put his pancreas idea in the back of his mind while cultivating an interest in some of the subjects he was learning about in Miller's lab, notably the action of nerves and reflexes. He had research ideas in these areas, and, just as he had consulted with Macleod about the diabetes idea in November, now in March he corresponded with C.S. Sherrington, a great British physiologist and Miller's former professor, about an idea he had to study reflex action in the limbs of kittens and dogs.[11]

In spite of these developments, Banting had decided by the spring that he wanted to get out of London, at least for a few months.

Perhaps he was unduly discouraged. Perhaps he had decided he just didn't like the city. From his boyhood flights to the Alliston fairground, right to the last trip of his life, Banting was prone to a temperamental restlessness, a desire physically to escape from the demands on him. At this time in London the most serious of his problems appears to have had little to do with medicine, research or even money, but revolved around Edith. She apparently kept visiting him most Saturdays until early May, but their relationship seems to have deteriorated. At some point she broke off the engagement and returned the ring. Just how deeply Fred loved Edith is unclear – perhaps they were just highschool and wartime sweethearts drifting apart – and it was probably unclear to both of them. But we can imagine Fred, in his moods of depression, meditating blackly on the crumbling of his dreams for stability and security and a happy family life. What would it be like to live in a house you had bought as a home for your bride and your family, then to find you had no bride?

Early in March 1921 Banting renewed contact with Macleod in Toronto. He hoped the professor remembered their discussion in November, and, "if your offer for facilities to do the research still holds good," hoped to spend the early summer months working in Macleod's laboratory. Macleod replied that he would be glad to have Banting come up "to see what you can do with the problem of Pancreatic Diabetes, which we spoke about."[12] By his own account, though, Banting was still not sure whether this was the course he wanted to take:

About the middle of March when things were going on in the worst possible way I heard of a proposed expedition that was going up to the far North in the Mackenzie River Valley to bore for oil. It was said that they might take a medical officer with them. I found the name of the man in St. Thomas who was to be in charge of the party. I was in desperate circumstances. I liked the thought of a trip to the North country. The possibilities of doing research seemed remote. I tossed a coin – three out of five – heads I was to do the research, tails I was to go to the Arctic to search for oil. Tails won, and I took the next train to St. Thomas to make a personal application in the hopes of obtaining the job. He explained that he was not sure of taking a medical officer but if they took one, I could have the job. I watched for the mailman every day for weeks. Finally a letter arrived saying that the party had decided not to take a doctor. Again my financial hopes dropped.

Bill Tew and I talked over the possibilities of joining the Indian Army Medical Service and even wrote for particulars.[13]

On sober second thought he was not ready to run all the way to India to escape his problems. Dr. Starr, who felt that Fred's real problem was his reluctance to settle down and stick with things in London, was still advising him to concentrate on building up his practice through the coming summer. Edith may have been saying the same things. Surely if one of Fred's worries was financial, it was folly to take a couple of months off to pursue a strange idea; no one had offered to pay him for the research work he would be doing.

Fred Banting was such a puzzling young doctor. At some times in his life there was no one in Canada with more courage and determination, or just plain stubbornness. At other times his insecurity and lack of confidence so overcame him that the desire to run away was almost overwhelming. Edith, and the others who were close to Fred, must have wondered whether the mood changes, the ups and downs, the tiresome uncertainties and hours and hours of worry, were peculiarities of Banting's character. Were they going to grow worse with age? Would they cripple him for life? Were they a kind of hangover from the war, something many veterans suffered and eventually grew out of? Would most men who have known ambition and lived through their twenties recognize the pattern? Would a sensitive, loving woman know how to handle it?

Going to Toronto to do some summer research was a middle way out. Banting would get out of town, but not burn his bridges. He could always come back in September. He decided to commit himself to the Toronto summer project and apparently went to the city to go over the plans in more detail with Macleod (he was a bit disappointed that Macleod discouraged a proposal to start some of the dogs early, over the Easter holidays; Macleod pointed out that no one would have the free time to care for them properly until Banting returned).[14] On one of these visits Banting was introduced to Macleod's two student research assistants, Clark Noble and Charley Best. Macleod asked them to help Banting with his project. They decided to split the job and tossed a coin to see who would go first. Best won the toss.

On Saturday morning, May 14, 1921, Banting locked up his

house, supervised a final examination for the fourth year medical students at Western, and then caught the noon train to Toronto. As a token of their appreciation for his work with them during the year, the students had given him a box of cigars.

The cigars are a reminder that Banting had not failed in London. He did not realize it, but he had been gradually succeeding in building up a practice while making a niche for himself in teaching and research at Western. With patients he was a friendly, warm, dedicated physician and surgeon, bound to be popular. At the University he was conscientious. Had he not been so unduly upset by his early troubles, had his romance not broken down, had he taken Starr's advice to stay with the London situation a little longer, Banting might soon have settled into a comfortable life. He would have been a competent small-city surgeon and part-time university lecturer in the tradition of practitioner-teachers. He would have been popular with his fellow medical men and probably become a leader in local medical circles. He would have found a wife, settled down, raised a family, and disappeared from history. He might have had a happier life than the one he led after his return to Toronto.

CHAPTER FOUR

The Discovery of Insulin

Banting, J.J.R. Macleod, and a student assistant, Charles Best, began work on Banting's research idea on May 17, 1921. Less than a year later, a summary of the work done by these three, plus four other researchers who had been added to the team, was presented to the elite of North American medicine gathered in Washington, D.C. The audience stood and applauded one of the greatest achievements of modern medicine. Banting was not present at that meeting to hear the applause. The nine months of research which produced the discovery of insulin, a discovery that forever changed the world for diabetics and was one of the most sensational achievements of modern medicine, had just about broken him. Banting had had the idea that started it all. But the wonderfully successful and exciting research that led to insulin was also for him a growing nightmare of uncertainty, confusion, fear and tragic conflict.

This chapter is a history of how the discovery was made. Any intelligent layman can follow the events and the reasoning; but there is a certain narrowing of focus here, and a necessary repetitiveness as a large number of dogs are depancreatized and receive pancreatic extract. No other chapter in this biography is nearly so technical. Many readers will find it not technical and detailed enough. They can turn to my much more elaborate history in *The Discovery of Insulin*. Readers fresh from that book can skim over this chapter.

Banting stayed with Fred and Lillian Hipwell for the first few weeks he was in Toronto. Stories that he did his first experiments in their house are extremely implausible. He may have taken some laboratory dogs home from time to time, and even tried a few tests with some of Hipwell's chemicals. But this was a serious project, and Banting was too well-trained to approach it quite that cavalierly.

It seemed like a fairly straightforward piece of mostly surgical research. Banting would operate on several dogs, cutting into the abdomen, locating the ducts leading from the pancreas to the duodenum, tying them shut, and then closing the incision. The dogs would recover to more or less normal health. But their pancreas, unable to secret digestive enzymes, would gradually shrivel or atrophy. Other dogs would have their pancreas completely removed. These dogs would quickly become diabetic. Banting would re-operate on the duct-ligated dogs to obtain the shrivelled-up pancreas. According to his theory, it would no longer contain the powerful external secretion, but might contain the internal secretion.

He would attempt to graft parts of that pancreas into the abdomen of the depancreatized, diabetic dogs. An alternative, or perhaps a follow-up procedure would be to make a liquid emulsion or extract of the atrophied pancreas and try injecting or feeding it to the diabetic animals. In either case, the key to the experiments would be to observe whether or not the diabetes was relieved. That could be determined by various tests, including measuring the amount of sugar in the urine and the blood, as well as more elaborate measurements of the constituents of the urine (particularly the "D:N ratio" of sugar to nitrogen). If everything worked and the diabetes was relieved, the experimenters would have found the mysterious internal secretion of the pancreas. And they might have a useful treatment for diabetes.

In the first piece of surgery, on May 17, Macleod showed Banting how to do a pancreatectomy on a dog. The accepted method was to do it in two stages. Go into the abdomen. Cut away most of the pancreas, but leave a small remnant. Pull the remnant up and stitch it in place under the skin. Close the incision. The remnant, still functioning, would keep the dog from becoming diabetic while it recovered from surgery. A week or so later do the second stage by snipping away the remnant. The now completely depancreatized dog would quickly become diabetic, dying in a week or so from the disease.

After helping with the first stage of a pancreatectomy on the first dog, Macleod left Banting and Best on their own. The surgery turned out to be easier to describe than to do. When Banting and

Best started work together on a dog they accidentally killed it with an overdose of anesthetic. Then Banting lost a dog from too much bleeding. The next dog survived its operation, but then the original dog died from infection. Then that surviving dog died. Finally, after a bloody, unsuccessful week, Banting learned the knack of the technique and got a dog healing well from its first-stage pancreatectomy.[1]

Knowing he could do the pancreatectomy, he began the critical duct-ligation surgery on other dogs. He ran into more trouble. Two of the first three dogs he ligated soon died from infection. The third, he realized, may not have had its ducts ligated at all: they are small and hard to find, and an inexperienced experimenter can easily ligate a piece of pancreatic tissue instead of a duct.

There were always more dogs. True, the University's supply was limited – Macleod thought Banting might use ten or twelve dogs in his research; in two weeks he had already worked on ten, losing seven of them – but there was nothing to stop a determined researcher from finding his own dogs. From time to time during the summer of 1921 Banting and Best looked for dogs on the streets of Toronto, paying $1 to $3 for unwanted animals, no questions asked. One night Banting used his tie as a leash to lead a newly obtained dog back to the lab. Such activities fed generations of stories in Toronto about family pets disappearing forever into the dreaded laboratories of the Medical School.

Macleod did not take part in any of the experiments after the first dog. But he was on hand, working in his department in the same building as Banting and Best. Banting's notebook reveals two consultations with Macleod to discuss the plan of work, including the professor's "parting instructions" on June 14. Macleod was leaving for a three-month visit to Scotland. Banting noted his summer address. He also noted the address of J.B. Collip, a biochemist who had happened to be seeing Macleod at the time of one of Banting's consultations. Collip knew a little bit about hormones and tissue extracts, sat in on the session, and was apparently interested enough that Banting thought of him as someone he might write to about the work. A florist's son from Belleville, Ontario, Collip was the same age as Banting. A far better student than Banting, he had sped through a Ph.D. in biochemistry at the University of Toronto, and was currently teaching in Edmonton at the University of Alberta. Collip had a sabbatical leave for 1921-22; he planned to spend the summer working in Massachusetts, then come back to Toronto to work with Macleod for several months.

The research seemed to be well in hand when Macleod left Toronto in mid-June. Several dogs had had their ducts ligated. It would take several more weeks before their pancreases had degenerated sufficiently to try the more important experiments. In the meantime Banting could keep practising his pancreatectomy technique, making animals diabetic and then learning about diabetes through the tests he and Best were doing of their urine and blood. Best, too, went off in mid-June to take a couple of weeks of militia training. He showed Banting how to do the tests on the dogs while he was away. On hand was one depancreatized dog, which seemed to be becoming increasingly diabetic. As Best left, he wrote a note to Banting suggesting that the test for the D:N ratio ought to indicate a fully diabetic dog in a day or two.

It did not, and as Banting started doing Best's tests on his own, he decided that his assistant's methods were inaccurate and sloppy. Dirty glassware and irregular solutions of chemicals seemed to be mucking up the results. It was not easy or pleasant to redo the tests. When Best reappeared at the lab later that month he was confronted by a blunt, angry Banting: "I told him that if he was going to work with me that he would have to show some interest, that his work was totally unsatisfactory, that he lacked accuracy and was too sloppy, and I ended up by telling him that before doing another single thing he must throw down the sink every solution that he had been using, wash every bit of glassware and make up new solutions that were truly 'normal.'"

Charley Best must have been surprised by Banting's anger. Best was a tall, blond, blue-eyed, clean-cut graduate of a good honours course in Physiology and Biochemistry. The twenty-two-year old son of a Canadian-born Maine doctor, he was sailing along through "Varsity," enjoying university life, getting increasingly good grades, having a fine 1921 summer of baseball, riding and outings with his beautiful fiancée, Margaret Mahon. He may have been interested in Banting's diabetes research because an aunt had died of the disease.

As Banting recalled their late-night confrontation in the lab, Best's first reaction to the dressing-down was a kind of mute anger. "I thought he was going to fight and I measured the height of his jaw. He delayed and I feared he was not going to fight." Suddenly Best turned away and went off to wash glassware. He worked all night (according to Banting's memory), leaving everything perfect in the morning.[2]

"We understood each other much better after this encounter," Banting wrote. The little confrontation apparently cleared the air, showed who was boss and began to cement what gradually became a working partnership. It was not a deeply personal relationship, or even a life-long friendship, but Banting and Best did work together without further friction. They got along so well in June, in fact, that Best stayed on rather than give way to the second student, Clark Noble. That arrangement was perfectly agreeable to Noble at the time. He regretted it for the rest of his life.

The shared hardships of the research strengthened the bond between Banting and Best. In retrospect, Banting was fortunate to be working in a lab which provided dogs for research, special metabolic cages for post-operative maintenance, a special animal operating room and a well-trained assistant like Best. For the time these were not primitive facilities by any means. Many researchers around the world with far better qualifications than Banting had to make do with far, far less. Banting did not see it that way. The dog quarters were in a smelly, dirty garret at the top of the Medical Building. The little animal operating room next to it became indescribably hot and sticky and stinking as the summer sun beat through the tar-and-gravel roof on researchers trying to do delicate, exacting surgery. Toronto's summer climate often seems imported from Alabama. On those days Banting may have begun his life-long habit of cutting off the sleeves of his lab coats to work bare-armed. He also cut off the sleeves of his pyjamas to sleep more comfortably.

Every aspect of the facility could be interpreted two ways. Banting never forgot how he and Best had had to scrub the whole animal operating room in May to make it usable. No one had done experiments in it for years. It seemed to be a dirty, unused, abandoned hole. In fact it had been gathering dust in disuse because it was such an advanced idea: an animal operating room put in ahead of its time, ahead of the University having anyone to use it.

There are no surviving descriptions of Banting and Best at work in the summer of 1921, only their own laconic comments, such as Best's report to Macleod: "We have found it next to impossible to keep a wound clean during the very hot weather. Conditions in the animal operating room are also not very good, as you know."[3] How could they keep the sweat from pouring down their faces and

65

arms and into the wounds? How could they keep the flies away? How could they breathe in the stench of dog urine and dog excrement and dog vomit and dead dog? Goddamn research had better work, Banting must have muttered many times over. He had endured worse, horribly worse, in France in 1918. But the heat and the smell of this research were bad enough.

They were almost defeated in the first week of July. They opened up one of their seven duct-ligated dogs and found that nothing had happened. Its pancreas had not atrophied at all. Banting had missed a duct, or his ligature had come loose, or the duct had re-formed. Nothing to do but open them all up – in some of the hottest July days in a hundred years. Five of the seven dogs had to be re-ligated. Two died. So did two depancreatized dogs. What was there to show for seven weeks of research? A lot of dead animals! What Best described as "very heavy casualties." Nothing to do but plod on grimly. Rest a while and then attack again.[4]

At the end of July they were finally ready to test Banting's idea. Dogs with duct-ligated and apparently degenerated pancreases were at hand. So were a couple of depancreatized, diabetic dogs. Banting's thoughts of grafting or transplanting were now abandoned, perhaps because of the heat, perhaps because of the alarming rate of dog wastage. Instead Banting and Best moved directly to a faster, easier experiment. They killed a duct-tied dog, number 391, to get its shrivelled-up pancreas, sliced and chilled the organ in Ringer's solution (a physiological salt solution), ground it up, and filtered the solution. The result was a liquid extract of degenerated pancreas. Banting and Best prepared to inject it into a diabetic dog.

Dog 410 was a white terrier, depancreatized in two stages on July 11 and 18. It was only mildly diabetic, but that seemed good enough. Its blood sugar at 10:15 a.m. on Saturday, July 30, was measured at .20 (a normal dog's blood sugar would be about .08 to .13). Banting injected four cubic centimetres of the extract into one of its veins. An hour later the blood sugar measured .12. The extract seemed to work. A second injection, and an hour later the reading was .11. Not much of a reduction, but at least it wasn't rising, as it might normally do in a diabetic dog. In the afternoon they tried feeding sugar to the dog. Would injections of extract still hold down the blood sugar, suggesting that the dog had regained the ability to burn it up? It wasn't easy to get the sugar and water down: Banting and Best nearly killed the terrier by first inserting a stomach tube into a lung. Then, despite hourly injections of extract, its blood sugar did rise back into the .18-.21 range. But perhaps it would have gone much higher without the injections. The dog wasn't secreting much sugar in its urine either, probably a good sign.

Some of their later accounts suggest that Banting and Best were very excited by this first test. If so, they were remarkably cool in deciding to break off work for the day at 6.15 p.m. When they came back to the lab in the morning dog 410 was in a coma. They took one blood sugar, getting a not very diabetic reading of .15, before the dog died. They did no autopsy, an inexcusable piece of sloppiness even on a Sunday. They later wrote that dog 410 was probably dying from infection at the time they decided to run the extract test.[5]

The other depancreatized dog, a collie (number 406), was close to death from diabetes and/or infection on Monday, August 1. Using extract made from another duct-ligated dog, Banting and Best gave the unconscious animal a large injection, eight cc. The dog's blood sugar started down. The collie awoke, stood and walked. Then, despite another injection, it lapsed into coma and died. Possibly another exciting result, but hard to know what had really happened that afternoon. The case of dog 406 was so inconclusive that Banting and Best never wrote it up.

On Wednesday, August 3, they began an experiment that finally worked well. The extract had definitely favourable results on another diabetic collie, dog 408. (To get the dog ready quickly, Banting abandoned the two-stage pancreatectomy, taking it all out at once. About this time Banting and Best also stopped paying much attention to their dogs' D:N ratios, apparently because the figures seldom seemed to work out. Urinary sugar estimates were also thrown off by the small amounts of urine excreted.) Control experiments on 408 showed that extracts made from liver and spleen did not have the same effect. Four times during four days the extract of degenerated pancreas, which Banting and Best started calling "isletin," drove down 408's blood sugar. The last time was during an all-night experiment; at the end of it the dog died of infection (they did an autopsy this time) and perhaps shock. Now, at last, there were results worth reporting to Professor Macleod.

Banting was brim full of ideas. "I have so much to tell you and ask you about that I scarcely know where to begin," he began his report to Macleod on August 9. He and Best had an extract that reduced the blood and urinary sugar and improved the clinical condition of diabetic dogs. He listed nineteen problems that were now "presenting themselves" for further research. They included the need to find "isletin's" chemical nature; the effect that the pancreas's external secretion, trypsin, had on the extract; the extract's mechanism of action; the graftability of pancreatic tissues; and – of course – clinical application: would the extract work on human diabetics?

Banting asked Macleod in his letter if he could stay on and work in his laboratory. But he also remarked on the urgent need for help to keep the place clean, and for gloves, gowns and a refitting of the animal operating room. He wanted Best, whose work had been excellent, to stay on with him. He was about to go to London to close out his affairs there "and have them off my mind," he told Macleod. He and Best were going to go ahead slowly while awaiting Macleod's wishes regarding the research. "Hoping to hear from you soon and eagerly awaiting your return. . . ."[6]

Why wait for the mail to go all the way to Scotland and back? Banting and Best started in right away on a big push of round-the-clock experiments, comparing the condition of two diabetic dogs, one treated with the extract, the other untreated. The untreated dog died in four days. The dog that got the extract, a yellow collie, number 92, seemed to respond beautifully. She was a frisky, friendly, cooperative patient, who became something of a laboratory pet. Banting and Best were able to try different strengths and mixtures of extract on her. She was still going strong when they ran out of extract.

There was no more degenerated pancreas on hand to make extract from. It wouldn't hurt to study the effect of extract made from fresh whole pancreas. Banting and Best's notebooks and charts and published article all show that this extract worked on dog 92 at least as well as the "isletin" made from degenerated pancreas. But Banting and Best had not expected the extract to work, and they were either too tired or too inattentive to study or think clearly about their data. They dismissed the extract of fresh whole pancreas as being much weaker than their normal extract.[7] If Banting had understood what his own experiment was showing him, the work would have gone ahead much more quickly. He would have realized, first, that his hypothesis about having to destroy the external secretion in the pancreas before being able to obtain the internal was very suspect; and second, that they could dispense with the cumbersome duct-ligation and degeneration process, and work with fresh whole pancreas instead.

Having missed a key fork in the road, Banting and Best tried another way of obtaining extract. They used a complicated procedure in which the hormone secretin was used to stimulate a dog's pancreas to produce digestive juice. If the pancreas exhausted itself of external secretion, they reasoned, only the internal secretion would remain. An extract could be made from it. The extract seemed to work beautifully on the diabetic collie, bringing it from extreme lassitude to wonderful friskiness. But an attempt to repeat the stimulation method using cats was a failure. There was no more extract. Finally dog 92 sickened and died; it had lived with its diabetes and injections for a remarkable 20 days. Banting remembered tearfully mourning the death of his pet.

Fred and Charley had some good and fine times together, partners on a pioneer voyage charting their course by the stars and sunrise as the city slept. But actually it had been a rough summer for Banting. Nobody was paying him for his time in the lab. He had no savings from London, was paying the mortgage on an empty house there, and was fairly heavily in debt to his family. The only money he made that summer was a few dollars doing tonsillectomies to help one of his medical friends, plus $25 from selling some of his instruments. Relations with Edith were apparently at a confusing impasse. If he saw her at all that summer she probably pestered him about when he was going to settle down, bring some stability to his life, grow up.

He had almost reverted to his student ways, it seemed. When he wasn't minding the Hipwell house for Fred and Lillian (*successful* cousin Fred, practising medicine and a homeowner), he was living in a tiny room in a Grenville Street boarding house. Trying to save money, he sponged meals from his friends, sometimes cooked over a bunsen burner in the lab, even went back to the Sunday night suppers at the Philathea Bible Class. Sometimes the Hipwells or the Philathea girls brought food to the lab. Banting seemed to be a young man who needed mothering.

He also needed fathering, in the sense of having an older man he could go to for advice. While Macleod was away that summer, Fred sometimes consulted with C.L. Starr about the work and how he should proceed. He did not have much in common with the only other researcher in the physiology department, Dr. Fidlar, a gentle,

69

somewhat eccentric scientist who had built an enormously complex apparatus to study the respiration of one frog. But one day Banting happened to drop in on Velyien Henderson, the Professor of Pharmacology and one of his former teachers. As a student Banting had not liked Henderson, who was something of an intimidating character in the classroom. But now the older man took a friendly interest in Banting's work, the two veterans may have swapped war stories, and the foundations of a lifelong friendship began to form.

As he had implied to Macleod, Banting was so confident in the future of his research that he was ready to burn his London bridge. Early in September he sold his house and most of its contents. That was the end of his attempt to make a living practising medicine. Banting was delighted to leave London forever.

Banting and Best started to work again in September, doing some duct-ligations. Then Macleod's letter arrived responding to their report. The professor was cautiously encouraging. He found their results "definitely positive" though "not absolutely certain," criticized some of their techniques, hoped they had gathered supporting data, and urged Banting to "continue along the same lines." Banting should concentrate on the preparation of the extract and not as yet take up the many problems he had mentioned in his letter. Macleod wanted Banting's work to be able to withstand the criticisms which had greeted other researchers' similarly promising findings. The problem was to "build up a stronghold of proof which others cannot pull down. . . . I am glad to see that you are to stay in Toronto and you may rest assured that I will do all in my power to help you."[8]

Having already done the one experiment Macleod authorized, and having no duct-ligated dogs ready to work on, Banting and Best were at loose ends, not quite sure what to do. They tried using the secretin-stimulation method to get extract quickly, played around with other methods of administration – rectal insertion and subcutaneous injection – and tried to find out whether trypsin, which they thought was the pancreas's external secretion, nullified the extract's effectiveness. The experiments were almost laughably sloppy, their results virtually worthless. Remember that we are dealing with two almost completely inexperienced researchers, waiting for supervision and direction.

Macleod arrived back in Toronto on September 21. A few days later Banting met with him to discuss the future. The meeting was a disaster. Whether Banting went into it with a chip on his shoulder, or whether tempers deteriorated as they talked, there is no doubt that the discussion became heated. Banting wanted better working conditions. Macleod had earlier explained to him that he could not afford to spend money on the old animal operating room which would shortly be replaced by facilities in a new anatomy building, then under construction. He also pointed out that Banting and Best had gone through more dogs than planned. It all cost money, and if extra resources went into Banting and Best's research, somebody else's project would have to suffer.

Banting got it into his head that Macleod did not think his research was important enough to spend more money on. Macleod was not saying that; he apparently said it was no more important than any other research in the department. To Banting, who had just abandoned his practice and his prospects in London, the research was the most important thing in his life. He said something to Macleod about finding out whether the University of Toronto thought his research was important. "As far as you are concerned," Macleod replied, "I am the University of Toronto."

"I told him that I had given up everything I had in the world to do the research, and that I was going to do it, and that if he did not provide what I asked I would go some place where they would."

"He said that I 'had better go'."

They argued about where Banting would go. Talking bravely or ignorantly, or both, he threatened to go to the Mayo Clinic in Minnesota or the Rockefeller Institute in New York. Macleod finally softened a bit and told Banting he would do what he could to meet his requests. Banting came out of the confrontation livid with anger. "I'll show that little son of a bitch that he is *not* the University of Toronto," he told Best.[9]

Between them, Macleod and Velyien Henderson managed to find the resources to keep the research going. Macleod got Banting and Best a better room to work in, fixed up the animal operating room, and gave them a part-time lab boy. He also persuaded the University to pay them both retroactively for the summer's research. Best got $170, his normal pay as a student assistant; Banting, the outsider, who had no university position, was paid $150. Henderson hired him for the 1921-22 academic year as a special assistant in Pharmacology, so Banting joined the staff of the University of Toronto with fairly light duties and quite decent remuneration of $250 a month.

Banting's job in Pharmacology seems to have been worked out by Henderson and probably Macleod as a handy way of getting Banting on the University payroll. It was not, as Banting later claimed, a case of Henderson valiantly coming to his rescue when Macleod had cast him out into the cold.

We are now in October. Banting and Best ligated more dogs. They had one ligated dog from September, and used its degenerated pancreas to try some of Macleod's suggestions, eliminating the possibility of diurnal variation or a dilution phenomenon as alternative explanations of the extract's effectiveness. By using extract made from different parts of the pancreas they thought they were showing that the more atrophied parts produced better extract, though in fact they had confused the two extracts they were using, mistaking "A" for "B" and vice versa.

Banting had invited Macleod or some of his associates to take part in the work. Macleod told him that he and Best should complete their project as planned before any others collaborated with them.

Through much of October, while waiting for the pancreases of the newly ligated dogs to degenerate, Banting and Best did background reading in the voluminous literature relevant to their work. Macleod supplied a bit of guidance. "The goddamned little bugger knows everything about this subject," Banting muttered one day to the departmental librarian as he chased down another reference Macleod had given him.[10]

It was Best who came across one of the most important articles, an account in French of the researches of N.C. Paulesco in Bucharest, Roumania. Paulesco described experiments with his pancreatic extract which preceded Banting and Best's work by several months. His results were just about as good, and in some cases better. As Best stumbled through the foreign language, however, he was most impressed by the problems he found with Paulesco's work, problems which he greatly exaggerated by mistranslating "non plus" to mean "no good." Banting and Best did not realize that Paulesco and others were either right on their heels or even ahead of them, depending on how you looked at it, in the race for insulin. In fact the Toronto researchers did not realize they were in a race.[11]

Banting gave a lot of thought to the problem of what to do next with the research. He finally decided to try his original idea of grafting pancreatic tissue. At this point Macleod apparently intervened, advising the pair to repeat and buttress their summer's experiments. They tried, got mixed results, lost a couple of depancreatized dogs from post-operative bleeding, and stopped again. Apparently assuming their project was finished, they started drafting an article about their research. Macleod asked them to give a talk about it at a meeting of the faculty's Physiological Journal Club on November 14. The date happened to be Banting's thirtieth birthday. "Half my life is over," Banting wrote in a little diary in the small hours of that morning. The big questions before him were whether to leave surgery and whether ever to marry. "At the present it behooves me to study and work at the internal secretion of the pancreas & if possible isolate it in a form that will be of use in treating Diabetes."[12]

The Journal Club talk did not go very well for Banting. He had no experience at public speaking and was nervous. And Macleod gave such a complete introduction to his research that Banting found himself with very little to say (according to one observer's memory, "Fred said that Macleod had covered everything so fully there was nothing left for him to say and sat down in a deadly silence"). In fact Macleod was so impressive in his presentation that some of the students apparently came away thinking that Macleod was responsible for the interesting research they had heard about.[13]

Of course it was work being done in Macleod's lab and under his supervision. Now that it was time to go beyond the original project he started to become more active in directing the research. At a conference with Banting and Best on November 15 he picked up a suggestion a junior colleague had made at the Journal Club meeting about the next step possibly being a longevity experiment. How long could they keep a depancreatized, diabetic dog alive on their extract? Banting and Best agreed to try and find out.

But there was no extract. It would take another month or more to make a new supply of extract by the duct-ligation and degeneration method. In the small hours of the 16th Banting hit upon what seemed like a brilliant idea. Knowing that the islet cells developed fairly early in foetal animals, and that the external secretion of the pancreas is not needed until digestion begins after birth, Banting reasoned that the foetal pancreas ought to contain the internal secretion of the pancreas free from neutralization by the external. He knew that cattle were often impregnated while being fattened for slaughter. So he and Best went to a local abattoir, cut out the pancreas of several calf foetuses, and brought them back to the lab to make extract.

It worked. Extract from foetal calf pancreas reduced blood and urinary sugar just as effectively as the extract of degenerated pancreas. Forget about duct-ligation and waiting for degeneration. Supplies of extract could be made easily from the foetal pancreas available at the abattoir.

Having made that breakthrough, Banting and Best began their longevity experiment, using dog number 27, which was made diabetic by depancreatization. There is no doubt Banting and Best were hoping the extract would soon be used to give longevity to human diabetics. Indeed, word had begun to spread outside of Toronto about their interesting work. One of the most prominent American diabetologists, Elliott Joslin of Boston, wrote Macleod asking whether the Toronto research gave him any reason to offer any hope to his diabetic patients. Joslin was using the best therapy available to treat diabetics, the principles of "undernutrition" developed a few years earlier by his countryman, Frederick M. Allen – the Allen therapy Banting had learned about in medical school in 1916. Banting had not known about the dark side of Allen's "starvation" system, as it was popularly called. The most severe diabetics could not metabolize enough food to live on; their diets had to be so restricted that keeping the diet to hold off the diabetes meant gradually starving to death. Joslin and other diabetologists were treating patients who had been reduced to living skeletons in a desperate attempt to prolong their lives. One way to help keep up their morale was to hold out hope that if they stayed alive long enough some better treatment might be discovered. Was Toronto about to produce that treatment, Joslin wondered?

Macleod answered him on November 21. The work was still inconclusive, but "I may say privately that I believe we have something that may be of real value in the treatment of Diabetes and that we are hurrying along the experiments as quickly as possible."[14] Two days later, while working on their dogs, Banting and Best decided to try a little extract on a human. Banting, who would always want to try things on himself, received 1½ cc. subcutaneously. At least the extract seemed harmless, for it caused no reaction. From about this time on, the research was heading intentionally toward an overwhelming question. Would the extract work on a human diabetic?

The pace picked up as Banting and Best began adjusting the extract to try to find its most potent and purest form. On December 2 and 3 they got it in either too potent a form (they later realized) or in

74

a particularly impure state, for the injections threw the longevity dog, number 27, into repeated convulsions and other symptoms of extreme shock. It finally died, killed by the extract. Banting and Best switched another test dog, number 33, onto longevity, and kept on going.

Now they started making the extract by mixing the pancreas in alcohol rather than in Ringer's solution. Macleod, who had first mentioned alcohol to them (it was a common solvent, often used in extractions), showed them how to evaporate the pancreas/alcohol mixture, leaving a residue which, redissolved in a salt solution, produced the injectable extract. Another day they decided to try using an adult dog's pancreas extracted with alcohol. This was effectively the same experiment they had tried in mid-August. Then they had misread the results. Now they realized it worked. All along, it turned out, you could get the "active principle" from chilled whole pancreas (soon they tried whole cow pancreas, obtained from the abattoir; it worked too). This finding was an experimental disproof of Banting's original hypothesis; the external secretion in the pancreas does not destroy the internal secretion (the reason is that it exists in the pancreas as inactive trypsinogen, not the proteo-lytic digestive enzyme trypsin). But Banting and Best were too busy trying to get to the next stage of the work to think about such theoretical questions. Who cared about the physiology if the extract could be made to work on diabetics?

J.B. Collip had returned to Toronto that autumn to work with Macleod on the relation between blood sugar levels and the acid-base balance. Having been in on that early discussion of Banting's work, he took an interest in its progress and several times offered to help. Banting and Collip were becoming friends, and Banting had asked Macleod if Collip could help. Macleod had thought it unwise. But now that Banting and Best's first project was over, and now that there was going to be no problem getting supplies of pancreas from which to make extract, Macleod invited Collip to join the group working on the pancreatic extract. He started about December 12, 1921.

Collip was a thoroughly-trained, experienced and inventive bio-chemist. He immediately began making effective extract, improving in minor but useful ways on Banting and Best's methods. Perhaps because his lab was in the Pathology Building, several blocks away from the dog quarters, Collip took up one of Macleod's suggestions and began experimenting on rabbits. He soon found that the extract lowered the blood sugar of a normal rabbit (Banting and Best had not thought to test it on normal animals). This finding gave the team an easy rabbit test of the extract's potency. Then, in his first dog experiment, Collip observed that the extract cleared up ketonuria, another feature of severe diabetes.[15]

The group of four were working as a team now, meeting most days for lunch, sharing their results and planning the next steps in the work. They knew it was important to see if the extract restored the liver's ability to store glucose in the form of glycogen, a function lost in diabetes. Collip volunteered to do the test. On December 22 he found an extract-treated diabetic dog's liver loaded with glycogen. This was an exciting result, for all along there had been considerable uncertainty about whether an extract that reduced blood and urinary sugar was actually working to alleviate diabetes. Perhaps it was just causing something to happen to the sugar levels. Now the group had evidence that the extract restored a physiological function lost in diabetes.

A few days after Collip joined the team, Banting began to suffer the first of what mounted into a shattering series of disappointments. He and Best had gone ahead testing other kinds of extract. Certain that only pancreatic extract worked, they tried to make it in larger quantities. Suddenly in the week of December 18-22 they found that none of their batches was effective. That same week they decided to try some older extract, which they knew to be potent, on a human diabetic. They apparently decided not to tell Macleod or Collip of their plans. On December 20 Banting phoned a diabetic classmate of his, Dr. Joe Gilchrist, who was beginning to go rapidly downhill from the disease. It would be too risky to inject him with the extract (think of dog 27!), but Gilchrist came into the lab that day and agreed to swallow some. It had no effect, and never would, for even today's insulin does not work when administered orally. Back at their animal experiments, Banting and Best failed for the seventh straight time to reduce an animal's blood sugar, then quit for Christmas. This was the day of Collip's good result with the glycogen experiment.[16]

Macleod had arranged for Banting to present the results of the work through mid-November to the American Physiological Society conference at Yale University on December 30. Banting's talk was entitled "The Beneficial Influences of Certain Pancreatic Extracts on Pancreatic Diabetes." Because of the prestige of the conference and the rumours that the Canadians were onto something important, the session attracted all of the big men in American diabetes research. In addition to several physiologists who had done extensive work with pancreatic extracts, the audience included the father of the undernutrition therapy, Dr. Frederick M. Allen, whose encyclopaedic research and exhaustive clinical work had made him unquestionably the world's leading diabetologist. If Allen had a rival in clinical practice in North America it was probably the gentle New Englander, Joslin, also present, who was particularly involved with juvenile diabetics. Banting's name was actually on the program twice at this conference, for his work at Western with F.R. Miller in neurophysiology had been written up by Miller with Banting listed as a co-author. But it was insignificant compared to the diabetes paper, which Banting would be giving on his own.

"When I was called upon to present our work I became almost paralyzed. I could not remember nor could I think. I had never spoken to an audience of this kind before." He had little experience addressing audiences of any kind, had no natural gifts as a speaker and, except for having this project to report on, had no business among scientists and doctors of this calibre. Banting was like a sandlot ballplayer suddenly brought to bat against the New York Yankees.

He struck out, doing so badly that Macleod, who chaired the meeting, stepped in during the question period to field queries and defend the reputation of his lab. There are no records of what was said at the meeting, but several of the audience remembered a fair bit of criticism of the Toronto work. Criticism was entirely likely in view of the many shortcomings in Banting and Best's experiments. To take only one example, they had done no temperature readings on their dogs and so would have been unable to field questions relating to the most common toxic effect other researchers had found with pancreatic extracts – that they caused fever.

In trying to defend the work, Macleod stressed the sheer number of times an injection of extract had lowered blood sugar, plus the fact that it seemed able to keep diabetic dogs alive (as it had with dog 92 in August and was now doing with dog 33). Macleod's defence had a greater impact than Banting's presentation ("Banting spoke haltingly, Macleod beautifully," Joslin remembered[17]), leading to a post-session feeling that Toronto was doing interesting work. Perhaps they would be reporting further progress soon. The paper had been neither a triumph nor a disaster, more like a statement of work-in-progress.

But Banting was humiliated by his personal failure. While the others slept on the trip back to Toronto, Banting sat up all night in the smoker brooding about what had happened to him. He had spent months working on those experiments, working day and night under the worst conditions, getting the good results, and then been incapable of presenting them. Instead Macleod had talked about Banting's work. He had even had the gall to call it "our" work, as though he had been there in the lab himself. How many experiments had Macleod actually done in the lab? None that Banting could remember. How much help and encouragement had he given? All Banting could recall were warnings, hesitation, discouragement, the quarrel in September. Wasn't the reality that Banting and Best did the work and Macleod mostly got in the way? Except when the work was being described to others – as at the Journal Club, or at New Haven, or in a session Banting remembered in Macleod's office with a distinguished visiting professor. Suddenly on those occasions it was "we," and "our" work, and people got the impression that Macleod was the mastermind of it all. The "talker and writer" was getting the credit while the real lab workers were ignored. A man of the people, Banting was probably predisposed to view events through a populist lens. Honest farmers were always being gulled by smooth-talking city-slickers. The men who went through hell at the front in the war never seemed to get the glory. The big shots always seemed to push the little man aside.

Banting convinced himself that he could have answered his critics if only Macleod had let him. Why hadn't Macleod let him? Putting the whole pattern together, Banting decided that Macleod was deliberately taking over the work. Back in Toronto he began telling his friends that he couldn't trust Macleod not to steal his results.[18]

The course of the work in January 1922 caused Banting's semi-paranoia to harden into fixed conviction. The enemy became not just Macleod, but Collip too. Collip was another slick scientist, a full professor like Macleod, much chummier with Macleod than the lowly Banting or Best could ever hope to be. Collip worked on his own in a separate lab and seemed to always tell Macleod first about the results of his experiments, instead of sharing them with Banting and Best. And Collip's results were so damned good, especially compared with the trouble Banting and Best had had with their extract before Christmas. Perhaps it was that skill of Collip's which had caused Macleod to suggest that he be responsible for getting the extract into a form suitable for human testing. That assignment, though, was also another step in the way in which Collip and Macleod seemed to be taking control of the vital areas of the work. Would they also take the credit?

Early in January there was a Journal Club meeting to discuss ketonuria. Macleod later realized that there had been some "strain" between Collip on the one hand and Banting and Best on the other that night. Was it about credit for the discovery that the extract could relieve ketonuria? Banting and Best had "discovered" the extract. Collip had "discovered" what it could do to ketonuria. Who should get the credit?[19]

Banting assumed he would share the thrill and the glory of the clinical testing. The idea of treating human diabetics with whatever he discovered had been part of his concept of the research from the beginning. He was the only member of the group with any recent medical training or experience. But events, and possibly people, were conspiring to edge him aside. It was Collip who would make the extract to be tested. Now Macleod's friend, the Professor of Medicine, Duncan Graham, ruled that someone other than Banting would do the testing! Graham rejected Banting's application for an appointment that would enable him to treat patients at Toronto General Hospital, the University's teaching hospital. Graham's ruling – that Banting, a surgeon who had never treated a diabetic and was not currently practising medicine, was not qualified to conduct advanced research on human diabetics – was technically sound, taken properly in the interests of the patients. To Banting, it was another sign that the big shots didn't want him.

He fought back, going directly to Macleod and somehow persuading him to have the first clinical test done with extract he and Best had made. Macleod persuaded Graham to let the trial take place. On January 11, 1922, Banting and Best took extract they had made and tested for potency on a dog across College Street to Ward H of Toronto General Hospital. Dr. Walter Campbell, a young University of Toronto graduate, handled the diabetic patients there. While Banting and Best waited outside the ward, Campbell's house physician, Dr. Ed Jeffrey, injected fifteen cc. of the mud-coloured extract into the buttocks of a fourteen-year old charity patient named Leonard Thompson. The boy's diabetes and diet had reduced him to 65 pounds of skin and bone. On his breath was the sweet, sickly smell of diabetic acidosis. The dose the doctors used was about half as much as would have been used on a dog of equal weight.

The injection had no immediate effect on Thompson's clinical condition. Banting and Best waited around hoping to get samples of the boy's blood and urine. They were told the hospital would do the tests and let them know the next day. "There did not seem to be anything to do so we went back to the laboratory," Banting wrote.[20]

It was just as well, for the results of the tests were not encouraging. Thompson's blood sugar dropped from .440 to .320, still a highly diabetic figure. There was a very slight decrease in the large amounts of sugar in his urine. The ketones in the urine were not affected. Thompson not only failed to show any visible clinical improvement, but developed a sterile abscess at the site of one of the injections. This was a toxic side-effect evidently caused by an almost completely ineffective extract. Although he was a very sick diabetic boy, the doctors decided not to give Thompson any more of this extract. Some evidence in the documents suggests that one or two other patients received Banting and Best's extract at about the same time, with so little effect that no one bothered to do sugar or urine tests. The pancreatic extract made by Frederick Banting and Charles Best to treat diabetes failed its one formal clinical test.[21]

J.J.R. Macleod never held Banting's ability or judgment in particularly high regard. With the failure of this test, Banting must have dropped even further in Macleod's esteem and must have known it. Banting had boldly intervened to stay the train of events that was shunting him aside, and his intervention had failed. He and Best had proven Macleod's good judgment in assigning Collip to work at purifying the extract, perhaps also Duncan Graham's good judgment in not authorizing Banting to treat diabetics. It was another crushing defeat for Banting.

The defeat was made worse when the first newspaper story about the research appeared. A reporter for the Toronto *Daily Star*, Roy Greenaway, had heard about the Thompson test and begun looking into these medical goings-on. Macleod was appalled at the prospect of publicity which might arouse premature and entirely false hopes in diabetics. He gave Greenaway a very cautious interview, stressing how preliminary the work was, being careful to describe the group's "hope that some day we may be able to help on a little bit" with diabetes. Greenaway's story was published on January 14. Here, for Banting, was another article full of "we"'s and "our"'s, and it implied that he and Best hadn't achieved very much. Surely the intent of Macleod's scheming was clear.

As his unhappiness mounted, Banting freely told other people that he suspected Macleod of stealing his work. Sometime in January Macleod finally learned that Banting was publicly accusing him of the high academic crime of taking credit for a subordinate's research. After a flurry of meetings involving Macleod, Graham, C.L. Starr, Velyien Henderson, Professor Andrew Hunter, and possibly others, Banting and Macleod agreed there had been many misunderstandings; now they would wipe the slate clean. Macleod thought it would settle the credit problem to have the names of the participants in the research listed in alphabetical order on the group's publications. Banting would therefore be first, Best second.[22]

There was not much for Banting to do while Collip worked to purify the extract. He did whatever experimental surgery the group needed – not much – looked after his and Best's longevity dog, 33, may have helped Best in preliminary work on extract which was then given to Collip, and fretted about his future. "Best and I became technicians under Macleod like the others," he wrote of these months many years later. "We were asked for the extract as it was required for their experiments. We were asked to provide depancreatized dogs and other surgical work. Neither plans nor experiments nor results were discussed with us."[23]

As he worked day after day, night after night, trying to purify the extract, Collip had no need to discuss anything with Banting. Banting had no expertise that would help Collip develop a complex extraction process. After showing him their method of preparing the extract early in December, neither Banting nor Best had contributed much of anything to the research. Indeed, they were now using some of Collip's improvements in making their own extract. To top it off, Banting had badly muddied the waters with the failed clinical test, apparently breaking the chain of responsibility in the group and causing all sorts of embarrassment and trouble for the others. Collip's attitude to Banting may have been just to ignore him, or it may have been openly critical, even scornful. Sometime in January, Collip realized that the severe, sometimes fatal convulsions the extract occasionally caused in rabbits stemmed from the effect potent doses had in reducing blood sugar *too* far, causing a hypo-glycemic reaction now known as "insulin shock." If Collip's discovery of this phenomenon and its antidote (sugar) came *after* the first Thompson test, he would have had particularly good reason to condemn Banting for having insisted on testing the extract before animal tests had revealed its lethal properties. He could properly have accused Banting of dangerous recklessness.

Late one January night, probably the 16th, Collip discovered how to purify the extract. He found he could "trap" the active principle in the extract. First he created a pancreas-alcohol solution in which the active principle was soluble but most of the contaminating particles were not. Then he raised the concentration of alcohol to a point at which the active principle itself was precipitated in powder form. "I experienced then and there all alone in the top story of the old Pathology Building perhaps the greatest thrill which has ever been given me to realize," Collip recalled in 1949.[24]

On January 23 Leonard Thompson was given his second injection of pancreatic extract. This time it was Collip's purified extract. The results were spectacular. The boy's blood sugar dropped to normal, the sugar in his urine almost disappeared, the ketones did disappear. The listless, semi-comatose child visibly brightened and became more active. He told his doctors he felt stronger. The doctors must have been thrilled, for they were seeing the first clear sign that the researchers had come up with something very, very big. They had a discovery to treat diabetes with.

It should have been a time for cheering and celebration. Instead, personal relations among the discoverers disintegrated almost beyond belief. Sometime between January 17 and 24, Collip told Banting and Best that he had made the breakthrough. They asked him how he had done it. He refused to tell them.

Putting the best face on Collip's attitude, he was tired and naive. In a worse light, he was arrogant, trying to rub their faces in his glory. In *The Discovery of Insulin* I speculate that Collip, like Banting, was tired and worried. There was no trust left on the team. Paranoia had begat paranoia. If the confrontation did not take place until the evening of January 24, as I now tend to believe, it is plausible that Collip and Macleod had gone ahead and had had Collip's purified extract tested on Thompson without telling Banting and Best.

It was too much for Banting. After all the work, all the failures, the plans, hopes, arguments, false starts, encouraging successes, tests, frustrations, *etcetera*, here was Collip, the latecomer, who had solved the puzzle. Collip had the secret and he wouldn't tell it to Banting. Most red-blooded Canadian men knew there was only one way to handle double-dealing like this. Collip's face was white as a sheet, Banting remembered. "He made as if to go. I grabbed him with one hand by the overcoat where it met in front and almost lifting him I sat him down hard on the chair. I do not remember all that was said but I remember telling him that it was a good job he was so much smaller – otherwise I would 'knock hell out of him'." "Banting was thoroughly angry and Collip was fortunate not to be seriously hurt," Best wrote. "I can remember restraining Banting with all the force at my command." Clark Noble once drew a cartoon of Banting sitting on Collip, throttling him. He titled it "The Discovery of Insulin."[25]

J.J.R. Macleod's wife once told friends about some of the trials of the insulin period. Her husband would be relaxing at home, the phone would ring, and he would have to rush off to deal with more quarrelling at the lab. No details of the immediate aftermath of Banting's attack on Collip survive. There is only a kind of peace treaty signed by all four of the researchers on January 25. Banting, Best and Collip agreed to work together, under Macleod's general direction, and in cooperation with the University's fledgling Connaught Antitoxin Laboratories, to develop the extract. There would be no change in policy without a joint conference. Banting, Best and Collip each promised not to take any step toward having the process independently patented (Banting's anger at Collip included a belief that he planned to try this; Collip may not have trusted Banting not to do the same).[26]

Banting and Collip had "had it out," as Canadians say, like any two boys would have had it out in the schoolyard or hockey players at centre ice. Surely the tension would be eased and the team could go on to exploit its wonderful triumph. Collip produced more extract to try on Walter Campbell's patients. Campbell and his associate, A.A. Fletcher, expanded the testing to half a dozen other diabetics. Working with J.G. Fitzgerald, the professor whose interest in antitoxins had caused the University to create the Connaught Laboratories in 1915, Collip prepared to make the extract in much larger quantities. Greenaway of the *Star* was continually pestering the team for more information, so they decided to publish a preliminary scientific report on their work. Written at the end of February, the article was entitled "Pancreatic Extracts in the Treatment of Diabetes Mellitus," by Banting, Best, Collip, Campbell and Fletcher. It appeared in the *Canadian Medical Association Journal* on March 22, 1922.

Macleod was directing several experiments designed to explore the extract's physiological effect and firm up the claim that Toronto had really discovered the internal secretion of the pancreas. Best, for example, was working on an experiment to test the extract's impact on a diabetic's respiration (he used Dr. Joe Gilchrist as his diabetic subject). Clark Noble had been added to the team to help study the substance's effect on hyperglycemic rabbits. Collip prepared the extract. Campbell and Fletcher handled the clinical testing. What was there for Banting to do? Not very much: a few pancreatectomies to create diabetes in dogs, some virtual make-work assisting Macleod in an experiment measuring fat content of the liver before and after extract. As Banting realized, there was almost nothing for him to do except serve as a technician for Macleod, Collip and Campbell, the real experts.

Banting believed they were all building on what he and Best had done. Despite the apparent reconciliation of January 25, Banting was still in a fighting mood, determined not to lose his rightful share of credit. Everyone was saying that Collip had made a workable pancreatic extract. Banting believed that he and Best had made a workable extract. They not only had all the evidence from their summer and fall series of experiments (and at least Banting had the satisfaction of seeing his and Best's first paper, "The Internal Secretion of the Pancreas," published in the February issue of the *Journal of Laboratory and Clinical Medicine*), but there was also that winter's longevity experiment. By the end of January, dog 33 had been kept alive for over eight weeks on Banting and Best's extract. Surely this dog was convincing proof that Banting and Best were the discoverers of an effective anti-diabetic extract.

It might have been, if Banting and Best's records of the dog's condition had been complete and clear. Instead, as Banting must have realized, they were very sporadic. Furthermore, as Macleod pointed out to Banting, the data he had did not rule out the possibility that the dog was surviving because it was not very diabetic. If Banting's pancreatectomy on the dog had not been complete, a fairly common flaw in pancreatectomies, enough pancreas could have survived to keep the dog alive with or without extract.

They decided to see. Dog 33 was killed on January 27. An "independent and impartial" pathologist did an autopsy. He found that Banting had missed a little piece of pancreas. It was just a tiny nodule of tissue, a few millimetres in diameter, adhering to the submucosa of the duodenum. Surely it was not enough to make a difference, Banting and Best thought. But they had to admit that it might have made a difference (tiny pieces of pancreas sometimes did; no one today can be sure whether or not this one did). The one piece of evidence Banting hoped to use to clinch his and Best's priority had to be discounted because of faulty surgery. "The experiment is not finally conclusive," he and Best admitted in their published account of it. Another failure. Everything had gone wrong.[27]

"It was an extremely trying time for me. Best was still intimate with Macleod and the others about the laboratory. I was out of the picture entirely. Macleod had taken over the whole physiological investigation. Collip had taken over the biochemistry. Professor Graham and Dr. Campbell had taken over the whole clinical aspect of the investigation. None of them wanted anything to do with me." Banting thought about giving it all up and going into practice "at some four corners where I would be useful and wanted." Sometimes he dreamed of going on to new research. What about cancer, he speculated, apparently while reading about it in Macleod's physiology text. On February 4, Banting jotted in one of his notebooks, "The cure of cancer is I think going to be brought about by the obtain [sic] of some substance (chemical or internal secretion) that will prevent multiplication of tissue cells." The next day he had an idea: "inject juice from cancer & see if it causes neighbouring cells to proliferate." Through February and into March he read desultorily about cancer.[28]

There was also his personal situation to ponder. His job in Velyien Henderson's Department of Pharmacology had certainly been a life-saver, but it was due to expire at the end of term. What could Banting do? Would Macleod want him in Physiology? In what capacity? A professor of physiology? Don't be ridiculous. A thirty-year old junior lecturer or demonstrator? Maybe.

To complicate everything, Edith was back in his life (she may never have been very far out of it), and in March they went through another agonizing round of uncertainty about their future. We know about it from tantalizingly vague jottings on Banting's desk calendar. For March 17: "The most human letter E ever wrote. Letter of farewell." Below that he wrote, "not very good – a little spirit." Perhaps he was referring to the letter, but in his 1940 manuscript, "The Story of Insulin," Banting admitted that the events of that winter had overcome him. The "little spirit" may have been the alcohol Banting was using as a sedative every night to black out his worry and unhappiness. His attendance at the lab fell off. But the lab did have this to offer: in a time of prohibition liquor was expensive and difficult to come by; full-strength alcohol was being used in making pancreatic extract. "On two occasions I actually stole a half a litre of pure 95% alcohol from the laboratory, diluted it with water and drank it in order to sleep. I do not think that there was one night during the month of March, 1922, when I went to bed sober."[29]

The group at the University decided to use a Latin root to name the extract, produced in the islets of Langerhans, *insulin*. The term was first used publicly in the paper J.J.R. Macleod presented at a meeting of the exclusive Association of American Physicians in Washington, D.C., on May 3, 1922. The occasion was close to being a formal announcement of the discovery. As they listened, the audience realized that the discovery of insulin at the University of Toronto was an epochal event in the development of modern medicine. The Toronto group received a standing vote of appreciation.[30]

Banting's name was on the paper Macleod delivered – in fact Banting came first because of his alphabetical precedence – along with the names of Best, Collip, Campbell, Fletcher, Macleod and Noble. But Banting was not there to glory in the applause. He was back in Toronto, he and Best having told the others that they couldn't afford to make the trip. Nobody believed this was the true reason.

CHAPTER FIVE

Banting Triumphant

B anting recovered from his boozy depression and began to fight back. Here is his melodramatic account, written in 1940, of the way he snapped out of his March despondency and drinking:

> About 10:30 on the night of March 31st Best came to my room at 34 Grenville. It was blue with smoke. I was partially finished my preparation for sleep. Best sized up the situation and proceeded to give me a setting out. He told me that MacLeod was vexed because he was not getting extract with which to work. Collip was unable to make an extract as he had not written down his procedure so was unable to repeat it. Campbell was held up entirely. . . . I told him I was not interested, that they could have the whole damn thing, and that I would finish the teaching term with Henderson and then look for a place where there were decent people to live with.
>
> Then Best said possibly the only thing that would have changed my attitude, "What happens to me?" "Your friend Macleod will look after you," I said. Best replied, "If you get out I get out." There was silence for some moments. I thought of all the joy of the early experiments which we had known together. Here was loyalty. I emptied my glass. "That is the last drink which I will ever take until insulin circulates in diabetic veins. Shake on it Charley. We start in tomorrow morning at nine-o'clock where we left off." Best was pleased. We sat down and as we had done hundreds of times, planned experiments.

Banting had garbled some facts, and may have sensationalized the encounter in memory, but there is no reason not to believe that it happened. Best later corroborated the story, adding that something similar happened on another occasion. This demonstration of camaraderie by Best at a time when Banting desperately needed it seems to have been crucial in Banting's later determination to share his glory with the younger man. When Banting had failed, Best came to his rescue.

The more important failure, upsetting all of that winter's plans for the development of insulin, and making possible an extraordinary reversal in Banting's fortunes during the next four months, was Collip's. He had indeed lost the ability to make effective extract. It probably happened about mid-March, after seven patients had been treated, the first paper drafted, and equipment for large-scale insulin production installed in the sub-basement of the Medical Building. When Collip tried to make these large batches he found they were not potent. Reverting to his small-scale laboratory methods, he started getting similar results: first very weak extract, then no potency at all. A laboratory problem became a human tragedy when one of the most severe diabetics, a little girl, drifted into a coma. The weak, partially prepared extract that the scientists had on hand brought her back to life momentarily. When it was used up, she fell back into coma and died.

Banting's claim that Collip lost the secret because he had not written it down makes a little sense (Collip was a fast, intuitive worker, not strong on methodical record-keeping), but was far too simplistic. Making insulin in 1922 was an adventure in the unknown, fraught with hidden pitfalls and variables, as everyone else who tried to do it found out in the next few months. In retrospect the real surprise was not that Collip failed in March, but that he had ever succeeded in January. In attempting to repeat his extraction he was like a chef trying to recreate a masterpiece using a wood stove and uncalibrated measuring cup, or a baseball player trying to hit a home run on every pitch. To add to his troubles, Collip had to spend precious time away from the lab when his family was laid low by the flu.

Plans for the development of the extract and ongoing research into its properties had to be suspended while everyone turned back to the problem of how to make it. This was when, in Banting's memory, Best persuaded him to come back to the lab. He must have come back with a certain sense of satisfaction – the big shots who had taken over had shot their bolt; now Banting and Best were needed again – combined with uncomprehending scorn at Collip's apparent sloppiness or stupidity: bugger finds the Holy Grail and then loses it. The January 25 agreement, following their fight, had only momentary success in patching up relations between Banting and Collip. Banting was so intensely angry at Collip that spring that another violent incident between them probably occurred. The most likely of several stories is that Banting grabbed Collip in the corridors of the Medical Building one day and said he'd kick his ass all the way to College Street if he didn't find the method. Passers-by pulled them apart.[1]

The fact was that Banting had never been quite as far out of the insulin picture as he saw himself in his self-pity and self-justifying recollections. He was accurate in suggesting that there was no significant role for him in the research and clinical testing before the production failure. But as word started to spread about the big discovery in Toronto, Banting was very well placed to move back into prominence, even dominance.

First, it was hard to talk or write about the discovery of insulin without using lines like these:

"How did they do it?"

"Well, it all started with Dr. Banting, and this idea he had. . . ."

It all started with Banting and his idea. He had the idea. His idea led to the discovery of insulin. He and Best did the experiments to test his idea, and it all worked. Sure, some others helped, just as people helped Edison or Marconi. But don't you call the man who had the idea for the invention the inventor? As an intelligent businessman on the University's Board of Governors once explained, offering his view of what must have happened, "If somebody came to our plant here with an idea that appealed to us we would give him a chance to work it out. We would place engineers at his disposal and would supply him with the necessary tools of steel and aid him with suggestions without which he might fall down, but we would regard him as the inventor."[2]

Outsiders could not easily understand the complex collaborative process that had led to the discovery of insulin. Even most outside medical men did not realize the flaw in the argument that it was Banting who had had the big, brilliant Idea, the one that had made all the difference. The flaw was this: Banting's idea of ligating the ducts to destroy the external secretion of the pancreas was both physiologically unsound and technically unimportant in the isolation of insulin. It was not an idea that worked, *except* in the sense that it started Banting and Best fiddling with pancreatic extracts. The results of their fiddling were good enough to convince Macleod to support more work and agree to Banting's request that Collip join them. These good results were obtained partly due to J.J.R. Macleod's advice; partly because it is difficult for anyone to make a totally inactive pancreatic extract; partly because of the new chemical technology which made it practical to obtain quick, numerous blood sugar readings; and partly because Banting and Best were unskilled enthusiasts who did not know enough to be cautious. When Collip succeeded in purifying Banting and Best's crude extract, then and only then had the Toronto team progressed beyond a stage in the search for the internal secretion which had already been reached by Paulesco and several other predecessors. As I argue at much greater length in *The Discovery of Insulin*, insulin emerged in 1921-22 as the result of collaboration among a number of researchers, directed by J.J.R. Macleod, who expanded upon and carried to triumphant success a project initiated by Banting with the help of Best. The single most important technical achievement was that made by Collip in the purification of the extract. On their own, Banting and Best would probably not have reached insulin. Their work would have been taken over and brought to a triumphant conclusion somewhere else.

A very few scientists, including such insiders as Macleod, Collip and their friends, understood how insulin had been discovered. In December 1922 a scathing exposure of the flaws in Banting and Best's early work was published in a long letter to the *British Medical Journal* from a Cambridge researcher, Dr. Ffrangcon Roberts. It was lost sight of in the celebration of insulin itself, however, and even historians and textbook writers who should have known better continued into the 1950s to credit Banting's idea with greater physiological significance than it had actually had.[4] Macleod chose not to show Roberts' criticisms to Banting. From all of his accounts of the discovery of insulin, and in Best's considered opinion, Banting never did understand the limitations of the duct-ligation idea. He had had the idea. He and Best had gone through stinking hell to get it to work out. Just when it worked, along came Macleod, who had never believed in it in the first place, to take over the work and the credit. The first and firmest believer in the Banting myth was Banting himself.

And Banting had too much grit in his character ever to give up the struggle for his place in the sun. Even in his periods of forlorn despair, Banting fought on by continuing to spread his view of what had happened: what he had done, how they had treated him. His version of the discovery process had that ring of plausibility. So, in at least a superficial way, did his belief that Macleod and Collip were running off with credit and glory that were rightfully his. Every layman knows or suspects that scientists are not beyond skulduggery. The idea that sophisticated, powerful professors might edge an innocent, trusting young researcher out of the limelight was not incredible. Everyone in the group must have realized very early on that the aura of insulin was bound to be very bright, very attractive. It was not hard to see how a conniving professor could give in to temptation and nudge Banting and Best to the rim of the circle.

And there was the attractiveness of Fred Banting himself, a likable young fellow despite his artlessness – perhaps because of his artlessness. Was there ever a more honest man than this rude, candid young doctor, explaining in his halting, unpolished way how the idea had come to him, how he had fought on against Macleod's resistance, his own lack of money, the heat and stench of the summer of '21, and was now being put out of the picture? At all times in his life Fred Banting was able to win the friendship and loyalty of other men. They liked him because of his candour, his manliness, his sincerity, his own loyalty to his friends. There was never any appearance of dissembling about Fred, no two ways about him. He said what he thought, and what he thought was true. He expected you to believe him, and if you didn't believe him you could get the hell out or be ready to fight about it. Most people who heard him tell the "true" story of the discovery of insulin believed him. Some of them, his coterie of well-placed friends, gave him very important advice as he recovered his bearings and found his way back to the forefront of the insulin work and the insulin glory.

Velyien Henderson may have been his closest confidant. Banting always gave Henderson extravagant thanks and credit for keeping him and insulin in Canada. Henderson was a quick-talking, sometimes affected, but manly and genuine man, who knew his way around the treacherous politics of the University, and was generally well regarded by his colleagues. Little is known about the advice he gave Banting, and less about his motives. It has been commonly said, particularly by Best, that Henderson disliked Macleod and played to Banting's paranoia. Perhaps he did. Others thought Henderson was more statesmanlike, helping temper the extremes of Banting's rage, playing a necessary mediating role between Banting and those in the University who scorned his scientific ignorance and his lack of polish.

Another of Banting's former instructors, Dr. G.W. "Billy" Ross, the therapeutics man, did play to Banting's ego. Ross had dabbled in research himself, announcing in 1909 his discovery of a serum to cure tuberculosis. The rather more solidly based discovery of insulin tremendously impressed Ross, who instantly idolized Banting. Not himself a distinguished figure in Canadian medicine, Ross had excellent medical/political contacts, some of them by virtue of the fact that his father, the Honourable Sir George William Ross, had been the most recent Liberal premier of Ontario. Ross junior knew how to pull levers and strings. It was Ross, for example, who seems to have alerted one of his patients, *Star* reporter Roy Greenaway, to the insulin work, and more particularly to Banting's side of the story. When Greenaway published his second major piece on insulin, on March 22, 1922 (to coincide with the *CMAJ* article), the subheading was "Banting stakes his all on the results." The story of the research heavily emphasized Banting's point of view. A follow-up story quoted a Toronto doctor, identifiable as Ross, on the "epoch-making" nature of "Dr. Banting's discovery," "one of the most brilliant pieces of research that has been done in the history of medicine." This was just the beginning of Ross's effort on Banting's behalf.

Cousin Fred Hipwell was another Toronto physician naturally determined to champion Banting's case. So was Dr. Joe Gilchrist, Banting's diabetic classmate, as well as such other classmates as his good friend Angus "Scotty" MacKay. Banting still went to C.L. Starr as a kind of father confessor, but was also taken in by another surgical friend, D.E. Robertson. Robertson, a practical, impulsive man, seems to have become increasingly impatient with the fooferaw about credit; to him it seemed to be getting in the way of the job of getting insulin into the bodies of diabetics.

Another impatient participant in the feuding was the head of the Connaught Laboratories and Professor of Hygiene, J.G. Fitzgerald. Fitzgerald formally became involved in the work at the time of the Banting-Collip fight, but may have been in contact with Banting as early as the summer of 1921.[4] Collip was the team's production expert in the spring of 1922, the liaison with Fitzgerald and Connaught. During the insulin famine the relationship between Fitzgerald and Collip seems to have become distinctly cool, perhaps because Collip was not spending much time in the Connaught facility.[5] The incident when Best brought Banting back to the lab might have started with Fitzgerald impatiently telling Best or Macleod that somebody had better get to work to do the job Collip didn't seem capable of handling.

All four of the discoverers worked long hours attempting to rediscover the knack of making insulin. Banting's notebooks indicate that his experiments with the use of glycerine in making extract did not amount to much. Macleod and Best seem to have worked together in deciding to abandon the use of an inconsistent vacuum still and resort to a procedure of evaporating alcohol from the extract solutions by a warm air current. Collip apparently suggested using acetone instead of alcohol. Banting always credited Best with the most important role in the rediscovery of the process. Later in life Best always claimed that role. Going beyond the cautious account in *The Discovery of Insulin*, I believe there is ground for speculating that Best, making use of the group's pooled knowledge and perhaps working directly with Banting, produced in mid-May the first batch of potent extract the group had seen in two months.

What did he do with it? Collip had given his finished extract to Walter Campbell for testing in Toronto General Hospital. Best, it seems, acting with or without Fitzgerald's or Macleod's consent, gave his to Banting. This was a major change of procedure which was a vital step in Banting's resurgence. Suddenly, for the first time, he had insulin to use clinically.

He had deliberately positioned himself, perhaps on the advice of his friends, to be ready to use insulin clinically. Earlier the fact that he was not practising medicine had helped disqualify him from the clinical work. It was not a permanent obstacle, for in the spring of 1922 Banting simply opened an office at 160 Bloor Street West and began the private practice of medicine. More significantly, in April an official from the Canadian government's Department of Soldiers Civil Re-Establishment discussed the insulin situation with Banting and others at Toronto, and then offered to make available patients and facilities at the Christie Street Military Hospital in Toronto for a special diabetes clinic. Banting was to be in charge of it. Now

Banting was not only practising medicine, but had better clinical facilities for using insulin than Campbell possessed at Toronto General Hospital. When Best started getting the insulin again, it was therefore hard to prevent it going to Banting for testing. Campbell and Toronto General were cut out of the picture.

The first human test of the rediscovered extract was probably on Joe Gilchrist, who had agreed to work with Banting at the Christie Street clinic, on May 15. The next week insulin was handed to an American physician, Dr. John R. Williams of Rochester, New York (just across Lake Ontario from Toronto), who had been promised extract as soon as it was available so he could try to save the life of a dying diabetic patient of his named James Havens. On May 21, 1922, Havens, the twenty-two year old son of a vice-president of Eastman-Kodak, became the first resident of the United States to receive insulin. When the first injection appeared to be ineffective, Banting himself went over to Rochester to see what was wrong. He advised sharply increasing the dose. The larger injections began working, and Banting promised to keep Havens supplied with extract – so long as there was no publicity, for fear of a deluge of requests from other diabetics.

It is not clear whether Macleod, Graham and Fitzgerald had voluntarily accepted the logic of Banting as the clinician in charge of insulin or whether they found themselves confronted with a *fait accompli* that they could not control. As head of Connaught, Fitzgerald may have played a critical role by throwing his support behind Banting and Best. He certainly did not seem to be supporting Collip, for at the end of May J.B. Collip left Toronto to go back to his job at the University of Alberta. Best took his place in charge of insulin production at Connaught. About this time Macleod in his correspondence begins referring to Banting as "my clinical associate." Macleod might have felt bittersweet relief in being able to direct the hundreds of inquiries about obtaining insulin, all of which someone had to answer, to Banting.

Banting later described the insulin position this way: "Things were stalemated. Best and I had control of the production of insulin and I had the clinic at Christie Street Hospital and had more private patients than I knew what to do with. So I decided that the Department of Medicine and the Toronto General Hospital could not have insulin for use on its wards until I had an appointment on the staff."[6] It is hard to believe that Banting (and Best) could have

94

adopted and enforced such a ruthless, ethically questionable position. It is true that Banting did control most of the insulin. At some time in these weeks it was agreed (apparently between the Connaught Laboratories and the discoverers) that two-thirds of Connaught's insulin production would go to Banting, to be split between his private practice and his Christie Street clinic. The remaining one-third would be made available for use in Toronto General Hospital and the Hospital for Sick Children.

Whether or not Banting was demanding an appointment as a condition of insulin being used at Toronto General, the doctors and the University hierarchy were beginning to realize that the situation was impossible. Insulin was being used by Banting entirely outside the control of the University of Toronto. The University had denied Banting the right to use insulin in its teaching hospital, had denied him an appointment in its Department of Medicine and (apparently) had not offered him any permanent appointment of any kind. What a way to treat a discoverer! Complicating matters further, Banting was beginning to get attractive offers to leave Toronto. In early May he was offered a position at the University of Buffalo. In early June, George Eastman of Eastman-Kodak urged Banting to come and work at the new medical school at the University of Rochester.[7] In the middle of that month Banting, Best and Clark Noble went to Battle Creek, Michigan, to talk to the staff at Dr. John Harvey Kellogg's Battle Creek Sanitarium. Kellogg, the inventor of cornflakes and peanut butter, offered to build Banting a special wing of the sanitarium and pay him $10,000 a year if he would join the staff.[8] Banting did not feel wanted by the University of Toronto. He and his insulin were wanted by almost everyone else. In fact, now that word of the discovery had spread across North America, diabetics and their doctors were clamouring for insulin. Hundreds, thousands of dying diabetics could have their lives saved by this wonderful substance.

If only the discoverers could produce more than the dribs and drabs available from the primitive rediscovered process. That spring the Toronto group had realized their limitations and decided to accept an offer from Eli Lilly and Company of Indianapolis to collaborate with them in the development of insulin. Toronto and Lilly were to pool all their knowledge; Lilly's incentive was a one-year monopoly in the United States market. To forestall other manufacturers and maintain quality control, the Toronto group would take out a patent on insulin, turning it over to the Board of Governors of the University for administration.

Banting did not dissent from these arrangements, except in suggesting that as a physician who had taken the Hippocratic oath he could not be party to any patenting of a discovery. The first patent application, therefore, was in the name of Best and Collip. (Banting's name had to be added later to avoid possible charges of misrepresentation. He was given elaborate assurances that no one would question his professional ethics.) Lilly chemists began work on the extract early in June. When their product was ready for clinical testing the plan was to begin supplying some of the leading American diabetologists who so keenly wanted insulin. A few of them were already trying to make the extract themselves. A substantial portion of the early Lilly product would also be shipped to Toronto to supplement whatever Best at Connaught could turn out.

If Banting accepted any of the offers he was getting from the United States, there might not be much further testing of insulin in Canada. Already the one juvenile diabetic Banting was treating, James Havens, was in Rochester, New York. The prospect of Banting and insulin leaving the University, and the city, and the country in which the discovery had been made was appalling. Public criticism of the men responsible for such a mess would be intense. The University of Toronto would have bungled the discovery of insulin. Faced with such a scenario, it was absolutely necessary to negotiate with Banting. What kind of university and hospital appointment would make Banting happy? "It seems to us that if we can keep a Diabetic Clinic in Toronto in present circumstances," President Falconer of the University wrote diplomatically to the chairman of the hospital board, "it will be of great advantage to everyone concerned and it would be a misfortune were it transferred to the United States."[9] A special committee of the Faculty of Medicine considered how to end the stalemate.

Realizing how fast his star was rising, Banting suggested that a new 50-100 bed diabetic wing, equipped with kitchens, labs and outpatient facilities, be added to Toronto General. Apparently thinking he could tap Eastman money in Rochester, he offered to help raise $500,000 to build it. Parallel to the clinic, the University should create a sub-department of Medicine, similar to its Paediatrics unit, to coordinate clinical and research work on diabetes and insulin. A senior physician in charge of the work would assign problems to his staff and "the results of such investigations [would] be published under the names of those who actually conducted them, or in other ways directly participated in planning them."[10]

Duncan Graham was opposed to giving Banting anything. Graham probably believed he had to protect his patients from an inexperienced, impulsive, probably unsound clinician. Over the weeks D.E. Robertson was instrumental in breaking down Graham's resistance. Their arguments about Banting nearly destroyed their friendship, but Robertson finally persuaded Graham that the dilemma – "Campbell knows all about diabetes but can not treat it, and Banting knows nothing about diabetes and can treat it," as Robertson phrased it[11] – could best be solved by some kind of compromise. Banting must have realized that he, too, could benefit from the compromise, for he and Gilchrist were woefully unprepared to conduct clinical trials of insulin in the same league with such world-class experts as Joslin or Frederick Allen, who would shortly be getting Lilly insulin. Without expert help Banting could flounder and look silly.

Late in June the University's medical establishment gave in, probably against its better judgment. Banting was offered an appointment under Duncan Graham, and in collaboration with Campbell and Fletcher, to conduct a 32-bed diabetic clinic at Toronto General Hospital. Banting was to receive the handsome salary of $6,000 a year, take on no new private patients, and be given a temporary University appointment in the Department of Medicine. Banting took his time accepting these terms, and the University of Toronto seldom does anything quickly, so the clinic did not start up until late August.

Banting's first priority in the summer of 1922 was to treat diabetics. They were starting to descend on Toronto from all over North America, begging for insulin, some of the rich offering to pay any price for it. "Diabetics swarm from all over," Fred wrote Charley that July, "and think we can conjure the extract from the ground."[12] After having been cramped by finding Macleod, Graham, Collip or someone else standing in his way all winter long, Banting suddenly found himself alone and in charge of the insulin situation. Collip was gone for good, Macleod had gone to New Brunswick to do research on fish pancreas, Graham had faded into the background and even Best was off getting a month's rest in Maine.

It would have been a good summer if only the insulin production had worked. It did not. The new process developed by Best and the others was primitive, hazardous (at one point they came close to blowing up the Medical Building), expensive and not at all reliable. The insulin made in the Meds basement was extremely impure, painful to take and often ineffective. Havens in Rochester, whose insulin was being shipped by overnight train from Toronto, suffered horribly from the injections, lost ground to his disease and hovered near coma and death. Joe Gilchrist and a few soldier-diabetics who received injections from time to time suffered badly from pain and large abscesses.

Banting agreed to take a few private patients, three of whom were terribly sick children brought up from the United States: Myra Blaustein, Ruth Whitehill and Teddy Ryder. More than sixty years later, Ted Ryder, who turned six in that summer of 1922, was interviewed as part of the research for this book. At the time he had been taking insulin longer than anyone alive in the world. Almost as remarkable was the fact that his ninety-three-year-old mother, Mildred Ryder, was also alive to be interviewed. She, of course, remembered more about Toronto than her son.

She remembered how Banting had told her physician brother-in-law that Ted should not come to Toronto until September when there might be more insulin available. "He won't be alive in September," Morton Ryder replied. Banting relented. Mildred Ryder remembered Banting's Bloor Street office – hardly an office at all, just a few supplies in an old kitchen cabinet. The doctor with the miracle drug did not seem awesome to her at all, and she noticed that the nurses and doctors at Toronto General Hospital hardly seemed to know who he was. In turn, Banting urged her to treat Ted in private quarters because they knew so little about diabetics' special diet at Toronto General. Banting would come over on a summer's evening to bring some insulin. He and Mrs. Ryder would sit at the one big table in the rented room, under a green shade, while he told her about his troubles with his girlfriend and how hard it had been to get along with Professor Macleod. Meanwhile little Ted, who had weighed only 26 pounds when he first got insulin on July 10, was responding nicely to his injections, as many as four a day.

Banting took yet another private patient when his old fellow medical officer, L.C. Palmer, who was practising medicine in Toronto, phoned one day:

> He wanted me to see a severe diabetic who had a very extensive
> infective gangrene of the leg. The only thing that would save her
> life was an operation yet the best surgeons in the City would not
> risk the operation. Would I see the case with him tomorrow?
> There was not anything in the world that I would not do for such
> a one as he. When the conversation was finished I leaned back in
> my chair and thought of the day that Palmer had taken me with
> him to the front line to reconoitre before the Battle of Cambrai
> Sept. 26 1918. . . .
> Such experiences draw men together and when he asked me to
> see his case I could not fail him. The patient was in even worse
> condition than I first thought. Her leg was in a bad condition but
> examination showed that her whole system was poisoned and
> that she was on the verge of diabetic coma. We rushed her to
> hospital. Five patients were taken off insulin and their doses
> given to this new one. The following day she was free from
> acetone. He did a rapid and beautiful amputation under gas and
> oxygen anaesthetic. I tested her every few hours and gave insulin
> when and in quantities indicated to control both acetone and
> sugar. The hours and then the days passed. She healed normally,
> the stitches were removed. She made an uninterrupted recovery.
> For years she went about on an artificial leg. It was the first major
> operation performed on a severe diabetic.[13]

The insulin supply faltered and then failed again in mid-July.
Fortunately the Lilly chemists, using more expertise and better
equipment than Toronto could command, were now able to make
insulin. Their first batch, labelled "Iletin," arrived in Toronto on
July 3 and was immediately put to use with the patients. Later in
the month, with Connaught's product proving ineffective and the
amputee, Charlotte Clarke, having been added to the list of those
relying on insulin, Banting rushed to Indianapolis to see how Lilly
was able to make good insulin and in hope of bringing more back.
"We had 150 units ready for him," J.K. Lilly wrote, "and when I
told him he could take it back with him, he fell on my shoulder and
wept. . . . Banting is really a fine chap."[14]

He seemed to be everywhere, doing everything, in the dog days of that summer of 1922. Sometimes he worked in the Connaught set-up in the basement of the Medical Building trying to make extract. Seeing the good equipment used to make insulin in India-napolis, he turned up in the downtown office of Sir Edmund Walker, chairman of the University's Board of Governors, demand-ing $10,000 to re-equip the insulin plant. When Walker demurred, Banting got angry. "Mr. Chairman, we got to get this still and I want to know if you damned Board of Governors will or will not accept the money if I get it for them."[15] Stalking out. On the train to New York. Dr. H. Rawle Geyelin phoning a rich parent of a diabetic who only asked how to fill out the cheque. On to Morristown, New Jersey, to compare notes with the great Frederick M. Allen. To Woods Hole, Massachusetts, for consultation with G.H.A. Clowes, the research director of Eli Lilly and Company whose foresight six months ago at the New Haven meeting had led to the collaboration. Finally to Boston to visit Joslin. Banting at the centre of things. A few weeks later, the Whitehills have a costume party to celebrate Teddy Ryder's sixth birthday. The last guest to arrive is a tall, slender creature wearing a long pink gown, white gloves to the elbows, a lorgnette, and a large white hat. Dr. Banting, again!

An American came to him one night and offered a million dollars for the rights to insulin. Rawle Geyelin told him that summer that if he moved to New York City he could easily clear $100,000 a year at part-time work in a clinic. Banting charged his Toronto patients regular fees: $100 for Charlotte Clarke, $25 a week to be on call night and day with his insulin-taking diabetics. This is Banting at his best. "His notion of medical ethics reveals a measure of proposed self-sacrifice that even orthodox practitioners regard as almost quix-otic," wrote a journalist in one of the early stories about him.[16]

Not all of his colleagues shared Banting's notion. Some months later, when the wife of a wealthy American publisher who had brought her diabetic child to Toronto, came down with appendicitis, she was referred to Billy Ross and then to the prominent surgeon, Herbert Bruce. Bruce charged her $500 for her appendectomy, and Ross added a consultation fee of $250.[17]

There was also Banting at his worst. Banting, a WASP country boy in a community whose educated elite set the tone of prejudice. Banting having to refuse desperate, importuning, wealthy Ameri-cans. Banting saying to his secretary one day, "You know, if I'd known so many Jews had diabetes, I don't think I'd ever have gone into it." Banting telling Mildred Ryder that he once had told Mrs. Whitehill how hard it was to keep fending off people who wanted insulin. "'And besides, they're mostly Jewish'," Banting said to Mrs. Whitehill. "'Dr. Banting,' she replied, 'Do you mean you don't know we are Jews?'" "If the floor could have opened up and swallowed me, I would have been happy," Banting told Mildred Ryder.

Banting had such a disarming air of honesty even in the telling of his prejudices. Mildred Ryder, Rawle Geyelin, and practically everyone else who met Banting that summer liked him. When they heard his story of how insulin had been discovered they tended to sympathize with him. Allen offered him a job at the Physiatric Institute in Morristown. Joslin became a firm Banting "booster." Both doctors gave Banting advice on the dietary regime he should use in treating his patients. George Clowes, the Lilly man, promised to orchestrate the American clinical testing program so that Toronto's work would be given priority. And, he wrote Banting, "you would not only get full credit for your work but it would be the first step toward securing the Nobel Prize in medicine for you and your associates."[18]

The Lilly chemists and facilities made possible a gradual easing of the insulin shortage in August. Clinical testing began in other centres. New supplies also made it possible for Banting finally to agree to treat Elizabeth Hughes, whose mother had written to Toronto several times inquiring about the situation. Elizabeth was the fourteen-year-old daughter of Charles Evans Hughes, defeated Republican candidate for the U.S. presidency in 1916, now serving as Secretary of State in the Harding administration. Since the onset of her diabetes in 1919 Elizabeth had been getting the best treatment Allen and Joslin could provide, rigidly following Allen's diet, and she and her parents hoping against hope that something would turn up before she died. In three years her weight had dropped from 75 pounds through the 60s, then the 50s, and in the spring of 1922 fell below 50 pounds. When there was enough insulin to bring Elizabeth to Toronto on August 15 they had cut the margin very finely: Banting met a living skeleton, almost five feet tall, whose skin was scaling and hair brittle and falling out from starvation. She had the prominent abdomen we see today in famine areas of Africa, had hardly any flesh left on her body, and was scarcely able to stand. Just three days away from turning fifteen, Elizabeth Hughes weighed 45 pounds.

She responded beautifully to Banting's injections of insulin, the sugar quickly disappearing from her urine, her blood sugar dropping to normal levels. The Toronto General Hospital diabetic clinic opened a week after Elizabeth's arrival in Toronto, so she became Banting's last private patient. In treating all of these patients Banting was an inexperienced physician who happened to have supplies of a life-saving substance. He knew next to nothing about the complexities of diabetes, or the intricate principles of dietary balance worked out by the pre-insulin diabetologists. The advice Joslin and Allen gave him that summer was to be careful: very gradually adjust the diet if and as a patient responded to the extract. Teddy Ryder was treated this way. With Elizabeth Hughes, however, Banting decided to throw caution to the winds and adopt the commonsense view that she needed fattening up, and insulin would enable her to do it. He put her on a normal diet, enriched by huge helpings of butter and cream. Elizabeth could hardly believe her good fortune, and her Joslin-trained private nurse was incredulous at Banting's liberality. Apparently because he was violating every principle of dietary treatment known to diabetics, Banting swore Elizabeth and her nurse to secrecy about the diet.

When the hospital's diabetic clinic began in late August, Banting transferred to it all his private patients except Elizabeth and the other American children. He and Duncan Graham almost immediately got into a thicket of misunderstandings and disputes about fees, bills for insulin (Connaught was charging $1.00 per cc. for the extract; the patients required two to eight cc. daily), correspondence from patients, the terms of Banting's appointment, the allotment of patients on the wards, and post-discharge treatment of patients. Best remembered a story, probably from this period, of Banting and Graham having quarrelled one day, with Graham accusing Banting of false representations. "I went over and lifted him up by the collar," Banting told Best, "and said, 'Professor, are you calling me a liar?' And if he had said 'Yes' I'd have smacked him, but he said 'No, just probably a mistake – I'm not calling you a liar.'"[19]

At one point Graham did tell Banting he was such a disruptive force in Toronto that he really should accept one of those fine offers and go to New York. Banting's reputation among the sophisticated, scholarly medical establishment in Toronto appears to have been that of a wild man, an uncontrollable force, likely to break out at any time causing unbelievable trouble. Others saw him as immature and troubled, badly advised, sometimes silly. He often confided in Duncan Graham's secretary, Stella Clutton, who told me how she lost patience with him one day. "Fred Banting, you're acting like a fifteen-year-old," the younger girl told him. "Why don't you grow up?" Graham later told his friends that if he had seen insulin and all the trouble it caused coming, he would have got out of its way.

Alan Brown, the physician-in-chief of the Hospital for Sick Children, did not like Banting either and resisted the idea of giving him an appointment there. According to Banting, that deadlock was finally broken when D.E. Robertson inveigled the two of them into a room together and said, "Now you two stubborn damn fools shake hands. We need insulin in this hospital and Banting needs cases."[20] His one notable case at Sick Children's was an eleven-year-old Canadian girl, Elsie Needham, diabetic for six months, who gorged herself on grapes and olives one day that October and was brought into the hospital in coma. Comatose diabetics died. Banting and Dr. Gladys Boyd gave the girl insulin. It drove her blood sugar so low that Banting got cold feet and gave her sugar. After several days of insulin and enemas, fever, delirium, and roller-coaster changes in her condition, Elsie Needham regained consciousness.[21] As the other clinicians were starting to experience with insulin, it was a wondrous thing to bring a human being back to life this way. Elsie Needham was the first Toronto example of what Elliott Joslin called the "near-resurrections" insulin caused.

Banting handled only a fraction of the cases in the Toronto General clinic. Most of the burden fell on Campbell, Fletcher and Graham. Diabetics continued to flock to Toronto to try to get treatment with the miracle substance. Those who approached Banting's private office were often interviewed by Dr. Fred Hipwell, who screened the requests, sending only the most severe cases to the clinic (many diabetics, particularly the older, maturity-onset ones, could do quite well on diet alone). Hundreds of letters and pleas for treatment went directly to Duncan Graham, who had to spend a large part of his time sorting out the neediest for admission. All of the physicians were rapidly becoming experts in diabetes and insulin therapy.

Banting was not a professional clinician, fascinated at the prospect of exploring the intricacies of insulin therapy. He saw insulin as a wonderfully powerful treatment, restoring diabetics to normality. For Banting, and perhaps other male doctors, one of the most impressive effects of insulin was in restoring a diabetic's sexual desire and potency. He liked to tell of how the Christie Street veterans had been leery of insulin until one of them returned from a weekend leave and announced that insulin had made him a man again. "By night every diabetic in the hospital was asking for insulin."[22]

Neither Banting nor those of his friends who began treating diabetics – Hipwell, Angus MacKay, Joe Gilchrist himself – joined what became an elaborate debate among the experts about the proper diet for insulin-taking diabetics. Common sense told Banting and his friends that the insulin-user should eat normally, adjusting his dosage to his diet rather than vice-versa. Fred told a story of being visited once by a diabetic who every year sent his doctor, Israel Rabinowitch (the first Montrealer to give insulin), five gallons of fine maple syrup. The patient himself still snacked on tasteless, thrice-cooked vegetables, prescribed for their bulk and lack of carbohydrates. "I thought to myself, 'My God and Rab a diabetic specialist.' I said to the old gentleman, 'I want you to do something for me. I want you to fill your syrup tin with five pounds of thrice-cooked cabbage and send it to Rabinowitch and tell him to eat it and you eat the maple syrup yourself and don't go hungry.' The poor old man gazed in amazement and I said to him, still seriously, 'I mean exactly what I say.' We talked for a few minutes and as he left he said, 'Do you still want me to speak to the Doctor about the cabbage?' 'I certainly do.' We shook hands and he was gone. I sat down and wrote to Rab."[23]

If literally true, Banting's recommendation was not good for his patient. But often his common sense may have been better medicine than the expertise of the trained, experienced clinician. In the late 1920s Rabinowitch himself became one of the first advocates of a normal diet for insulin users, an approach widely favoured today. And Banting had another good story illustrating the shrewdly realistic approach he and his friends used:

> There were two places in Toronto where a patient was given modern, balanced diets as early as 1923, namely the Western Hospital where Dr. F.W. Hipwell was in charge of the outpatient diabetics and at the old Grace Hospital where Dr. Angus MacKay was in charge.
>
> About three years after insulin was in general use I met Dr.

Edward Jeffrey in the corridor of the Pathology building. . . . He was in charge of the outpatient diabetics at the Toronto General. About his first words were "I don't think much of your insulin." "What is the trouble?" I asked. And then he explained that he saw diabetics in the outpatient Department, referred them on to the wards, as long as they were in hospital they got along fine they gained and remained sugar free – but as soon as they were out of hospital they again showed sugar and had to be put back in hospital. He explained that they were poor people and could not buy fresh vegetables like celery, tomatoes & lettuce, and cream and butter, and hence they broke diet. He asked, "What should I do with them?" "Send them all to the Outpatient department of the Western or Grace hospitals. They will likely land there ultimately." Jeffrey is not blessed with too much sense of humour and said, "Oh, I can't do that." I then explained that he should find what the patient has on his table at home and how much sugar was excreted and based on the sugar excretion give enough insulin to enable the patient to eat the diet and whatever he did if possible to keep the patient at work. He was perfectly sure that the reports were true and that I was a wild person.[24]

Banting's confidence in the soundness of his judgment was continually bolstered during the summer of 1922 by Elizabeth Hughes' wonderful progress. This most pedigreed of juvenile diabetics – both in the family sense and in her classic case history, recorded in minute detail from the onset of her disease – kept on responding beautifully to her injections of insulin and her high-calorie diet. As the flesh came back on her bones, she gained two to two and a half pounds a week, started to grow taller, and learned to give herself the insulin injections. To it all she added a bubbling, joyous enthusiasm and zest for recovery, making her an absolutely model patient.

Elizabeth naturally adored Banting. "He is so very nice, and so modest," she wrote her mother, "that it's all you can do to make him say anything about what you're most interested in." One of the highlights of her Toronto convalescence was an evening out they had together. Banting showed Elizabeth his office, and then the room over it where he now lived, its walls lined with his books and paintings. "It seems that his hobby is books and painting in his spare time and I just wish you could have seen those oil paintings he does. They are simply beautiful, showing great talent, and if he hadn't already gained distinction from being a famous doctor, he certainly would, to my thinking, gain distinction as an artist of some note."[25]

Banting was gaining medical distinction as Elizabeth gained weight. He showed her off to visiting physiologists, such as H.H. Dale, who had been sent to Canada by the British Medical Research Council to investigate insulin, and her treatment in Toronto received international newspaper publicity. Neither Elizabeth nor Banting liked to be bothered by the reporters: "Haven't they been horrible though? I hate to be written up like that all over the country and I think its cheapening to the discovery. Poor Dr. Banting's even gotten to the place where doctors are beginning to kid him about advertising his discovery through me. Isn't that perfectly horrid, though?"[26] But their stories did indeed advertise Dr. Banting as the man who had found insulin.

Banting's finest hour as a clinician came late in November 1922, when the leading North American diabetologists – Allen, Joslin, J.R. Williams, Rollin Woodyatt, Russell Wilder, H.R. Geyelin and others – came to Toronto for three days of discussion on insulin and their experiences with it. Fred Banting, who had six months' experience treating diabetics, took an active role in their discussions. He presented the case of Miss Hughes in great detail, and then, on the last day of the conference, presented Miss Hughes herself:

Well all the doctors came at last just as we were about to sit down to lunch.... They all stood in the door and just stared at me until I got so nervous I didn't know what to do. It seems to me that everytime I looked up I met the eye of one of theirs fixed on me.... Dr. Allen said with his mouth wide open – Oh! – and that's all he did. He just kept saying over and over again that he had never seen such a great change in anyone. . . . And Dr. Joslin is the sweetest man, all he could do was to look over at me and smile and say that he never saw anybody with Diabetes look so well. Of course those two doctors took the leading part over here as the others didn't have anything special to do with me and so naturally they remained in the background but marvelled just the same.... When Dr. Banting came in for a few minutes last evening to give us the one hundred ccs. of this wonderful extract he said that they had had the honor of hearing Dr. Joslin say at one of their meetings up here after he had seen me that I was the most wonderful case of Diabetes he had ever seen treated. Now think of that coming from a man like that. . . ."[27]

Think of all that the man who couldn't treat diabetes had done. He had engineered the outstanding achievement with insulin so far, the case of Miss Hughes. He was responsible for the next most interesting case, an articulate physician named Joseph Gilchrist. He had treated the first American, Jim Havens, done that amputation on Charlotte Clarke, brought Elsie Needham out of coma. He had more solid achievements in a few months than in all his life before that.

Banting now began to experience the heartfelt outpouring of diabetics' gratitude. Insulin was salvation to severe diabetics. The man or men who discovered insulin were their saviours.

"I owe my life to you . . ."

"May God Bless You and enable you to continue with your wonderful discovery."

"I feel so thankful to you for all you have done for me – for saving my life through God's great gift to you."

"Your discovery of insulin was the greatest thing I have had come into my life so far. It saved my child's life. . . ."

"I thank God and You for the New Lease of Life."

"When you think quietly about the matter it must give you a pretty fine sensation to feel that your work has been the means of making it possible to bring people back from what has always been certain death."[28]

Banting got mail from all over the world thanking him for the discovery of insulin. Wherever he went, grateful diabetics thanked him personally. His physical appearance was too distinctive to give him anonymity. In Toronto he was apt to be recognized on a street corner and thanked for saving a total stranger's life.

By late autumn of 1922 insulin was being tested clinically across the continent and the medical profession and public were beginning to herald what seemed to be the defeat of diabetes. Invitations poured into Toronto to have Dr. Banting come and describe how it had happened. Less than a year after the series of failures that had brought him to the fringes of the insulin work and the edge of a nervous breakdown, Banting was the most applauded medical man in North America. Listen to the applause:

On December 21, 1922, Banting spoke to doctors in New York

city: "Six hundred usually reserved New York physicians disturbed the scientific calm of the Academy of Medicine last night with an extraordinary tribute to Professor [*sic*] F.G. Banting, of Toronto, discoverer of the new insulin treatment for Diabetes. The Canadian scientist, a low-voiced man apparently in his early thirties, was compelled to arise and bow his acknowledgements three times before the vigorous applause of his professional audience subsided." Dr. Frederick Allen spoke at that meeting, saying of Banting, "He has made one of the greatest discoveries of modern medicine, and the name Banting will be written large in medical history. The best men have been trying without success for thirty years to do what he has done in less than two."[29]

A few days later Banting was back in Toronto where a meeting of the Federation of American Societies for Experimental Biology was being held. "Medical scientists from all parts of the Continent cheered Dr. F.G. Banting of Toronto yesterday, and hailed him one of the greatest benefactors of modern times. The discoverer of the insulin treatment for diabetes was given a tremendous ovation when he was forced to speak. . . . All afternoon eminent scientists have discussed his treatment and joined in declaring that it was one of the greatest developments in modern medicine." Allen paid him another glowing tribute.[30]

On January 16, 1923, Banting addressed the Harvard Medical Society at Peter Bent Brigham Hospital. A young Canadian medical student, Harold Segall, recorded the event in his diary: "The place was overflowing with people. . . . At 8:15 Dr. Joslin walked in with Banting – a typical stale looking Torontonian. . . . Banting was greeted with applause such as I have never heard at a medical meeting. It increased steadily in volume as the Hero of Insulin stood with bowed head waiting for the end of the uncomfortable pleasure. . . . Joslin was evidently greatly moved, tears rolling down his cheeks. . . . I wish I had more vitality in me, so that I might write a better account of this epoch making address by an ordinary looking quiet fellow. Banting looked a great man when he stood with his back to the blackboard resting his arms on the chalk ledge, frowning a little as he recalled the details of the human cases. . . ."[31]

CHAPTER SIX

The Hero of Insulin

"Banting is . . . greatly in the limelight here and seems to bask in it." J.J.R. Macleod wrote J.B. Collip in February 1923.[1] The two scientists who had contributed at least as much as Banting to the discovery of insulin, and were both deeply involved in ongoing insulin research, were understandably skeptical at the acclaim Banting was receiving. They probably did not understand Banting's own ambivalence about his fame. They knew he was certainly an odd choice to be in any limelight, but did not realize how nearly impossible it was for him to "bask" in it.

In most ways he was just an ordinary product of Alliston, Ontario, who knew nothing about hob-nobbing with the high and mighty, who had never owned more than one suit at a time in his life. Alliston was naturally proud of the achievement of its native son. The townfolk knew Fred Banting had been involved in a great discovery, and put on a big tribute to him at the Opera Hall. There seemed to be a bit of puzzlement about how Fred had managed such a big thing, because no one remembered him as being specially remarkable or promising. His mother told reporters that he was just an ordinary boy despite his honours and glory:

A little while ago, when he was home, I said to him, "You with your name in the paper! Are you the same little fellow who used to gather eggs on the farm, and go around with your arm around your mother's waist?" And he is just the same. He's still a little boy. When he was at home he would come into our room and, sitting on the edge of the bed, tell his parents everything. He still does that. He has never given his parents a moment of worry or trouble, and I am sure now he never will.[2]

(Nothing better illustrated the difficulty that ordinary folk had in coming to grips with Fred's fame than one issue of the Alliston *Herald* in February 1924. The first page contained an account of Banting, "Alliston's illustrious son," opening the new library. The other lead story that week was a "Case of Divine Healing," describing how a Rochester New York woman had been led by God to Alliston. Pastor Barnewell of the local Pentecostal Church, using "no other agency than prayer and faith," succeeded in having the Lord remove four tumours from the woman's body. One of them was about the size of a man's fist.)

Insulin threw Fred into dazzling new circles outside of Alliston. D.E. Robertson had taken him in hand the day Elizabeth Hughes and her mother arrived in Toronto, leading him to a first-rate tailor and ordering a proper blue suit and overcoat. Within a few months blue was not enough: formal dress was required at most functions honouring the Hero of Insulin. Banting hated formal dress. "No one ever got an idea in a boiled shirt," he liked to grumble. On one of the early occasions when formality was required, a dinner in Ottawa, he found he had forgotten to bring the pants to his tuxedo, and could not rent a pair. He could not avoid attending a dinner which was in his honour. There was nothing to do but wear his blue slacks with his black tuxedo and hope the guest beside him, the Prime Minister of Canada, would not notice.

Mackenzie King did not notice the gaffe in dress. He was more observant in noting that Banting was not quite sure of his role – that he was being suitably modest, but that the modesty was being a little overdone. "I asked Banting where he lived and he said in an attic." Best was having the same kind of problem, King noted in his diary, but on the whole the talk was good and they were both "good types."[3]

By the time of that dinner Banting was beginning to loathe the attention he was getting from the press. Apart from the personal bother involved in being pestered by newsmen doing their duty, Banting shared the dismay and anger all of the Toronto group felt about the way the premature press coverage of insulin had misled diabetics, causing no end of misunderstanding and extra work for the researchers. When reporters met him at the station in Ottawa on this trip he refused to talk to them. Though often halting and inarticulate, Banting sometimes drew on his wit and his education for a nifty turn of phrase. He told the reporters that they had printed so much "rot" about insulin that to talk to them would be "simply casting pearls before swine." Was it true that Banting would be lunching in Rideau Hall with the Governor General? "Not for newspaper purposes."

He did have lunch with Lord Byng, the Governor General. They may have compared notes on newspapermen. In any case, the day caused Banting to jot down his feelings on his desk calendar:

> Nobility and public people are alright but I pity them from the bottom of my heart. Of all people, they have the least liberty. They can't do anything without those damned newspaper reporters trumpeting far & wide.
>
> There are so many things that are dearest to oneself that should never see daylight and those reporters in their wild passion for a story would even enter the holy of holies.
>
> Poor Lord Byng.[4]

Public speaking was about as difficult an ordeal for Banting as dealing with the press. He was not naturally at home before an audience, tending to be quiet, slow-talking and nervous. He worried a lot before a speech, and was restless afterwards. "Every speech I have ever given," he wrote in 1936, "has been preceded and followed by hyperacidity, diuresis, diarrhoea and diaphoresis." Seale Harris remembered an occasion when he gave a good speech preceded and followed by Canadian Club whiskey.[5] In this early period of his fame Banting felt that he had to live up to the public's expectations, doing his duty of publicizing his discovery. As we see below, the thought that the publicity helped make the discovery more firmly *his* may have occasionally crossed his mind.

Fame was very tiring. By February 1923 Banting was wishing he could get away from the limelight and find some peace and quiet. "This is an awful life," he wrote in his desk calendar the day after a thousand Torontonians cheered him at a Canadian Club luncheon. "One responsibility after another – too many things are crowding me – I have not enough time to myself." The desire to get away from it all became a refrain for the rest of Banting's life, just as it had been in London in 1920-21. Often, we will see, he acted on it; but until his last flight, he always came back to his responsibilities.

The adulation continued for the rest of his life. He was the "Greatest Living Canadian" or some variant thereof in five separate surveys done in the 1920s and 1930s. The Prime Minister usually came second. Some recent academic writing suggests that Banting fitted his countrymen's need for "a cultural hero of mythic proportions," "a hero of the archetypal mythical pattern."[6] The more prosaic, occamesque, explanation of Banting's stature as a hero is that most people thought he had made one of the greatest medical discoveries of the age. In point of fact the earliest and loudest applause for Banting's achievement had come from his fellow physicians – who themselves no doubt needed mythic heroes, but also were honestly applauding insulin. Nor was the applause confined to Canadians, for doctors and newspaper readers throughout North America gloried in the story of the ordinary, country-born doctor who carried his brilliant idea through adversity to triumph and immortality.

It has been suggested that profiles of Banting instinctively or unconsciously stressed those aspects of his character which fit the heroic myths Canadians unconsciously revered. He was a plain rural boy, a hard worker, he loved his mother, he had triumphed over adversity. Of course this was all factually correct, and it would have been hard to write about Banting without mentioning these aspects of his life. But newspapermen did go much further, sometimes to almost comic extremes, in trying to make virtues out of Banting's plainness. How wonderfully modest and humble he was! If he came from simple surroundings, and hid his intellectual light during his schoolboy years, the journalists saw these as common themes in the careers of great men. And of course we cannot expect great men to cooperate smoothly with the press. After one of Banting's curt refusals to be interviewed, a reporter idolized him anyway:

> In his visit to London, Ontario, Banting gave an excellent dual impersonation of an oyster in one of its most silent moments and a turtle retreating into its shell when confronted by a reporter. . . .
>
> He is so modest that he is almost violent. But one can't help liking him. All the honour he has received has not turned his head. He is not conceited. He is not really self-conscious. He is genuinely modest and utterly uninterested in publicity. He reminds one a little of a small boy asked to recite something in front of the class when he wants to go swimming. . . . He has something of Shaw's contempt for what people think about him, and one can't help liking him for it. It is a refreshing rudeness.[7]

The process at work here is not so much deliberate or intuitive myth-making as it is the journalist's or everyman's assumption that great events must be authored by great and praiseworthy men. Stephen Leacock wrote the classic account of one such man, an ordinary farmer on whose land gold seemed to have been discovered. Suddenly Tomlinson of Tomlinson's Creek was a "Wizard of Finance":

> Anyone who had known him in the olden days on his bush farm beside Tomlinson's Creek in the country of the Great Lakes would have recognized him in a moment. There was still on his face that strange, puzzled look that it habitually wore, only now, of course, the financial papers were calling it "unfathomable." There was a certain way in which his eye roved to and fro inquiringly that might have looked like perplexity, were it not that the *Financial Undertone* had recognized it as the "searching look of a captain of industry." One might have thought that for all the goodness in it there was something simple in his face, were it not that the *Commercial and Pictorial Review* had called the face "inscrutable," and had proved it so with an illustration that left no doubt of the matter. Indeed, the face of Tomlinson of Tomlinson's Creek, now Tomlinson the Wizard of Finance, was not commonly spoken of as a *face* by the paragraphers of the Saturday magazine sections, but was more usually referred to as a mask; and it would appear that Napoleon the First had one also. The Saturday editors were never tired of describing the strange, impressive personality of Tomlinson, the great dominating character of the newest and highest finance. . . .
>
> Some writers grew lyric about him. What visions, they asked, could one but read them, must lie behind the quiet, dreaming eyes of that inscrutable face?[8]

When Canada's Wizard of Science returned to Alliston to a hero's welcome in February 1923 the Toronto *Star* reporter observed how "from behind his glasses looked forth a pair of eyes which even in their most casual glance gave the impression of penetrating beneath the surface of things and reading secrets not revealed to ordinary eyes."[9]

In Leacock's story the riches of Tomlinson's farm turn out to be fool's gold; the Wizard of Finance happily disappears back to his farm and his obscurity. Banting could escape from time to time, but he could never go back, for insulin was the real thing. And he, of

113

course, was its discoverer. A generation of medical textbook writers printed his version of the idea as though it had been the physiological insight necessary to the discovery of insulin. In 1980 a very distinguished British medical man who had met Banting several times kept marvelling to me about how the Canadian had had "the simplicity of genius" in going to the heart of a scientific question. Those who knew Banting better, or knew their science better, realized he was a very attractive Tomlinson from the third line of Essa Township.

The *sine qua non* of Banting's popularity was the persistence of the belief that he was the genius who had discovered insulin. It was an appealing belief, we have seen, greatly strengthened by Banting's prominence as the doctor who gave insulin in the summer and fall of 1922. But it was not a universally held belief, for at least a few others, notably Macleod and Collip, knew what had really happened. They were not without friends or influence.

It was vitally important to Banting, and to his friends, that he stay on top in the ongoing discussion of who had discovered insulin, and that his top position be certified by appropriate public and institutional recognition. Remember: Banting's plainness, his dislike of the limelight, his modest demeanour, and his other humble traits, were always tempered by his belief in his own achievement. Yes, dammit, he had done great things, and he did deserve honour and glory. He sure as hell deserved it more than J.J.R. Macleod or J.B. Collip.

The debate about credit for insulin flared briefly and semi-publicly in the autumn of 1922. Macleod was back in Toronto. Banting was riding high as the great insulin doctor. The great British physiologist, Sir William Bayliss, lit the tinder with a letter to *The Times* claiming that chief credit for the discovery should go to Macleod. He dismissed Banting as a lesser and later collaborator. The article was quoted in the Toronto *Star*. When Best went to Macleod and complained that Bayliss had been unfair to Banting, Macleod replied, "Banting will have to get used to it." Whatever Macleod meant by the statement – that Banting would have to live with distortions in the press, or that he would have to live with second billing – it was a red flag to Banting. He rounded up Greenaway of the *Star* and went to see Macleod. When Macleod refused to comment on the offensive article, Banting asked Greenaway to leave the room, then had it out with Macleod. Since the spring he had compiled a new list of injustices: disparaging comments by Macleod that had come back to him, Macleod's denying Banting *carte blanche* to spend part of the insulin research grant, an article by Macleod neglecting Banting's work. He was convinced that Macleod was again manipulating the situation. Banting threatened to cause a public controversy unless Macleod contradicted Bayliss's letter.

Macleod gave in and gave Greenaway a carefully worded statement. The *Star* published it under the heading, "Gives Dr. Banting Credit for Insulin," and Greenaway interpreted it as a firm statement settling the matter of credit. In fact Macleod only gave Banting credit for the initial duct-ligation experiment. Banting realized this and insisted that Macleod give him full credit for the discovery of insulin as it was being used in the treatment of diabetes. Macleod refused.[10]

Until now – the autumn of 1922 – there had been no serious discussion of Charles Best's role in the discovery. After their showdown in June of 1921, Banting and Best had worked smoothly together, apparently without friction, as partners who became friends. They had taken in movies and plays and dinners, and had sometimes double-dated, although Fred's complicated relations with women had always put a bit of a damper on that side of things. They published four joint papers about their work. Banting usually described these early experiments as the work of Banting and Best. He always remembered, too, that Best had come to his aid when he was down. A man must not easily forget that kind of personal loyalty.

On the other hand, Banting had moved into the clinical use of insulin on his own (Best's 1922-23 job was to produce insulin at Connaught, a constantly frustrating effort which, in total, amounted to something of a disappointment. Substantial quantities of Lilly insulin had to be imported into Toronto well into 1923), and he saw no reason at all to share credit for his idea, or for such subsidiary ideas as the turn to foetal pancreas in November 1921. He did not always remember to emphasize Best's role in the discovery. As I conclude in *The Discovery of Insulin*, Banting saw Best as the comrade who had gone through the wars with him and had rescued him when he lay wounded. Thinking of this in the dispute with Macleod, and being in a mood to give the professor a lesson in credit-sharing, Banting issued a statement clarifying Best's role in the work:

> While the idea, it is true, is mine, Mr. Best must have equal credit for the success we have attained. I never would have been able to do anything had it not been for him. We have worked side by side, sharing ideas and developing them together, and but for his unflagging devotion and enthusiasm and his patient and meticulous work we would never have made the progress we have.
>
> From the very beginning it has been a case of Banting and Best, and if our hopes are realized I desire to see Mr. Best given all the honour that would be his due.[11]

We will never know all the details of the quarrelling that September. Macleod referred to Banting's "fresh outbreak" having stirred up "unbelievable trouble." Banting had "succeeded so well in sowing the seeds of distrust in me," Macleod wrote, "that it will be necessary for me not to take any step that could possibly be misinterpreted."[12] Colonel Albert Gooderham, a prominent member of the University's Board of Governors who was helping administer the discovery by serving as chairman of the Insulin Committee, tried to clear the air. He asked Banting, Best and Macleod to each write down their version of what had happened. Banting had actually started trying to write up his side of the story several months earlier.

When he finished his account, he had produced 3,500 words of self-justification that were virtually impossible to reconcile with Macleod's history of the same events. Banting did not directly accuse Macleod of unethical or improper behaviour, and was perfectly willing to credit him with excellent work in organizing the physiological *investigation* of insulin. But the *discovery* belonged to Banting, perhaps to Banting and Best. His harshest accusations were directed at Collip, whom he charged with having wanted to patent the extract. In a somewhat meek conclusion Banting implied that many of the misunderstandings between himself and Macleod might have been cleared up if only the professor had trusted him and been more cooperative.[13]

Trust and cooperation were never restored. The next round that fall was a quarrel over laboratory space. Banting wanted to supplement his clinical work with research. Macleod, who was supervising a large number of research projects probing the nature and action of insulin, did not have room for him in the Physiology Department (in which Banting had no appointment; his only University position, Senior Demonstrator in Medicine, was solely to legitimize his work at the Toronto General Hospital clinic). Nobody else in the University seemed to want to give him lab space. He was "on the verge of starting a private laboratory outside of the University on my own initiative," he wrote, when Velyien Henderson once again came to his rescue. Henderson provided Banting with space and Macleod agreed to pay the costs of Banting's work.[14] From mid-October 1922 Banting again had lab space at the University. He also had a new assistant, Miss Sadie Gairns, a native of Toronto who had taken her first degree in Household Science and then done a Master of Arts in Physiology with Macleod. Banting would have preferred a male assistant, Henderson told Miss Gairns when he offered her the job, but there was not enough money to pay for one.

Banting was now doing research on his own, free for the first time from what he had thought was the stifling supervision of Macleod. In the first of his post-discovery experiments with insulin, Banting injected some rabbits with insulin plus diphtheria and typhoid toxin. The rabbits died. Studying alternative methods of administering insulin, he diluted insulin in alcohol and gave it by mouth to a dog. Result: an intoxicated dog, which staggered around in its cage and then collapsed. "Dead drunk," Banting noted. Neither oral administration of insulin nor rectal insertion had any effect.[15]

He began searching for the cause of diabetes. Deciding that diabetes probably developed when the islet cells of the pancreas could not produce insulin, he experimented with ways of irritating the pancreas to try to show this. On November 10, 1922, for example, he tried to inject hot water into the pancreatic blood vessels of a live dog on the operating table. When that did not seem feasible, he simply injected a hot saline solution all over the pancreatic tissue. "I should judge that the greater part of the pancreas was 'parboiled'," he wrote in his notebook. Soon he devised a more sophisticated procedure to measure the effect of heat on the pancreas. It involved entering the abdomen, cutting away part of the pancreas, wrapping rubber tubing around the organ, then closing the incision with both ends of the tube extruding. With the dog hanging suspended in mid-air, Banting could "irrigate" its pancreas more or less at will.

He was working on the hypothesis that an excessive blood supply, hyperemia, caused hypersecretion of insulin from the islet cells and their consequent exhaustion. He elaborated on it in a short paper, written about December, in which he further argued that the relationship between excess weight and diabetes stems from the drag on the transverse mesocolon in obesity. This pressure, Banting felt, would cause congestion in the pancreas leading to degeneration of the islets. So the "rational treatment for Diabetes," he suggested, was low sugar intake, insulin if necessary, and the wearing of a snug abdominal belt to relieve the drag on the pancreas.[16]

Banting did not publish this paper, which was just as well. His research and reasoning were pathetically ill-informed, bearing the same relationship to serious physiological inquiry that a farmer's tinkering with a beat-up Ford would to advanced engineering.

Banting did discuss his theories with two distinguished physiologists. On November 24, 1922, over dinner at the prestigious York Club, he told J.J.R. Macleod and the visiting Nobel laureate, August Krogh, of his hypothesis. Krogh politely suggested that there must be some other mechanism than congestion which produced hypersecretion of insulin. Perhaps it was nerve or hormonal stimulation. Banting challenged Krogh to prove that such a mechanism acted on internal secretions, thought he had won his point when Krogh admitted there was no proof, and went home with his hypothesis unshaken. We can only speculate on the impression the evening's conversation had on Krogh, who soon afterwards wrote an important nomination for the Nobel Prize. He nominated both Banting and Macleod, arguing that Banting could not have reached insulin without Macleod's help.[17]

As Banting continued his researches in the winter of 1922-23, the question of his future in the University became entwined with the issue of how the great discoverer would be honoured. Why had the University of Toronto not heaped honour and praise upon Banting, newspapermen began to wonder in the autumn of 1922? What would the University, what would the Province of Ontario, what would the Canadian people themselves do to honour the discovery and the discoverer?

Banting wanted his future to be in research. It was a natural enough desire in view of how well the "diabetus" idea had panned out. In view of Banting's training, how the insulin research had actually gone, and the fumblings he was currently engaged in, it was quixotic, naive, almost absurd, to believe that Banting could function effectively on the frontiers of medical science. Banting was trained and qualified to practise medicine and surgery. He would have chosen the post-insulin career most suited to his abilities if he had left the University of Toronto to practise medicine.

Fred apparently did not see this, and would not have listened to the person most qualified to tell it to him, J.J.R. Macleod. Or, insofar as he might have realized his limitations, he could point out that the discoverer of insulin would never be able to practise medicine normally. He would be besieged by diabetics, and would have to become a diabetes specialist, imprisoned by his fame. Banting may have known that even insulin would not arm him with long-term staying power in this specialty. He had never had much interest in diabetes anyway. While the insulin experience obviously quickened his interest, it was in finding more cures, not in staying with the disease he thought he had conquered. In his own and his friends' eyes he was not so much a diabetes doctor as a discoverer, a research man who had had an idea. Whether or not the idea he was working on, about the cause of diabetes, would lead to anything significant, there were other diseases and other ideas – remember the thoughts he had had about cancer early in 1922. There might be other internal secretions to be found. Give him the financial support and the free time necessary to devote his life to research, and he would surely come up with something.

Another possible course for Banting would have been to get out of Toronto and get some advanced training in medical science and research. It was the path Charles Best was advised to follow, and soon did. For Banting it was too late. The world-renowned discoverer of insulin could not possibly become a graduate student again. And why should he? Wasn't success at medical research a matter of the quality of your ideas, not the quantity of books you had read? The only advanced degree Banting earned – he got many honorary degrees – was his M.D. from the University of Toronto, awarded in 1922 for some of his insulin work.

The University of Toronto took no initiative in the Banting situation. Whether the inaction was normal academic ponderousness or stemmed from more considered doubts about Banting's ability cannot be determined. The nearly fanatical discretion exercised by President Sir Robert Falconer and many of the institution's leading governors and professors in that era has made it difficult to penetrate their thinking on the Banting matter. Some University people, particularly laymen serving on the Board of Governors, undoubtedly believed that Banting was a great genius who ought to be given unlimited research facilities. Anyone who talked to the most powerful and respected medical scientists in the University – Macleod, Duncan Graham, even C.L. Starr – would have heard a different opinion, not only of Banting, but of how insulin had been discovered. None of these men would have considered Banting as anything like his equal; all would have been unenthusiastic, not to say appalled, at the prospect of the University offering him a permanent, senior appointment. Apparently some governors did sound out informed opinion, for Billy Ross discerned a "Mugwump" element on the Board of Governors who were reluctant to acknowledge that Banting was wholly responsible for the discovery.[18]

It may have been the threat of such sentiments that caused Banting's friends, notably Ross and Velyien Henderson, to plan and execute a campaign to combine public recognition of Banting with the granting of a university sinecure. The idea was to have the Ontario government recognize Banting by funding a special research chair at the University of Toronto, separate from all the regular departments, which he would hold for the rest of his career. "Will *not* work with or have anything to do with Prof Macleod," Banting noted the first time he considered a research position. When Henderson presented the idea to Falconer, Banting heard that Macleod was "jealous as h— and raises the objection to Defries that Collip his dear disciple in selfishness will be left out if the government take any step in such a manner as they propose."[19] The only comfort Macleod might have taken from the proposal, when he thought about it, was that Banting would not be attached to his department. Banting's post in the University would have to be independent of the regular departments for a very good reason: he was not qualified to be a professor in any of them.

The campaign to honour Banting hinged on recognizing him as the sole discoverer of insulin. He had given a copy of the version of the discovery he had written in September 1922 to Billy Ross. Ross circulated it judiciously among leading Canadian politicians. The Banting group wanted to influence federal as well as provincial politicians, for the government of Canada should surely lead the way in recognizing this greatest of all scientific achievements by a

Canadian. To reinforce his assault on Ottawa, Ross wrote to the leading American diabetologists, plus Charles Evans Hughes, saying that Canada was thinking of honouring Banting and, in effect, soliciting their testimonials about his achievement as the discoverer of insulin. Ross did not ask for their views on any of the other participants. No politician received J.J.R. Macleod's account of the discovery of insulin.

Ross also solicited the active support of Sir William Mulock, former vice-chancellor (soon to be chancellor) of the University, former federal cabinet minister, newly appointed Chief Justice of Ontario, and a powerful figure in the Liberal party. Mulock had given the Prime Minister, Mackenzie King, his first job in government. During his term as Postmaster General, Mulock had usefully assisted Guglielmo Marconi when he was having difficulties with the British government. Mulock had indirect links with the Banting family, having long ago helped Fred's father with a mortgage. The octogenarian politician enthusiastically took up Banting's case with Mackenzie King. He saw Banting as another Marconi — and more, a Canadian boy who had done this great thing for the benefit of humanity. Certainly Canada had to honour him.

How could the nation reward its brilliant scientist? Until very recently Canadians of the distinction insulin conveyed would be recommended for titles from the king. Influenced by wartime hysteria about profiteering baronets, however, the government of Canada had decided in 1919 no longer to request titles for Canadians. So Banting's friends could not urge that he be knighted. The next best recognition would be financial. As Ross and Mulock knew, it was a fairly common Canadian practice for the friends of prominent political figures to raise special funds to enable them to stay in public life without financial worry. Why not ease Banting's burdens so that he could stay in the research life without financial worry? But do it from public rather than private funds, by giving Banting some kind of annuity for life, just as the state was rewarding its military heroes.

Banting had given Ross his account of the discovery, was involved in his friends' planning, and wrote at least one letter supporting the request for testimonials. For Banting the justification of the campaign was to ensure that he not lose the credit rightfully his. Ross and Mulock were genuinely hero-worshipping. Imagine Banting telling the story of insulin to those who idolized him, and then

121

mentioning that he had this idea about cancer that he'd like to try. The result is Mulock writing to King: "Banting in the matter of research has the research instinct. In part is I think almost a genius in matters of research work. Those who know him so describe him, a simple, unaffected, shy and thoughtful man, contemplate his solving the cancer problem. Is it not worth taking the chance of enabling him to devote himself to the work?"[20]

Imagine Banting telling the same story to Frederick M. Allen and Elliott Joslin, both of whom were too dazzled by what insulin was doing in their practices and too busy using it to rethink the discovery process. They wrote glowing, powerful testimonials:

> From Allen: Insulin is performing miracles. . . . Banting holds clear and undisputable priority in the discovery of insulin, which undoubtedly will rank among the leading achievements of modern medicine. . . . In meeting Dr. Banting I have been impressed by his very promising ability, and he will not stop with this one discovery.

> From Joslin: All that I imagined and more than I hoped could be accomplished Dr. F.G. Banting has done. . . . Not many weeks ago Dr. Banting spent a night at my house and sat up until two o'clock in the morning, telling me about other undeveloped and as yet unmatured work which may be as remarkable as that he has already accomplished. Please let me know if I can do anything to promote a grant to Dr. Banting from your Government.[21]

Testimonials from other leading American diabetes doctors were almost as effusive. Charles Evans Hughes, one of the greatest American statesmen of the time, wrote Mackenzie King about what insulin had done for Elizabeth, saying "I cannot adequately express my gratitude for Dr. Banting's work."[22] With friends like this, who needed to worry about his enemies? Especially when no one was asking for their views.

King did take the precaution of asking Sir Robert Falconer to confirm the belief "that what is of greatest significance in the discovery is due to Dr. Banting." The president's reply was so tactful ("There is of course the case of Mr. Best, and furthermore Dr. Collip of Alberta, who did valuable work on the chemical side in connection with its refinement. Whether you should recognize these gentlemen in addition to some extent is a matter for you to decide") that it became effectively meaningless.[23] Banting himself was beginning to worry about Best being left out of the glory. Best had no powerful friends in Toronto. Banting's friends tended to see Best as an assistant rather than a partner, and happily and deliberately left him to fend for himself. But when the Premier of Ontario, E.C. Drury, came to his lab to discuss with Banting the idea of setting up a research chair for him, Banting asked Drury that it be named not just the Banting Chair, but the Banting and Best Chair.

Neither Collip nor Macleod was at all comfortable with the scheming to recognize Banting. They did not make their private objections public. Perhaps they felt it would be hopelessly difficult to challenge Banting. Perhaps they sensed that history would vindicate them. Almost certainly they felt that an all-out public dispute about credit for insulin would be a discredit to all the participants. Neither man had friends with the Canadian political connections that would make possible a little quiet diplomacy on behalf of the other discoverers. Both of them were deeply involved in continuing research, with Macleod being specially burdened as the secretary of the University's Insulin Committee. He was also fed up with feuding, commenting in a letter to a friend that "if every discovery entails as much squabbling over priority etc. as this one has, it will put the job of trying to make them out of fashion."[24] So the only people who could challenge Banting's and his friends' claims left the political field, refusing to do battle.

Some other sentiments may have been involved in the Banting-admiration movement. In later life, Best believed that Banting had been deliberately singled out by Mulock, Ross *et al.*, because he was the Ontarian in the group. Macleod was a foreigner, Collip now worked in far-off Alberta, Best had been born in the United States. So Banting's prominence had something to do with local chauvinism in Toronto.

Best may have been right, but in fairness to Banting's friends little evidence has been found of their having thought in these categories. Expressions of xenophobia or chauvinism such as criticisms of Macleod as a foreigner are surprising in the insulin story by their absence. The only exception is Velyien Henderson's comment to his wife when Macleod resigned his chair in 1928: "I do not want to see another cocky overbearing foreigner in Physiol. no matter whether he be English or American." Canadian nationalism was present, of course, in Canadians' deep pride in their countryman's achievement, as well as in a strong feeling that Canada had to reward its talented men lest they emigrate to the United States. The latter sentiment was particularly prevalent in the early 1920s, a time of substantial and continuing exodus of highly trained Canadians to greener American pastures.

The insulin question may also have become entwined with public concern about the nature and management of the University of Toronto. The modernization of the Faculty of Medicine, including the appointment of its first "full-time" professors, had led to powerful resistance from the old guard of Toronto medical practitioners. Billy Ross was among that old guard. He introduced Banting to some of the other disaffected and highly political doctors, particularly the ambitious surgeon, Herbert Bruce, who then did useful lobbying on Banting's behalf. They may have seen Banting as someone they could use to oppose the new establishment in the Faculty of Medicine, men such as Macleod and Graham. The problem was that Banting idolized the full-time Professor of Surgery, C.L. Starr, who was one of the old guard's chief targets. There is one confused note in Banting's desk calendar after a long talk with D.E. Robertson about the University crisis: "I am persuaded that there is some right on both sides. Macleod is certain selfish & I do not believe that Bruce or Ross could be any such thing yet Graham & Starr like Macleod & hate the former."[25] More generally, it must have cheered the old-fashioned medicos, like Ross and Bruce, to see a great discovery made by an old-fashioned ordinary doctor like Banting, rather than those high and mighty professional researchers.

Finally, Ross and Mulock were highly placed Liberals. Many of the University issues had turned into partisan conflicts in Ontario, with the Liberals championing the old ways and the left-out little man against the modernization and meritocratic elitism of the provincial Conservatives. Advancing the cause of Fred Banting, a simple, much put-upon, Ontario genius, against an arrogant, ruthless scientific Establishment was a good Liberal cause. At times the Ross-Mulock machinations came close to being a Liberal party conspiracy.

As the honouring game developed, Banting went to bat for Best from time to time, but never consistently or totally. Otherwise, he was content with his friends' work and was grateful to them for the rest of his life. There is only one hint in his papers of second thoughts. Late in May 1923 Banting, Macleod and Elliott Joslin all gave lectures on diabetes in New York City. Afterwards Joslin apparently told Banting about some impending article or talk or occasion where Joslin planned to give him and Best full credit for insulin. That night Banting scribbled out a letter to Joslin:

My dear Dr Joslin

Some unused pages of my diary are all I have but I know you will not mind.

I cannot go to bed without writing to you.

I cannot tell you the feeling you caused in me today when you spoke to me and I know Best will be so happy too. There is only one thing that mars my happyness (and I want to tell you) and that is that from what you said only our two names are to be mentioned. I wish you could mention all the names and especially Prof. Macleod. I feel so different about so many things now. Possibly I was selfish and did not get the proper prospective.

I have recently learned that Prof. Macleod is being criticized by some, and I am very sorry and would do anything to save him from it because he is such a wonderful man & has done so much for Insulin & for diabetics. Personally I want to sink any personal element because of this fact.

I want to take the opertunity of this personal confidential note to express to you Dr. Joslin my appreciation of your kindness to me.

I have received a great deal of inspiration from the kindly, unselfish altruistic personality with which you seek to investigate teach and treat diabetes.[26]

In the hard light of morning Banting evidently had second thoughts. There is no sign the letter was sent.

The Joslin letter suggests that Banting sometimes had doubts about the merits of his case. Another private view describes his more typical mood that spring. A Toronto physician, Dr. John Harris McPhedran, invited Banting to dinner one night in March, and described him in his diary as follows:

Banting whose name will go down in Medical circles as the discoverer of the hormone Insulin is a very shy modest man with a keen sense of humour & much evidence of tenacity of purpose. He is loyal to an institution namely the University of Toronto which he believes has used him badly, inasmuch as he refused an offer to go to an American Institution at $10,000 per annum, with charge of 100 beds and a staff of thirty assistants, provided of course I suppose that this Institute get control of Insulin. To a man hard up it was very tempting but he has remained here & will remain I believe. He does not look brilliant but must be a man of ideas.

The fame and the fortune came together for Banting in the first six months of 1923. A shower of prizes and medals began to descend on him from Toronto and other universities. Queen's University of Kingston, Ontario, gave him his first honorary degree in May. More important, the Ontario government announced that month that it was establishing the Banting and Best Chair of Medical Research at the University, funded with a direct annual grant of $10,000. Banting was to be a permanent Professor of Medical Research, at an annual salary of $5,000.

Ross continued to apply pressure on Ottawa for an annuity. In a typical gesture to add more legitimacy to Banting's cause, Ross arranged to have the Toronto Academy of Medicine pass a special resolution declaring that Banting and Best had priority in the discovery of insulin. On June 27, 1923, the Canadian House of Commons unanimously voted to grant Banting, in recognition of the discovery of insulin, a lifetime annuity of $7,500, "sufficient to permit Dr. Banting to devote his life to medical research." Banting was now an independently wealthy medical researcher – $12,500 went a long way in the 1920s, and even further in the 1930s – with a lifetime appointment to do nothing but research. Such was his countrymen's and his friends' gratitude to him for the discovery of insulin. "Banting is not likely to be robbed of the credit of this great discovery," Mulock wrote Ross. "The press is now speaking so splendidly of Banting's work, that he renders some risk of having his head turned. However I fancy he is a level-headed fellow. Genius is always modest."[27]

News of the annuity reached Banting at sea, on the *Empress of France*, where he was bound for England for a summer of conferences and sightseeing and resting. "I wish they would give you an equal amount," he wrote Best. "Surely blessings are falling on us fast enough now. We must keep our heads."

A blizzard of cables and letters followed him across the ocean. The directors of the Canadian National Exhibition wanted him to preside at the opening ceremonies in Toronto in August. Ross telegraphed to say he had accepted on behalf of Fred, just as Hipwell telegraphed advising against accepting – "nothing to gain but honor, might lose much through advertising." The tireless Ross lobbied to get the Academy of Medicine to support Banting's appearance, persuaded the CNE officials to downplay the "circus parade" aspects of the occasion, and persuaded Banting to accept this opportunity to advance the prestige of the medical profession. Then news arrived of Best's extreme disappointment at not having shared in the largesse of the government of Canada. Best and Fitzgerald were trying to get Prime Minister King to reconsider, but had no luck. Best was sure he had been victimized by Ross's method of soliciting testimonials for only Banting's work. "Dr. Ross could just as well of had the thing come through Banting and Best. . . . You say that Dr. Ross is a friend of mine. I can not see it."[28]

Banting was disturbed by Best's letter, assured him "that you will be looked after in some way," and wrote Fitzgerald that the Connaught Laboratories should do some of the looking after. Banting would make sure Best was given due place at the Exhibition ceremony – "which I wish was in Hades." Fred was fed up: "All I want in the world at present is to get down to work quietly and uninterruptedly in a lab. Any person can have any damned thing they like if I can only be left alone. I have some new remote ideas in a new field and am going to give up practice and everything pertaining to Insulin, and am sick of it all."[29]

There are traces of evidence that Banting had hoped to bring more than glory with him on this trip to England. Banting's desk calendar records that on June 2, with Edith Roach's brother and sister, he went to Port Hope where Edith was now teaching, and brought her back to Toronto. "Took Edith home to Alliston with me," he wrote the next day. "We went to church that night." He rushed off to speak in Philadelphia and Washington, making only one more relevant entry in his calendar, on June 6: "I certainly dont know what to do about Edith. She is certainly the only woman that ever got me properly & she certainly has – and yet . . ."

Edith's cousin, Spencer Clark, remembered this as the time Banting made an all-out effort to persuade her to marry him and come abroad for their honeymoon. She did not go. Whether she turned him down flatly, or agreed to renew the engagement is not known. Several of Banting's friends said they could tell the state of his relationship with Edith by whether or not he was wearing the diamond ring on his watch chain. But no one was able to remember exactly when Fred had the ring and when Edith had it. The balance of evidence tilts towards suggesting that the engagement was still off. Banting saw several other girls later in June, including Isabel Knight and someone named "Leila." He and some classmates appear to have had a good time in mixed company during a few days in Montreal, with at least one of them being reluctant to stop. "Was very much afraid of Old Bills actions on the train," Banting noted, "He brought a kitten home from Montreal with him."[30]

Spencer Clark also remembered that friends had advised Fred not to try to mix a honeymoon with all his other activities on this trip to Britain. Good advice, for Banting was having a dazzling and strenuous array of new experiences in the old country, a visit he later described as "one of the most trying ordeals through which I have ever passed." He was spending day after day being introduced to the leading medical men of England and Scotland, meeting them at luncheons, dinners, in their labs, during tours of hospitals, at Oxford and Cambridge colleges. He met C.S. Sherrington, A.V. Hill, the Haldanes, father and son, Sir Almoth Wright, Bayliss, Starling, and dozens of others. His guide was often Velyien Henderson, also over for the summer, perhaps partly for the help he could give to the green Banting. "I am waiting for Prof. V.E.," Banting scribbled to Hipwell one day in July. "Thank God he will be here tonight. Freddie he is a peach. I know of none better. . . . I'll be glad to get home where I can have a little peace and quiet. Everything is fine but I like home and the ordinary life."[31]

Part of Banting's ordeal was meeting scientists who were not only masters of their trade, but also highly cultured. "Before going to Cambridge," he reminisced in 1940,

Henderson told me that we would visit the laboratory of Sir Gowland Hopkins who had just isolated some new sulphur-creating compounds. I acquainted myself through reading on this subject and was pleased that I was able to understand what he was talking about as we went through his laboratory. He invited us to one of the colleges for dinner which was a novel experience and after dinner we went into the college grounds over a bridge and sat under a tree. It was a gloriously warm evening. I remember J.B.S. Haldane was one of the party. I had got along well in

The Banting farmhouse, on the second concession, Essa township, Simcoe County, where Fred was born on November 14, 1891.
University of Toronto Library

Fred Banting and his brother, Thompson, about 1900.
University of Toronto Library.

Left: Margaret and William Banting of Alliston, Ontario. *University of Toronto Library*

Right: Wes Dungey and Fred Banting, 1910 or 1911. *University of Toronto Library*

ALLISTON 1915

Fred in uniform, Edith Roach, Ella Knight, and Sam Graham. He left for the wars in 1917. *Spencer Clark*

Even when his right arm was lacerated by shrapnel, near Cambrai on September 28, 1918, Banting continued to write his mother. *University of Toronto Library*

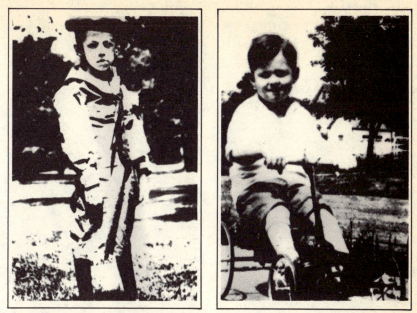

Teddy Ryder, one of Banting's first patients, in July 1922 and July 1923.
University of Toronto Library

Edward Ryder and his mother, Mildred, 1983, *Toronto Star*

Best, Banting, and dog, April 1922.
University of Toronto Library

Banting and Best's first paper.

J.B. Collip's method. His refusal to tell it to Banting caused a fight in the lab.

The paper announcing the discovery of insulin. Read in Washington, D.C., May 3, 1922. The audience cheered. Banting was not present.

J. J. R. Macleod. *Drs. C. J. and Barbara Wyatt*

The illuminated address presented by the Nobe Committee. *University of Toronto Library*

THE DISCOVERER OF INSULIN

Images of Banting, for the rest of
his life after insulin, the most
famous man in Canada. A fame
difficult to live with.
University of Toronto Library

A. Y. Jackson and Banting sketching aboard the *Beothic* during their Arctic voyage, 1927. *University of Toronto Library*

An Arthur Lismer drawing at the Arts and Letters Club, to celebrate the birth of William Robertson Banting, 1929. *University of Toronto Library*

Banting, drawn by A. Y. Jackson, about 1931. *University of Toronto Library*

Opposite: Frederick Banting and Marion Robertson Banting on their wedding day, June 4, 1924. A very sudden decision to marry right away. *University of Toronto Library*

An early Banting sketch in the style of the Group of Seven.
Cecilia Long

Pack ice, Baffin Bay, 1927. *Cecilia Long*

Sketching in Quebec. Cap Aux Oles, 1930 or 1931. *R. Hipwell*

Sketching in Quebec. Ste. Tite des Caps, 1937. Banting's considerable talent as an artist never had a chance to develop beyond Jackson's influence. *Cecilia Long*

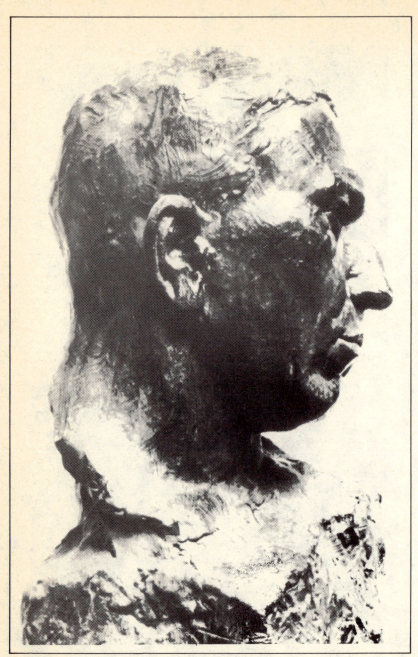

Banting by Frances Loring. The heroic discoverer.

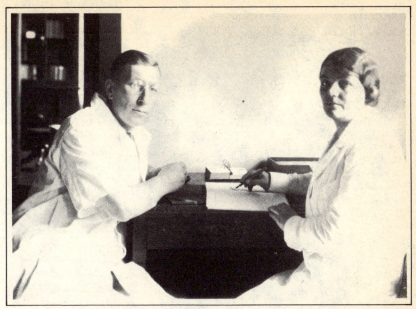

Banting with Sadie Gairns, his researcher, secretary, and administrator.
University of Toronto Library

Banting visits I. P. Pavlov at his villa near Leningrad, 1935. *University of Toronto Library*

81   July 13/35

The Georgian Military Road.
is very old. It runs from
Ordzhonikidze to Tiflis,
through the Gudaur Pass
at an elevation of
7,800 ft. A motor trip over
this road is a memorable
occasion because of
the beauty of the scenery
of the interesting things
seen by the wayside. The road is good and
is being constantly kept
in repair or improved
by native workmen who
are thin, dark men who
wear heavy large fur
caps and overcoats even
on a hot day in summer.
They work slowly with
two wheeled carts & long
handled shovels. The road
is made of stone — cobble
with a layer of gravel on top. In places where it
was being repaired or new road was being built
little heaps of stone were
dumped by the roadside &
men sat with hammers
smashing the larger stones to
the proper size. They held
the stone with their feet &
when crushed kicked it
or threw it with the feet
onto the new pile.

best also on account
seen by the wayside.

with a layer of gravel on top.
was being repaired or

Banting's travel diary: the old Georgian military road, Russia, July 1935.
University of Toronto Library

Fishing. *University of Toronto Library*

Above: With the "BOF" group from
the Arts and Letters Club.
C. A. G. Matthews

Left: At a kitchen table. *University of
Toronto Library*

Second marriage: With Henrietta, Lady Banting, probably soon after their June 1939 wedding. *University of Toronto Library*

Opposite page: Top: Wartime research. An oxygen mask being tested at the National Research Council, Ottawa, 1940. *National Research Council*

Middle: Wartime research. Banting's mustard gas wound, 1940. There were fears he would lose his leg. *University of Toronto Library*

Bottom: On duty again. Banting and I. M. Rabinowitch, about to leave for England, November 1939. *University of Western Ontario*

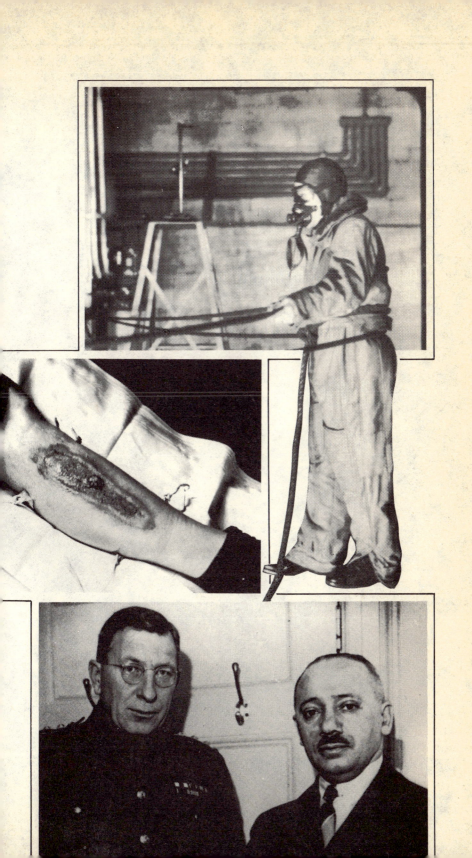

The last photograph, February 14, 1941. *University of Toronto Library*
The crash. *Public Archives of Canada, C-9703*
The funeral, March 3, 1941. *C. A. G. Matthews*

conversation in the laboratory where the subject of conversation was on biochemistry, but when I listened to discussions on music, plays, books, paintings, history, international affairs and politics, I was hopelessly ignorant. I marvelled at the versatility of these men. That night I resolved that I would set aside at least one hour each day for study on subjects outside my own particular work.

At Oxford there was a link with home, even with the farm country north of Toronto, when he visited the residence of Sir William Osler. Banting never met Osler, who died in 1919. On this trip Lady Osler invited him to stay with her at Norham Gardens, the famous "Open Arms." He slept in Osler's own bed, but could not rest:

To have been in the same house, slept in the same bed, bathed in the same tub, shaved by the same mirror, talked on the same veranda, viewed the same books and pictures as Sir William Osler fills one with an inspiration that puts sleep to flight. Above me is the picture of his sainted father and mother. How proud they were of him! Lady Osler is charming. He had wonderful surroundings, friends, books & a beautiful home – Because he was the kind of man to whom all things were beautiful & to whom all people were good. He gave to others & it came back to him.[32]

By far the most memorable meeting of the trip came a few days later. The Canadian High Commissioner in London, P.C. Larkin, briefed Banting on the etiquette of an "audience." He was asked to appear at Buckingham Palace at 10.00 in the morning of July 18. There was frantic last-minute shopping for a silk hat, gloves and the other appurtenances of morning dress. A very nervous Banting ("I do not mind admitting that I was nervous") arrived at the palace as directed. He began to feel at ease when his contact, the King's second secretary, turned out to have baggy trousers, scuffed shoes and a diabetic relative.

At length I was taken upstairs and along the wide corridor and through heavy double doors into a room with a single table in the centre. I was announced and left alone with his majesty. It was a curious thing but I wondered if we were being watched and I thought that there should have been a guard or someone present. It occurred to me that I did not like to be alone with him for if anything happened to him I would be blamed. I had exactly the same sensation as if I had in my hand a fragile vessel of inestimable value. His majesty was most gracious and in a moment I was completely at ease and we were talking about doctors, hospitals and research work. I was amazed at the amount of knowledge the man had and I was amused at the fact that he knew the incomes of some of the eminent surgeons and the cost of maintaining some of the hospitals. He gave me the feeling that he was genuinely interested.[33]

On his way out Banting was met by a reporter. "'Is Dr. Banting coming soon?' I looked and half pointed over my shoulder and said 'Pretty soon'." Banting strode past the reporters and photographers and into a waiting cab. As it pulled away, the press rushed out, realizing they had missed him. He waved. What could a person say to newspaper reporters about one's king? The episode got him tagged by the London reporters as the "world's shyest genius"; the label amused those of his friends who remembered his antics with his friends in Montreal.

Banting was not able to keep the reporters from attending his first medical talk in Britain, an appearance before an international congress of surgeons meeting in London. On the afternoon of the opening day of the conference the group heard a beautifully fluent talk in French, delivered without notes to a riveted audience by the suave Dr. Serge Voronoff. Voronoff was the French surgeon who claimed to be able to rejuvenate old men with transplants of monkey testicles. Voronoff on monkey glands was followed immediately by Banting on insulin. Banting was much less impressive than Voronoff. "Dr. Banting . . . was painfully embarrassed," a reporter wrote, "broke brisquely into his exposition without preliminary remark and literally fled from the hall after two minutes of nerve-cramped, graceless, almost inaudible explanation of his discovery. It was two minutes after he left before the assembly, realizing it was over, broke into hand-clapping." The reporter kindly labelled Banting "a doer, not a speaker," assumed he was over-wrought from severe laboratory work, and judged him to be one of the new North American breed of men who scorn fine phrases to get on with their great achievements. Banting himself never forgot how badly he had done compared with Voronoff.[34]

Banting did a better job on July 24 in Edinburgh at the Eleventh International Physiological Congress. He and Macleod shared a session in which they discussed their recent work. Banting's contribution was to give short papers on experiments he and Best had done on insulin in blood and on the work he and Sadie Gairns had attempted on factors influencing insulin production in the pancreas. This presentation was distinctly secondary to Macleod's keynote address on insulin, which had been delivered earlier that day. Macleod had given a masterful summary of the Toronto work, and of what was known about insulin. "Very fair, but not at all unselfish," Banting commented on the address, which he attended; his and Best's work was given three paragraphs in Macleod's very long talk.

Henderson took Banting straight from his Edinburgh session to the station for an overnight trip to Portsmouth and a presentation at the British Medical Association's convention. He was on more familiar turf here, talking insulin with other clinicians. "I was in very good form & got the stuff off my chest very well." During the discussion period one of the British doctors remarked on how they would all be able to say "I heard Banting's address on insulin" when they remembered the Portsmouth meeting of the BMA.[35]

The Edinburgh Congress had been the more important meeting in terms of the people who were there to hear the papers. A group from the Caroline Institute in Stockholm, Sweden, had taken in all the insulin sessions, listening very carefully. Their attendance probably sparked rumours, reported in Canada, that Banting, and perhaps Macleod, were candidates for the Nobel Prize. The press did not catch up to Banting to quiz him on the prospect, but he did feel bound to tell a reporter there was no truth in a story published in the New York *World* about insulin having more rejuvenative powers than monkey glands. Perhaps it did on diabetics, he allowed, but his name was not to be connected with the kind of thing Voronoff was trying to do with his "old reprobates."[36]

Banting probably saw some of the old reprobates the night he took in the Folies Bergère in Paris. He spent a few days there after the work in England. His sightseeing included the Louvre, Sainte Chapelle, Versailles, Napoleon's tomb, some of the 1918 battlefields, and Freddies, also known as the Lapine Agile, a nightclub where dangling skeletons were lowered in among the dancers. The highlight of his visit was to Louis Pasteur's tomb in the Pasteur Institute. "To me it was hallowed ground. Pasteur had been for years my idol. I thought what a benefit his life had been to mankind. The scientific spirit of France culminated in Pasteur, the greatest of all medical research workers."

One of Banting's last visits before leaving England for Canada was to Mrs. Read, the mother of Katherine, who seems to have been one of the girls who had refused his presents during the war. The daughter was not at home. "I am very sorry that it was my misfortune not to see Katherine, but possibly it is all for the best for both of us and fate has been kind. I am but slightly interested in them and the odd girl that does raise my interest usually, when analysed & facts are known, proves to be unimaginative, unschooled, unthinking or unloving or something wrong with them."[37]

He gave a lot of thought to women during the voyage home, if only because his shipboard reading was H. Rider Haggard's *She*. There didn't seem to be any equivalents of Haggard's enchanted temptress aboard: only one "interesting" woman, Banting noted, "but as she is likely a hot-air American with a little brains & a lot of talk I don't think she is worth the trouble of meeting." There was a "lovely child" aboard, a prettyish but chubby redhead named Miles from Montreal. She danced well. There is no mention of Edith in Fred's calendar-diary after June.

His ship docked at Quebec on August 18. The newspapermen who boarded it could not find the hero of insulin; he was hiding in another doctor's cabin. When the reporters finally caught up to him he said he thought he had set a record in not giving a single interview in England. But how could the press do its job if celebrities treated them like this? "Well, why not just leave a fellow alone?"[38]

There was one big public appearance before he could try to be left alone. The Canadian National Exhibition, advertised as the world's greatest fair, opened in Toronto on August 25. There was a record opening day attendance of 76,500. It was a joint Warriors' and Scientists' Day, with the veterans parading to the Exhibition grounds, where Banting – "a representative of the Canadians who, by their brains and labour, are winning for Canada that great heritage which is now hers to achieve" – spoke from the main bandstand. He issued a plea for support for medical research to enable talented Canadians to stay in the country. It had been written for him by Beaumont Cornell, a classmate and friend. "The mingling of Dr. Banting's address with the music of the parading warriors was a vivid suggestion of the manner in which the present generation of Canadians is successfully engaging problems of war and peace."

The special medals for achievers at the 1923 CNE bore a likeness of Banting on one side, the Dufferin Gate on the other.[39]

Banting finally settled down to intensive research in the autumn of 1923. The course of his work is discussed in the next chapter. Toward the end of October he took a day off to visit his parents in Alliston. He drove back to the city early the next day, Friday the 26th, and went directly to his Bloor Street office. The phone was ringing. When Banting answered it, a friend congratulated him and told him to open the paper. There was the news that Frederick G. Banting and J.J.R. Macleod had been awarded the Nobel Prize in Physiology or Medicine for the discovery of insulin. Banting's reaction on learning that he had won the greatest of all scientific honours was intense anger:

MacLeod! MacLeod! MacLeod! No mention of Best. I rushed out and drove as fast as possible to the laboratory. I was going to tell MacLeod what I thought of him. When I arrived at the building Fitzgerald was on the steps. He came to meet me and knowing I was furious he took me by the arm. I told him that I would not accept the Prize; that I was going to cable Stockholm that not only would I not accept but that they . . . could go to hell. I defied Fitzgerald to name one idea in the whole research from beginning to end that had originated in MacLeod's brain – or to name one experiment that he had done with his own hands.

Fitzgerald had no chance to talk but when he had an opportunity he said "there is a gentleman waiting to see you in my office." It was Col. Albert Gooderham. The weight of his presence cooled me down. He was one man whose calm and strong personality always reminded me of my father. He congratulated me and said "Banting, you have just got 11 days to get to Stockholm. There is a boat sailing tomorrow from Quebec & you can make it. I want you to be there for you are the first Canadian to win the Nobel Prize. I will pay all your expenses – only I do not want anything said about it."

I thanked him and told him that I could not accept. That I would not go to Stockholm and that I would not accept the Nobel Prize.

He was one of the few men who knew the whole story and he said that he understood my feelings and that he agreed with me but that there were other considerations that must be taken into

133

account. I must think first of my country – what would the people of Canada think if the first Canadian to receive this honour were to turn it down? Then there was science to consider – what would the world think of scientists who would because of differences of opinion disagree about a Prize? I had not thought of this aspect of the situation. He did not ask me to decide immediately but asked me not to do anything rash, & "better wait 24 hours."

Best was in Boston. He was to address the Harvard Medical students that night. Poor Best I knew he would be disappointed. I said to Fitzgerald & Gooderham – whatever I do Best will share with me. Fitzgerald suggested sending Charley a wire.[40]

After Best had finished his talk at Harvard, Joslin got up and read the telegram from Banting: "... I ascribe to Best equal share in the discovery stop hurt that he is not so acknowledged by Nobel trustees stop will share with him." A few days later Macleod announced that he was sharing his half of the Prize with Collip.

Banting considered making his anger public. Perhaps if the Toronto *Star*'s reporter on the story, Ernest Hemingway, had been more energetic and less interested in leaving Toronto forever, he could have pried the inside dope out of Banting. Banting may have had another blunt show-down with Macleod over the professor's statement to the press that Collip's share in the work was "equal" with that of the others, for Macleod soon issued a clarification to the effect that Collip was entitled to a "fair share" of the credit. It happened that the Toronto Academy of Medicine had planned a special dinner to honour Macleod on November 6. Banting and some of his friends boycotted the dinner, claiming (incorrectly) that the Academy must have had foreknowledge of the award. Some of Banting's friends wanted him to at least allow them to challenge Macleod's claim to a share of the Prize. To his credit, Banting calmed down and urged them to let it pass. "While I feel that the whole thing has been a great injustice to Best, and whereas I cannot understand Professor Macleod in this matter, the University of Toronto and Science in general would be discredited for their rangling. At the present time the outburst of indignation is subsiding, and any additional controversy would do only harm, since nothing can actually be done about the award."[41]

On November 26 the University of Toronto awarded its Nobel laureates honorary Doctor of Science degrees. (Falconer had refused

Banting's urgings to give Best a D.Sc. too, offering instead to give him a lesser honorary degree. Best turned it down). Banting spoke with appropriate dignity. He did refer to Velyien Henderson as "the truest friend and best guide of all," going on to say pointedly, "If you are proud Insulin has remained Canadian it is to him it is responsible." But he also talked about how Macleod's approval of his work resembled the stamp of the Bank of England. He said nothing of his deep bitterness that his name would be forever wedded with Macleod's in mention of the Nobel Prize for the discovery of insulin. He could not have guessed how successful he and Best would be during the next sixty years in unjustly discrediting J.J.R. Macleod. Even the stewards of the Nobel Prize themselves mistakenly came to believe that the 1923 award should have gone to Banting and Best.[42]

The Prize money was announced as being approximately $40,000. The reduced exchange rate of the Swedish kroner against the Canadian dollar, however, meant that it was substantially less, approximately $30,000. Banting's one-quarter share was $7,750. Nineteen twenty-three had been a very good year for him financially, his total income apparently being over $30,000 (the earnings had been swollen by such sums as a retroactive grant from the province in funding his research chair). He was out of debt and building up substantial savings. The story in Stevenson's biography that Banting had to borrow money to pay his 1923 income tax may be true, but only in the sense that he did not want to cash any of the more than $15,000 worth of bonds he had purchased.[43]

CHAPTER SEVEN

The Elixir of Life

Banting settled down to work in the autumn of 1923 as Canada's first Professor of Medical Research. He had a good salary, a skilled assistant in Sadie Gairns, enough financial support from insulin royalties to cover all his research needs, and the goodwill of his friends and patrons at the University. He was located in Velyien Henderson's Pharmacology Department in the main medical building on campus. He had little more to do with diabetes, having transferred his private practice entirely to Fred Hipwell. His professional ambition was to make new contributions to knowledge and health care through his research. The most important unresolved question in his personal life was whether or not he would marry.

His experiments on the pancreas and insulin had continued fitfully through the previous winter and spring. More studies were made of hyperemia's effect on the pancreas through the use of Banting's "irrigation system" to heat the pancreas of a living dog. X-rays were used to attempt to destroy the islet cells of a pancreas. A large number of rabbits were de-cerebrated, apparently in a search for some kind of antidote to insulin shock. Banting must have found the hypoglycemic condition puzzling, for he seemed to be able to get very low blood sugar – .018 and .009, double-checked, in two dogs – without causing a reaction. This is impossible.

On April 27, 1923, Banting finally started an experiment that involved grafting a dog's pancreas. It was probably part of the procedure he had originally intended to use in the search for the internal secretion. He cut away all but a small portion of a dog's pancreas, sutured the remnant under the skin, then observed the dog as first the nerve and then the original blood supply to the

136

remnant were cut off. The islet cells in the little piece of pancreas apparently continued to supply insulin. The experiment fizzled over the summer of 1923, however, while Banting was in England, when someone operated on the dog by mistake and it died.[2]

After a few more experiments in the autumn of 1923, Banting wrote up his research. The paper, "Factors Influencing the Production of Insulin," was finally published in the *American Journal of Physiology* early in 1924. It was Banting's only substantial work on the pancreas or insulin after the discovery. As part of his determination to share credit with his collaborators, he insisted over her objections that Sadie Gairns' name be on the paper. Banting had abandoned his congestion hypothesis about the cause of diabetes, and offered only a few muddled conclusions, none of them substantiated, about hyperemia and insulin secretion. The paper contributed nothing. It must have caused those who read it carefully to wonder about Banting's qualifications as a researcher.

On October 31, 1923, Canada's just-proclaimed Nobel laureate spoke in London, Ontario, where he had conceived his great idea exactly three years earlier. "Three years ago I became engaged, two years ago last May I was wed, and today I apply for a divorce from insulin," he announced. He was already embarked on the search for something far more important than insulin. He had apparently been mulling over ideas while in England that summer, and in September began a new notebook with some thoughts on bacterial action. Banting speculated that all bacterial toxins are "somewhat similar. . . . The problem is to either find out where these toxins act & prevent their action or find out where the antitoxin is formed & help the body to form it."[3]

He decided that the heart of the matter was in the adrenal cortex. The adrenal or suprarenal glands are two small capsule-like organs situated above the kidneys. They have two functionally distinct parts, the inner medulla and the outer covering or cortex. It had been known since the 1850s that animals cannot live without their adrenals. When the powerful and fascinating hormone, adrenaline or epinephrine, was first isolated around the turn of the century as the internal secretion of the adrenal medulla, researchers were disappointed to find that it would not keep adrenalectomized animals alive. They gradually learned that the adrenal cortex, not the medulla, is essential to maintain life. Something produced in the cortex, probably another hormone or internal secretion, made the difference between life and death (and would also probably treat Addison's disease). Banting apparently reasoned from this fact to the hypothesis that the secretion of the adrenal cortex was the universal antitoxin, or at least made possible its production.

He tested his hypothesis a few days later. At the Connaught Laboratories' farm he removed the adrenals from a dying horse and made an extract of the cortex. Four guinea pigs were injected with lethal doses of diphtheria toxin plus the cortical extract. Would the extract counter the effect of the toxin?

Yes! Three of the pigs died quickly, but Banting did not think they showed signs of dying from diphtheria. Better yet, the fourth pig lived for a week. It should have been dead within 96 hours at the most. Fitzgerald of the Connaught said it had received 60 killing doses of the toxin.

"There is something fishy about the whole thing," Banting noted – as indeed there must have been. Somebody was pretty excited, though, for a few days after these experiments the Ontario Minister of Health told a gathering of medical men that he had been conferring with Banting and that Banting "now has something better than insulin to offer the world. It is a marvelous thing, but I am not at liberty to make further mention of it. Dr. Banting has about completed work on his new discovery. An announcement will be made soon."[4]

The news that Banting had discovered something better than insulin was picked up by a wire service and reported all over North America and Britain. G.H.A. Clowes of Eli Lilly wired Toronto congratulating him. "Hope you will give us a chance to co-operate with you as we did on insulin." The rumour that the discovery would be a cure for pernicious anemia – a dreaded disease of the 1920s – caused hundreds of sufferers to write Banting and several to make the trip to Toronto.[5]

Velyien Henderson spoke to the press on Banting's behalf. He issued only a qualified denial. "Dr. Banting had something so good that we didn't believe it." They were about to repeat the experiments and would have a better sense of the results in five or six weeks. "It is unwise for the public to expect a new discovery of the type of insulin in any period of time under two years," Henderson warned, adding that even Pasteur took three or four years for each discovery. Banting's work was not on pernicious anemia (actually Beaumont Cornell was working on it in Banting's lab), but much more theoretical.

"We expect to have something in six months which may be a revolutionary idea in medical science, but can't talk about it yet."[6]

In the lab they were repeating the guinea pig, cortical extract, diphtheria toxin experiments. "Pig sits hunched up, hair ruffled, doomed," Banting scrawled of one of the subjects. They were all doomed (including the one that had to be chloroformed because the other pigs had chewed its feet), but those that got the extract seemed to live a few hours longer than the others. Perhaps the extract worked to inhibit the diphtheria, but was itself toxic to the pigs. Maybe the problem was to get impurities out of the extract, just as it had been with the pancreatic extracts. Some of the same methods were tried – switching to alcohol as a solvent and evaporating it in a warm air current – but these new extracts seemed to shorten rather than prolong the lives of the pigs. Many more guinea pigs were sacrificed that fall. Less lethal experiments involved studying the extract's effect on the contractions of muscular tissue suspended in Ringer's solution. An apparatus called a kymograph, which made stylus tracings on smoked paper wrapped around a drum, recorded the results. The object was to compare the tracings made by Banting's extract, which he wanted to be adrenaline-free, with those made by adrenaline itself.

One day someone snapped a picture, used on the dust jacket of this book, of Banting at his kymograph. There he sits, in his friends' eyes Canada's wizard of science, the Edison of the north, on the verge of discovering the key to life itself. The friends and the hopes were not so much the product of a country having its first love affair with science and research, as they were the heirs to the North American belief that a good enough genius, like Edison, can invent anything. To get the Canadian line of descent right we would need a photograph from half a century earlier of Robert Fraser, a farmer from the Alliston area, with his perpetual motion machine.[7]

Banting abandoned the guinea pig experiments after a month or two and reverted to a more orthodox technique, similar to his 1921 pancreas experiments, in his search for the adrenal elixir. The insulin experiments had involved trying to keep depancreatized dogs alive with an extract of pancreas. Banting now did adrenalectomies on dogs, and then gave them doses of his extract of adrenal cortex to try to keep them alive. Just as he earlier believed he had discovered a technique for eliminating the powerful external secretion from his pancreatic extract, so he seems to have felt that his

139

method of making the extract from fresh cortex prevented contamination by adrenaline.

It wasn't going to be the insulin research all over again. No matter how carefully Banting did his surgery, no matter how they fiddled with the extract, the dogs died very quickly, within a day or two of the adrenalectomy. By spring 1924 Banting had gone through many dogs, and had nothing to show for his work. He had had an intimation that something like this could happen; during the Nobel accolades in November he had written Rawle Geyelin that "I stand in a very precarious position, with so many people expecting something and I have nothing to offer." In March 1924 Beaumont Cornell, who was working with Banting, told an acquaintance that Banting "is now obsessed with the idea of doing something big by himself so that no honour will go to Macleod." Cornell believed, the acquaintance recorded, "that so much adulation has had a bad effect on Banting & has made him very unhappy."[8]

Sadie Gairns, who assisted in all these experiments, doing the same job Best had done in the insulin work, shared Cornell's opinion that Banting's research might have been more productive if he had not been constantly interrupted by people making demands on his time. He was still giving talks about insulin, writing articles about insulin, receiving honorary degrees for insulin, conferring with visitors about insulin, and taking part in University discussions about fund-raising to take advantage of the public's gratitude for insulin. Desperate to accomplish something in the lab, Banting increasingly resented the distractions, and began to proclaim a view of medical research as a calling requiring single-minded dedication. "The man who wishes to make a success in research work must be prepared to work. He must sever his connections with labor unions that restrict the hours of his labor. He must be prepared to live, move, and have his being in the laboratory, eating and sleeping beside his work if need be."

"Matrimony and research have seldom gone together," he added in an article written in the winter of 1923-24, and quoted Osler's advice that struggling medical students should put their affections in cold storage.[9] He probably wrote the article at one of the many troubled times in his affairs with women. Despite the rhetoric, Banting was anything but a confirmed bachelor. He deeply believed in the virtues of home, hearth and family, and would not hesitate to get married if he could only find the right wife.

There were willing candidates. The genius of insulin was a handsome enough thirty-two-year-old doctor: a little stooped and coarse-featured, in some lights almost horse-faced; but in other lights almost dapper or dignified, certainly a smiler, with an attractive twinkle in his eye. Also, of course, he was world-famous and financially comfortable. Altogether Dr. Banting was one of the most eligible bachelors any girl would ever meet. Many pretty girls took up nursing for a few years, hoping to settle down with a handsome doctor husband. Enough of these girls went after Dr. Banting to create scenes from situation comedy. Fred would have to conspire with Sadie Gairns, for example, to slip out of the Medical Building without being caught by the love-sick nurse from the diabetic clinic who waited for him at the end of a day. The escape became particularly difficult when she took to waiting in his car.

One of Banting's earlier biographers, Seale Harris, portrays him during these post-insulin months as "a Lothario long starved," welcoming the nursing girls:

It was not just one nurse who caught Banting's fancy, but two or three. Starting out modestly enough with a different invitation to a girl to dine with him, he found the going easier than he had supposed, and in no time at all he was up to his ears in complications, with dates and romantic manoeuvres filling whatever moments he had left after his rounds as a celebrity, leaving out in the cold, for the nonce, the monastic devotion to science of which he was such an advocate. Fortunately for his purposes the nurses in whom he was most interested had different nights off, so he could take out first one and then another without danger of conflict, except on one or two sad occasions when the nights off coincided and he had to wound the feelings of one by favoring another.[10]

Harris's story may be accurate – he spent some time with Banting in 1923 – but may equally likely be exaggerated. There is certainly one dalliance about which specific, though very ambiguous, evidence exists. Early in 1924 Beau Cornell, who had distinctly bohemian connections, introduced Banting to an old flame, whom we shall call Katharine Barrie. "She appeared to be the wonderful girl that he told me she was," Banting wrote. One day she asked Banting to visit her, saying she had something she wanted to talk to him about. Banting later drafted a memoir of their encounter. She is sitting on the bed in her tiny attic room, he is on the only chair, telling him her life story – "She had tried every kind of pleasure in her search for happyness" – when the memoir breaks off.[11] Banting's papers also contain four letters from Katharine Barrie. She appears to have been an unwed mother whose infant died during the months Banting knew her. There is nothing clearly compromising in her letters to Banting, only one ambiguous passage in a letter of April 22, 1924, from Brockville, Ontario, addressed to him as "Dear Man":

> How good you are to listen to all this. How good you are anyway. I think you just splendid. The world praises you, and yet the world knows but a small part of you. You are a much greater man than the printers have said. An obscure woman's heart has an understanding with God about you. . . .
>
> I shall always be grateful to you and pleased beyond telling if you will let me call you friend. How I shall strive to be worthy – to do and say what would meet with your approval – in some small measure to deserve you.
>
> Katharine

By this date Banting's affection was being lavished in another direction. His eye had fallen on an X-ray technician at Toronto General Hospital, the beautiful and vivacious Miss Marion Robertson. Marion was a tall, slim, fair-haired, blue-eyed doctor's daughter from the nearby town of Elora, Ontario. She had all the social graces, was well connected in Toronto medical circles through her father, and could talk intelligently about medicine because of her job. She was also powerfully attracted to Banting. Several of his friends remembered Marion saying soon after she met Fred that she would marry him.

Fred fell in love with Marion. But he had known and loved Edith Roach for too many years to make a simple transfer of affection. He seems to have loved the two women, or at least to have felt bound by ties to Edith. Affairs rushed toward a confused climax. At one point Banting wanted Marion and Edith to meet, and took Marion to Edith's apartment. Edith did not want to meet Marion. Matters came to a head in May 1924, just as Edith's mother died. Between losing her mother and having to put up with Fred, Edith was driven to the verge of a nervous breakdown. Her brother, it is said, had to order Banting out of the Roach home, insisting that he never bother her again.

That is the oral history. From the written record it appears that

Edith, or her family, or both, were determined not to let Fred Banting merrily take his diamond ring, walk out of Edith's life, and marry Marion. He must have been vulnerable to Edith in some way. Perhaps he was liable for a breach-of-promise suit. As the ambiguous evidence presented below may suggest, she might have had claims on him arising from some sexual episode in their relationship. The final settlement of Fred and Edith's romance took three days in May 1924, and generated two documents. One is a handwritten agreement, dated May 13 but apparently drafted on the 11th, signed by Edith Roach and Fred Banting, witnessed by her brother, H.C. Roach, which reads as follows:

We the undersigned do hereby agree not to interfere with each other in any way from now on, and for the sum of two thousand dollars ($2,000) and the ring Miss Edith Roach gives up all claims on Dr. Frederick Banting, when the said sum is paid in full, and that he on his part agrees to give up any claims on Miss Edith Roach. Either party agree not to use any private information that they may possess to harm the other. This agreement is drawn up with the understanding that both parties wish to avoid any further complications.

The other document is Edith's farewell letter to Fred, the only letter of hers he kept, written on May 12. After talking about the death of her mother, she said goodbye:

The bitterness has gone out of my heart and as time goes by I know that only the good old memories of our love will remain for these I will cherish and the unpleasant ones must die from neglect. A little more than a week ago I buried my mother; yesterday I felt that I buried you and my love too, but no, the love for the old Fred has conquered to-night and I think will always be with me, the love of our youth. When I come through Alliston, coming down from home, I always gaze with longing and pleasure at the banks of the old river and at the old house. These are the memories I want to live and I pray that they may soften and not harden us both.

The time may come when like yourself I may turn to another. It is and will be hard to be sure but if it is to come I pray that it won't be too late. I believe that things happen in this world for a purpose. The way is hard but there is a reason for it all, and this thought gives me strength. Won't you try to see it this way too and it will help.

You may have thought me hard yesterday Fred. I don't think deep in your heart that you did. You will never know what it cost me to go through with it. I had to do it and I don't think you understand, but then none of us understand each other perfectly. My mind heart and soul is at peace. I believe peace to be the secret of happiness and I wish you would believe it too and obtain peace. I think we are both stronger in character than we were two years ago and if that is true we have not failed for life is character building. I have regained my self-control and my self-respect and I am confident I can smile and go forward and make my life count something, though perhaps little. I have faith in you, trust, respect and admiration, for your good points are many and these will stay with me.

We have had our ups and downs and have hurt each other as it is only possible for people who love deeply to hurt, but I hope the storm is over. We have loved each other through it all, even be it only the love of our old selves. That will never quite die. I am your friend, I hope I always will be. I believe that you try to do what you believe to be right. As for our private affairs I trust you to do and to say only that for which you have good cause, and nothing which may lead to any future trouble for either of us, remembering the words of our agreement, and you may trust me to do the same.

It will be 13 years this next summer since we first met. The times that you have made me supremely happy during those years are beyond number and are the times that really count. I am glad I have had them and I do not regret. It is better to have loved and lost than never to have loved at all, but I don't feel that we have really lost.

May God bless you and keep you Fred and make you a greater man.

Yours sincerely
Edith

Nothing more is known about the relationship. Edith and Fred apparently never saw each other again. Some years later, Edith finally married. She never had children, and never talked about Fred. Fred came to wish he had married Edith.

The adrenal research took a sudden turn for the better in the weeks just after the break-up with Edith. On May 15, dog number 24 had lived almost three days since its adrenalectomy, apparently on injections of Banting's extract. "Either there is suprarenal tissue left in body – tho' I do not believe it, or else the extract contains the active principle of the cortex," Banting wrote in his notebook. He and Sadie Gairns kept the dog under 24-hour observation, Banting doing the night shift, Miss Gairns coming in during the day.

Here is the lone researcher with his dog in the small, quiet hours of the morning. "This room is cold," Banting writes at 2 a.m. on the 18th. If only the dog will live. The dog begins to sicken the next day. They give it more extract. "If this dog revives after this extract one cannot help but believe that there is something in it." Despite more injections, despite artificial respiration, the dog dies. It had survived 175½ hours after the operation. Banting did not yet know that with good surgical technique other researchers were having little trouble keeping adrenalectomized dogs alive that long, without using any extract. Many, many researchers, commanding far more expertise than Banting, were trying to isolate the hormone(s) of the adrenal cortex.

Fred and Marion were planning to get married in time for a long honeymoon trip centring on a conference in the Caribbean. Banting had put his past with Edith behind him. But that was not his whole past. On June 3, someone mailed this typewritten letter to Marion Robertson:

Dear Girl

I hear that you are keeping company with a famous doctor. Well he is famous for more than one thing and I hope your friendship will not grow into anything more serious because if it does you will be sorry. He has ruined my life and to get even with him I intend to sue him for breach of promise if he ever gets married and as I hear you are a nice girl I know you won't want to be dragged through that. I am not the only girl he has fooled, so others may be heard from. Let him deny if he can. And he will hear from me and no woman will be proud to see what I can tell in the paper about her husband. It is time the people knew the other side of him. Don't let him fool you. You will hear my name some day and then you will know who wrote this letter and I think you will thank me for it.

On the basis of its unusual salutation, "Dear Girl," I believe the letter was written by the woman who had addressed Banting as "Dear Man" a few weeks earlier, Katharine Barrie. It is completely inconceivable that Edith would have written it.

On the morning of June 4 Banting came into the lab and told Sadie Gairns he was going to be married that afternoon. "Don't tell anyone till after it's over," he said. "Well, for goodness sake!" she said. At 3 p.m., Fred and Marion were married in the home of Marion's uncle, Dr. James Caven. Only the immediate families were present. Some of the girls who had known Fred at the Philathea Bible Class apparently found out about the event and gathered outside to coo when the great man came down the steps with his bride. "This seemed just the beginning of a beautiful romance," one of them remembered. "Now we just had to sit back and watch him burst into fame."

One story of the wedding is that it was speeded up to avoid press coverage. Another possibility hinges on the excellence of Toronto's postal service in 1924. Marion probably received the anonymous letter on the day it was mailed, June 3. She may have been so upset by it that Fred could only finally put things right by deciding they would get married right away – tomorrow. Whatever happened, the most famous Canadian and his beautiful bride spent the first days of their married life at the Preston Springs Hotel, a spa about sixty miles west of Toronto. On the first full day of his marriage Fred had to sit down and write a few paragraphs to go into a colleague's book on diabetes.[12]

The newlyweds were soon off to the United States, where Fred got an honorary degree from Yale, gave a paper in Atlantic City and renewed acquaintances with some of the diabetics who had been in Toronto, including Teddy Ryder and his family. Fred and Marion made the usual post-nuptial circuit of visits to relatives, and in mid-July were off to the tropics for their real honeymoon. It was to be courtesy of the United Fruit Company, whose International Conference on Health Problems in Tropic America Banting had agreed to attend.

The trip was a classic medical junket of the 1920s. The United Fruit Company, the great banana business, was trying to demonstrate a commitment to improving the health of the people of Latin America. Accordingly, it had assembled prominent medical men from the Americas, Great Britain, France and Germany, for ten days of conferring at the posh Myrtle Bank Hotel in Kingston, Jamaica. There was a visit to Havana en route and a long tour of several of the company's banana republics afterwards. The doctors brought their wives, the company paid the bills, and for every medical session to be sat through there were half a dozen dances, parties, champagne suppers and sightseeing excursions.

The Bantings' experiences survive mostly through Marion's pen. To her the trip was blue seas, big full moons, dusky brown girls, beautiful and famous people, elegant hotels, sparkling harbour lights, dancing to marimba bands, and a lot of wretched natives living in unpleasant slums. Fred had a more stolid approach to the summer's activities. On the cruise from New York to Havana he had to get a speech ready. On shore the medical men toured hospitals, universities and a leper colony, and talked a lot about tropical diseases. A confrontation on the first day of the Kingston conference, when the Cuban scientist, Aristides Agramonte, challenged the bold, incorrect claims of Hideyo Noguchi to have found the cause of yellow fever, was enough in itself to put an otherwise insubstantial conference on the map of medical history. Banting worried about his own paper on insulin and diabetes, finally getting help with it from one of his fellow conferees, Colonel Bailey K. Ashford. He confessed to Ashford how little he really knew about medicine, how green he was in this kind of gathering. "Good God, man! – it's the substance, not the words," Ashford told him. Banting's revised talk went off without difficulty and was given a fairly warm reception.[13]

He dutifully took in most of the sessions, and exchanged ideas as best he could with his fellow scientists. Sir Aldo Castelloni, author of the standard text on tropical medicine, suggested they collaborate on studies of sprue, a tropical disease sometimes linked with the pancreas. The conference session on cancer also got him thinking, and he began jotting down ideas to pursue back in Toronto. With regard to diabetes, his observations led him to reason, incorrectly, that because the rising incidence of diabetes in the tropics apparently coincided with the increased use of refined white sugar instead of raw sugar-cane, refined white sugar was specially likely to cause diabetes. He dabbled with this idea from time to time for the rest of his life.[14]

He also asked himself what a diabetes expert was doing at a conference on tropical diseases:

Why I am here
Is not quite clear
Since diabetes
Of all diseases
is not contagious
in any stages

he scribbled one day in the earliest surviving demonstration of a talent for arch doggerel.[15]

Banting was there, clearly, because the United Fruit Company wanted its conference graced by a recent, high-profile Nobel laureate. To do this it was willing to give Fred and Marion, like the others in the conference, the equivalent of a free six-week Caribbean cruise. Fred took part in most of the social activities of the trip, especially the sightseeing, and became thoroughly tanned. Seale Harris, who also attended the conference, remembered that Banting found the poverty and horrible diseases of Latin America shocking, the ruins of Mayan civilization both awesome and depressing. Marion recorded that Guatemala appeared to her husband as "a fool of a country." Honduras, where a revolution was raging in the streets while the gringoes passed by, could not have appeared much wiser.[16]

Fred was not inclined to keep pace with his wife's ardent, joyous socializing. Marion loved parties, dinners, people, music, dancing. While Fred had learned to dance over the years, he still had his farmer's feet, and never really enjoyed it. "Night after night," Seale Harris wrote, "he sat up gloomily till the wee small hours, playing wallflower on the edge of the dance floor, while his wife, sought after and admired, was having a wonderful time. . . . To a sympathetic fellow watcher in Jamaica [probably Harris himself] who inquired why he did not join his wife on the dance floor he passed the whole thing off as a joke, saying that dancing was strenuous business on a hot night and that he preferred to let his be done by proxy."[17]

One day the whole hectic pace was too much for him. After a full program of sightseeing with the other doctors, he got back late for a round of evening socializing that Marion, who had stayed in the hotel, had arranged. "I was not able to take it," he wrote in their travel diary, "and Marion & I had one hell of a row."

The diary suggests that the honeymooners were not quite as

unhappy as Harris's biography, enriched by hindsight, implies. August 4: "Had a quiet evening by our two selves – the best evening since we left home"; August 11: "For the first time we have a table for two and its perfectly great." Fred's reference to a row was inked over.[18] Surely even honeymooners have a row from time to time. On the other hand, Harris probably felt comfortable with hindsight because Banting had probably later told him, as he certainly told many others, that he knew from his wedding night with Marion that the marriage was a mistake.

They returned to Toronto early in September and settled into an apartment on Avenue Road. Fred bought a lot and during the next year or so had a comfortable three-storey brick and sandstone home built for them at 46 Bedford Road, just north of Bloor Street and the University. Dr. and Mrs. Banting settled down to the routine of their life together. As befitted a doctor's wife of the 1920s, Marion left the paid work force. She would keep house for her famous husband, the Professor of Medical Research, as he threw himself again into the job of making discoveries.

Banting tried his first cancer experiments that fall, working with his friend Scotty MacKay. They got some human tumour tissue, froze it, made an extract, and injected it into the breasts of several dogs, rabbits and guinea pigs. When nothing much happened, they apparently dropped the work.[19]

Much more serious was the ongoing search for the magic adrenal-cortical antitoxin. More dogs had their adrenal glands cut out, were injected with the extract and died. Banting tried taking the adrenals out differently, tried making the extract differently, at one point imitated his insulin experiments in trying extracts of foetal calf adrenals, hoping there would be no adrenaline in them. Nothing worked. "There seems to be but one constant result after suprarenalectomy," he noted one day in frustration, "namely – death."[20]

He pressed on. Much of the research was little more than maintaining a death-watch on the adrenalectomized animals. Banting's adrenal notebooks are a depressing catalogue of the death-throes of sick dogs. Page after page is filled with restless dogs, vomiting dogs, trembling and convulsing dogs, ravenously hungry dogs, dogs refusing food and drink, dogs coughing, grunting, licking their wounds, snapping at flies, salivating, having bowel movements, hemorrhaging, lying prostrate, wagging their tails, twitching, frothing at the mouth, dogs dying, dogs found dead in their cage.

Organized anti-vivisectionism had worried medical researchers in Toronto at the time of the insulin experiments – so much so that Macleod had advised Banting and Best to move their dogs from building to building surreptitiously lest they be observed by the animal welfare enthusiasts. Although the "anti-vivs" tried to carry on a campaign to discredit insulin, they only seemed silly, for here was about as good a demonstration as there could possibly be of the worthwhile sacrifice of animals to humanitarian ends. The post-insulin dog research was more problematic. The anti-vivisectionists noticed and publicized the extreme pain inflicted on dogs in Banting's 1922-23 experiments "parboiling" the pancreas of living animals. To them the discoverer of insulin was a cruel vivisector, a butcher of helpless creatures.

Had they known all the details of the later dog experiments, the animal lovers would have been further horrified. As it was, some of them carried on the agitation in Toronto, sometimes to Banting's face. At one point during the post-insulin research, for example, he began taking German lessons and found that his instructor was an anti-vivisectionist. In his 1940 memoir, "The Story of Insulin," he recalled a visiting Englishman who refused to shake hands with him. He invited one or the other of these anti-vivisectionists to his lab to see the animals at first hand. He wrote about the encounter as follows:

I first took him to the animal room in the attic on the fourth floor. The dogs . . . gave us a hearty reception. There were seven dogs in the row of seven cages. Five of the dogs had been operated upon and I asked him to choose the two which had not. He hesitated and then said "I can pick two that have." I said "Go ahead, point them out." He pointed to the only two that had not been operated on. The reason for this mistake was that these two dogs had been admitted only on the previous couple of days. They had been taken from the street, uncared for and beaten about. They had not become accustomed to us, nor had they been in long enough to show the care that was taken of dogs in the laboratory.

I then opened the cage doors and let the dogs out and turned them over to show their operation wounds. At last I opened the cage second from the door and out jumped my prize dog. She had had three or four operations and many dozens of samples of blood

150

taken. She was displeased at the attention shown to the other animals and was relieved when her time came and she realized that she was not being neglected. I told the stranger that this was the dog from which I must draw the blood. She jumped up and down and ran about. I went to the top of the spiral attic stairs and sat down on the top step as was the custom and the dog came under into my arms. I carried her down and lowered her to the floor. She ran up and down while the stranger descended. As we walked along the corridor the dog ran back and forth. We then went down the broad staircase to the first floor and then to the open door which led out to the campus and the wide, wide world. The dog ran about but every moment looked back at me to see if I were ready.

I told the antivivisectionist that this dog had had many operations, that it had had more samples of blood taken than possibly any dog that ever existed and that it had had many injections of extract which possibly caused it pain and from an experimental point of view, that it was to me at least the most valuable dog in the world – but that if he could take the dog away without using force, that he could have the dog and thus save it from the vivisector.

He weakly snapped his fingers and called her but she paid not the slightest attention. I had made a bold statement but I knew my dog, and I believe that dog knew me. Often in after-life when torn to pieces by humans I have been grateful for the trust and faithfulness of a dog.

Banting sets this story during the insulin research. During most of the adrenal research it would not be very plausible. Similarly, Banting's general comments about animal research, written in his maturity and probably at a time of higher standards of care, hardly reflect the reality of his methods in the mid-1920s:

I have always been in sympathy with much of their [the antivivisectionists'] work and I find myself very tolerably disposed to those of them who have sufficient intelligence to prevent them from becoming too extreme. I have always felt that a dog should be, as far as possible, treated like a human with regard to operation, after care, nursing, drawing of blood, etc., and that nothing should be done to cause pain unless necessary and that an anaesthetic should be used as it would be in the case of a private patient or a patient in hospital. I have always advocated that no person should be allowed to operate on a dog, who has not received training as a surgeon. Absolute antiseptic or aseptic techniques should always be observed. No operation should be performed except it be for a specific purpose. No laboratory man should be employed to care for animals unless he has a natural fondness for them.[21]

Banting was rough on animals, sometimes inflicting needless, cruel pain. He was also fond of them, especially pet dogs. His attitudes to animals and animal research came directly out of his farm experience. Animals existed to serve man. You raised them and slaughtered them (and ate many of them). Not pretty, but necessary. Nothing to get upset about. This treatment of animals was far more justified, for example, than the pain and suffering inflicted on them by people hunting purely for sport. So long as there was a sensible purpose, there was nothing wrong with killing or experimenting on animals. Banting thought all his experiments, including the cruel ones, were purposeful. He also thought he knew enough about the real mistreatment of animals not to worry overmuch about a little rough handling of a few dogs.

Of course the fifty-six dogs Banting killed in his adrenal research were an insignificant number. Several thousand dogs had been sacrificed by researchers around the world in the search for the internal secretion of the pancreas before the Toronto group found it. Now an equal or greater number of dogs would give their lives in the gradual isolation of the adrenocortical hormones, which several teams of researchers achieved in the 1930s. At the University of Toronto, J.J.R. Macleod had begun to take steps toward tighter control of animal research in the early 1920s. He had set up a faculty screening committee and was resigned to licensing legislation for researchers in Ontario.[22] But then the concern for the animals seems to have diminished, partly perhaps because of the acclaim for the insulin achievement. Banting had *carte blanche* to do anything he wanted to his animals.

By 1924-25 the chief question about medical research at the University was not how someone like Banting might be restricted, but how he could be given more support in his quest for more life-saving discoveries. Plans to raise money for Banting had been

152

afoot since insulin burst upon the world in 1922-23. It took many months, though, for the pillars of the University to find the most appropriate way of taking over and refashioning a scheme for a $1,000,000 life insurance endowment policy on Banting which had been planned and publicized by a self-interested life insurance salesman. Finally, in the spring of 1925, driven largely by the enthusiasm of Sir William Mulock, an all-out campaign began to raise an endowment for the just-created Banting Research Foundation. It set out to raise $500,000, the income from which would be used to give Banting further support in his research, and also to support future Bantings, at Toronto and other Canadian universities, who had good ideas but no money. They would not have to suffer the hardships Fred could describe in such vivid detail.

There was some hope of reuniting Banting and Best as a research team after Best finished his studies, but it was of equal concern to support those other Bantings who were being drawn out of obscurity by the flame of insulin's triumph. There was a lot of excitement about the work of a local doctor, W. Easson Brown, who in 1923 seemed to have discovered a great new anesthetic in ethylene – and tried it on an eager human volunteer, Fred Banting. Then there was the all-out attack Fred's classmate and sometimes speech-writer and friend of fascinating women, Beaumont Cornell, was making on pernicious anemia. Cornell, a native of the new Athens, in Ontario, like Banting a son of the soil, was dividing his time between medical research and writing novels. In 1923 and 1924 he was convinced that he had discovered a bacillus that caused "p.a." If he had, the discovery would be almost as big as insulin – "I really think I've hit it Fred, and just here let me say once and for all to you, if I have hit it, I'm in the peculiar position of not feeling the least bit chesty. I've been conscious all through this thing of an outside and no doubt divine power assisting me. All praise to Him."[23] Other doctors came to Banting and the University with ideas, some of them being cancer-cure quacks, others like W.J. MacDonald of St. Catharines, Ontario, apparently being onto something. In Mac-Donald's case he had a liver extract that seemed to reduce high blood pressure. A lot of money and energy would be required to test the extract, and a lot of bad feeling created by the accusation that MacDonald had stolen it from a professor at Western University, before it was found to be useless. Unfortunately no one thought to try it carefully on Cornell's pernicious anemia, which by the end of the decade was shown to be a B_{12}-deficiency syndrome, almost completely conquerable by liver in the diet.

The campaign for donations to the Banting Research Foundation reflected the great expectations insulin had created in Toronto. President Falconer told the world that Banting was only at the beginning of his discoveries. A future University president, Canon H.J. Cody, argued that if only the public would support research, "Who can say that we shall not have other wonderful discoveries for the honour of Toronto and the benefit of humanity? What Canadians have done Canadians can do. We have a splendid body of students. There is no reason why there should not be other Bantings and Bests amongst them." Sir William Mulock saw other diseases being conquered as a result of the Foundation's work: "If it should happen that by reason of such contributions some great discovery should be made for the effectual treatment of, say, cancer, pernicious anaemia, hardening of the arteries or some other of what are still deadly diseases, what happiness would come to each contributor." The Toronto newspapers were also infected with the fund-raisers' enthusiasm: the *Star*, for example, hailed "an enterprise which may prove, as time goes on, one of most momentous consequence, not only to Toronto but to the whole human race . . . the release of all the creative scientific research energies of a great intellectual community." In fund-raising which featured only token contributions and efforts from outside of Toronto (Charles Evans Hughes gave $500; other grateful Americans added a few thousand), the target was exceeded by about 20 per cent.[24]

Banting did not participate formally in the campaign. It was enough for the public to know that he was working away in his lab, getting ready to score another touchdown against death. Friends had talked him out of his first inclination to give all of his Nobel Prize money to medical research. He insisted on giving $1,000 to the Banting Research Foundation over Mulock's objection that he had already done more than enough for humanity, and began a life-long habit of digging into his own pocket to buy equipment or underwrite the salaries of his assistants and fellow researchers.

Over the years he gave innumerable lectures and wrote several articles on the general theme of medical research, gradually developing a standard speech. It was a paean to science and the progress obtained through research, as well as a description of the kind of man needed for the research life. Banting saw the ideal medical researcher as a combination of what he had been and what he wanted to become. Reasoning from the night of October 31, 1920, for example, he stressed the importance of having ideas in research: "The idea is the most valuable thing in research. We do not know from whence they come. They do not come when commanded. They must be sought after, but they do not always reward the searcher with their presence." The research man had to spend a lot of time thinking. The best time to think, Banting thought, was late at night, "for then one is free from those disturbing elements which interrupt a clear consecutive trend of thought. These are the best hours of all, when the imagination is allowed to run riot on the problem that blocks the progress of research, when the hewn stones of scientific fact are turned over and over, and fitted in so that the mosaic figure of truth, designed by Mother Nature long ago, be formed from the chaos."

A fan of detective stories, Banting urged his audiences to read Sherlock Holmes, and he compared medical research to the "secret service" arm of medical science. The research worker, then, would have extraordinary qualities:

> The research worker like the secret service man must be thoroughly informed of all present knowledge on the subject he is to investigate. He must have keen powers of observation. He must have daring, originality, persistance and common sense. He must have initiative, for though he may at times have to obey authority, if he is to be a success he must, if necessary, depart from tradition and follow his own scheme of campaign. With self-detachment, self-abandonment, and self-abnegation he must pursue his own idea and ideal. Above all he must work with intensity, integrity, breadth, patience, thoughtfulness and faithfulness.

Finally, according to Banting, the research quest came down to a matter of hard work and determination. Drawing on his Methodist heritage of belief in the power of man's questing free will, and on the poetry of Ella Wheeler Wilcox, he usually concluded his reflections on research with this thought:

> I am a firm believer in the theory that you can do or be anything that you wish in this world, within reason, if you are prepared to make the sacrifices, think and work hard enough and long enough.

There is no chance, no destiny, no fate
Can circumvent, can hinder or control
The firm resolve of a determined soul.
Gifts count as nothing. Will alone is great.
All things give way before it soon or late.[25]

The lines were inspiring, but untrue. No amount of will, no amount of resolve and determination, could take the place of good postgraduate training or a skilled biochemist. Banting toyed with the thought that his adrenal research was promising enough to be the subject of the Nobel address he had agreed to give in Stockholm in September. But when Sadie Gairns found that a control dog treated with saline alone stayed alive longer than any of the others, he gave it up and reworked his discovery of insulin material for the umpteenth time.

After an idyllic several weeks' touring the continent with the Fitzgeralds in the summer of 1925, Fred and Marion went on to Stockholm. Banting's chief memory of the Nobel dinner in his honour, recorded in 1940, was of the prodigious amount of alcohol the Swedes expected a guest to consume. Possibly some of that liquor helped cause the newspaper reports from Stockholm of Banting having said science might find a gland juice comparable with the elixir of life.[26] Perhaps Banting never said any such thing. But perhaps he did say it: for two years he had been looking for that gland juice in the adrenal cortex. He never found it. In a few years other researchers did begin isolating very powerful hormones from that gland. But by then Banting had moved on to something else, which did not work very well either. He was never going to find "something big by himself." He was never going to find anything better than insulin.

CHAPTER EIGHT

Canadian to the Core

T he failures at research would never be for want of trying. Banting never fell into the pattern of the burned-out researcher or academic who sees less and less of his lab or desk in gradually surrendering to the seductions of the easy, tenured life. Hard work and determination were supposed to produce success. The will and energy were there. The Professor of Medical Research put in very long hours in his lab, often working around the clock and on weekends, trying to justify his salary. Then he would get away from it all with long holiday trips.

While he was in England in the summer of 1925, Banting visited the laboratory of William Gye, a prominent researcher doing interesting work on cancer with support from the newly created Imperial Cancer Research Fund. Since 1922 Banting had wondered occasionally about finding a cure for cancer. Now he was intrigued by Gye's investigations of a tumour in certain kinds of chicken, known as Rous sarcoma. Peyton Rous of the Rockefeller Institute had demonstrated in 1911 that this tumour could be transmitted through injections of cell-free filtrate from one bird to another. It seemed to be a strain of cancer caused by one of the mysterious sub-cellular products later called viruses. The idea that this could happen was not well received – Rous finally got a Nobel Prize for his work, but not until 1966 – and in the 1920s Gye was on the frontier of cancer research in giving major attention to Rous sarcoma.

Banting decided to take up the same problem. Superficially it seemed attractively simple. By transmitting Rous sarcoma, you could create cancer easily in the laboratory. Then you could try to find a way of stopping its creation, try to find some agent – vaccine, serum, antitoxin, whatever – that would protect a chicken against

157

Rous sarcoma. If all cancer was like Rous sarcoma (i.e., was another microbe-caused transmittable disease), and you could cure or prevent Rous, then you would have unlocked the whole treasure-house.

It took Banting a while to gear up for the work. Special pure-bred Plymouth Rock chickens had to be obtained from the Ontario Agricultural College. Then high-powered centrifuges and microscopes, necessary to isolate and observe the cancer-causing agent, had to be ordered from abroad. Banting and Sadie Gairns began work on some chickens in the winter of 1925-26, but did not undertake the cancer research in earnest until about 1928. Encouraging results would be a long time coming.

The discouraging adrenal experiments were gradually wound down. Banting and Sadie Gairns described the work in a long paper on "Suprarenal Insufficiency" which was published in the *American Journal of Physiology* in 1926. It contributed little to the literature, was seldom cited by other researchers, and effectively camouflaged Banting's dashed hope of isolating a universal anti-toxin.

While marking time at the start of the cancer project, Banting dabbled with experiments he had started early in 1925 to try to isolate a substance in the uterus that caused the onset of labour. For a while it seemed that an extract made from the decidua (the mucous membrane lining the uterus) of pregnant rabbits contained some unknown but potent substance. After many pregnant rabbits and many frustrating experiments, especially the one which gave the same potent results with an extract of rabbit brain, Fred gave up. There was nothing worth publishing in this work, not even the record of negative results. "This has been one of the worst years I have ever lived," Banting wrote Best, who was studying in England, in the spring of 1926. "But let us hope that 'They also serve who only stand and wait.'"[1]

Banting's only success at the University in these post-insulin years was in continuing to blacken the reputation of J.J.R. Macleod. To the end of his life Banting despised and vilified Macleod. The references in his speeches were never to Macleod by name, but the inferences were clear enough. When Banting talked about the lack of support others had given him in the insulin research, he meant Macleod. When he talked about having once worked with a senior professor who had no ideas but took credit for his students' work, he meant Macleod. When he talked about lab directors who failed to train creative researchers, he meant Macleod. The only two Nobel laureates the University of Toronto has yet had, its Professor of Physiology and its Professor of Medical Research in the 1920s, not only did not work together, but probably did not speak to each other. University people took care not to invite Banting and Macleod, or Mrs. Banting and Mrs. Macleod, to the same social functions. Fred Banting was never entertained in the Macleod home.

J.J.R. Macleod did not fight back openly, but went on with his teaching and his very substantial writing and research activities, mostly relating to carbohydrate metabolism and insulin. He attracted some excellent students to the University (unfortunately those of them who were Jewish soon realized they could not hope for a career in an institution permeated with genteel anti-semitism, and left for private practice or more tolerant cities), and wrote two important books about insulin and diabetes, in both of which he presented his own dry, scientific version of how the discovery had really happened.

There is little doubt that Macleod felt the repercussions of Banting's hostility, becoming a professor who had to live under the question mark Banting had created about his integrity. At the time and for years afterwards the atmosphere around the researchers at Toronto was polluted with ugly gossip about what "really" happened during the insulin research. Most of it reflected Banting's slurs on Macleod, though the Macleod-Collip champions managed to spread a share of counter-rumours about Banting and Best as bumbling incompetents. It was a sad and ugly situation, and for Banting in particular the broken relationship meant a real, if unrealized, professional handicap. In his anger and bull-headedness and pride, he had cut himself off from the best medical researcher in the University. Such friends and patrons as Velyien Henderson and D.E. Robertson were no substitute. Without Macleod, or someone of equal competence to help him, Banting could not achieve very much.

Banting's hatred of Macleod was an enduring blind spot in his judgment. Toward several other sometimes enemies his attitudes changed markedly. The insulin fight of 1922 had shattered a budding friendship with Bert Collip. After a conversation with Fitzgerald of the Connaught one day in the summer of 1925, Banting wrote Collip to congratulate him on his recent research on parathyroid hormone. In passing, he mentioned he hoped they would meet and let the past be buried. Collip replied in kind, regretting the "unfortunate misunderstandings of the hectic winter of '22."[2] A year later, when Banting was visiting Alberta he and Collip took in the Calgary Stampede together. Their friendship began to blossom.

Later on the same trip, Banting and Duncan Graham were both at a University of Toronto alumni dinner during the Canadian Medical Association's Victoria convention. "Some joker arose and nominated the two of us to represent the University of Toronto and present their felicitations to the banquet of the University of Western Ontario. To my amazement and surprise Professor Graham rose, came to where I was seated and we left arm in arm. We remained arm and arm for the distance to the other building. He introduced me as the link between the two great universities and asked me to make a speech." Banting was delighted.[3]

He did not see a lot of Charley Best in those years. Unlike Banting, Best realized that his insulin fame did not mean that he was yet equipped for a career in medical research. Getting good advice from H.H. Dale, the distinguished British physiologist who had visited Toronto in 1922 to learn about insulin, Best quickly took his medical degree in Toronto, then got out of town to do advanced graduate work. Charley and his bride, Margaret, spent the mid-1920s in England, where Best did his Ph.D. under Dale's supervision. The two or three surviving letters from Banting to Best in these years are friendly and chatty, though not intimate in the way Banting often was with his classmates or old war buddies. Banting and Best had talked about doing more research together – and friends like Henderson, who realized how badly Banting needed a biochemist, speculated that money from the Banting Research Foundation might support a renewed collaboration – but nothing came of it. When Best came back to Toronto in 1927 he resumed his job as head of insulin production at Connaught, took a position in Fitzgerald's School of Hygiene, and began a separate career in his own right as a productive researcher.

The frustration Banting felt at his failure to achieve anything in the lab in the mid-1920s deepened into black unhappiness as it became clear that his marriage had been a mistake. Whether or not there had been sexual incompatibility from their wedding night, as Fred sometimes hinted, Dr. and Mrs. Banting soon realized that they did not have nearly as much in common as their whirlwind courtship had led them to believe.

Fred held traditional attitudes toward marriage and family life. He expected his wife would be a lot like his mother had been—a quiet homebody who did all the woman's work very well, bore and raised a flock of children, never complained, let her husband do the man's jobs. Fred was going to be a hard-working medical researcher just as his father had been a hard-working farmer. He expected to come home at night, take his shoes off at the door, and sit down to a good supper (or, adjusting to modern city ways, a hot dinner). After the meal he'd read and smoke and sit by the fire, or maybe get together with some of the other fellows to chew the fat, or maybe go back to the lab and do some more work. His wife would be waiting for him when he came home. Whenever women who knew Fred in the 1920s talked about his image of an ideal wife, they said he wanted a marriage partner who would be like an Airedale to him, utterly loyal and unquestioning. He used the same image from time to time himself.

Marion was not the Airedale, homebody type. She was an outgoing, feminine, "modern" woman, who expected to enjoy the social whirl of modern Toronto. She had married the most prominent man in all of Canada, and was ready, probably eager, for the pleasant consequences of great social prominence. High status in Toronto surely meant a crowded calendar: dinner parties, dances, receptions . . . occasions . . . mingling with beautifully-dressed, beautifully-mannered, interesting and gracious people. You could hire help to keep the house going. Make sure you do your duty and impress your husband's friends by being a good hostess in your own right. Certainly it's something of a waste to sit around a house doing nothing, or spend the best years of your life "confined" by pregnancy.

Fred had been attracted by Marion's conversational and social skills and her refined tastes—all characteristics of the new woman of the 1920s—but then had not wanted her to use them. They were only for special occasions. At most times, he expected, she should be utterly traditional, like his mother. Occasionally she would be on display as his beautiful, intellectual wife, and he would be proud of her. Normally, her job was to be a dutiful Airedale-like wife. Fred's infatuation with Marion had been a 1920s "talkie" variant of the Beautiful Doll syndrome.

Marion must have been even more shocked by the reality of their marriage. She thought she had married a charming, brilliant, en-

161

gaging discoverer. Now she found that he was a conservative, taciturn, authoritarian countryman, with a countryman's manners and tastes. She was repelled by the way he would come home from the lab, take off his shoes, and refuse to be charming to the ladies she had in for tea. When was dinner? Fred would sit down at the table without even changing from the clothes he wore to the lab. Yes, he wore a gown over them in the lab, but a sensitive person could probably detect the dog odour and the odd dog hair. Cutting the roast in the same clothes he wore when he cut into the dogs.

Why couldn't Fred at least dress for dinner? Why couldn't he be friendly to Marion's friends? Why did he have so little to say? Why didn't he like going out more often in the evenings, dressing well, meeting important and interesting people? Why did he shun his wife and her friends, but have lots of time to go out with "the boys" and come home at all hours reeking with beer? Marion was remembered by her friends as "fastidious beyond words." She found her husband's manners and attitudes crude and gross. They were so thoroughly incompatible in temperament and values that it is hard to believe their sex life was satisfactory either. As well, they almost certainly quarrelled about money, with Fred accusing Marion of having extravagant tastes, and Marion objecting to his control of the family funds. Finally, there was the darkest side, the fights and anger and frustration that apparently led Fred, according to Marion's father's sworn testimony, to do what angry men often did to disobedient wives: he hit his wife.[4]

So the marriage was a dreadful mistake. But not a mistake anyone could easily correct in the conservative Canada of the 1920s, where it was a matter of nationalist pride that divorce was far less frequent than in the immoral United States. Respectable Canadians had no easy exit from a bad marriage. Adultery was virtually the only ground for divorce, and until 1931 even a parting on those terms required a special Act of the Canadian Parliament.

Fred and Marion had little choice but to begin making the adjustments necessary to endure each other. More and more often they went their own ways, Fred to the lab, Marion spending some of her excess energy as a leader in the Girl Guide movement. They lived in separate rooms in the Bedford Road house, but dutifully kept up appearances at the University and with some of their friends. Others, like the Hipwells, knew something was badly wrong. Velyien Henderson may or may not have known, depending on how one interprets a report to his wife after seeing the Bantings one night in 1928: "Marion is working very hard at Girl Guides, and Fred says it is a Godsend. She is as spoony a wife as can possibly be. I much prefer spooning in private." There were undoubtedly good times when Fred and Marion rekindled some of the old romance in a desperate effort to make it work. And there must have been the nightmarish times when she was left to cry hopelessly.

His marriage was one of the few aspects of his life that Fred did not later write about at length. Or if he did, the documents were later destroyed. Two surviving story fragments appear to draw on these unhappy years. In one a doctor is just finishing dinner, "all dressed up with a party of swells who are about to depart for the opening of the Royal Winter Fair." The doctor is called out to see a patient, and his wife says "the same things . . . that he so often heard: 'Now I will not go without you' . . . 'I don't know why we cannot do things together' . . . 'they will all be so disappointed' . . . 'Well, I do not think that you wanted to go any way' . . . 'One of his girl friends has just called him and I guess some one will have to be my Beau'. . ." In a second fragment Banting is reflecting on the kinds of people whose marriage vows are kept with "an Airedale trueness": "But the man who only sees his wife when she is dressed for dinner, who is the Teller to hand out money for her every whim, who has nothing in common but the name, who has no sincere interest in what she is doing, . . . has the devil's own job to remain true and faithful."[5]

Other fiction writers had imitated a reality which was in some ways eerily close to Banting's. In 1925 Sinclair Lewis published an instantly classic American novel about doctors and medical research, *Arrowsmith*. Late in the story Dr. Martin Arrowsmith marries the beautiful socialite, Joyce Lanyon, and then is bewildered at the way her desires interfere with his simple hope of living plainly and getting on with research:

She expected him to remember her birthday, her taste in wine, her liking for flowers, and her objection to viewing the process of shaving. She wanted a room to herself; she insisted that he knock before entering; and she demanded that he admire her hats.

When he was so interested in the work at [the] Institute that he had a clerk telephone that he would not be able to meet her for dinner, she was tight-lipped with rage.

. . . It was confusing to find how starkly she discriminated

163

between his caresses when he was absorbed in her and his hasty interest when he wanted to go to sleep.[6]

Banting might or might not have read *Arrowsmith*. He did spend a lot of time in his third-floor study with his books and his paints. He had accumulated a fairly good library of medical books and Canadiana, and became a fairly wide reader, partly to carry out his resolve to become more cultured. He often talked about his interest in Canadian history, especially in the Indians and their approach to medicine. Sometimes he jotted down a few notes from his reading, and began talking about some day writing a book about Indian medicine or medical history.

Beaumont Cornell had published novels in 1922 (*Renaissance*) and 1923 (*Lantern Marsh*), and received a certain amount of critical attention as a budding Canadian creative writer. There was Cornell, the medical researcher as author. By the mid-20s and for the rest of his life, Banting the medical researcher aspired to be a published author, often remarking that he thought writing the highest form of creative achievement. Not just Cornell's influence, but his own loneliness, his desire to express his thoughts and emotions, and his frequent bouts of sleeplessness impelled Banting toward trying to write. His favourite reading was not history or medical tomes, but detective fiction; his earliest literary efforts were attempts to bring to life Simon, or Silas, Eagles, an analytical chemist, half-Indian, who has a particularly keen sense of smell. Si lives with Stanford Cornell at Number 1 Carlton Street in Toronto, and, according to his creator is,

basically a lonely man, who would sometimes spend days and nights in the lab, often sleeping there on a couch. . . . He relaxed by painting and sketching. Although some of his things were quite good he never exhibited them. Everything he did he did with all his might; but it was true that irregular meals, lack of exercise, sleeping on his couch, etc., were undermining his health. He spent the greater part of his salary on extra apparatus. Smoked very heavily, even though he had a heavy cough.

Banting jotted down various Holmesian deductions Si could make – the outside paper of a cigarette which is smoked rapidly and nervously burns extra quickly; when a man crosses his legs in a certain way you can see a pulsating vein and tell if he is lying – but only finished one story that he tried to have published. "Si and the Cold Draught" was an almost unreadable tale in which the victim dies after drinking liquid air (the cold draught). Banting sent the story to an editor at the International Magazine Company in 1927. It was rejected as being "rather prosaic . . . a little difficult to follow in spots . . . too reminiscent of Sherlock Holmes . . . rather flat and uninteresting, mechanically constructed, without much atmosphere and allure." The editor suggested that Banting arrange a collaboration with a professional "fictioneer," and Banting did talk to several local writers, including Greenaway of the *Star*, who had become something of a family friend, about the possibility of collaborating with him. He also composed a Si fragment in which the great detective is trying to write and has come to "the conclusion that he would write what he wanted rather than what the editor wanted. He loved with a tender love the stories of the pioneer Canadian life, with the thrills of adventure, the struggle against nature, and the hardy ancestral stock. His fore-fathers had been among the first to settle in the district of Simcoe."[7]

Banting's interests often turned to Simcoe County and his boyhood on the farm in Alliston. With much less self-consciousness and more literary ease than in his fiction, he wrote out most of the stories used in the first chapter of this biography. He often talked about someday writing a full autobiography and once got about eighty pages into it. He realized, too, that some of the tall tales from Alliston days could be used for fiction. There was the story of old Jerry McGague of West Essa, for example, who bought a box of dry soda biscuits one day in town, was so hungry he ate them all on the way home, was so thirsty when he got home that he drank a pitcher of water, and then, when the biscuits swelled up, died of a bursted stomach. This was to be the first in a series of what Banting planned to call "Thirsty Tales."[8]

To quench his own thirst as he scribbled in the night upstairs at 46 Bedford Road, he kept a bottle of rye whiskey hidden behind one of the baseboards. His drinking, which had been a temporary problem during the insulin strain, was a steady fact of his life, but there is no evidence that it was a problem during these years. He was a heavy chain smoker, mostly of plain-tipped Buckingham cigarettes, sometimes of a pipe.

His favourite relaxation would always be his painting. During his 160 Bloor Street days at the height of the insulin work, he would sit in his upper room sketching while he dictated letters to his secretary. He liked to hang his own works on his walls, and one night made someone else's work – a painting of maple sugaring, which was in the hallway of his rented premises – partly his own by painting in snow in appropriate places.[9] During his travels as the discoverer of insulin Banting saw a lot of North American and European art galleries, and began buying art. His early purchases were not good, for his standards were uninformed and undiscriminating. He brought his simple patriotism to his taste in art, and shortly after winning the Nobel Prize commissioned one of his earliest mentors, Gordon Payne, of Ingersoll, Ontario, to paint for him a picture of a beaver at work. He may have had a series in mind, for Banting's aim, Payne told the press, was to combine art and patriotism by perpetuating Canada on canvas. Payne travelled 150 miles north to Algonquin Park to do his field work, and duly completed a large canvas for Banting entitled "The Beaver Dam."[10] Banting himself sat for a portrait in oils, commissioned by his classmates and later given to the University. The Toronto artist, Curtis Williamson, did a wretched job, worse than Banting could have done if he had ever attempted a self-portrait.

Other Toronto-based artists were painting Algonquin Park and the Canadian outdoors more effectively than Gordon Payne in the early 1920s. Banting was on the spot in Toronto in the years when the exhibitions of the work of Tom Thomson and the Group of Seven upset most of the conventions of Canadian scholasticism. As its members proclaimed, more than a little self-consciously, the first truly Canadian art movement came to life in Toronto in the late teens and early twenties. Arthur Lismer, Lawren Harris, J.E.H. MacDonald, A.Y. Jackson, *et al.*, friends of the drowned Tom Thomson, set out to paint the Canadian landscape as Canadians should see it – simply, starkly, colourfully, modernly. They began exhibiting as a group in Toronto in 1920. Stories of outrage and resistance to their work, and a hard struggle to win acceptance, are largely myths, reflecting both natural exaggeration by sensitive artists and a dollop of canny self-promotion.

The Group in fact had an immediate, immense impact on the Canadian art scene. They overcame adversity just about as quickly as young Fred Banting had when he did his early medical research in Toronto. Just as Banting's success depended on others more than he could realize or admit, so the Group had not had an immaculate conception on Algonquin Park's Canoe Lake, where Thomson painted and drowned. There was also a market for their work, just as there was a public for Banting's fame. Many well-to-do Canadians in the 1920s were looking back to the outdoors, to nature, to the simple life before cities and crowds and formality. The Group of Seven was popular partly because they supplied agreeable lenses. Within five years of the Group's first showing, it had become effectively the national establishment of Canadian painting, praised and patronized even as its members still affected their radical, outsiders' image.

Banting essayed a first small public showing of his own painting in January 1925, by contributing two small canvasses to a Hart House Sketching Club exhibit of the work of University of Toronto staff and students. A critic for the *Star Weekly* found most of the University artists predictably academic, but saw the influence of Tom Thomson in one of Banting's sketches, that of Lawren Harris in the other. There was "just a soupçon of the Seven" in Banting's northern Ontario landscape, and altogether it seemed that the doctor had made a reasonably successful "portage from test-tubes to paint-tubes." Another *Star* writer was less kind, suggesting that the only school Banting represented was the Medical School.[11]

Banting's first encounter with Lawren Harris came about the time of this exhibition. He found a highly formalized Harris canvas of Lake Superior hills intensely unsettling, going back to see it several times and always wanting to put his foot through it. Banting's eye-doctor, James MacCallum, happened to be an important patron of the Group of Seven; he heard Banting's opinion of Harris's painting and urged him to talk about it with the artist. MacCallum arranged for Banting and Harris to meet. Banting told Harris he couldn't understand why he'd painted the picture; Harris explained that he was trying to be creative the way Banting had been as a scientist, by transforming old realities into new. Beau Cornell was trying to do the same thing with literature. Banting found he could see similarities between creative scientists and creative artists. "Like all great scientists he was essentially an artist," he wrote of Si Eagles.

In April 1925 Lawren Harris nominated Banting for membership in the Arts and Letters Club of Toronto. His seconder was Barker Fairley, a German professor and talented painter who was the moving spirit in University art circles. The Arts and Letters Club, whose quarters were only a block or two away from the University, was *the* gathering spot for Toronto painters, writers and musicians in the 1920s. Men only, of course. It was a dining club, whose members' energies spilled into skits, celebrations, sketching trips and constant good fellowship. The Group of Seven were all members. So, in fact, were most of their fiercest critics, lunchers at what came to be called "the knockers' table." Banting was not a leading participant in the club's activities – he had no musical or acting abilities – but was a good companion at table, for he loved the singing, the story-telling and the good drinking of men relaxing. Luncheon bantering (Lismer once did a sketch of "Dr. Bantering") and first-naming and caricaturing at the Arts and Letters Club would be a refreshing change from the stuffy formality of the University or the social and sexual tension of life at 46 Bedford Road. For several years in the late 1920s Banting was a member of the club's executive committee.

Banting initiated one of the great friendships of his life when he went to see A.Y. Jackson one day in the mid-1920s. He diffidently introduced himself, and wondered if he could see some of Jackson's war paintings. Jackson showed him several, and Banting bought one. Alec or Alex Jackson, as his friends called him, was a life-long bachelor, eight years older than Banting, particularly convivial in male company, a passionate ideologue of the Group's quest for recognition. The famous painter and the famous doctor hit it off together from the beginning. Perhaps they swapped stories of their early struggles. They shared the myth about themselves and each other, of having risen to triumph against the Establishment. *I was ready to go to the States too. . . . Hell of a thing to get people to wake up in this country and see what's right in front of their eyes. . . . But by God I love this country. . . .* Banting would never say how much he had been helped by J.J.R. Macleod in his insulin work. A.Y. Jackson never told Banting that one of his own earlier patrons, who had purchased some of his sketches and invited him to his home for dinner, was J.J.R. Macleod. Both of the Nobel laureates in medicine had in fact been members of the Arts and Letters Club. J.J.R. Macleod had joined in March 1921, just before the insulin work started. In the spring of 1923 he had let his membership lapse.[12]

In March 1927 Jackson invited Banting to come to Quebec with him on a sketching trip. They went to the village of St. Jean Port

Jolie on the windswept south shore of the St. Lawrence below Quebec City, and tried to work outdoors in one of the coldest Marches in memory. Under these conditions Banting lost all the hesitation he had felt about painting being no fit activity for a manly man. "I found Banting one day crouching beside a rail fence with a little sketch box and the wind drifting snow over it," Jackson recalled. "Collar pulled up and hat pulled down, he was working away as I came up to him and said, 'Well, how do you like it?' He said, 'And I thought this was a sissy game.'"[13]

Banting went on this and other sketching trips under an alias, as Frederick Grant. When he was recognized he would be a cousin or brother of the insulin Banting. The trouble with being Frederick Banting the famous Professor of Medical Research at the University was that you lived in a world of people who, as Lewis put it in *Arrowsmith*, wore severe collars, made addresses and never cursed. And you also had to live with a woman like Marion, or Joyce Lanyon, and all her funny ideas. As he came to know A.Y. Jackson, Banting was like Martin Arrowsmith finding a true friend in Terry Wickett. The Wickett of *Arrowsmith* was "rough, he was surly, he was colloquial, he despised many fine and gracious things, he offended many fine and gracious people, but these acerbities made up the haircloth robe wherewith he defended a devotion to such holy work as no cowled monk ever knew."[14] A.Y. Jackson could almost have been Sinclair Lewis's model. When Banting went off painting with Jackson, it was not exactly the same as Arrowsmith and Wickett moving to the Vermont woods to do research at the end of the novel, but it was very similar. Away with the artificialities of civilization and women, on with the flannel shirt, back to nature, to the wild, to rugged things, and to doing fine and beautiful things. Ernest Hemingway would have understood too, both in a literary way and in remembering his own need to get away from Toronto and such institutions as the *Star* newspaper.

Where can the rugged Canadian look to define himself? Only and always to the north. Ever since a friendly critic had remarked that the Group of Seven's final objective was probably to paint at the North Pole, Alex Jackson had been thinking about going to the Arctic. He managed to persuade the Canadian Department of the Interior to find room for him on the steamer *Beothic*, scheduled to resupply the ports in Canada's Eastern Arctic in the summer of 1927. That year was proving no more successful for Banting in the lab or at home than 1926 had been. He had had his appetite for the north whetted by a brief trip to Alaska following a CMA convention in British Columbia the summer before, and longed to accompany Jackson. Officials of the Department of the Interior must have been startled to receive a letter from the discoverer of insulin applying to serve as Medical Officer of the *Beothic*.

They already had one. But Ottawa decided to accommodate Dr. Banting as a guest. In a generation not far removed from hazardous polar exploration, the Arctic was still far from a tourist attraction. Canada's official Arctic Expeditions, which were still part exploration and part assertion of sovereignty, were serious and sometimes dangerous affairs. The telegram from Ottawa came less than a week before sailing: "Can offer nothing luxurious. If you are prepared to face hazards of the north and assume the responsibility Department will be glad to have you."

Fred was elated at the prospect of getting right away from everything, his first pure holiday, he thought, "free from speeches, lectures, & labs, since 1918." Charles Best, back in Toronto and settling down to the life of an active medical researcher, seemed unimpressed at Banting's disappearance to the north just after telling everyone he would be spending the summer in his lab. "An artist friend of his is a member of the party," Best wrote H.H. Dale. "I imagine they will sketch ice bergs and polar bears." Fred gave Marion money for a trip to the British Isles while he was gone.[15]

The 2,700-ton *Beothic*, specially plated for work in the Arctic icefields, sailed from North Sydney, Nova Scotia, on July 16, 1927. As soon as they had cleared the wharf, Dr. Banting shouted "No more white collars," tore off his collar, and threw it overboard. In posturing worthy of a Stephen Leacock satire,* several other collars were thrown in. Fred went to his cabin and put on a grey shirt and a pair of old army breeches. "Good bye to civilization for two months at least!" he exclaimed to his travel diary.

Banting and Jackson shared a large stateroom with the large-girthed government botanist, O.M. Malte. Malte had done good business with Sydney's bootleggers before the *Beothic* sailed, and found nearly continuous occasion through the trip to celebrate important botanical observations with a glass of rum. The *Beothic*'s steward acted as bootlegger to the less well-prepared. Banting, still a

---

*"Collarless, tieless, hatless, gold watchless, the relaxed doctor shouted 'No more demands on me,' and threw himself overboard."

Methodist man of the world in some respects, reported that the Mounties on board were "an exceptionally fine bunch of boys – clean, keen, alert, wholesome trusting sportsmen – no filthy stories, they played bridge without stakes, very temperate."

Jackson and Banting could not keep up with the scenery as they tried to sketch the first icebergs north of Newfoundland. It was their first lesson in the difficulty of doing serious sketching (using oil on small wooden panels) of moving objects from a moving ship, and they had to revert to pencil drawings. Jackson often redid his drawings and sketches on canvas; Banting never mastered the technique, or just could not be bothered. The *Beothic*'s first call was at Godhavn in Greenland, where Banting and Jackson saw their first Eskimos, kayaks and huskies. "It was wonderful," Fred wrote that night, "to gaze about at this little northland village with the bay and its icebergs beyond. Dogs everywhere, gaily legginged and beaded natives smiling at us. Alex would chuckle and about a dozen times he said, 'I just want to laugh. It hardly seems possible that we are here.' It was difficult to realize that it was not a dream." They bought four "primitive Eskimo artist paintings," paying $1.50 each. "There was a Danish artist at Godhavn," Jackson wrote in his diary, "he seemed to me like a guy digging lead out of a gold mine, it was rather obvious stuff."[16]

The *Beothic* steamed north through the Davis Strait and Baffin Bay, visited Etah, Greenland, a famous stop for Arctic explorers which turned out to consist of four sealskin tents, and pushed on into the Kane Basin to the most northern outpost in the world, the RCMP station on the Bache peninsula of Ellesmere Island. Supplies were unloaded and RCMP officers exchanged. Sergeant Joy of the Mounted, famous across Canada as the Mountie at the top of the world to whom everyone radioed Christmas greetings (surely he responded in his Christmas eve broadcasts by proclaiming "Joy to the world . . ."), was being brought out. On July 31, Banting and Jackson went ashore at Bache. Banting, who gloried in being on frontiers – medicine, art, now geography – reflected that he probably stood closer to the North Pole than any man on the continent. Later in the voyage, Joy, who had made a 1,500-mile trip that year across and around Ellesmere Island and was peeved at having to come south, filled the tourists with stories of the Arctic explorers and his opinion that Canada's own Arctic Expeditions were expensive and purposeless, the supplies given the police posts usually cheap and rotten.[17] The painters found Bache a disappointment, offering only a little starved and shrivelled vegetation, with fog enveloping most of the hills. But Jackson kept a promise he had made to his sponsor in sketching and then painting the Bache post with the *Beothic* in the harbour.

They nearly became trapped in the ice at Bache, and a few days later failed in an attempt to reach Melville Island, southwest of Ellesmere. They were storm-bound for several days at Beechey Island, where in 1845-46 Franklin and his men had spent their last winter, and half a dozen Arctic expeditions had since left their litter. Picture Jackson and Banting sketching the ruins of the boats left for Franklin, investigating the whiskey bottle Captain Bernier of the Canadian Arctic Expedition had left in 1922, adding their names to the paper in it, their noses telling them the bottle was still pungent.

On the return trip the *Beothic* stopped at the chief Baffin Island posts: Arctic Bay, Pond Inlet, Clyde, Pangnirtung and Lake Harbour. There was less threat of ice, more time for sketching, and better hills to sketch – sharp peaks with glaciers instead of the flat, low sedimentary rock of the more northern islands. Banting, who studied Jackson's methods carefully and began to imitate him to the point where their work is sometimes indistinguishable, was starting to come along as a painter, Jackson thought. They were both fascinated by the forms and colours of the Arctic, especially the stark rocks and the interplay of light and ice. For Jackson, however, the trip seems to have meant more in the development of his sense of Canadian geography and nationalism than his evolution as a painter. Neither artist was particularly interested in the fauna of the Arctic, although Banting did procure a long narwhale tusk which still resides in the Arts and Letters Club as his gift from the North.

They found the Eskimos, a number of whom hitched rides from post to post on the *Beothic*, so interesting that Jackson wished they had a portrait man aboard. They are "much more paintable than Injuns and much more likable," he wrote and marvelled at the medley of costumes worn by the Eskimos who came out over the ice to the ship at Arctic Bay:

They trade them awful junk at the H.B. – old print dresses of twenty years ago, skirts down to their ankles, red, blue, pink, seal skin pants, the loose Arctic shirt with the bag at the back for the papoose, old army tunics, and every cap imaginable. And all hopping from one chunk of ice to another, throwing their dogs across the wide spaces. Old girls who you would hardly think could walk, jumping like two-year olds, and five-year old kids following them. . . . If the space was too wide, they jumped on a smaller piece and gave it a shove with one foot as they stepped on. As a show it was a marvel.

A lot of the shipboard talk was about the fate of the Eskimo in the white man's Arctic. The civil servants and RCMP men in the north had little use for the traders of the Hudson's Bay Company, men who seemed only interested in the north and the natives for the money they could make. Banting's and Jackson's diaries record only hostile comments on the fur traders, opinions Banting reflected in forming his own conclusions about the state of the Inuit. He was particularly interested in the situation at Arctic Bay, especially after the furs gathered at that post by the Hudson's Bay Company were brought on board the *Beothic* to be shipped out. Normally no one knew how well, or how badly, the company did at any post. Now the visitors compared the pathetic dress of the Eskimos on the ice flows with the company's fabulous haul in furs. Banting meditated in his journal:

Arctic Bay is a Hudson Bay Post. The company have systematically possessed themselves of this country. They have at each post an interpreter who puts before the native the company's views & teaches them that the great company will look after them & is their savior. While at the same time they hire them at ten dollars per year to "retain" them as their men. They buy their furs very cheap – in trade – tea – tobacco – woollens etc – which are by no means as good for the native as his former life without these things. At this port we took on 23 bales of fox furs & there are said to be one hundred skins per bale – They sell at $50 to $60 per skin. 2300 x 50 = $115,000.

Now where does the native come in? He hunts $100,000 worth of furs & the Company take the profits. Why can not the government do as the Swedish [Banting meant the Danish] government [in Greenland] – take charge of the sales & give the profits to the upkeep of the natives. They do not want or need education or religion, but a little guidance in provisions for the winter.

They are hospitable, easy going, will give one anything they have and if the Government were to put proper men in each post to lead them – they are easily led – the whole scheme would be self-supporting & at the same time to the benefit of the native.

A native cannot live on white man's food or in white man's dress.

Banting gave the natives and their problems considerable thought in the next few weeks, for at the beginning of the trip when he had asked if there was anything he could do to be useful, the Deputy Minister of the Interior had said it would be valuable to have his opinion of the effect of the white man's food and clothing on the Eskimo.

As the *Beothic* headed south through the Labrador Sea, the travellers who had found the ice so exciting six weeks earlier now couldn't be bothered looking out at a dozen icebergs. Jackson, whose trip diary was both more reflective and more thorough than Banting's (Fred gave up with two weeks left to go), meditated on some of the paradoxes of the cruise: "Strange, we have been voyaging in one of the most romantic countries in the world and yet nearly everyone on the expedition has been taking the artificial stimulus of detective stories to while away the times. I would like a couple of weeks paddling, swimming, and chopping wood on the Georgian Bay, to get the old muscles in shape. An occasional scramble over rocks is all I have had in the way of exercise."

The lack of exercise did not prevent Jackson from bursting with enthusiasm when Greenaway of the Toronto *Star* met them in Montreal. Greenaway found Jackson more virile than ever, more in love with Canada than ever, now that he and Banting had pushed the frontier of Canadian art to within 10 degrees of the Pole (there was a skit that winter at the Arts and Letters Club on the "Sevenization of the North Pole and the Groupification of the Eskimos"). There was no reason for young Canadians to go to Europe to take art lessons any more, Jackson said; he himself never wanted to work in Europe again. In passing, he gave Greenaway a separate sensational story by condemning his native Montreal as Canada's most bigoted city, where the Group of Seven would starve for lack of critical appreciation. "All the people who are thinking in art or literature in Canada these days gravitate to Toronto, not to Montreal."

Gravitating to Toronto on the train with Banting that night, Greenaway wrote a throwaway story on Banting's painting in the north, the weather, and the scenery. Banting looked it over – he had promised not to make statements to the press that were not cleared by the Department of the Interior – found it innocuous, and Greenaway wired it ahead to Toronto when the train stopped at Kingston. Then, on a post-prandial discussion, perhaps fuelled with bootleg booze left from the *Beothic*, Banting told Greenaway the real story of the way the Hudson's Bay Company was exploiting the Eskimo in the north. Banting thought it was an off-the-record talk among friends (Vincent Massey, who knew Banting from the Arts and Letters Club, rode with them part of the way). Greenaway saw it as a continuation of the interviews begun in Montreal, and remembered warning Banting that he was saying pretty strong things about the powerful company. He also took notes.

Learning that Banting had been seen talking to reporters, the assistant Deputy Minister of the Interior phoned him in Toronto the next day to remind him of the agreement. Banting said the only thing he had approved was a totally inoffensive story for the *Star*. Then he went out and bought the *Star* to check the inoffensive story. The paper's black headline was: BANTING REGRETS HUDSON BAY USE OF ESKIMO. Greenaway's long, copyright story contained almost all of the charges Banting had earlier recorded in his diary, along with complaints that there was scarcely a real Canadian among the English and Scotsmen in the Hudson's Bay Company. The story was loaded with long, direct quotes. It was a serious attack on Canada's most important northern commercial enterprise by Canada's most famous medical man.

The Governors of the Hudson's Bay Company were outraged, and denied Banting's charges as false and slanderous. The Department of the Interior was also outraged and let the press know its view that the Banting interview was in "bad taste," for he had not made any such report to the department, whose guest he had been. Banting was furious at Greenaway, frightened that the Hudson's Bay Company might sue him for slander, and embarrassed at the bad taste of it all. He and Greenaway had a highly unpleasant rehashing of what had happened, which included Banting slamming the door of his house in Greenaway's face. Banting did not forgive Greenaway, may have tried to have him fired – Greenaway was saved by being able to produce his notebooks – and did not speak to him for the next ten years. Greenaway, who must himself have been worried to hear that Banting was boasting of how he could get Sir William Mulock to have Joe Atkinson, proprietor of the Liberal *Star*, fire the upstart reporter, was equally bitter, and in his memoirs wrote that Banting was one of the few liars he had ever met.[18]

Banting wrote and rushed to Ottawa to explain what had happened – "I have been milked and deceived by a reporter and friend . . . one of the few newspapermen I do trust – but never again. . . . I cannot tell you how badly I feel." He eventually submitted two reports to the department on the health of the Eskimo. In them he stood his ground, charging that white men's food was not good for the native diet, white men's clothing was not efficient, and that exploitation as a result of the fur trading system would eventually lead to the extinction of the Eskimo race. He made several minor recommendations about health care in the north, as well as urging the government to take over the whole of the fur trade and use the profits to finance measures "to improve rather than destroy the chances of the Eskimo race."

The Hudson's Bay Company took the situation seriously, not least because Interior asked for its views on Banting's charges. The Governor of the company held a long meeting with Banting in Toronto, which he felt led to Banting's modifying his views. Banting told Jackson that it was a stand-off, with the two of them exchanging slurs on each other's lack of experience in the north and Banting instancing the United Fruit Company's treatment of its workers as far better than the Hudson's Bay Company's. Early in 1928 the company sent Ottawa a long, point-by-point rebuttal of Banting's sweeping conclusions, conclusions it noted that were "founded upon a single visit to Baffin Land, of short duration, and upon hearsay information of a somewhat vague character. . . ." Banting in fact knew little about Eskimo dress and diet, the company argued, or about Eskimo demographics, or about the economics of the fur trade (the Arctic Bay pelts were the product of a rare superb year; the posts had to be maintained in all the other years). Above all he knew nothing about Eskimo life before the contact with the whites: "Dr. Banting apparently assumes that, in a state of isolation, the Eskimo live in a happy, carefree state, immune from disease, comfortably clothed, comfortably housed, and with sufficient food exactly suited to their needs."[19]

That was the end of the affair. A few years later Banting wrote an account of his trip for the first issue of the *Canadian Geographical*

Journal, had it vetted by the Department of the Interior, and now presented a more balanced view of the Eskimo's situation ("The white man has introduced many new things which have added greatly to the comfort and pleasure of the Eskimoes"), concluding that changes should come slowly and the government had things well in hand.* Earlier Banting had taken a simplistic and fairly widely-held position in the debate on the impact of the white man's ways on natives. The company was correct in charging him with viewing the Eskimo as a simple, healthy child of nature who would have been better off in every way had civilization never reached him. The whole point of Banting's own flight from civilization, after all, was to get away from its corrupting, confining, deadening ways.

In 1928 Banting and Jackson fled west and north, joining a prominent mining engineer, Mackenzie Bell, for a visit to mineral claims on Great Slave Lake in the North-West Territories. It seems to have been a less exciting adventure – Jackson apparently did not bother with a journal – in several ways. The mosquitos, horseflies and blackflies on Great Slave Lake in July played havoc with most attempts to sketch. "What really stopped you was when they'd get in your paint," Jackson remembered. "After a while you were painting with yellow black flies, blue black flies and red black flies."[20] The natives of the area, Slave and Dogrib Indians, were living in wretched poverty and that summer were being literally decimated by a flu epidemic. Banting recorded all the stories he was told of their degradation, immorality and unreliability with little comment or query. "The poor old red man is doomed," he concluded. "Even here where civilization has scarcely permeated they cannot stand up under the strain."

The highlight of the trip was crossing Great Slave Lake to the Yellowknife River and returning in an old, leaky motor-scow. Both times the party had to take shelter on tiny islands. On one they found iron deposits. Here is Banting playing prospector, wandering around with his little hammer trying to find ore, Jackson putting down his paintbrush, asking for the hammer, knocking off a huge chunk of the red ore right beside him: "Is this what you're looking for?" Here is a party of traders, including a Levantine with a sick

*Lloyd Stevenson draws attention to the criticisms that the famous Arctic explorer, Vilhjalmur Stefansson, offered of the article of Banting's in his 1936 book, *Adventures in Error*. In fact Stefansson's points were minor nit-picking, made pompously and as part of an almost unreadable potboiler.

wife, storm-bound at the same island, who find the other party of strangers includes a world-famous doctor. The doctor finds himself in the middle of Great Slave Lake treating a beautiful black-eyed Moslem girl wearing a flowing white veil. Here is some of Banting's very worst prose as he tries to describe an overnight trip back to Resolution:

> Erstwhile the fingers of the Goddess of heaven waves to us a farewell, their green and yellow streamers extending like a veil in the wind as she opened and closed her hand. The cold breath of the North chilled us to the bone. The multitude of islands in all directions and of all sizes and height remind us that they were but mountain tops of former days and that we were now sailing suspended, high in the valleys where perchance once strolled fair lovers even at this o'clock.

Roughing it was not easy for citified guys. The twelve-mile hike carrying packs into the Pine Point ore deposits – lots of ore, but impossibly expensive to get out unless a railway could be built (as it finally was, thirty-five years later) – was hard on all of them. Banting's stomach had trouble standing the strain of camp grub and he was constantly taking bicarbonate of soda. But it was a good trip: "Last night I broke my glasses – stuck them together with copper wire and electric tape. For the past five or six days I have been having a lot of hyperacidity, likely due to the fat bacon and once boiled beans. My nose is still stiff and sore from sunburn. Behind my ears is nearly raw from mosquito bites – but I can walk 25 miles, paddle, or carry a pack – apart from these minor ailments I feel fine."

He felt fine, too, about all the memorable conversation on this trip: the way they talked about Canada's vast resources, the great work to be done developing the country, the need to keep most immigrants out, and Canadians' intolerable inferiority complex about their country. "Mack thinks we should be nationalists – It is the best way of being Imperialists. The greatest way we can help the Empire is by developing a true Canadian spirit. Promote our own resources, timber, power, mines, fisheries, agriculture, ranching, oil, salt, clays." Canadian resources, Canadian science, Canadian art, the Canadian north. The travellers were all, as Banting wrote of Bell, Canadian to the core.

Banting's marriage did not seem a total failure, for shortly after he returned to Toronto Marion found that she was pregnant. A son,

William Robertson Banting, was born in April 1929.

For Banting there was another important change in the Toronto scene. The Canadianization of the University of Toronto crept forward another step as a result of J.J.R. Macleod's decision in 1928 to go back to Scotland. He had had the attractive offer of the Regius Chair in Physiology at his home university of Aberdeen, which in itself was probably enough to draw him back. But he had also had enough of Canada, and the University of Toronto, and Fred Banting. The only semblance of a joint display of their talents which appeared after insulin was when they both contributed to a Hart House exhibit of doctors' art in 1926 or 1927. Once again Banting's virile Canadianism attracted more attention than Macleod's restrained traditionalism. He never said much about Banting as a painter or a scientist, but did tell one of his students that he felt he had to either leave Toronto or take legal action. On his part, Banting did not attend the glittering farewell dinner the University community held for Macleod – having replied to the invitation, it is said, by asking that an empty chair represent him.

When Macleod settled into his chair in the club car of the train out of Toronto he took the quiet satisfaction of shuffling his feet – "To wipe away the dirt of this city," he told a curious friend. He never came back. His Canadian years left him with a case of severe arthritis, which made him a semi-invalid. He could not do much research, and would not even have been able to paint. He died in 1935.

Charles Best's British patrons, H.H. Dale and A.V. Hill, strongly recommended that the University of Toronto promote him as Macleod's replacement. A possible American candidate for the job declined to be considered. Recommendations for some other candidates came with the usual qualifications. "Samson Wright is a Jew and may not be acceptable on that ground."[21] With Macleod himself recommending Best as showing more promise than anyone he could think of, the University decided to take the risk of pitchforking a thirty-year-old into a prominent senior position. In 1929 Best became Professor of Physiology and head of the small department. Banting and Best were now both at the top and alone in Toronto.

Sir William Mulock had fretted from time to time that Banting's immortality as insulin's discoverer might not be secure. He once sent Banting a clipping, for example, in which Macleod was reported to have referred to "Dr. Banting's . . . discovery of insulin."

179

Mulock urged Banting to save that clipping and if possible get a transcript of Macleod's talk.[22] Early in 1930 Mulock and Banting went through several rounds of discussion about the wording of a plaque to be put in room 221 of the Medical Building, where Banting and Best had worked in the summer of 1921. Mulock wanted it to identify 221 as the room in which insulin was "discovered." Banting, supported by Best, felt it would be better to be cautious lest someone reopen the whole controversy. He suggested that the plaque read "In this room, in 1921, Banting and Best carried out the early experiments which led to the discovery of insulin." Mulock was not satisfied. After an evening's discussion at Mulock's home Banting would not make any further suggestion. Someone else seems to have drafted a more detailed wording, subtly tilting the credit Banting's way. The plaque finally read:

> On the 30th October, 1920, Frederick Grant Banting originated the hypothesis that the failure theretofore to isolate the internal secretion of the pancreas had been due to its destruction by the ferments liberated during the process of extraction.
>
> He devised an experimental method by which this destruction could be avoided and the internal secretion (now known as insulin) obtained.
>
> In May, 1921, Banting and Charles Herbert Best, both graduates of the University of Toronto, conducted in this room the experiments which culminated in the isolation of insulin.[23]

Banting had not done anything to extend his reputation beyond insulin. He did not have to, for the glory from insulin would follow him everywhere and be with him always. The public always assumed, for example, that he was an expert on diabetes. Requests for consultation came from the high and mighty – Mackenzie King and Mulock both referred diabetic friends to Banting – and from the humble: a diabetic bargeman on the Athabaska River, a pioneering prospector for whom Banting's train was stopped in British Columbia. Diabetologists such as Elliott Joslin kept him informed of their triumphs with insulin, and he was one of the first to receive a sample when J.J. Abel at Johns Hopkins made the important advance of crystallizing insulin.[24]

Some of his early insulin patients kept in touch with letters. Some, like the Ryder family, looked him up when they visited Toronto. Others entertained him on his trips to the United States.

He had known about but never met some of the diabetics who now hailed him: in 1928, while visiting Vincent Massey, serving as Canada's first Minister in Washington, Banting was introduced to the daughter of Mr. and Mrs. Robert Bacon, the child who had received insulin after Bacon's $10,000 donation for insulin equipment at the University. "She was one of the most beautiful girls I have ever seen and the picture of health," Banting remembered.[25] While he was in the North-West Territories that summer another former patient sent him a set of dress pearl studs and handkerchiefs. He probably wore them later that fall when he made a special trip to Edinburgh to deliver the Cameron Prize Lecture, having received another of the most illustrious awards in medical research. The only subject he could talk about was the discovery of insulin, one which he told his audience was to him "impersonal and dissociated entirely from my present existence."

Having to give that formal lecture before an audience which was behaving very noisily during the preliminaries was one of the most worrisome of all his public performances:

I was finally called upon. When I stood up there was the loudest clamour to which I have ever listened. I had become more and more nervous. I remember that my knees knocked together and I had to spread my legs. When the noise suddenly stopped I tried to begin the lecture. There was dead silence – a pin could be heard to drop. My tongue stuck to the roof of my mouth. Not a sound came. My mouth was dry as ashes. I took a sip of water from a glass. Finally I got started. In a few sentences I forgot myself in the lecture.[26]

In other ways Banting was becoming more sure of himself by the late 1920s. He was not going to be pushed around by the University of Toronto, for example. In 1929 when a professor of biochemistry, George Hunter, was about to leave the University to take a job at Alberta, Banting offered him a few months' temporary work in his lab during the transition. President Falconer and the Board of Governors turned down Banting's recommendation and refused to sanction the appointment. "I cannot understand their action in this matter, except that they imply that I am not fit to manage the Chair of Medical Research," Banting wrote Falconer. "I would ask you therefore to accept this my resignation."[27]

A well-run university, as Toronto was in those years, cannot afford to let its ornaments resign. Especially not when it is planning to advertise their glory to the world by naming buildings after them. A big new medical building was being erected on College Street across from Toronto General Hospital. The University, the hospital, the Banting Research Foundation and the Province of Ontario were financing the construction. Banting tried his hand at some of the fund-raising. In the late 1920s he had met the mining millionaire, Harry Oakes, at the Arts and Letters Club, and got him interested in donating $150,000 toward a new medical building. The money never materialized. One story had it that Sir Robert Falconer failed utterly to hit it off with Oakes the way Banting had; another version contended that the University would not allow the new building to be named after Oakes. Another plan for that building – to make it a grand research institute in which all the University's medical research would be concentrated – was also aborted because of the objections of the established departments. The new building went ahead anyway because office and laboratory space was badly needed, not least by Banting. He had started his career as Professor of Medical Research in quarters made available by Velyien Henderson, then had moved to three small rooms in the old Pathology Building on the hospital grounds. His "Chair" and its financial resources were now attracting so many students and others to work with Banting that he was presiding over a departmental-sized establishment. In 1930 it was officially changed into the Banting and Best *Department* of Medical Research (usually known as the Department of Medical Research or the Banting Department) and given quarters, along with several other departments, in the new building. The Governors decided to keep the idea of an "institute" alive, however, by applying the term to the whole building. And, though reluctant to name buildings after wealthy benefactors, they decided to begin immortalizing in brick and concrete the names of some of the University's most illustrious sons. Who was obviously the most illustrious medical son? So the new medical building would be named the Banting Institute.

Banting did not run the Banting Institute. Indeed, the Banting Institute was not an institute and Banting had not wanted his name on the building. But his objections had been overridden.

The Banting Institute was opened on September 17, 1930, with a twelve-hour orgy of academic pomp, speech-making and banqueting. The spotlight shone most brightly on Banting, who would have the top floor of the Institute as his research kingdom. Asserting that if the ultimate happiness was to have nothing to do but full-time creative scientific work, one of the visiting dignitaries opined that Dr. Banting must therefore be the happiest man in the world. The keynote speaker, Lord Moynihan of Leeds, drew attention to how Banting wore his "crown of immortality" with "becoming humility."

The immortal Banting said nothing to the press or the public. The *Mail and Empire* commented that "the noted hater of public attention . . . shifted restlessly in his chair and smiled uncomfortably through thick-lensed glasses like a small boy caught stealing jam." This time the discomfort was more somatic than usual; shortly after the ceremonies Banting was admitted to Toronto General Hospital where D.E. Robertson, in a nine-minute operation, took out his appendix. Someone joked that Banting and the Institute were opened together.[28]

CHAPTER NINE

Banting *versus* Banting

B anting's studies of excrement were a by-product of his cancer research. He and his assistants began collecting infants' dirty diapers and painstakingly analyzing their contents as a consequence of his fanciful speculations about the cause of tumour growth. Some other work was starting to develop nicely, but in his department Banting's own research adventures seemed to reach a low point in absurdity just about the time his relations with Marion became more complicated. Soon Banting's problems with women would ignite one of the most surprising scandals that Torontonians had ever witnessed.

His first cancer hypothesis, formulated as the chicken work began in 1926, was that tumour growth was the result of some "combination of a male and female protein element in such a manner that the cells are stimulated to divide."[1] This fancy led him to a series of experiments trying to create a "spermotoxin" which would immunize female rabbits against male rabbit sperm. Switching to his newly established colony of cancerous chickens, he experimented with rooster sperm and ovary extracts. On the off-chance that there was some anti-cancerous active principle in that old adrenal cortical extract, it was tried a couple of times on the stricken chickens. It did not work.[2]

Banting then became interested in the action of enzymes – proteins serving as catalysts in certain chemical reactions in the body – as the clue to tumour growth. He speculated that some growth-stimulating enzyme was active in cancer cases. If the active principle of the tumour was an enzyme, then the problem was to find an anti-enzyme that would neutralize it.[3] Banting found himself studying the anti-enzyme properties of different animal serums through

184

observing their impact on the digestive enzyme trypsin.

A cousin's conversation auspicated his interest in diarrhoea when she visited the lab and got into a discussion with him on the art of chicken raising. The secret of her success was to keep baby chicks at a warm, constant temperature. Chilled chicks seemed to get diarrhoea and die. Banting began thinking that perhaps the cause of diarrhoea was the action in the bowel of serum exudates, whose anti-tryptic properties seemed to vary with temperature.[4] Perhaps they stopped the digestive enzymes from acting properly, leading to increased bacterial action and severe diarrhoea with its sometimes fatal consequences.

It happened that infant diarrhoea was a serious problem in Toronto in the summer of 1929. So Banting began to study babies' feces in the hope that his theory could be proven out and be practically useful in treating diarrhoea.

His own baby, Bill, contributed to his research by supplying the first dirty diaper to be analysed for its trypsin content (the stool was transferred to a glass plate, dried on the glass with a fan, and then kept in a desiccator until the examination was made). The soiled diapers of several dozen babies at the Hospital for Sick Children were then systematically analysed for their trypsin content (and, too, in search of the "antitrypsin" which Banting thought might exist as a separate substance in serum). When there seemed to be a correlation between the severity of the diarrhoea and the lack of trypsin in the stool, Banting was encouraged to believe that administration of trypsin would be a therapy for infant diarrhoea.

In September 1929 trypsin was given orally and by injection to two infants suffering from severe diarrhoea at the Hospital for Sick Children. Repeated treatments seemed to cause some improvement, but within ten days both babies had died. No more trypsin was given. The serum and excrement research supplied the only two scientific papers Banting published during the eight years between 1926 and 1934. They were entitled "The Antitryptic Properties of Blood Serum," and "A Study of the Enzymes of Stool in Intestinal Intoxication." Neither was of any consequence. Both in fact ended with admissions that later research seemed to have made the original hypothesis and early results untenable, as indeed it had. Sometimes there is a fine line between serious medical research and the stuff of bathroom jokes.

Or light fiction: One of the key figures in Robertson Davies' popular 1981 novel about Toronto university life, *Rebel Angels*, is Ozias Froats, a scientist attempting to find the secret of human individuality through studies of excrement. Froats, the "Turd-Skinner" as he is known, is something of a public scandal to the University, but is in fact a magus-figure whose researches leave him at the end of the story on the brink of receiving the Nobel Prize. Neither Davies nor Froats seems to have realized how extensively the University's only native-born Nobel laureate had earlier dabbled in "Filth Therapy."

In fact Banting had the capacity to outdo a satirist's imagination as he swung wildly from one "flyer" to another in his research interests. Another of his proposals was to investigate the chemical composition of royal jelly, in hope of finding the secret of its remarkable growth-inducing properties. Perhaps it could influence young mammals as well as young bees. Nothing came of the talk, except another embarrassing newspaper article, at this time.[6]

Banting sometimes realized how unlikely his work was to lead to more triumphs. One night in 1928 he told a friend how much it bothered him to be continually being asked if he had come up with something new. "I feel as if I ought to go back to the four corners and be a country doctor," he said, "at least until something else comes up. . . ." The opening of the Banting Institute added to his worries. Now that he worked in a splendid facility he felt more than ever the need to justify his position. He still wanted to do research, but would have preferred a little out-of-the-way lab where he could tinker and improvise, to the whole floor of the thoroughly modern medical building in the midst of Toronto that he commanded as head of the Department of Medical Research.[7]

The expansion of Banting's activities as a director of research gradually did lead to better, more soundly based work becoming associated with his name. The cronies who had come into his lab in early years, such as Beaumont Cornell, went on to other things (in Cornell's case two marriages, a good book on pernicious anemia, and the abandonment of the literary life for a high-income medical practice in Indiana). Or, as with Billy Ross, they carried on harmlessly at part-time research that never amounted to anything. From the beginning Sadie Gairns, a meticulous, well-organized researcher, had probably had a tempering influence, saving Banting from some of his enthusiasms and misjudgments. Her considerable administrative abilities also helped smooth his transition from a lone laboratory researcher to head of a full-fledged department. Gradually other researchers, many with training in chemistry or biochemistry, such as E.J. King, Colin Lucas and George Hunter, became attached to Banting's department and began turning out work of reasonable quality.

The new work from Banting's department tended to be technical and modest in scope. Papers with titles such as "Constitution of Hexosemonophosphoric Ester" (E.J. King and W.T.J. Morgan, 1929), or "The Use of Picric Acid as an Artificial Standard in Colorometric Estimation of Silica" (King and Lucas, 1928) were probably more substantial contributions to medical science than Banting's limp reports of grand attempts to grab another brass ring. Earl King, a brilliant biochemist, was the best and most active of the early associates, signing his name, for example, to fourteen of the fifteen papers published by Banting's whole group in the 1930-31 university year. By that time other young men had joined Banting who would do important work with him in the future. In 1928, G. Edward Hall, a graduate of the Ontario Agricultural College, came to work with Banting on an Ontario government scholarship. His first project was to study the relationship between heat and diarrhoea in young chicks. (There were many familiar reference points as the farm boys moved from the barnyards of their boyhood to the big city medical research laboratories.) A University of Toronto medical graduate, Wilbur R. "Bill" Franks, who had some ideas on cancer research, found Banting agreeable to letting him give them a try. In the early 1930s a young Queen's University professor, G. Harold Ettinger, began spending summers in the department; his first project was a study of the effects of electric shock, which was funded by the Hydro-Electric Power Commission of Ontario.

The best example of an investigation that developed from tinkering to concerted, careful research, and perhaps the most important research in Banting's department before the war, was work on silicosis. A lung disease caused by irritation arising from the inhalation of fine particles of silica contained in mineral dust, silicosis was an occupational hazard of several kinds of mining. Banting first became interested in it after a chance conversation with the University's Professor of Mining Engineering, H.E.T. Haultain, while they were installing the centrifuge for the cancer work. Silicosis was a baffling disease that might strike down one man after two years in the mines while leaving his partner still healthy-lunged twenty years later. Banting and Haultain thought about trying to invent a better mask to filter out silicates so they would never get into the lungs, but also got interested in following up some work Haultain had heard about on the solubility of silicates in the body. They decided to create silicosis in animals and test whether various chemical compounds could impede or cure the disease. To create the silicosis it was necessary to invent a special dust box, its air filled with particles from ground-up, specially chosen quartz crystals. Rabbits were exposed to the dust for several hundred hours, killed, and their lungs measured for silica. Treatments of acid and alkali compounds were given to some of the rabbits to see if they reduced the amounts of silica.

The results at first seemed favourable – they always seemed to be favourable at first in Banting's research – but then became irregular and positively contradictory. Banting realized that a large part of his problem lay in inadequate methods for measuring silica in tissues. He asked Earl King to find better measuring techniques. Many of King's early articles described the methods he developed and the findings they made possible about silica in the lungs and body. Other workers elaborated on the dust box experiments, the whole situation being further complicated by the fact that the dust boxes created a lot of silica in the rabbits' lung tissue, but no silicosis. Banting largely withdrew from the work after the early experiments, but encouraged ongoing assaults on the problem.[8]

Banting continued to spend long hours, days and nights in the lab. It could be a handy excuse to get out of all sorts of unpleasant or tedious situations, for Fred might have to go in at any time of the day or night to check an experiment or feed the chickens. The unhappy relationship with Marion did not improve. The birth of the marriage's only child, Bill, in April 1929, did not bring Fred and Marion closer together. At times it seemed to draw them further apart, sparking desperately bitter quarrelling. At home Fred became more and more reclusive, virtually living in his study. Sometimes he dined with Marion; other times, according to stories, she brought him up his meals. After July 1930 he slept upstairs in what became effectively his own apartment. He and Marion no longer had intercourse.[9]

He escaped in annual sketching trips with Jackson. They often went to Georgian Bay or the French River, north of Toronto, but in 1930 and 1931 Banting again went with Jackson on his spring excursions into the Quebec villages on the St. Lawrence below Quebec City. For Banting the trips were a return to the simple, rural life of his boyhood. They stayed in farmhouses or rustic hotels, ate pea soup and roast beef, wore farmers' clothes, and spent long days getting healthy again trooping around the Quebec countryside.

It has been snowing all day. This evening Alex and I went for a walk. It was dark for there are no street lights. The houses were outlined in the snow and light shone from the windows. One could not see the drifts of soft snow that have been piled up today and one minute we were walking on hard packed snow while the next we were wading thigh deep. It was blowing a real western blizzard, and it made me think of those days of long ago when it was necessary to leave the old farm house on such a winter's night. This house creaks with the wind like our old barn. They are not particular – the French – about such noises. This old bed with its straw mattress and home-spun quilts squeaks so loud at every move that it wakes me up.[10]

The French-Canadian villagers appeared to him much as the Arctic Eskimos had, as simple, happy practitioners of an old way of life which was being threatened by civilization.

The old coal-oil lamp is one of the softest and best lights that there is after all. . . . It would not be Saint Fidèle if things were changed and modernized. . . . Now that the road is through tourists will come and before long some carrier will drop a few bugs. Civilization is a danger and will demand changes by its spread even in places like St. Fidèle. . . .

I hate to leave this country. There are so many fine things about the people. Life is less complicated. They have simple faith, large families, little of this world's goods, and happyness. They work long hours and steadily but not too hard. They are never in a hurry. They pay very little taxes and no income tax and get much of their luxuries duty free. The sons that have gone to the States and come home in big cars and wealthy cause much unhappyness and envy.[11]

Jackson and Banting wanted to paint the old, unspoiled Quebec. They liked villages where people drove the old red cutters and still had colourful painted doors on the houses, or had painted the whole house red or pink or yellow. Tall, peaked houses and old barns were a good subject. The buildings and sleighs, of course, needed to be set in the right mixture of roads, hills and river. In 1931 after wandering around the village of St. Irenée, Banting noted in his diary that they had found "everything necessary for the French Canadian landscape – bake ovens, old houses, old horses, wood sleighs, (one) red cutter, barns, stables, outsheds, dugouts, wood piles, the river, hills, and winding roads."[12] Jackson always painted this landscape in the spring because he was fascinated by the texture of the melting snow and the effects of sunlight on it.

The trouble with spring painting in Quebec was that winter was never very far away. There were many days when it was snowing or too cold to work outside. Even on the relatively good days, Banting noted,

> There is plenty of hard work to painting. It is often very cold and I have even lit matches to warm my hands. The light may change halfway through a sketch and then it is a terrible job to finish it. When one stands up for a sketch one gets tired and when one sits the snow melts and finally wets the seat of one's trousers and it is mighty cold and uncomfortable. Then again if one sits on a stone, tailor fashion, one's leg goes to sleep. It is also cold on the hands, and sometimes one can hardly hold the brush. Alex is a terrible fellow to walk and I trail along behind. It is tiring and makes one's back ache at times. But!! after a day's sketching one eats, sleeps and feels satisfied – even if the sketches are poor.

And remember they were tough guys: "I'm one of these rough birds from the big open spaces," Jackson wrote a friend from St. Irenée, "and me and Fred Banting we just say 'hell' when the north wind blows."[13]

Banting was never very satisfied with his own sketches, often writing, as Jackson did, about "messing" or "dirtying" the birch boards they sketched on. In fact some Bantings would be impressive enough had they not been so much like Jacksons. Banting was a talented imitator of Jackson; he could capture light, colour, form, the texture of snow and wood with the same simple, bold, yet subtle appreciation of his subjects. The results were usually simple, colourful, well-composed and picturesque sketches. Banting imitated Jackson, leaning a bit more than the master did to tranquillity and satisfaction, but even Jackson was not quite as innovative or radical as he sometimes claimed. He said he disdained the "Christmas card" approach to painting Quebec, but was firmly in the tradition of artists trying to capture the simple life of old Quebec. Jackson's paintings were used on Christmas cards in the 1920s and 1930s. So were several of Banting's, appearing in Rous and Mann's Canadian Artists Series. He received $13.77 royalties for the use of his sketches, apparently the only money he ever made from painting. He would not sell sketches, keeping most of them for himself, giving some to friends and relatives. He no longer bought or collected anyone else's work.

On their sketching trips Banting deferred entirely to Jackson's judgments. He would note wryly that even the children could tell who the painter was, as they always chose to cluster around Jackson rather than Banting. Jackson enjoyed Banting's company, for Fred was always keen, had almost as much patience and endurance as he did, and liked the evening story-telling just as much. The two admired each other as creative people, understood each other's periodic need to be left alone, and never exchanged angry words.

Banting would take a sketch to Jackson and demand to know what was wrong with it. "He was learning to simplify and keep his colours fresh," Jackson remembered after Banting's death. "Apart from that he was not concerned with theory or the philosophy of art."* Banting lamented to his diary on the outcome of it all: "To sketch one must be able to draw, get tone, get colour, get relations, get design, and get simplification. That is all there is to it. It is strange that Alex and I can do the same scene and when the sketches are finished he has an improvement on the original while I have a poor imitation . . . I fear that I will never become an artist."[14]

He talked to Jackson many times about retiring and doing nothing but painting. The mood often came on him, when he needed a holiday, when he had just begun one, or when he was feeling the benefits of the sun and wind and good nights' sleep: "The more I think of the city the more I want to live in the country, and the more I think of being a professor of research the more I want to be an artist. . . ."[15]

Jackson thought that Banting's chief pleasure as an artist was not

---

*Banting was once asked by an aspiring artist for his opinion of some designs. He replied that he liked those designs built on "Canadian motives [sic]. I would suggest that you develop your work along the lines of Ontario life, or beaver or wheatfields, buffalo, lumbering, or, in other words, portray Canadian background. Snakes and Venus and chariots are things of the old world and are not so creative or original as would be the life in Canada of today or the historical pageant of the past." (FGB to Percy Garrett, Aug. 24, 1931).

in what anyone felt about his sketches, but in the sheer enjoyment of making them, "in mixing up a lot of colours in a sketch box and all the adventures that led up to it, the freedom from responsibility, scrambling over unknown country, getting burned by the March sun, smoking a pipe before the camp-fire or the welcome at a little hotel and the good meals and looking over the day's work." On a brilliantly sunny March day Fred and Alex would walk five miles, sketch a little, walk and sketch some more. At mid-day Alex would take out his little saw and cut some dead branches; they'd build a fire on the snow and warm themselves. "We toasted our sandwiches," Fred wrote, "had lunch and would not have traded places with members of parliament."[16]

By the 1930s Banting was one of Canada's best-known amateur painters, even mentioned briefly in published surveys of the art scene. In his best work, where he varies light and colour and breaks away from Christmas-card sketching, it is clear that Banting has considerable talent; perhaps he could have developed beyond Jackson's influence and come into his own as a painter. He was not exactly an eighth member of the Group of Seven (which had at least ten professional members during its life), but seemed increasingly close to the artists in temperament. On his fortieth birthday, in November 1931, he wrote out a few thoughts about his love of life – "only for the brief space of half an hour have I during the past forty years considered suicide" – and then added a comment which captures the essence of his and his friends' Canadianism: "But even more precious than life is my native Canada. She is a funny country to love with her frozen north, her rocky barren tracts, her mountains and her lakes. She is always toddling along behind the neighbour to the south. Her people are to me the best in the world but I would love Canada if there were no people – sometimes I feel that I would prefer it."[17]

His artist friends, his own instincts, and possibly his training as a scientist, combined to begin to make Banting less conventional in other ways than painting. Brought up as a devout Methodist, he gradually drifted away from Christian observance. Many of the members of the Group and the Toronto cultural community – including friends like Beaumont Cornell – had left the orthodox churches, some to become pantheists, many of them to find a satisfactory way-station in the flexible combination of theism, spiritualism and mysticism that called itself theosophy.* Banting did not go this far, apparently becoming a commonsense agnostic, possibly a pantheist. "Nature is God and God is Nature," he wrote in one of his 1930 meditations. He never set out his views systematically, but left a number of samples. The death of his mother-in-law in 1930, for example, sparked some late-night philosophizing about life after death: "Is there a spirit and a future life? The Maker must have a terrible time amusing the souls of those billions that he has made and taken unto himself. He does not do it with other life that he has made. I think we just stop."[18]

With nothing after death to look forward to, it seemed important to get the most out of life. By 1930 or so Banting had rebelled against much of the puritanism of his upbringing in matters of personal morality. Again reflecting the influence of the radical bohemianism of friends like Cornell, there might already have been smidgeons of left-wing politics. But mostly Banting had decided to embark on a quasi-bohemian commitment to drink deep draughts from the cup of life. Away with the artificialities and restraints of conventional civilized life:

One has to exceed the limit to know where the limit is.
One has to sin to know what sin is.
By living we know life.
By fighting we know strife.
By striving we know gain.
By losing we know shame.
By dying we know death, the last knowledge of all.[19]†

If nothing else, Banting's moral code functioned as a rationale for

*As some scholars have known, but laymen do not understand, Canada's prime minister, Mackenzie King, was far from unique in his covert spiritualist beliefs in the 1920s and 1930s. He was unusual mostly in writing everything down in such detail, and then having had his diaries ransacked by unsympathetic historians. Actually King was close to the mainstream of his generation's rebellion against religious orthodoxy.
†In a meditation written sometime in the 1930s Banting described his rebellion and his sins this way: "I once had a high school teacher who told his class repeatedly that we should do anything for a new experience – and many of us followed his instruction – I think that it is a good rule. I have done many things of which I am not proud. But they have given me that thing of incalculable value – experience. I have robbed, I have stolen, I have borne false witness, I have spent a night in the police station, I have committed adultery, I have coveted, I have been drunk, I have broken the sabbath. I have never committed murder nor rape, but apart from these two I think I have done every thing that is forbidden in religious teaching.
But religion as we have it is a man made ritual, a selfish, self-seeking expostulation of

his adultery. He had told Marion that the only way they could continue to live together would be if she let him lead his life exactly as he wanted to without accounting to her. She could do the same.[20] About 1930 or 1931, perhaps earlier, Fred began spending a lot of his time with a woman writer in Toronto, Miss Blodwen Davies.

Blodwen was a struggling freelancer, determined to prove to her parents that she could make her own way in life, who specialized in turning out light travel literature about the charming, storied, romantic cities and regions of Canada. Born in Quebec in 1897, Blodwen had come to Toronto in the 1920s and was drawn by their avant-garde aura into the Seven's social circle. She was not particularly attractive physically, being prematurely white-haired and either willowy or droopy depending on who described her. But she was intoxicated by art and ideas and idealism, a kind of original groupie to the Seven, the starry-eyed, innocent, vulnerable adorer. She may also have had the slim ankles that Fred once said were the feature he admired most in a woman.

Blodwen is said to have met Banting while researching a biography of Tom Thomson; she asked for his advice on the medical evidence surrounding Thomson's mysterious drowning. Another version of their meeting has Fred telling A.Y. Jackson of his unhappiness in love and at the lab and his intense desire to be a writer, and constantly pestering Jackson for advice. The taciturn Jackson, who liked to keep his distance from his friends' personal problems, referred Fred to Blodwen, a professional writer. They were bound to meet anyway in the small Toronto cultural circle centring on the Arts and Letters Club and its members' activities.

Blodwen gave Fred advice, or vice versa. One thing led to another. Marion later told her father about the close friendship between Fred and the writer: Fred visiting Blodwen in her apartment, no doubt to discuss writing; Blodwen being invited to dinner at the Bantings and then going up to Fred's "apartment" with him for the rest of the evening, no doubt to discuss writing; the "manifestations of affection" they often displayed in Marion's presence. Marion made the best of a bad situation – Fred had at least freed her to see other men too – and was on civil, perhaps friendly, terms with Blodwen.

---

introverted egotists – god's anointed, whose pose in puffed miniatures as saints & examples. Of all the curses which the Middle ages of darkness left to us as a heritage – it is religious custom – baptism marriage and burial, churches and religious dogma."

Blodwen later told Fred about the time, early in their relationship, when she awoke one morning "knowing that you meant to me all that all men could mean to me. . . . That night you came to see me and expressed the most beautiful thought that was ever put into words to me." She wrote a poem about Fred, which she entitled "Music where there was no music before." It was Whitmanesque and not too badly done:

When you stand straight and tall
Talking gently,
Your long fingers stressing what you say,
And speak of dreams and works, and lives saved by the
    unaccountable scores
And show me the narrow path by which you rose out of
    the darkness of your unhappy loves
Why then in spirit I am crouching at your feet in worship
Because you are my god

. . .

When in the dusk you lean and seek my lips
Hungry for yours,
When your strong arms enwrap me and press me
Throbbing to your breast
And all is lost, forgotten, in the white flame that wraps
    us round
Ah! then you are my lover

When softly by I come and take you in my arms,
Draw your dear head upon my shoulder
Play in your soft, pale hair with yearning fingers,
Until you close your eyes and rest unmoving there.
When soft I lay my lips against that broad, white brow
As though a sleeping child lay on my breast,
Know you not, then, you are my son?

In the other three stanzas Fred was her husband, her father, her friend – all that all men could be to her.[21]

One night in October 1931, Marion Banting went directly from a Girl Guide meeting to join Fred at a party at Blodwen's. Marion was introduced there to Donat M. LeBourdais, a writer friend of Blodwen's who worked as education director for the Canadian National

195

Committee on Mental Hygiene. LeBourdais already knew Fred from the Arts and Letters Club, where they had often dined at the same table. He met Marion again a month or so later at a Hart House concert, and another day had tea with her, Blodwen and A.Y. Jackson at Blodwen's apartment. In December LeBourdais escorted Marion to another Hart House concert, and then on New Year's Eve was invited to 46 Bedford for dinner with the Bantings and several others. After dinner Fred and Blodwen and Marion and "D.M." went to the Arts and Letters Club's New Year's Eve dance, and then on a round of visits lasting until seven in the morning. "It was sort of tacitly understood that Mrs. Banting was my partner and Miss Davies was the doctor's partner," LeBourdais said later. On New Year's Day Marion phoned to ask him to come to tea with Fred and Blodwen.

That day or the next, Fred and Marion had another of their quarrels. Fred recorded it in doggerel, dated January 2:

See here
My dear,
This will not do
You can't have me
I can't have you

I drink
You shrink
You think me bea[s]t
and call me low
Because I feast.[22]

Throughout January, Marion and D.M. saw each other fairly often. Marion would invite him over in the evening. Fred would come in, sometimes have tea with them, sometimes go to bed early. Marion often dropped in on D.M. in his nearby Yorkville Avenue apartment and they would talk about concerts, books, politics, or she would read chapters of the manuscript of the biography of Vilhjalmur Stefansson that LeBourdais was writing. He loaned her his copy of Bernard Shaw's *The Intelligent Woman's Guide to Socialism*.

D.M. was giving weekly broadcasts about mental health for a local radio station, CFRB. On Monday, February 8, 1932, Marion phoned and asked him if she could come over and read the script of his Saturday broadcast, which she had missed. She went to his rooms between six and seven o'clock in the early evening.

They had not been together very long before there was a loud knocking on the door to LeBourdais's apartment, then the smash of glass as someone broke the panel in the door. A hand reached in and opened the door from the inside. In rushed Fred Banting and two strange men – private detectives he had hired. Seeing LeBourdais in front of him, Banting grabbed him by the throat and pushed him over the back of his couch.

"Doctor, you can't take a dead man into Court," one of the detectives said.

As LeBourdais remembered the night, the dialogue went like this:

Fred: "Where is Marion?"

D.M.: "There she is." She was behind him.

Fred: "I am going to divorce you."

Marion: "Fred, you didn't need to do this. You don't have to do this; why didn't you come to me and talk this thing over?"

Fred: "Yah, yah, yah, yah, yah."

Marion asked D.M. and the detectives to leave them alone for a while. About ten minutes later Fred came into D.M.'s bedroom demanding that he sign a statement. LeBourdais refused, saying he was not going to help Fred drag Marion's name through the mud. "He said to me," LeBourdais testified, "that he was going to broadcast me from the housetops, that I would lose my job, he would get me fired, and he would tell the world. He was a bit incoherent."

Later that evening Marion went to see Sir William Mulock, Chief Justice of Ontario as well as Chancellor of the University. Fred spent the night with Angus MacKay. The next day he picked up his clothes at 46 Bedford and also saw Mulock. On Wednesday the 10th, alert readers of the *Star* who noticed a small item in the "Legal" column of the classified ads were stunned to realize that something had gone seriously wrong with the Banting marriage:

I, F.G. Banting, M.D., formerly of 46 Bedford
Road, Toronto, will not be responsible for any
debts contracted in my name after this date
without my written order.

Toronto phone lines must have been humming. *Have you seen the Star?* Half a century later people who could not remember any details of the aftermath told me how horrifying it was when Fred Banting publicly refused to pay his wife's debts.

The University's most prominent psychologist, Dr. William Blatz, acted as go-between. He knew Fred from the University and D.M. from the Committee on Mental Hygiene. Fred was absolutely determined to divorce Marion, "to blow the whole thing wide open," Blatz said later. Would Marion and LeBourdais defend themselves in a divorce action? Blatz talked to her about how messy a public fight would be, how much damage it would do because of Fred's position at the University and in the profession. It was an unhappy marriage anyway, probably better off ended. Perhaps if Marion would agree not to defend, Blatz could persuade Fred to be more reasonable about custody of Bill, as well as provide some financial support. Everything had to be said with the utmost care in these meetings, where lawyers were often present, for any evidence of collusion in obtaining the divorce could upset all the arrangements and make the mess worse. Nor were there as yet many precedents for handling these matters in Ontario, because divorce actions had only been transferred from federal jurisdiction to the Supreme Court of Ontario in 1931.

Marion decided not to defend against Fred's suit. Fred and his lawyers did not question Blatz's suggestion that a payment to her of $250 a month, possession of the house, and custody of Bill would be a reasonable settlement with Marion. They assured Blatz, who assured Marion and D.M., that if the divorce was not contested the whole proceeding would be carried out in camera. There would be no unpleasant newspaper publicity. Sir William Mulock would make sure of that. LeBourdais decided to go along with the arrangement because Marion wanted him to, because he was assured there would be no publicity, and because he thought it would be the best way to protect Marion's name and reputation.

So no defendants appeared to question the evidence presented in Assize Court on April 25 by the two detectives, H.A. Sherman and L. Eckley, of H.A. Sherman Ltd., Secret Service. They told of several earlier meetings between Marion and D.M. that they had observed, and of how on February 8 they had seen her enter his apartment, had waited until the lights went out, and then phoned Dr. Banting. When they broke into the apartment, according to the detectives, they flashed a light around. They saw Mrs. Banting and Mr. LeBourdais reclining on a chesterfield. "Mrs. Banting's dress was above her knees, and Mr. LeBourdais's coat and vest were open, and his trousers were partially so," Sherman testified. "Mr. LeBourdais's trousers were undone, and he was fastening the button, the top of the fly," Eckley added. "He seemed to endeavor to button his fly."

Banting was not required to testify. In his sworn affidavit he said that he had previously objected to Marion seeing so much of Le-Bourdais, that she had deceived him in making her visits to his apartment, and that she admitted to him after February 8 that she had had "a love affair" with LeBourdais. Fred had asked for custody of Bill, but now he told the judge that Marion could have custody if she would give Bill a good home. The judge awarded Fred custody anyway, saying he need not enforce it. A decree nisi was granted, meaning that the divorce would become absolute in six months unless formal objections were filed. The arrangements for an un-contested settlement of the matter in Banting *versus* Banting seemed to have worked.

They began coming unstuck that afternoon. The Toronto *Telegram* published a short but front-page account of the proceedings, naming LeBourdais and mentioning the fact of the raid. Chief Justice Mulock's assurances that there would be no publicity had not been borne out, apparently because he had not understood the limits of judicial prerogative under the new divorce law. A few days later, when Blatz met with Fred to discuss the financial settlement, Banting objected to the $250 figure and said he would only pay $125 monthly plus $50 when Bill was with Marion. Bill could stay with Marion during the school year and then with Fred in the summer. Marion could have the house and car. Blatz went with Fred and Marion and acted as mediator the day they divided the furniture.

Marion's father, Dr. William Robertson of Elora, had urged her from the beginning to contest the action. Now that it was all public knowledge, she and LeBourdais must have realized that the admission of guilt in their refusal to defend meant a permanent blackening of their reputations. During the summer of 1932 they reconsidered their situation. At the same time, Dr. Robertson "caused inquiries to be made," as he put it, into Fred's relations with Blodwen and the events leading up to February 8. The inquiries were probably made by private detectives. Fred was not being particularly discreet in his relations with Blodwen at this time. When a close associate finally urged him to be more careful for the sake of the department, he allowed that he might meet her in the park instead of her apartment.

That October, one week before the divorce was to become absolute, D.M. LeBourdais and William Robertson filed motions of intervention. Both men charged that the divorce was being obtained by collusion. LeBourdais now wanted to defend himself, flatly denying the detectives' testimony.

The breakdown in the delicate divorce arrangement was bad enough. It was made much, much worse by the decision of the Toronto *Star* to publish all the details of the interventions and the ensuing proceedings. And to publish it all as front-page news. Publicity of any kind, such as the *Telegram*'s April story, was bad enough. This publicity, the revealing of all the intimate details of the Banting mess to the readers of the largest circulation newspaper in Toronto, was dreadful. It was scandal – seamy, sexy scandal – stuff that only appeared in Canadian newspapers as the sordid adventures of Hollywood stars and Chicago heiresses. It was not supposed to happen in good grey Canada. But now it was happening to the most famous Canadian, the ornament of the country's leading university, the humble benefactor of mankind. So an angry Fred had threatened to broadcast Marion's sins from the housetops. Well, the newspapers were doing it with a vengeance, dragging her name, his name, everyone else's name, through the mud of public scandal, literally shouting the names from the streetcorners.

Toronto newspapers had been protective enough of the private lives of the prominent and powerful over the years to make the *Star*'s coverage of the Banting divorce seem unusually attentive. Well, it was an unusual situation, partly because the divorce legislation was so recent, and partly because no one at the *Star*, or any other Toronto newspaper, had any particular regard for Dr. Banting. He had been offensively rude to the press for years; he had been particularly offensive to Roy Greenaway, a star *Star* reporter, five years earlier in the Hudson's Bay Company affair. Why go to bat for Banting? Let him look out for himself, and if he didn't want the heat he should have stayed out of the courtroom. In any case, the *Telegram* had started it all with the report of the original trial. If the *Star* did not publish, the *Telegram* probably would anyway. Better to do a good, thorough job of Banting coverage than none at all.

Sir William Mulock is said to have tried to stop the press. A writer friend of Banting's who was then with the *Star* told me of being present when Mulock, very much against the writer's advice, insisted that Joe Atkinson, the *Star*'s publisher, keep the divorce out of the paper. Atkinson was a fellow Liberal who had benefitted from Mulock's past patronage. He flatly turned Mulock down. Leaving the *Star* building, the furious nonagenarian Chief Justice was extremely rough on his drowsy chauffeur, poking him very sharply with his cane.

The newspaper stories meant luscious suspense for gossip-hungry Torontonians, daily dread for the participants, especially Fred. What will they publish next? How much will they find out? How bad is it going to be?

Pretty bad. LeBourdais claimed that the detectives had lied about what they had seen in his apartment. The lights had not been out. Marion had not taken off her coat or hat. She had sat at his desk reading a manuscript, and was just standing up to leave when the commotion began.[23] There had never at any time been improper relations between Marion Banting and D.M. LeBourdais. He had refused to sign Fred's statement of February 8 because Fred had no evidence. In a second affidavit later in October, LeBourdais named Bill Blatz as the go-between, thereby bringing him into the public muck. A month later, on November 28, it all hit Banting's fan with a vengeance when Marion's father's affidavit was read in court.

It detailed the breakdown in the marriage, charged that Dr. Banting had "cruelly and frequently assaulted" his wife, described the friendship between Fred and Blodwen as Marion had seen it, denied all improprieties between Marion and LeBourdais, and detailed Blatz's collusive persuadings. "Not only is my daughter not guilty of the charges made against her, but I am further convinced that the plaintiff Banting is guilty of improper relationships with the woman writer, and that these [divorce] proceedings were taken in an effort to get rid of my daughter in order that he might marry the writer."

The *Star* printed every word. Its competitor printed less, but did it in larger type. DR. BANTING CRUEL TO WIFE, FATHER CLAIMS, was the headline on the colourful front page of the evening edition, known as "The Pink Tely." The affidavit was a little vague on details, so there may have been countless dinner conversations about whether or not Dr. Banting had stopped beating his wife.

Perhaps in hope of finding out, the *Star* sent one reporter after another to try to interview Banting. The cheekiest young reporter, Gordon Sinclair, finally caught up with Banting twice. The first time a crowd of football players interrupted practice on the back campus to listen to Banting berate Sinclair about the *Star*'s lack of conscience or decency. The second time Banting was painting a house. The ladder he was standing on wavered in his anger as he yelled at Sinclair to get the hell away. Sinclair prudently stayed out of paint range.[24]

Lacking more details and having to worry about libel, the daily newspapers were limited to factual court reporting. But Canada's leading scandal tabloid, *Hush*, virtually an underground newspaper in those days, did have a little fun in its December 10 story:

> While the artistic world had been aware of the close friendship existing between Dr. Banting and Miss Blodwen Davies for many months, it assumed the association to be one actuated by kindred intellectual tastes and not merely a sordid, sex attraction, such as is now alleged by Dr. Banting's father-in-law. The world will never believe this charge against the great humanitarian.

> Both Dr. Banting and Miss Davies were considered to have similar mental "auras", far above the heights attainable by the rabble. If they sought the privacy of each other's company in the attic of the Banting home, the accepted belief was that it was to discuss some new abstruse theory propounded by their friend, Dr. Blatz, revel in the delights of psyco-analysis or the effects of the Freudian or Neitche doctrines on the nudist colonies of Europe.

> Instead, it would appear from Dr. Robertson's deposition that they were drawn together for the purpose of satisfying the passions inherent in man and woman.

There were few more publicly moral cities anywhere in the 1930s than the town known as Toronto the Good. Divorce was anything but commonplace. Even divorced men whose wives had been the guilty party were divorced men, tainted men. *He's divorced, don't you know?* Divorced men who had been guilty themselves were something like pariahs in polite society. Never know whose wife or daughter they'd be trying to seduce next. They would not be welcome on the staff of institutions charged with being *in loco parentis* to the young and impressionable, such as the University of Toronto. Could even Banting have retained his position had he been the guilty party in a divorce? As it was, there were faculty members who thought that Dr. Robertson's revelations would be enough to do him in. "Now he'll have to go." To Banting it was a time of "dire trouble" at the University; one of his old enemies who came to his defence was Duncan Graham. His old friends from the Philathea Bible Class who read about it in the papers found it all so sad and confusing. They couldn't believe it. Fred didn't deserve this. "He didn't belong in the gutter with those people. He was on a pinnacle. He was too good for those people."[25]

The couple's friends chose sides, giving a slant to events and personalities that was still obvious during conversations half a century later. Marion's partisans remembered that Fred was a cruel, heartless bastard in the way he treated her. Even if she did have an affair with LeBourdais, she was certainly more sinned against than sinning. Fred had the Establishment, the University of Toronto, and especially Sir William Mulock on his side. Marion had nobody but her father, and the most innocent of the principals, D.M. LeBourdais. Fred's friends remembered Marion as a flirt and tease, who ought to have learned how to amuse herself domestically when Fred had to spend his long hours in the lab. If it hadn't been LeBourdais, Fred had told them, as he also told LeBourdais, it might have been any one of half a dozen others. "I chose you because you weren't married," Banting told LeBourdais.

LeBourdais was in fact married, though his wife was living in California. She intervened in the proceedings too, trying to protect her husband's good name. He was a bit hampered in his ability to defend himself, however, by the fact that he had been having an affair with someone else during part of the time he would have to testify about. Opinion at the Arts and Letters Club on the matter of Banting *versus* Banting and LeBourdais was split down the middle, with D.M. having enough support to make Fred feel not quite comfortable there. For several years after 1932 he seldom went into the club. Jackson, who did not often talk about his friends' affairs, was heard to say only that Fred should never have married Marion. "You know he's awfully dour."[26]

The judge ruled that the interventions and charges of collusion did not justify a new trial. He saw no reason to set aside sworn testimony about Marion's relations with LeBourdais in favour of a story she had later told her father. As for Blatz's role, the judge said during the hearing, "Any other reputable man would have done all he could to avoid a scandal." There was not any adequate evidence in law of collusion. If there had been, the judge mentioned, precedent might have caused the Crown, in the form of the Attorney General, to intervene. On December 2, 1932, the divorce was made absolute.

On December 5, lawyers for Marion or her father or LeBourdais filed notice of appeal. But there was never an appeal hearing. In March 1933 the court was informed that a settlement had been reached. It is not clear what had happened. Certainly Marion and her father must have had second thoughts. Perhaps lawyers advised that the legal case in appeal was not very strong. Then there is the persistent story, told by Marion's friends, that the Chief Justice of Ontario, Sir William Mulock, had determined to use all his influence to make sure that the divorce was not upset. How he might have applied pressure is not clear – though one wishes it were, for his role in the affair is almost stranger than fiction. Had a new trial been held, there is a strong likelihood that his name would have been brought in, and tossed into the muck, as having provided the initial assurance that it could all be kept quiet. It is not clear, either, how Fred was responding to the situation, except that he threatened from time to time to deepen the scandal with further charges of serious adultery (a prospect that Fred's friends, whom he had sometimes encouraged to be Marion's escort, found distinctly alarming. "My God, I've sat with her in the front row of the Royal Alex").

Whether Fred would have been able to sustain a more elaborate case against Marion will never be known. He thought he could. The marriage had been so bad for so long, and Marion was such a social creature, that she probably had drifted into one or more affairs, just as Fred had. In a deposition which never had to be used in court, Blatz swore that he had asked her if she could defend her behaviour against any possible action Fred brought against her. She said she could not.

On the other hand, both Marion and LeBourdais maintained complete innocence in their private conversations with Blatz. It seems that Marion was drifting towards an affair with D.M. LeBourdais in the early months of 1932, but nothing compromising had actually developed by the time of the raid.[27] Fred's detectives cheerfully stretched the truth for their fee: LeBourdais noted later a case in which a judge called one of them notoriously untruthful. Fred's outrage at Marion may have been trumped up, or it may have been fuelled by his belief that she had been sleeping around for several years.

Marion and her father were probably right in believing that Fred and Blodwen had hoped to get something going between Marion and D.M. They may have planned the whole thing, as Marion's father charged, with Fred promising Blodwen he would marry her after the divorce. Or Fred's anger may have been an unforeseen reaction to Marion's behaviour. Trying so hard to be liberal, to be a proper bohemian, he encouraged Marion to have a male friend the way he had a lady friend. But when he began to believe, probably wrongly, that he had encouraged her right into an affair, he turned out to be just another conservative man with a double standard. Fred was a much-maligned husband seeking comfort and consolation with Blodwen. Marion was a loose and treacherous woman climbing into LeBourdais's bed.

In retrospect the Banting divorce takes on an aura of the ridiculous: a play on Canada's absurd divorce laws and the voluble virtue of the Toronto bourgeoisie. For Fred and Marion and the child, Bill, the absurdities only caused more pain. Fred, in particular, was deeply conscious of his public humiliation. His moral radicalism was only a veneer. He deeply wanted to be an upstanding, respected family man as his father had been. Now he was branded, possibly as a scarlet adulterer, certainly as a pink wife-beater. He worried deeply about how his mother would react on learning of the scandal. As good and wise mothers will, she took it in stride: "Well, dear, if living with Marion has made you so unhappy, perhaps it's best that you separate."

That was the calm view of old age. To the younger people involved in the Banting divorce, Fred and Marion and LeBourdais and all their friends, Banting *versus* Banting was one of the unhappiest, messiest situations they would be involved with in their lifetimes.

CHAPTER TEN

Banting *versus* Capitalism

After the divorce was granted, in December 1932, Fred took a short sketching holiday along the Massachusetts coast to lick his wounds. In the midst of the Great Depression of the 1930s he was deeply depressed personally, emotionally drained and more than normally misanthropic. Noticing that Champlain had passed through Massachusetts in 1606, he decided that his fellow man had scarcely improved since then. "The Indian was a good, wise fellow. This depression which we hear so much about may yet bring us back to common sense and simple life. One hates to think of the drastic methods used in Russia, but they have much sense and drastic methods may have been necessary. Why can we not get some common sense without the unlovely side? I think the first step should be to muzzle newspapers, and control them. Democracy as practiced in Canada & the U.S. is a farce."

He gloried in being alone to think over his past and present and what he could do with the rest of his life. There was a lot of reliving the past implied in this meditation on modern life and conventions:

> One must do what everyone else does or be dubbed eccentric, idiotic, insane, countryfied. One can be the most deceptful liar and yet by a close and careful adherance to social conventions and polished manners occupy the highest place in society. The Lieut. Gov. of the Province of Ontario at the present moment [Dr. Herbert Bruce] is a fine example. . . . My X wife is another example. She is essentially untrue & deceptful yet clever, polished and in the social sense a perfect lady.
>
> There would be some excuse for the existence of such people if they contributed to the general good and general happyness of people but they do not.

One may not agree with conventions from a rhetorical view-point but from a practical point one cannot disregard them. For example one may believe in free love & yet find the law does not permit its practice. . . . We are thus enslaved by convention & tradition. How is one to be honest? Tolerant yes. But honesty is incompatable with modern social life.

Banting spent some time in Boston, taking in the art gallery and then visiting the Deaconess Hospital where Elliott Joslin based his large practice treating diabetics. He found Joslin's new associate, Dr. Priscilla White, interesting to talk to – "young (about 28-30), quite pretty with a good face, very quiet, fine figure, and Dr. Joslyn uses her as a ready reference for everything. . . . . She reminds me of Sadie" – and he admired Joslin's single-minded devotion to his work. Banting had been doing a lot of thinking about his own career: "I think even yet – over forty as I am – that I may discover something – Could I but do something worth while then I feel that I could be myself again. I have lost eight years of my life."

He found two antidotes to adversity and depression. One was to spend more time with his male friends – Fred Hipwell, Scotty MacKay, Gordon Cameron, and one or two others – than he had for years. "Talking with friends is like letting the pus out of a wound." He also threw himself back into the work of his lab. He was determined to solve the cancer problem, and he became the active leader in a broad, complex attack on silicosis. He was inspired, in part, by a talk he heard his friend Lawren Harris give in Toronto about art and creativity: "There is nothing he said about art that he could not have said concerning research. It resolves itself into this: – that we poor mortals must *work* on to the best of our ability – in the hope that we will be selected by the power from without to fulfil some of the creative arts – be they in the field of art, music, research or literature – Keep oneself prepared and receptive for ideas."[1]

Marion kept the name Banting, lived at 46 Bedford Road for a time, then sold that house and moved to Oakville, a few miles outside of Toronto. Although Fred is said to have continued to support her, she went back to work, becoming the head of the Shoppers' Service at Simpson's department store, an ideal job for a sophisticated, feminine woman who knew the kinds of things that men and women of good taste liked to have around them. Young Bill was enrolled in Bill Blatz's special experimental school at what became the University's Institute for Child Study. He spent weekends with his father.

Blodwen Davies had worshipped Fred. Thinking back to the beginning of their affair, she wrote, "I remember saying to myself if he ever failed me, I would have no faith in God himself."

Fred failed her. He did not marry her, and he broke her heart.

He apparently did not see much of her in the winter of 1932-33, and in the spring when they did meet he was abrupt and cold. "You came, that last night I saw you, literally with your watch in your hand. . . . I had the most complete confidence in you and to lose it was the bitterest thing I've known. I'm afraid I'm proud but I won't take second best from any man. I'd rather go on alone for the rest of my life."[2] In emotional turmoil near the end of April, she rushed away from Toronto. Fred kept the pained letters she wrote to him, first from Buffalo, then New York.

Exactly why he had cooled to Blodwen is not known. Certainly the divorce publicity had made things difficult, practically impossible. If Fred married Blodwen now, wouldn't it suggest to the whole world that Marion and her father had been right all along?

Apart from that problem, and also apart from Blodwen's physical and personal limitations, Banting was developing an interesting dalliance with the good-looking Boston diabetologist, Priscilla White. They met for the second time at a conference in Montreal in February 1933, where they skipped one of Israel Rabinowitch's papers to go sleigh-riding. They corresponded that spring, comparing interests and ideas and patients (she was treating Teddy Ryder), and may have met again at another conference. To Priscilla White, who had dedicated her life to looking after juvenile diabetics, Fred Banting was the man who had done the greatest thing imaginable – given her diabetic children the means to stay alive. She idolized Banting, fell in love with him, and even overlooked his curious disinterest in diabetes and diabetics. Theirs was a platonic relationship, though, not least because Dr. White met with shocked disapproval from her boss, Dr. Joslin, who did not believe she should allow herself to be seen as a companion of the immoral, divorced Banting. After several meetings over the course of a year or two, Banting and Priscilla White drifted apart.[3]

When Blodwen fled Toronto to try to pull herself together, Fred did not have the sense to let it end. He wrote and explained himself. His letter has not survived. Her reply has: ". . . you've broken me all up again with your letter. If there were things bothering you all winter, why couldn't you confide in me? Couldn't you trust me to understand, no matter what it was? I've felt so long I was shut out. I felt you resented the fact that you wanted me and wished you could get along without me. I was so unhappy month after month. . . ."

She thought they had patched things up – "life is worth living again" – but when she got back to Toronto it all fell apart again. The love affair ended with two long letters from Blodwen to Fred, bathetic and eloquent in about equal measure:

Monday, July 10, 1933.

I have waited for you tonight and you have not come. You have strange ideas about how to hold a woman's love. No intelligent woman would accept what you have offered in return for what you expect. Tonight I realized that nothing I have had from you since I returned home compensates for the distress I am suffering in this unequal and unhappy partnership. . . . I tried to give you all the sympathy & tenderness I could when you were unhappy. Now I am in trouble, the worst trouble I have ever known, & you have neither pity nor tenderness, even though I have begged for your help to get me over this difficult time. I know now I never want to see you again. My heart is broken because you are so different to the man I idealized and depended upon for affection, for those things that would have made life tolerable and even happy. If I am to carry out the thing I should do in the next six weeks it must be without any recurrence of the distress I feel tonight. I hope some day to be able to forget these times & remember only what I want to remember. Please don't try to see me. There is nothing more to say but what will cause more pain to each of us. . . . Goodbye. I hope some day to be able to think about happier things. I don't know why I should be punished so for the best impulses of my life. Perhaps some day I shall know.

Saturday, July 15, 1933.

You know and I know that the incident of Monday was not of itself important. . . . but as a physician and as a man you know something of what I've been up against and in your heart you know you could have eased the strain all these months past instead of increasing it. You have withheld the kindness that would have made me happy and then hated me because I could not smile as though I was enjoying life. If I could have smiled I could have defended myself. I met your conditions or tried to. In fairness you might have made some concessions instead of coming to me reserved and arrogant. . . .

I cannot bear to stand by and see you going through this phase. I know, better than anyone else, the humanity, the awareness, the intelligence, the latent power there is in you. I dreamed of you being very great, not only in reputation, but in power tempered with wisdom, in will tempered with gentleness, in a rich humanity that would make you beloved of everyone you come in contact with. You can fight your way to place, but not to power: Insulin should be but an incident in your life, the stepping stone to an influence such as no Canadian has ever yet exercised over the hearts and minds of this country. But you are stopping the channels of your intelligence with your grudges and rancour. You are fumbling in the dark when you could be walking in the sun with your heart and mind open. There is my sharpest pain, Fred, to feel you are being less than you could be.[4]*

Blodwen stayed on the periphery of Fred's life, seeing and writing to him now and then as she revised her book on Tom Thomson ("The Story of a Man Who Looked for Beauty and for Truth in the Wilderness"), and delved further into the intricacies of theosophy. She and Fred had often talked about divine mysteries and she had probably been instrumental in his attending the odd meeting of the Toronto Theosophical Society – where he would have met Lawren Harris and many of his other Arts and Letters Club friends.[5] Over the years she tried several times to explain to him what must have happened that night of October 31, 1920. The idea for insulin had come to him as a kind of revelation, a flash of insight into the fundamental principles of the universe. It was the scientist, like the artist, having a special vision not given to ordinary men, a moment of what the great Canadian theosophist, Maurice Bucke, had labelled

*Do these letters hint at a pregnancy that was going to be terminated? They can be read that way, and there is reinforcement in the fact that Fred lent or gave Blodwen $300 about this time. But the letters can also be read several other ways. Blodwen may have had a physical ailment, been under special stress in her writing career, or been enduring the illness of a close relative. As well, Fred does not seem to have believed in abortion. An impecunious young couple, friends of his, once went to him to ask his advice about whether to use the services of an abortionist they had found. He congratulated them on the good news that a child was coming, poured a round of drinks, and talked them out of the abortion. In fact Banting so badly wanted more children of his own that the one way Blodwen might have fulfilled her heart's desire would have been to get pregnant and be made an honest woman.

"Cosmic Consciousness." Bucke, Banting, Lawren Harris (you could see it in his paintings), Tom Thomson and finally Blodwen, so she came to believe, had broken through and become cosmically conscious.

Fred was more interested in achieving another research break-through. He did not believe the theosophical gobbledygook, but it was tempting to hope that fundamental ideas would somehow present themselves, as the insulin idea had, to help unlock other medical mysteries, such as the cancer puzzle. The Rous sarcoma research had been grindingly slow, with most of the drudgery falling to Sadie Gairns as she transplanted tumour-causing material from one Plymouth Rock hen to another, three to six chickens a week, week after week, year after year. She observed the results day after day, year upon year, and kept meticulous records, almost invariably of the growth of a malignant tumour leading to the death of the fowl. In all, 1,768 chickens were transplanted in Banting's lab from 1928 to 1933.

The interesting, sometimes exciting birds were the ones whose fate varied from the norm. A very few chickens – 7 in the first 1,768 – would resist repeated transplants of tumourous tissue. Were they immune to Rous sarcoma? Had they produced antibodies which nullified the Rous virus? If they had, could you make up an antitoxin or serum that would protect other chickens from Rous sarcoma? Would it protect other chickens from other kinds of tumours, such as the interesting Fujinami strain? Would anything work when you tried experiments across species, using mice instead of chickens?

The answers were almost all negative. Whenever a result looked promising, it turned out to be difficult to repeat, explicable on the basis of some other hypothesis, or simply a break-through into a blind alley. About the best that could be said of Banting's cancer work was that he was in good company, associated with Peyton Rous, William Gye and a growing legion of researchers in the 1930s, all of whom were finding the enigma of cancer in general, and these strange virus-induced cancers in particular, overwhelm-ingly complex. Most cancer researchers in the 1930s, and for many decades afterwards, got results similar to Banting's. Take a legion of the blind, set them to work trying to climb an unknown obstacle, let the obstacle be Mount Everest, and the research results would be similar.

Banting filled one notebook after another with ideas about the tumour work. He tried to create quiet time for thinking, when good ideas might come to him, and even on holidays seldom put the research entirely out of his mind. His travel diaries and sketch books contain many entries beginning "I had another idea last night. . . ." Once in Toronto he jotted on his desk calendar that it was "a good thing to have a sleepless night at times. It gives me a chance to think. Whereas most of one's ideas are wrong or do not amount to much one should keep on trying. If one idea out of a hundred is worth anything then it is worth while. It is like fishing. . . ."

He fished and fished for the answer to cancer. Nothing took the hook. "Tumour work in the lab is so terribly slow that it is hard to keep one's zeal from flagging," he wrote in the summer of 1933. "The months required for an experiment which may end in failure are sickening in the extreme. But some one has to do them. . . ." They only had to be thought through more carefully, he would often conclude. "Most people experiment too much and think too little. . . . I could write a book on the foolish experiments that I have done."[6]

The least foolish, most productive of the experiments Banting directed were those in the silicosis project. It became much more important in 1933 when the Ontario Mining Association, led by McIntyre-Porcupine Mines, asked Banting's group to coordinate a broad attack on the problem. Banting became effectively the chairman of a well-funded multi-faceted research effort, eventually involving more than seventy workers both inside and outside his department, which generated both pioneering and lasting studies of many aspects of silicosis.

The work soon caused a flurry of attention. Bill Franks took time from his cancer experiments to think about silicosis. An idea man and a tinkerer, much like Banting, Franks decided it should be possible to remove silica dust from the air by electrical precipitation. He designed a portable precipitator that he hoped could be used to treat the air in mines after blasting. Late in 1933 Franks was just about to supervise field testing of his machine when, first, his wife gave birth to twins, and second, the newspapers suddenly reported from London, England, that the silicosis problem had been solved – by the machine invented by Dr. F.G. Banting of insulin fame!

Banting was in Europe on holidays. Clouds of reporters descended on the lab in Toronto. Letters of congratulation poured in. Inquiries about the invention arrived from mining organizations around the world. Franks damned the press for being misleading and sensational, and Sadie Gairns refused to give them Banting's itinerary. As he puzzled over what could have happened, Banting realized that in England he had talked about the silicosis work only to William Gye, the cancer researcher. Had Gye told the press? Yes. Or, rather, he had told another medical man about the work at a tea party; a journalist overheard, thus the garbled report. "I am desperately unhappy to have been such a *bloody fool* to be careless & ask you to forgive me," Gye wrote Banting.[7]

The newspaper stories were doubly premature. Not only had Franks' machine not been tested, but when tested it did not work well enough to be practical. It disappeared into the crowded limbo of theoretically sound failed inventions, though not before Franks spun out several interesting papers on photometric methods of studying dust. Meanwhile King, Irwin and others were carrying out extensive studies of mineral dust in the lung, much of the work involving the complicated problem of how different dusts and gases interact with one another and then with the living tissue. They were on the forefront of an important area of research in the 1930s, and their publications were well received by experts in Britain and other countries.[8] Naturally much of the glory reflected on the head of the lab in which all the silicosis work was going on, F.G. Banting.

In fact his name was on very few of the silicosis articles, or any of the other papers coming out of his department. As he gradually changed from being an active experimenter to being head of a large department of active experimenters, Banting became almost obsessive about not taking credit for other people's work. He was not going to do to them what he believed J.J.R. Macleod had done to him. Unless he had actually been in the lab doing experiments he would not have his name on the reports of results. This position was not particularly consistent with Banting's view that ideas counted for more than experiments, but it did guarantee that he would never be accused of appropriating someone else's glory.

To the young researchers in the department, Banting's attitude was refreshing and liberating. They would always get all the credit they deserved, from a chief who stressed teamwork and collaboration and would fiercely argue with them that he *not* have his name on their papers. It was an ultra-egalitarian, democratic approach to publishing research results, not commonly followed in Banting's time or since, and still represents a radical position in a continuing debate. It may have made Banting a rare director of research in never once having been accused of having his name on someone else's work.

On the other hand, Banting did not fade into the background as the faceless head of a large department. In nice counterpoint to his local notoriety as a bohemian wife-abuser, Banting found his scientific stature continuing to grow. In some ways he was in a position like the cave man in the *New Yorker* cartoon, of whom another cave man is saying, "I don't care if he did invent the wheel. What's he done since?" The silicosis research implied he was doing more things, and to most people the wheel was big enough. Through the 1930s more medals, memberships and other honours descended upon Banting without apparent effort or prompting on his part.

The Royal Society of Canada gave him its Flavelle Medal in 1931, the Canadian Medical Association its F.N.G. Starr Gold Medal in 1936. He fulfilled the ambition of his army days when he was made a Fellow of the Royal College of Surgeons of England in 1930. In 1934 the Ancient Society of London Apothecaries bestowed upon him their Apothecaries Medal. Then in 1935 he received what President Cody of the University called "the blue ribbon of scientific scholarship the world over" in being elected to membership in the Royal Society of London. Few realized how odd it was that twelve years were required for the Royal Society to recognize the inventor of the wheel, as it were, and deem this Nobel laureate acceptable. In fact a complex internal battle had been fought for several years among the British insiders over the order in which the insulin discoverers would come up for membership.* H.H. Dale told Banting that his election was due as much to the recent work coming out of his department as to insulin. Other correspondents welcomed the honour as finally putting an end to the insulin controversy; the question mark about Banting's scientific credentials had finally been removed.[9]

To most Canadians the only question mark about Banting the

---

*Macleod had been elected in 1923. Banting's 1935 election came two years after Collip's, and there might have been a wider gap had not Sir Henry Dale, Secretary of the Royal Society, blocked Macleod's attempt to advance Collip's claim until Banting's name was on the list of candidates and apt soon to be approved. Banting knew in late 1931 that he was up for election to the Royal Society. The knowledge might have been a factor in his spurt of publication in 1933-34 and the renewed ambition mentioned obliquely in Blodwen's anguished letters.

scientist was whether his own country had done enough to honour him. The country went a step further in 1934. The Conservative Prime Minister, R.B. Bennett, had decided to renew the granting of titles to Canadians, a practice suspended since 1919. For years it had been assumed that Banting's work merited a title under the old dispensation. Therefore it was not surprising when in the king's birthday honours list, released in June 1934, the title of Knight Commander of the Civil Division of the Order of the British Empire was bestowed on Fred Banting. "All I can say is that I feel it to be an added responsibility," he told a reporter. He was too much of a North American democrat to put much stock in rank or titles, and had earlier said he hoped he would never have to face the problem of accepting or declining one. Those close to him felt he was gratified with the honour in 1934 because it showed he was not in disgrace from his divorce. "I don't suppose in the whole history of the country has there ever been a more popular honour conferred upon a distinguished Canadian," an acquaintance wrote in one of the many congratulatory letters. He added that he hoped the knighthood hadn't interfered with Banting's ability to sing "The Old Black Bull."[10]

It had not. There was never a less pretentious Canadian knight than Sir Frederick Banting, for whom the title meant no difference at all. He never used it himself, and did not like being addressed as Sir Frederick. He was Fred or Freddie to his friends, Dr. Banting to others. He lived quietly in a comfortable apartment near the University and hospital, employing a housekeeper to cook and clean for him. Without a wife to look after his clothes he was usually rumpled and poorly dressed. One former member of the department remembers once running into Banting at Eaton's where he was about to buy a cheap overcoat that would have been a better fit on a high-school boy. "I told him it looked like hell and talked him into buying a Burberry – he said it was no better. Then he had no money. . . ."[11] He was not prominent socially, spending most of his evenings at home or with his old friends. They were that small group of "the boys" – Fred Hipwell, Gord Cameron, Scotty MacKay, Cec Rae and a few others – mostly the 1T7 gang, who played a little bridge or poker and drank a lot of beer and sang the old songs together, and gathered religiously every November 11 to remember dead comrades. Banting was content with a narrow circle of friends and his privacy, in fact often wished he had more of it. He had many family obligations – relatives coming and going, his aged mother in Alliston (his father had died in 1929), his son Bill's visits – quite apart from the bustle of the lab and his high visibility on the streets of Toronto. "I got to get time alone," he complained in his sketchbook in January 1935, "and it seems the only way to get it is to get away. I think I'll get a quiet simple warm room somewhere that no one knows about – a place where I can go and be absolutely alone. I would like to get out of Toronto except that I would like to see Scottie and Freddie sometimes. . . . The older I get the more I want fewer friends and better friends."[12]

He satisfied his yearnings for privacy, for a break, for a little adventure, by taking several long trips. In the autumn of 1933 he spent more than ten weeks in Britain and Europe, attending a cancer congress in Madrid, then holidaying in Spain and Italy. He was fascinated by the art galleries of the Mediterranean countries. The Prado in Madrid took three visits to see properly, and Banting came away convinced that Goya had done all the best that modern art was capable of doing. The Raphaels and Andrea del Sartos in Florence's Uffizi were wonderful, in a class by themselves. Leonardo da Vinci was a little disappointing, Botticelli surprisingly good. Banting felt he had never before appreciated Italian art. He realized that the European masters had left nothing more to be done with the human body – though landscape work seemed to have lagged behind and was a field in which the best Canadian painters, his friends, were the equal or better of the Europeans. Perhaps his greatest "aesthetic" shock was to be cruising through a room of small Dutch paintings in the Uffizi and come across a painting he thought he owned. What the Britnell galleries in Toronto had sold to him as an original Diaz was in fact a copy of an obscure Dutch work. Banting was not impressed to see students in the galleries learning their craft by making copies of the great masters.[13]

He did quite a bit of sketching and pen-and-ink drawing in Spain, though often found the crowds of children who would gather around him too distracting. He had trouble making up his mind about Spain and Spaniards. They seemed to be another carefree and happy people – "large families, large hearts, large voices, and a large amount of time to do as they want to do" – but a little too mired in poverty, ignorance and illiteracy for the taste of a Canadian Protestant. He found he did not like the cruelty of the bull-fight, and was continually disgusted at the evidence of the way kings and churchmen had oppressed the people in the past.

Banting was touring Europe in the year Hitler came to power and Mussolini was at the height of his glory in Italy. He decided that there was too much turmoil in Germany to go there, but could not avoid having his attention drawn to the German situation. A Scottish shipmate on the *Duchess of Bedford* who had recently been in Germany blamed it all on the Jews in Berlin having so much power. A young German in Florence told Banting that Polish Jews who made money in Germany and put it away in Swiss banks were the key to the problem; Hitler was the greatest man in all of Europe. In England, though, Banting had trouble getting to see H.H. Dale because the Britisher was busy interviewing refugee Jewish scientists. Fred soon began to wonder how anyone who studied the scientific accomplishments of European Jewry could be anti-semitic. Not long afterwards he, too, would be worried about finding employment for refugee scientists.

Banting's prejudice against Jews was giving way to other strong ethnic dislikes. He only spent a few days passing through France on his 1933 trip, but loathed every minute of his time there and every contact with the French. "The Jews are gentlemen in comparison to this scheming, begging snivelling race who beg one minute and parade in silks the next. . . . Even Pasteur is going down in my estimation." Banting had not liked the French very much during the war, he remembered, and the country seemed to have gone downhill since. Italy, by contrast, seemed to be making astonishing progress under the fascist socialism of Benito Mussolini. Banting loved everything about Italy, from its art to its "good, efficient & fast train service," and wrote long passages in his diary about the way Italy was waking from the years of sleep and domination by the Catholic Church. "There are no beggars in Italy. She has a growing army, a growing air force, a growing navy. She has national consciousness, a national spirit and a national pride. . . . There is no graft in Italy. Women are emancipating [*sic*]. The church has been forced to abandon its control of the temporal and give better service to the spiritual. All this has happened in ten years. What will the next ten years bring forth?"

There was enough violence abroad to make Banting wonder about the next ten years bringing forth another war. He was anything but a sophisticated political thinker, but liked to talk geopolitics, and shared a common fear in the 1930s that the democracies lacked leadership. Typically, his Cook's tours around Rome caused him to meditate on the fate of the Roman Empire, and to wonder if England might be suffering from the same rot. Britain seemed too pacific at world conferences:

> Are English statesmen too compromising? It seems to me the Mussolinis and Hitlers – the shirted, square-chinned gentlemen are the men who will get there. France with her hang dog whine, lacks leadership and gets her way with indulgent England. The American pop gun, gum chewers want their pound of flesh. England pays [the war debts]. The gentle people pay their taxes. I think England needs awakening – a Hitler or a Mussolini. Japan is growing & suffering from growing pains. China is still snoring. Russia has shed her feathers & growing in a new plumage & soon will fly. Canada is an infant in arms.

His travels and conversations in Europe that fall convinced Banting that war would break out again. "And in our time. It is not a pleasant thought. But it is a fair bet that boys now of 10-15 will be in uniform as their fathers were." He asked himself about the role of science in a future war. Would some kind of germ or drug or gas be developed that could cripple an enemy, some "diabolical poison" that airplanes could drop over enemy territory? Whatever happened, scientific brains would probably be the chief factor in winning the coming war.

Why should anyone take this middle-aged physician's confused and amateurish observations seriously? Partly because he went home to Canada and warned his fellow medical men of the need to think about a future war and the role chemical or germ warfare would play,[14] then, as we will see, became the leader of the country's scientific effort when that war did break out. Partly, too, because he is not unattractive in his thirst to understand a confused and confusing world. Canada could not send a Christopher Isherwood or an Eric Ambler figure to ride the trains of Europe in the summer of 1933. Instead we have a solitary, quiet, unobtrusive doctor, hiding his fame, wandering around making simple pictures and drawings of ordinary life, writing page after page in his travel diary. Stooping a bit, thickening at the waist, bespectacled; a friendly gent, too middle class to be interested in the cabarets or wicked women of Europe, but glad to strike up a conversation with a friendly bartender or fellow traveller. Even wanders into a nightclub in his

Marseilles hotel to get a free drink and chats with "a very dolled up fine looking negress singer – absolutely clean in her talk and spoke like a Bohemian." Properly disgusted by the "overdressed, fat, elderly, hairy-faced dames with their poodles" on the promenade at Nice. Watching the young Americans blow into a hotel and liven it up with their jazz. Trying to make sense of it all. Worrying about the work at home, and finally glad to be going home. Writing on his last night in France, Banting thought about the prospect back in Canada:

Tomorrow God willing I leave this God forsaken country for home and sunshine, real people and friends. Except for the Daily Star, Toronto is the finest city in the world. In the sleeplessness of last night I thought of all the worry and discomfort that this rag of a newspaper had caused me. It is the one evil that I would like to irradicate from our fair city. The Star to me, typefies all that is underhand, unreliable, untrue, and deceitful. It has been at the root of all the unfavourable things that have ever happened to me. And I hate the whole institution of the Toronto Daily Star. I wonder if the time of retribution will ever come? . . . It is rotten to the core and the core is Atkinson. . . . The editor of "Hush" is a gentleman in comparison. The one consolation is that the people of Toronto seem to pay little attention to the Star. The common sense of most of the people prevails and the Star has little influence in city politics or politics in general.

On the westward crossing Banting spent a lot of time talking with a Canadian senator, who was deeply worried about what would happen to his alcoholic, playboy son. At age twenty-two the young man was well along on the road to self-destruction. Such were the problems of the rich. And Fred did not like the company of a prominent Toronto business family, the woman of the pair being "decidedly Frenchy." They were ostentatious and silly. "They have a Pomeranian pug dog that ought to be thrown overboard. It is unfortunate that there is not a good-sized cat to tear it to pieces and eat it."

So the wealthy products of North American capitalism were not very impressive. Unlike some prominent medical men, Banting had never courted their company or their patronage, and he had no social aspirations. Many of his artistic friends, such as A.Y. Jackson, held recognizably left-wing political views, decrying a society that worshipped money while forcing its creative people to scramble and beg on the margins. Capitalist money-grubbing seemed to corrupt and cheapen the ideals of social life – as Banting had seen in the way the Toronto *Star*, owned by a sanctimonious millionaire, Joseph Atkinson, allowed no restraints to stand in the way of its grubbing for more dollars. "Consider our men of industry," Banting wrote of Atkinson. "I have in mind a bald-headed old sinner who wants to open every board meeting with prayer and close it with another million to his bank account. He does not drink, smoke or swear and has never been found out in a scandal but is a church-goer and prays and I would not trust him for he is pre-eminently selfish, narrow, scheming, skunkish and sanctimonious. Watch him through the rest of his miserable career. He holds high places but his is a money aristocracy. He will die dead. What then is success? The massing of a fortune?"[15]

Was there an alternative? Was there a society that truly believed in art and artists and science and all the ideas Banting and his friends thought should be valued? By the late 1920s, and increasingly as the depression of the 1930s seemed to signify the failure of Western capitalism, many idealists began looking to the Union of Soviet Socialist Republics as a possible alternative society. There the Communists seemed to be trying to make the beautiful dream of socialism a reality.

Everyone knew that the first fruits of the 1917 Bolshevik revolution had been war, famine and pestilence. But now, in the years of Stalin's ambitious five-year plans, in the years when the Western world was mired in its own economic disaster, it seemed to many as though Soviet communism was worth taking a good look at. Perhaps it was a window into mankind's future. Banting had heard lectures about the Russian experiment in the late 1920s and had often expressed a desire to see the country for himself. In 1935 he had to cross the Atlantic to be inducted into the Royal Society of London. He arranged to go on from England to Russia, ostensibly to attend the Fifteenth Physiological Congress in Moscow, but mainly, he wrote, to witness at first-hand "the greatest experiment of all time."[16] He left from Hay's Wharf, London, on Saturday June 22, aboard the USSR Steamship *Smolny*.

As Banting described the voyage to Leningrad in his travel diary, it was an unconscious parody of tourist journeys to Communist Russia in the early 1930s, beginning with the fine red sunset on the first full day out of England. A red sunset to go with the *Smolny's* "Red Room": its red-carpeted, red-tableclothed recreation room, decorated with pictures of Marx, Engels, Lenin and Stalin. The Red Room was presumably the site of the captain's speech to his passengers, in which he talked about the wonderful progress of the Soviet Union and its merchant marine. There was hardly any need for discipline aboard his ship, the captain said, and when it was in port its sailors spent their leaves visiting cinema, operas, museums and art galleries. The truth about the latest political murders in the Soviet Union (in the aftermath of Kirov's assassination) was that a counter-revolutionary conspiracy had to be dealt with. "One hundred and sixty millions of people – all enthusiastic about their country – are not going to be disturbed or ruled again by a small group of selfish power-seekers," Banting dutifully recorded.

He was writing it all down, trying to read Leontiev's introduction to Marxist political economy, and talking for hours with his fellow travellers, a motley collection of professors, journalists and artists, mostly Jewish he observed, mostly enthusiastic about communism's achievements since the Revolution.

> In the afternoon Prof. Delahaye (lecturer in psychology – Cambridge) gave a talk of conditions in Russia from personal observations. . . . He told how children's toys were selected by doctor, artist, teacher, and children.
>
> In Russia man cannot exploit man, but a man can exploit the work of his own brain. The Russian system is built upon a plan, a theory, a philosophy, not, like the Italian, on sentiment. "To each according to his need; from each according to his ability." Leaders in Russia do not command or dominate. They are chosen because of the brain, judgement and integrity. Russians discuss everything for hours, all interested or contributing parties are allowed full speech. . . .
>
> Undoubtedly this system is better than our system – except for the selfish man. It is not good for the lazy man. He who does not work in Russia does not eat. Crime in Russia since the new regime has been inaugurated has decreased tremendously.

Banting was determined to keep an open mind to everything he heard or saw. He felt there surely would be "something to learn from them that would help to solve the difficulties of the capitalist countries." His only regret, about which he was anything but open-minded, was that the group of four Canadians aboard included a reporter from the Toronto *Star*. "That cursed paper is here to pest[er] me even at this distance." Fortunately Miss Gibb of the *Star* did not recognize him (he must have been using his alias, Frederick Grant) and went on her own way after Leningrad.

The passengers tipped the crew by taking up a collection "for the assistance of political prisoners in capitalist countries." Banting was to do his touring before the Physiological Congress in Leningrad, so went on to Moscow. First, though, he paid a call on the Soviet Union's greatest scientist, the famed physiologist I.P. Pavlov. After touring Pavlov's Institute of Experimental Medicine, Banting, Delahaye and some other travelling companions were driven by Intourist Lincoln to Pavlov's villa outside Leningrad. It was a large white building.

> Guards came out to open the huge iron gates and we drove into a court-yard. As we alighted from the car there was a great noise and the whole house seemed to shake. There beside us and adjoining the front steps was a large barred cage containing two gorillas. The gentleman gorilla was vexed at our arrival and tried to shake his house down. A boy came with a whip and he ceased his riot. We were shown into a vestry and a "Director" came to tell us that we could not see Pavlov and the Russians again held a meeting. After a few minutes a message came that the Professor would see us immediately and we all hurried upstairs.

> To my surprise, on reaching the top, the professor came rushing forward and shook hands and bowed and led us at a half trot through a hall and three rooms into a sort of study. He talked rapidly all the time in Russian. He was delighted to see us. He sat on a setee in the corner and poured forth rapid Russian gesticulating all the time and laughing in a hearty manner. He told all about his ailments and that his heart was giving him some trouble, but that as soon as this illness was over that he would be better than ever. His beard flew up and down. His eyes were bright and expressive. His whole face was animated. There was a lypona on the back of his right hand, third knuckle, about the size of a half walnut. He did not appear like the quiet thinking scientist that I had pictured him. We sat in an adoring half circle. It was hero worship. . . .

> One of the group snapped several pictures of Banting on the sofa

with the eighty-five-year-old Russian. The visitors toured the labs at the villa and the huge animal quarters ("The pups are to be kept and studied," Banting noted, "much like Blatz's child study"), before returning to the city. It all left Banting a little "overawed," wondering at the tribute involved in a government "which the world considers so harsh and inhuman" paying such honour to a scientist, wondering too if Pavlov might not be happier in his old lab than in the combination tomb and shrine the government was building for him.

The cinema-like presentation of the new Russia continued through Banting's arrival in Moscow. Just as he got to his room in the Hotel National a parade of marching, singing athletes began passing by in the street below. The Canadian visitor stood on his balcony and watched for two hours of marching and singing:

> Some carried rifles, some red flags, floats, huge pictures of Lenin and Stalin, designs, banners, miniature airplanes, a huge boxing-glove, tennis rackets, foot-balls. Some wore red stars on their bosoms; some whole groups of men had heads close-cropped; some groups wore full, blue pullover overalls. One group had dogs, dumbells; some groups were mounted on bicycles; even their band played while riding. Some had packsacks, some coils of rope as bondoliers. Many carried flowers or branches. All were very much tanned, the strong muscles or full round breasts giving shape to their uniforms however scanty the latter might be. . . . airplanes, fifty in one lot, came roaring over. . . . Smaller flights followed at intervals. I have never seen such a spectacular sight. . . . There may have been a hundred and fifty thousand marchers. . . . They sing magnificently. It was stupendous.

In Moscow Banting was taken on tours of impressive new Soviet factories, museums and art galleries ("most interesting was the work of the modern school. Some of it was just plain crude but some was extremely powerful"), the marriage and divorce courts, an abortion clinic, and an institution for the treatment of former prostitutes. The Soviets loved to present their achievements statistically. At this haven, Banting was told, 2,005 prostitutes had been cured and rehabilitated. "Of these, 52% became respectable workers, 19% became social workers, 12% obtained standing and joined the Communist party, 17% studied in the University." Both the horses and the children of Moscow, "good barometers of general well-being," seemed happy and well looked after. He could hardly believe the range of his Intourist guide's knowledge of English literature. She had read Scott, Dickens, Shakespeare, and even tried Chaucer. "Fancy these people reading such things."

Banting spent most of July 1935 on a great circular tour of south-central Russia, travelling alone by rail and boat, shepherded by Intourist guides during stopovers. From Moscow he went to Gorki, then cruised down the Volga through Kazan, Samarra and Saratov to Stalingrad ("immediately whipped off to visit a tractor factory.... Ford has nothing on this place for machinery"), then to Rostov-on-Don, Ordjhinokidze and, after a picturesque drive over the old Georgian military road, to Tiflis deep in the southern Caucasus. The waiting room in the railway station at Tiflis was "like a private sitting room . . . beautifully furnished, and was for 'Officials and First Class Foreigners'. The Russians do distinguish classes of people, regardless of the talk about class distinction."

Only the first and second class passengers had sleeping accommodations on the boat that took Banting across the Black Sea from Batum to Yalta. He shared his first-class cabin with a Red Army officer, and decided that the sleeping peasants on the decks probably got fresher air to breathe than he did. The lavatories on the boat were particularly foul. "A revolution is needed among the plumbers of Russia." From the resort town of Yalta there were side trips to delightfully picturesque Tartar mountain villages, the caves of Peter the Hermit, and the Czar's summer palace. The palace had been converted into a tuberculosis sanitarium, though its wine cellars were still intact and the visitors were treated to a tasting of the royal vintages. Another motor trip to Sebastopol, then long train rides north to Kiev and Moscow completed the circuit.

Most of his sightseeing was standard inspections of show-case factories, apartments, schools, crêches and hospitals. On these excursions Banting saw the Soviet Union at its absolute best, with everything explained to him in excellent English by attractive, cultured and deeply committed female guides. Many of the North Americans he met in Russia, especially in Moscow, were also deeply committed communists, expatriates working to build a new society.

But Banting also observed peasants filing off like cattle to work in the fields, mud huts in the countryside, run-down urban housing, cities and villages almost untouched by the Revolution, children whose protruding abdomens meant rickets or starvation. "The cities by the Volga all have their group of poorly-dressed, ragged dirty creatures who have a fish sticking out of one pocket and some black bread under an arm. . . . At Kazan there is a great deal of malaria, malnutrition, rickets, infant and child mortality." He also experienced a fair share of tourist helplessness in the face of Russian officialdom. "The accomplishments of the Soviet Union are all the more outstanding when one considers the Russian mind," he wrote in one of his more perceptive comments. "The abject stupidity of some of the minor officials is astonishing. How Russia gets anything done is remarkable on account of the time it requires to get started . . . A five-year plan is necessary, for unless the people know exactly what was going to happen a long time before it happened, it would never happen. The great weakness of the future of the Soviet Union is bureaucracy. How to avoid such weakness is impossible to say. The people are very, very patient."

As a tourist travelling first class, Banting had had the best of everything in Russia and knew it. He decided that class distinctions were a natural, inevitable phenomenon, and that the great distinction Russia enjoyed was that it was offering everyone the opportunity to move from class to class. Many of the medical people who came for the Physiological Congress in Leningrad, which opened on August 8, had had less time to experience the Soviet Union, and were not as indoctrinated as Banting with the rationalizations and explanations the guides offered. How could the splendour of the Soviet Union's reception of visiting scientists be justified in the midst of egalitarian poverty, they wondered? Banting explained:

The reception was a very grand affair. The Congress delegates gathered in the Ethnological museum and after walking among the cases of specimens and meeting many friends and a lot of new people the mass moved into a very large room in which there were tables ladened with food of all sorts. Cold roast chicken, ham, fruits, bread, cavier, wine. The flowers, silverware & luxury were in contrast to the drab appearance of the guests. Scientists and their wives are not noted for their tidyness. . . . Some of the delegates thought it a crime that such affluence should be displayed when many people in Leningrad were poor half dressed & starving. Such conclusions are irroneous. There are no poor except the lazy in all Russia. There are no breadlines. There is no unemployment. It is true that many people live on simple fare &

ware shabby clothes. Many of the scientists themselves have had periods in their lives when they ate simply & dressed poorly. There would have been a great to do if the same members were given bread, fish, and cucumbers.

Unfortunately Banting's zeal as a diarist was beginning to wane by Congress time, and he kept no record of the meetings or his socializing with fellow delegates. So nothing is known of his relations with the several other Canadians who attended the Congress, including one of his classmates, Dr. Norman Bethune, who in a few years would become almost as famous as Banting. Bethune and Banting had a lot in common: they had been born one year and fifty miles apart in rural Ontario north of Toronto, had been wounded during war service, had become surgeons, painted for relaxation, and were divorced. They had both abandoned the Christian faith of their upbringing (Bethune was a Presbyterian minister's son), and both travelled to Russia to see whether this was the future at work. A principal difference between them was that Banting had long ago achieved his world fame. Norman Bethune in 1935 was a not particularly well-known Montreal thoracic surgeon of highly debatable competence. He was not a diarist either, apparently, and left no record of whatever talking and drinking the classmates might have done together in Russia as they compared notes on their reactions to communism.

Banting had his final experience with Soviet bureaucracy when he was told that there was no room for him on the *Siberia*, sailing from Leningrad for London. Intourist promised to send him back by plane, but the weather interfered. Finally Banting and one companion, a doctor from Bombay, were given a large amount of food and put on a train heading west. "Russian trains are the slowest in the world." When they crossed the frontier into Poland the smart dress of the Polish officials reminded Banting how accustomed he had become to the poor clothes of the Russians. There were barefoot peasant women working in the Polish fields, but the view from the train was of a cleaner, more prosperous countryside than in Russia. The German countryside was even more prosperous – "spick and span, clean, organized, scientific, . . . a veritable garden." This was Banting's only visit to Germany. From his train he noticed the swastika flag flying everywhere. After three days and three nights on the train, riding through communism, fascism and crumbling democracy, Banting arrived in London on August 26, 1935. Four days later he left for Canada.

He brought back impressions of Russia that were fairly typical of the conclusions of many of the well-intentioned Western idealists who saw Soviet communism in these years, visitors ranging from Beatrice and Sidney Webb through Lincoln Steffens and Julian Huxley. Like these others, Banting's "open-mindedness" in Russia had actually been a will to believe, a suspension of most critical judgment. He did not look for the dark side of the Soviet dictatorship and had no opportunity to observe it. The harsh side of ordinary Russian life could be blamed on centuries of oppression under the old regime. The poverty was the legacy of Czarism; all the signs of progress were communism in action. Russia was not yet utopia, but the battle had been fairly joined. "It is everywhere apparent that there are master minds behind the scenes in the Soviet Union," Banting had concluded one day in his diary:

> There is improvement along the whole battle front. Heavy industry becomes a salient. Education forms another salient. Music and art and architecture are mustering for a drive. Medicine, public health, and dentistry have captured a difficult piece of ground but are now advancing rapidly with education on one flank and culture on the other. The intelligence department of research has drawn to its ranks some brilliant and active minds that are in touch with every tactic and are already giving the world new truth. . . .

On his Volga boat trip, he had closed a meditation about class distinction with the thought that the Russians he was seeing

> do not suffer from an inferiority complex. They have passed through a hell on earth. They have won and are winning and as a consequence they have a beginning consciousness of their power. But they are anxious to learn and always open for knowledge. I have never experienced such a thrill as that of observing this nation of one hundred and sixty millions of people in their awakening. There is enthusiasm among the whole people, especially in the young. They are wholesome, clean-minded, and they crave knowledge.

In Canada Banting wanted to share his enthusiasm for the USSR. His speeches, articles and interviews revealed as good a propagandist

227

as the Communist regime could hope for. He praised the Soviet Union indiscriminately, sometimes ridiculously. He was on his most solid ground in talking about the USSR's system of socialized medicine and its drive to increase its medical personnel. When he turned to the Red Army, telling reporters that it was "primarily an educational institution. . . . it is marvellous how this army takes uncouth lads from the four corners of the country – boys who can scarcely read or write, and turns them into artists, musicians and scholars," Banting was just silly.[17] Usually he concentrated on how the Soviets were supporting science and building for the future. His most revealing eulogy of these greener red pastures came in comparisons between the scientists' situation there and in Canada:

> One cannot help but compare conditions in the USSR & in Canada. They are forging ahead to peaceful prosperity, culture, art & science. We are standing still. They have so much common sense. We are so bound by tradition, public opinion, domination of newly rich. A scientist here who wishes to devote his life to science and medical research or industrial research depends on the droppings that he can beg from the rich man's table. Science cannot promise dividends, but it pays better than a mine or industrials. It gets no votes for a government, hence it gets but meager support. It sells no full page advertisements to our daily newspapers, hence they exploit its workers or garble a scoop for their headlines regardless of their worth.

Privately Banting could get even more carried away. Soon after his return from Russia, Sir Frederick announced in the living room of the Lieutenant-Governor of Ontario, Dr. Herbert Bruce, "I am a communist."[18]

Bruce's reaction to the proclamation is not known. Undoubtedly some of Fred's down-to-earth friends thought he had gone round the bend. He was not a Communist or a communist and when it appeared as though he might be publicly labelled one, alarming his friends and raising the prospect of more newspaper controversy, he began to tone down his ardour for Russia. It had never been whole-hearted in any case, for in all his meditations and comments he had deplored the revolutionary violence that had launched the Bolshevik regime. Fred was a loyal subject of the king, and believed in democratic, normal methods of change. Like many of the fellow-travellers who thought they saw a working future in Russia, he preferred to live in the Canadian present. He didn't want to import communism wholesale. It was appropriate, maybe necessary, for Russia. Yes, it would certainly be sensible if Canada honoured its scientists and doctors the way Russia did, and if the greedy capitalists and their newspapers were kept under control. Perhaps a slow transition to socialism, such as the British seemed to Banting to be experiencing, would be the answer. In a late-1936 address on "The Trend of Civilization," Banting suggested this as a kind of happy medium between the extremes of fascism and communism – the kind of trend a loyal, tolerant British subject could support. There was no need to be a "fanatic" and "go off the deep end" about political ideas.[19]

Norman Bethune, on the other hand, did not back away from the implication of accepting communism. He came back from Russia full of the same enthusiasms as Banting. He wrote, for example, that "Russia presents today the most exciting spectacle of the evolutionary, emergent and heroic spirit of man which has appeared on this earth since the Reformation."[20] In the autumn of 1935 he became more deeply involved in studying the principles of what he realized was a modern religion. He soon swallowed his individualism, his dislike of crowds and regimentation, and dove into card-carrying Communism. Within a year he was operating a blood transfusion service for the Republican side in the Spanish Civil War. From Spain he went to China where he became a kind of guerilla surgeon to Communist forces fighting the Japanese invaders. Bethune died there of septicemia in 1939 and was made a heroic cult-figure by Mao Tse-tung.

Banting and Bethune had at least one contact after 1935. Bethune visited Fred in his lab in Toronto. There may have been other meetings. Bethune is said to have urged Banting to come to Spain or China, telling him he'd really be a hero there. Banting wasn't interested.

Banting and Bethune were both symbols of their generation's struggle to come to terms with personal and political life after the Great War smashed so much that they and most others had been taught to believe. God was dead, and so were many of His teachings, especially about sex and marriage. Their classmate, Beaumont Cornell, had anticipated the dilemma they all shared when he ended his 1923 novel, *Lantern Marsh*, with crimson flames burning away the familiar marshland of an Ontario farm community and rural boyhood. For Cornell's hero, and for Banting and Bethune, life became a lonely odyssey.

The struggle to come to terms with reality was worse for Bethune, a deeply disturbed egotist, whose jaunty amorality masked an obsessive insecurity and fear of failure. Bethune's paintings were angry, intense, dark. Banting's were tranquil and picturesque. Bethune would become an angry, mean drunk; Banting a mellow, companionable one. Bethune desperately needed something to believe in. He found his faith and his fulfillment, his martyrdom in communism, joining the red conflagration. Bethune had to believe. He had said that to deny the Russian experiment was "to deny your faith in man, and that is the unforgivable sin, the final apostasy."[21]

Banting had no special faith in man in the abstract. He had his research and his department, his friends and his country to believe in. He soldiered on with his daily life. There were periods of insecurity, depression and despair, but you got up the next morning and did the day's duties and stayed away from *Star* reporters. At the end of the day you could relax with friends and drinks, or just by being alone. During his travels in Russia, Banting had reflected on the way the people seemed to do everything in crowds. "One thing I cannot understand," he wrote to himself, "is how they can exist without sometimes being alone to think."

CHAPTER ELEVEN

Maturity

H is country would not leave him alone. In 1937 Banting agreed to serve on Canada's National Research Council. While maintaining and enlarging the research activities of his department at the University, he became the first national spokesman for medical research in Canada. The few years before the outbreak of Hitler's War were some of the best for Banting, culminating in his second marriage. He had had no illusions about the prospect of European war, however, and when it began in September 1939 he was standing at the head of the line to volunteer his services.

The National Research Council was a semi-independent, government-funded body, formed in 1916 to coordinate and encourage all kinds of scientific research in Canada. By today's standards its early years were unbelievably lean and its activities minuscule. But by 1935 the NRC did have its own research laboratories in Ottawa, a substantial if poorly paid scientific staff, and a budget of about $400,000 annually. That year became a turning point in its history when the government appointed General Andrew G.L. McNaughton president of the Council. McNaughton was an engineer, artilleryman, scientist, inventor and professional soldier, who had risen to the rank of brigadier-general during the First World War and had served as Chief of the General Staff of the Canadian army from 1929 to 1935. McNaughton was an enthusiastic supporter of scientific research, was determined to prepare the Council to give scientific leadership if war came, and managed to pry more money out of Ottawa to finance an expanded role.

When Banting joined the NRC it had no general involvement in medical research – no public agency in Canada was involved in the field – but it had gradually become active in funding tuberculosis work, slipped into radiology and radium therapy, and was entering such fields as parasitology through agricultural research. When McNaughton asked Banting to join the Council, he probably already had in mind an organized, direct NRC role in medical research. Late in 1936 he had proposed that the Council create a special Associate Committee, parallel to its other associate committees, which would become the sole coordinating body for medical research across Canada. After carefully orchestrated consultations with professional bodies such as the Canadian Medical Association, the Associate Committee on Medical Research was formally created early in 1938.

Banting had agreed to serve as chairman of the Associate Committee reluctantly, apparently telling McNaughton he wasn't qualified for the job and didn't really deserve his reputation. Why couldn't McNaughton himself chair the committee? "You've got a reputation in this field and I haven't," the general told Banting. "Whether it's deserved or not makes no difference. You've got it. You can do this better [than I] and it's your duty to do so." Banting could not resist an appeal to his duty. He stood up, virtually coming to attention, and said, "Yes, sir. I'll do it." The founders of the Associate Committee assumed that in a few years it would grow out of the NRC coccoon into a Medical Research Council, similar to the MRC in Great Britain.[1]

Banting took advantage of his access to McNaughton to raise with him the military-medical issue of biological warfare. Since 1933 he had been reading and talking with other scientists about the possibilities of spreading disease against an enemy, the talk usually hinging on some of the alleged attempts at germ warfare in the Great War. The Germans were said to have caused a cholera epidemic in Poland, for example, by sending contaminated sugar to their prisoners there, who spread it among the peasants. In 1917 the Roumanians were said to have discovered stocks of anthrax and glanders microbes at the German embassy in Bucharest. And so on. Poison gas, of course, which was chemical warfare, had been used by both sides.

McNaughton urged Banting to prepare a memorandum on the subject, which could be passed on to the Canadian and British military authorities to put them on their guard. Banting's confidential memorandum of September 16, 1937, was a seven-page elaboration of a thesis that "undoubtedly the next development in war will

232

be the utilization of epidemic disease as a means of destroying an enemy." Airplanes could drop waterborne diseases such as typhoid, cholera or dysentry into city reservoirs. It might be possible to spread such airborne diseases as spinal meningitis. Above all, there was the danger of insect-borne epidemics such as plague:

Fleas could be produced in billions by artificial culture; by feeding fleas on plague bacillus they would become infected. These infected fleas in the chilled hungry state could be dropped on enemy troops or civilians and an epidemic of plague would result with certainty. A second means of transmission of plague would be by means of rats harbouring infected fleas. . . .

Yellow fever and malaria are transmitted by mosquitoes. The mosquitoes can be grown and infected in a laboratory, preserved for months by chilling. . . .

In the hands of specialists in tropical medicine such diseases as sleeping-sickness, which is transmitted by the tse-tse fly and Kala-azor, which is spread by a sand fly, might, through research, be applicable to medical warfare. . . .

Recent advances in knowledge of virus diseases added to the horrible possibilities, and there were so very many ways in which disease could be spread:

In warfare virus diseases, for example, psittacosis, could be adsorbed on dust and introduced into the enemy territory by means of dust bombs. . . .

By the invention of an automatically air-cooled shell, bacteria such as gas gangrene, tetanus and rabies could be added to the danger of the wounds inflicted, so that even a scratch would be deadly. In the same manner snake venom might be used. . . .

. . . Bacterial diseases, such as anthrax, and foot-and-mouth disease, affecting cattle, and glanders, affecting horses can be as readily disseminated as the diseases affecting man. Diseases of grains must also be considered.

. . . A secret agent . . . could readily carry on his person small glass ampules containing most dangerous bacteria or viruses. . . . In the re-armament program for self-defence due consideration should be given to these possibilities and facts.[2]

McNaughton was impressed by Banting's speculations and arranged for him to address the officers association of the Royal

Canadian Army Medical Corps (RCAMC) on the subject. There was already an anti-gas warfare project at the NRC, thanks to McNaughton. Banting's warnings caused an officer in the RCAMC to make a special study of biological warfare. Captain A.K. Hunter's confidential review of the possibilities of bacteriological warfare raised many questions about just how easily infectious diseases could actually be spread, and concluded that the best defence would be a public threat to respond in kind. In Britain the Committee of Imperial Defence and the Medical Research Council had already considered the subject, and dismissed much of the Sunday newspaper and other speculation about biological warfare, most of which was similar to Banting's, as being largely ill-informed and exaggerated. The practical difficulties of waging war with bacteria were so great, the British concluded,* that beyond keeping sensible reserves of vaccines and paying more attention to crop and livestock diseases, little needed to be done.[3]

This was hypothesizing about a hypothetical war. Banting's job as chairman of the NRC's Associate Committee on Medical Research was to stimulate normal peacetime research. Before he could do that, though, he had to find out what researchers were doing in Canada. Therefore in the autumn of 1938 Banting and the Associate Committee's secretary, Dr. C.B. Stewart, toured Canada from Halifax to Vancouver, visiting universities, hospitals, provincial public health laboratories, and one or two private researchers, trying to find out who was doing what and how their work could be encouraged.

They found less medical research going on in all of Canada than would be done in one moderately productive physiology or biochemistry department today. The University of Toronto and McGill University were reasonably well-established centres of research, Western and Queen's and the University of Alberta had small but

---

*In 1937, for example, the MRC concluded: "If bombs or shells were used most germs would be killed by the heat of the explosion; if glass containers, dropped from airplanes, were used the infected area would be small, and distribution to many people would be unlikely. Even if bacteria were sprayed in the form of liquid droplets from aircraft so as to cover an area of some square miles at a time, the risk of widespread infection would not appear to be great. The spread of infection by agents as a species of sabotage would, perhaps, prove a more successful method, but one involving considerable difficulties. Even if it were possible by one or other of these methods to start a centre of infection, propagation of an epidemic demands not merely the creation of an initial centre of infection, but the existence of environmental conditions that favour the spread of disease from that centre."

234

active facilities. One or two particularly dedicated men might scrounge some time from teaching at the University of Manitoba or Dalhousie University to sustain a research program. But almost everyone was handicapped by too many students, too few technicians, and always too little money. The trip itself was a gruelling ordeal for Banting because he was expected to give speeches on medical research at every stop, sometimes two or three a day. The twenty-five talks he gave in November 1938 were an all-time record, he wrote his mother. "I often think of father and the way he worked & had pleasure in work. My life is different but the principle is the same."[4] To make the trip even more difficult, Banting felt he could not, as an agent of the National Research Council, be characteristically rude to reporters. Fortunately he got along fairly well in his press interviews, the trip producing only one sensational story about his working on a cure for cancer. After the reporters were gone and the formal dinners were over, Fred could get together with old friends like Miller from Western or Collip at McGill, unwind, have a few drinks and reminisce.

Banting was doing some of his best work in this capacity as an ambassador of medical science. Most researchers found it pleasant and flattering to talk over their projects with someone who stood so high in the medical world. He went out of his way to meet medical students, and his friendly, natural manner made an excellent impression. There was no harm done to medical research in Canada, probably considerable good, by his earnest public pleas for more research, more openings to keep bright young Canadians from emigrating to the United States, and more money to pay for research. Although he was popularly revered as the lone genius who had realized his brilliant idea under the most primitive conditions, he was now well aware that modern research was collaborative and expensive. New discoveries did not emerge overnight, and while the science was free, the laboratories had to be paid for. There was surely something wrong with the priorities of a nation spending a million dollars a week subsidizing over-expanded railways, but having almost nothing available to support humanitarian research.

By this time in his life Banting had become reasonably experienced in human relations and knew how to exercise down-to-earth diplomacy when he wanted to. When two researchers in Manitoba were competing to work on the same problem, Banting urged Dr. P.H.T. Thorlakson to mediate it this way:

You should take the earliest opportunity of inviting McDonald and Cameron to that room in your basement and supply each one with a liberal quantity of whatever spiritous liquors they like best. The first hour of the meeting should be spent in social amenities and nothing should be said concerning research until the lubrication has permeated. You can use your judgment as to whether or not two or three equally congenial people are present. This treatment may have to be repeated at intervals, but I think it is the best solution of the personality problem. Malice is soluble in alcohol.

(Unfortunately Banting was wrong in his generalization. "I applied the treatment you recommended with no apparent success," Thorlakson reported back "because the more liquor Cameron consumed the more critical and unbending he became. In fact the only effect that I could discern during the evening was that alcohol stiffened his spine."[5])

The 1938 trip led to a decision to create National Research Council grants in aid of medical research in Canada. There was evidently some internal debate as to whether it would be better to centralize state-supported medical research in NRC labs, as the British and American medical research bodies were tending to do. C.B. Stewart remembered that Banting threw his influence on the side of decentralization. For the first year's grants, given out in 1939, researchers across Canada asked for a total of $120,000. This was far too much for the Associate Committee to fund; it had less than $50,000 available. But that was the beginning. As this is written, less than half a century later, Canada's Medical Research Council operates on a budget of more than $100 million annually.[6]

There was naturally less time for Banting's own research. The Rous sarcoma work went along as frustratingly as ever, generating a lot of notebook ideas but no results worth publishing. Nobody else in the department took up Banting's cancer ideas, but Franks continued his own approach to cancer, as did a brilliant emigré member of the department, Dr. Bruno Mendel, who had arrived from Germany in 1935 with his own laboratory equipment as well as enough money to pay for the costs of his research.

Most of the time Banting spent with active experiments after 1936 was on projects involving cardiac failure. Harold Ettinger, Ed Hall and a student, George Manning, carried out a series of studies of factors producing heart damage. They measured the impact of massive injections of acetylcholine on animal hearts, did extensive testing of an idea of Banting's that over-stimulation of the vagus nerve can cause heart damage, and then went on into studies of the effects of pulmonary embolism. By the end of the decade the work on experimental heart disease had expanded to include studies of nutrition and atherosclerosis. Much of the experimenting had grown out of the new capacity researchers had for studying the heart after the development of the electrocardiograph. This work in the early days of cardiac physiology was useful and interesting, not spectacular, and led to the last series of original articles with Banting's name on them.

He was mostly an "idea" man in this research, who had to be persuaded to let his name be added to articles written by Ettinger, Manning or Hall. Sometimes, though, he had time for the old lab routine: during one stretch of round-the-clock dog research he shared the 8 p.m. to 8 a.m. shift with George Manning, catching a little sleep on the couch in the lab, offering the young researcher an illicit alcoholic libation at 3 a.m., making pen and ink drawings of the early morning view from the fifth floor of the Banting Institute.[7]

Ed Hall, who had upgraded his qualifications by taking his M.D. and Ph.D. in the teaching departments of the University, became the moving force in the department's physiological investigations after Ettinger returned to Queen's. He led the group into another area of research late in the decade when another new machine, the electroencephalograph, opened up many possibilities for investigating the brain and brain damage. One of the phenomena they began to study was the use of shock therapy in schizophrenia and other mental disorders. Two of the drugs used to induce convulsions or seizures which seemed to clear the brain's circuits were metrazol and insulin. Banting's involvement with the studies of insulin shock was largely confined to one case of insulin-resistant schizophrenia; he wondered whether the patient's blood serum would make others insulin-resistant. This was his only return to the magic hormone that had made his name. The utility of insulin and other chemical shock therapies for mental illness before the consciousness-altering drugs were developed is now regarded skeptically, not least for having been agonizingly painful treatments of relatively helpless patients.

Banting was not greatly interested either in mental illness or insulin, and did not have his name on any of the articles. His only publications on insulin in the 1930s were a couple of popular rehashes of the discovery days. By 1939 he had nothing more to say about insulin. "I simply cannot do it. I am not interested in the subject," he wrote an editor who had asked for an article from him on insulin and diabetes. "I have nothing to say that has not already been said a thousand times by people who have the gift of writing or talking. My knowledge of insulin is out of date. I have not done an experiment on it during the past 14 years. My whole attention is upon other problems in medical research." The public would never understand. When Banting refused to comment on a new insulin-substitute, saying he knew nothing about the subject, a reporter wrote it off as humility from "the man who knows more about diabetes than anyone else in the world."[8]

The silicosis project became the most exciting work in the department in the late 1930s. The researchers had been exploring the mechanism by which the bits of silica in mine dust cause damage to the lung. The particles apparently dissolved in the lung to form silicic acid, which then caused the fibrosis. If it was not practical to keep the dust particles from entering the lung, perhaps the silica could be prevented from dissolving. Early in 1937 two chemists from McIntyre-Porcupine Mines, who were working with Banting's group, discovered that metallic aluminum dust almost completely prevented silicious material from dissolving in a test tube solution. They immediately tested the powder on rabbits, exposing some to quartz dust plus aluminum dust, a control group to the quartz dust alone. The latter rabbits gradually developed silicosis; the former did not. The researchers' attention immediately focused on the aluminum dust treatment. Another series of elaborate, more carefully controlled rabbit tests confirmed the earlier results. The aluminum dust prevented silicosis from developing, seemed to arrest established cases and by itself did not damage the lungs. The dust seemed to be effective because it thoroughly coated the quartz particles, preventing them from becoming involved in any reactions in the lung.

The group moved on to develop methods of spreading aluminum dust in the air and eventually to clinical trials. Banting had kept in touch with the progress of the work, and was eager to investigate the possibility of aluminum dust being used as a prophylactic device in the mines. He adamantly refused the researchers' requests to present the first paper on the new preventive measure, however, sticking to his determination never to report for the first time the findings of others. He did not live to see the development of the aluminum dust treatment, which was taken over (and patented) by the McIntyre group, and widely used in the mines of Ontario and several countries until the 1970s. There was some decline in the incidence of silicosis among Ontario miners; whether or not it was because of the prophylaxis is not known. A retrospective study of the treatment in 1980 concluded that the animal studies of the late 1930s were well done and convincing, but that the human data, compiled after Banting's researchers had dropped the work, provided no evidence one way or the other. To a later generation the best approach to silica particles in lungs was to keep them out.[9]

Banting's people had done good work for the time on many aspects of the silicosis problem. The key to the achievement was the talent of those who had gathered around Banting. Because the Department of Medical Research was there, because Banting with his reputation was there, because more money was gradually becoming available, the group had expanded, diversified and developed into a reasonably impressive research unit, in both silicosis studies and generally. There was a fairly steady turnover of personnel, as researchers who did a year or two with Banting decided to go on to other jobs or more advanced training. But by 1939 Hall, Franks, Mendel, Dudley Irwin and Colin Lucas were attacking a long list of problems, using the skills of almost forty workers. Banting still dug into his pocket on occasion, often to give personal loans, but now considerable outside money was being attracted to fund the research. Granting agencies ranged from the Rockefeller Foundation and Eli Lilly and Company through the Scottish Rite Masons, Northern Jurisdiction. Students who worked in the Department of Medical Research got reasonably good professional training; from time to time Banting's hallways were graced by quite distinguished scientists, such as biochemist Hans Krebs, who spent a few weeks in Toronto working on depancreatized pigeons in 1939.[10]

There was still room for flyers and fancies. Banting finally got work started on royal jelly in 1938 when a graduate of the Ontario Agricultural College expressed interest in it; Banting immediately gave him a fellowship. A Canada-wide cooperative effort among apiarists produced nearly 100 grams of crude royal jelly. Colin Lucas and the student, G.F. Townsend, completed a chemical analysis of the substance and were beginning experiments in feeding it to other species when the war interrupted the work. Townsend got a job as Provincial Apiarist for Ontario.

The Department of Medical Research also looked into drowning in 1938, when a public health worker asked for advice on resuscitation methods. In one version of the results, the work was stimulated by Billy Banting's wondering how ducks could eat under water without drowning. Another story has one of Banting's student researchers, Bernard Leibel, claiming he could make a dog drown with ten drops of water. Banting bet Leibel all the change in his pocket that he couldn't. Leibel showed him how a few drops of water can cause a spasm of the glottis in the larynx and death by asphyxiation. Banting enthusiastically set Leibel and others to work on the physiology of experimental drowning. The sacrifice of a number of laboratory rabbits and rats seemed to disclose a number of useful techniques to try in drowning crises, ranging from tracheotomy to injections of belladonna to stimulate the heart. NEW BANTING SERUM AID IN DROWNING CASES headlined the *Telegram*, after Banting approached the Toronto police about the possibility of using his methods in drowning emergencies. The idea seemed to be that a flying squad of researchers would rush to the scene to revive the dead. Nothing much came of it. Laryngeal spasm is not a problem in most ordinary drownings. The last research article with Banting's name on it was a paper by himself, Hall, J.N. Janes, Leibel and D.W. Lougheed entitled "Physiological Studies in Experimental Drowning (A Preliminary Report)", published in the *Canadian Medical Association Journal* in 1938.[11]

Banting brought neither enthusiasm nor any flair for administration to the job of running his substantial department. He did bring his considerable capacity for hard work, combined with a willingness to delegate jobs to anyone willing to do them. The most willing was Sadie Gairns, who had gradually assumed the position of departmental secretary/administrator. A short, dark-haired, energetic lady, Miss Gairns was devoted to Banting. Over the years they came to know one another intimately. Sadie Gairns demonstrated more Airedale-type loyalty to Banting than any of the other women in his life, becoming like an adoring little sister whose energies are dedicated to keeping a weak and sometimes stumbling big brother out of trouble. She handled departmental detail, advised Banting on departmental policy, fronted for him when he was misanthropic or depressed, kept up the tumour work and advised him on his private life.

Banting occasionally fought with Sadie Gairns, too – she retaliated with silence – but realized how indispensable she was to him.

> I do not know what in the world I would do without her. . . . She advises. She provides the detail. She controls. She is so right in her instincts as a woman in so many cases that as a man I am ashamed to be professor of Med. Res. No man could possibly have a more loyal true and brave supporter than I have in Miss Gairns. She gives to me so much & demands of me so little that it embarrasses me to express my feelings concerning the relationship. It amounts to this – When she is content then I know that I am right. When she doubts, I doubt, but when she condemns, I pity. Her only fault is that she is too much of efficiency. She demands too close to the 100 percent. She is too honest for this world.[12]

One day when Banting and Sadie Gairns were walking through Queen's Park, a distant acquaintance came up to them and said, "Dr. Banting, I believe – and Mrs. Banting too?" "Not my wife," said Banting. "My secretary, much more important, and more difficult to replace."

Banting needed Sadie to cover for him from time to time. Although most people who knew him in the late thirties were impressed by how he had matured and relaxed from the impossible, insecure character of insulin days, he was still hot-tempered, bullheaded and blunt to the point of violence. There are so many stories about Banting throwing a reporter out of his office that it may have happened several times. Those who worked in the department for any length of time also remember being fired several times. There were occasions when Banting was too depressed to see any of his associates, perhaps days when he was too hungover to face the world. He usually bounced back in a day or so, apologized to anyone he might have offended when he was not himself, and went on with life.

To most of the people who worked with him in these years, Banting was a hell of a good fellow, friendly, kind, unpretentious. He took an interest in everyone's projects and loved to toss around ideas. He was the first to admit he didn't know a damn thing about somebody's special area, but he was curious and would listen and get enthusiastic, and be specially encouraging to the young men.

Perhaps he saw himself in the shy summer student, or in the farmboy who wandered in one day and got a tour of the whole department from Banting himself. Velyien Henderson once tore apart a paper given by young George Manning. "Don't pay any attention to the old bastard," Banting advised Manning. "He doesn't like undergraduate students." Another time, when Duncan Graham would not let one of the junior men in the department carry out a research proposal using patients at the hospital, Banting advised telling Graham to go to hell; on second thought he advised the researcher that the University of Toronto was full of bigotry and bigots and it would be better to go somewhere else. What a contrast Banting the democrat was to Henderson, Graham or most of the aloof, Olympian professors at the University.[13]

Every year he would have the gang from the lab up for a beer and hot dog party. Sometimes at the end of a day in the lab, after 4 o'clock tea, he'd get together with two or three of the boys, someone would produce a bottle or some laboratory alcohol, and they'd have a round or two. There was a memorable bus trip back from Kingston once, with Dr. Banting leading the researchers in loud and bawdy song. Another night at a dinner at the Military Institute he really tied one on, and they had a hell of a time getting him into a cab and home. The next day he apologized to everyone in the lab for anything he might have said or done the night before. Forty years later Norman Stephenson couldn't get over how Dr. Banting, who hadn't offended him at all that night, would have the humility to apologize to even the most junior member of the staff. In his reminiscences of the department, Bill Franks constantly referred to the "family" atmosphere Banting created, and the "exquisite times" they had together, "just damn good fellowship." It was important to Franks and to a lot of the men who worked with Banting that he was a man you could get drunk with.

He was not a man you could do collaborative research with very profitably, for he was not very well informed about the frontiers of medical research, did not have creative ideas and could contribute little to the substance of a student's professional development. More and more often in these years he realized it and found he could go a long way by admitting his ignorance. Sometimes it was even useful to researchers caught up in a thicket of ideas and procedures to have someone ask them to start over and please explain it all simply; then Dr. Banting's plain wisdom seemed to shine through as he took you back to first principles. Some of his former associates insist that Banting's methods were far more effective than the aloof use of students as semi-technicians which they believe characterized the labs of Macleod and then Best. Others are scornful of the poor quality of training anyone who worked too closely with Banting was likely to get.

The reconciliation of these views seems to lie in the way Banting, as a lab director, was one of the boys. If he had been a baseball manager he would have been too friendly with his players to have exercised any discipline. He would have given all his rookies a chance, told everyone to get up there and knock hell out of the bastards, been a terror to the umpires, and bought the first round of beer after every victory. Most of his players would have loved him and some would have thrived on being left alone, but the team would have been only as good as its natural talent. It would have finished in the middle of the pack, or worse, except in the years when the boys got lucky.

For Banting these were probably the happiest years professionally since his schoolboy or college days. But only by comparison, for he was still often overwhelmed by the pressures of his daily routine. One hot, sleepless night in the summer of 1938, when he was meditating about cancer research, having had a new idea, he wrote out an excellent description of his daily life as Sir Frederick Banting, Head of the Department of Medical Research:

The lab has changed. I will have to get a new laboratory. When I go to it I find that it is not a lab but an office. There are a pile of letters to answer, phone numbers to call up, people waiting to have an interview, routine work that must be done. Some person wants me to give him some money, someone wants a signature, someone wants to know what to do about a friend of a great aunt's cousin who has a cancer, or who has gone insane. Someone has a cure for diarrhoea, cancer, or anterior polyio myelitis. Some anti-vivisectionist damns. Some of the staff are sick or want a raise in salary or want a holiday. Some newspaperman wants a exclusive story, "inside dope." Some one has written an article and they wish it commented upon. Some member of the staff has an idea and they wish to discuss it. Some visitor from China, the USA, England, has arrived and "cannot visit Canada without seeing the distinguished discoverer of Insulin!" Some person wants a job in the department, and has applied on a previous occasion.

– I must write a letter of introduction for someone I have never seen before to someone I have never seen (& hope I never do see).

– But despite all this I plan an experiment. I will draw blood from my immune birds at 10.00 A.M., inject it at 11.15 A.M. – do transplants at 11.45. Have luncheon at 12.45 at the Military Institute, keep an appointment at 2.00 P.M. to see a visitor from Peru or Brazil. At 3.00 P.M. a man has been trying to get me for 4 days, he has telephoned five times and has come and is waiting – he wants to sell me stock in a gold mine in the Yellowknife area. It is dirt cheap and will be worth millions. . . .

– And here is a poor returned soldier out of luck – without a job. "You have had luck," why not share it with a pal? You were down in your luck once. But now you're up and you have gone "high hat."

And here is an invitation to attend a luncheon for a politician. You must of necessity go for he is a friend of the Prime Minister and of the Cabinet and it is necessary to "keep in right" or you will not get the grant for research –

And at 3:30 there is a meeting of the committee on a resperator and at 4.00 "you must be at the advisory council meeting and at 4.45 there is a meeting of the post graduate committee on degrees."

– "I am sorry to interrupt but will you call the carpenter for he does not know what is to be done about the shelves in room 509."

– "The professor of cosmography of Columbia University is waiting to see you about an international convention in 1939."

– "And a life insurance agent is also waiting."

And such is life! would anyone care to live it as I do?

– A letter from my home town asks for a scholarship for the school – a letter from a church asks for a donation – a artist wants to sell his pictures – a dear friend of the family who has known me "all my life" wants a loan – an editor of a magazine wants an article – a movie man wants a few feet of film of me in the lab, a broadcaster wants the outstanding incidence of my life to put into a skit – the National Research Council wants me to approve the minutes of the last meeting. What a life!

. . .

At times I feel like a wrung out dishrag.

– exhausted with giving and nothing left to draw from.

At the end of each day I am tired and would like to sleep but cannot – unless soothed to rest with alcohol.
Reading – it is out of the question.
Painting – I have no time or energy left.
Writing – only when it relieves my midnight pent up feelings.
Experiments – no time at all.
– and yet I am supposed to be an experimental physiologist.[14]

Banting had not looked after his body particularly carefully over the years. He smoked extremely heavily, several packs a day, and had developed a chronic cough. He took no physical exercise, in fact did not believe in exercise, writing to himself that "exercise for the most part is a fad like all this talk of diet." Unrelieved physical and mental tension was probably the source of his chronic sleeplessness. He often treated stress and insomnia in these years with alcohol. As he had briefly done in the worst of the insulin days, Banting now routinely used liquor as a sedative. In 1940 he estimated his daily consumption at ten ounces of rye whiskey. By and large the nocturnal drinking did not interfere with his daily activities. He did not drink to keep going through the day, nor did he go on binges. None of the surviving members of his research group believes he was an alcoholic; some argue that he exaggerated his intake, partly because of his upbringing. "His drinking habits would not raise a single eyebrow in today's society," one of his colleagues claims.

Perhaps. It is certainly true that Banting did not disgrace himself in public. The ten-ounce estimate remains, as does Banting's own concern about his drinking. One night, for example, he scribbled these verses in pencil on the back of a notepad:

> Sleep only comes on exhaustion
> And this infalible rule
> Suggests that the end of all things
> Is to be a bloody fool
>
> And alcohol comes into the picture
> for by this simple means
> One gains the fools paradise
> And repose from ambition & dreams.[15]

There is one story, credible but unconfirmed, that he took his anxieties to a psychiatrist, who advised him to keep on with his writing as a release from pent-up tension. Whether or not he had been advised to write as therapy (the consultation with the psychiatrist may have been as little as a talk with Bill Blatz about insomnia), Banting filled many notebooks and pads with meditations, opinions, drafts of stories, fragments of autobiography and increasingly detailed diary entries. The trouble with writing to relax, though, was that Banting found liquor helped clear his head so he could do it well; so he often drank while he was writing. Sometimes it helped improve the writing:

> I never thought that I would come
> to writing poetry for fun.
> Or ever writing it at all
> I blame it on King Alcohol.[16]

It was the integrity of his character more than the alcohol, I believe, which caused him to put so much of himself on paper and then keep every scrap of it. Banting wanted to write about life as it really was, his own real life, thought and feelings. One of his meditations one night in 1938 was about autobiography, and may hint at the kind of history of his life he would have wanted written: "If a man were thoroughly and absolutely honest there would be nothing like an autobiography to find out the real, the true, the ideal, the motivation of a man of action. . . . Because of the sordid, the weakness of human nature, the frailties of human life, the physiological urge which impels us, few, if any autobiographies are absolutely true. Some are daring, some are revealing, some are almost truthful but none is the true picture of the struggling human soul with weakness, strength, ideas, shortcomings, imperfections."[17]

In 1936 Banting moved to a house he bought at 205 Rosedale Heights Drive, overlooking the city, a comfortable home on the same fashionable street as the Hipwells. He began enjoying puttering in his long, steep garden, and also put his surgeon's fingers to work carving wood as a hobby. He may have been influenced to take up the craft by his sculptor friends, Frances Loring and Florence Wylie, two bohemian artists, who lived and worked in an old church nearby in Moore Park. Banting sometimes came to "the Girls'" famous Saturday night parties, where he became noted for his recitations of Robert Service, and agreed to sit while Frances Loring sculpted his portrait. The Loring bust shows an heroic intellect at work, high-foreheaded, almost straining with the effort of thought, ruggedly Canadian. Some critics see it as Loring's best work, one of the best pieces of sculpture done in Canada.[18]

There was one more sketching trip in Quebec with A.Y. Jackson, to St. Tite des Cap in March 1937. Banting did quite a few sketches, some of his best, but his diary of the trip reveals how haunted he was by the lab:

March 20: I have usually found it possible to forget the laboratory when I leave it. This trip is different. I cannot get the laboratory and its financial requirements, its experiments, and its people out of my mind.

I have not got into the habit of sleeping properly. In the evening I am tired & can go to bed and to sleep but I awaken in six or seven hours and cannot go to sleep again. It is in those early hours that I think of the laboratory. I had a long uninterrupted think on the cancer problem this morning. . . .

March 22: Got a letter from Sadie containing all the news of the lab. She needs a holiday more than I do. . . .

March 23: I am glad to be here but I cannot get myself free of the lab and its problems. I think I would sooner be home than anyplace at present. If I could only get one important piece of work done I would be pleased and happy to get away. Then I have to provide financially for the upkeep of the thing. I wonder if there are any of the workers in the lab that realize and appreciate where the money has come from & where the next money is coming from – & if they appreciate their opportunities.[19]

There was always the relaxation with the old friends in Toronto, perhaps Banting's best, most constant therapy. A psychologist once told him that no one ever went insane who had an intimate friend he could confide in. Banting had always done a lot of confiding in bull sessions, after a few drinks. Some of his new, or renewed, friends in the late thirties were a group at the Arts and Letters Club, which he started frequenting again. There were some fine, beery times when the BOF group, known as Birds Of a Feather, or Bloody Old Fools, got together at Jack McLaren's cottage. One of the group remembered in the 1980s that he had last seen Sir Frederick Banting, KBE, sitting on the floor of the McLaren cottage drenched in beer from the keg he was going to show them all how to tap properly.

The restless search for fellowship was often simply the result of a middle-aged bachelor's loneliness. His son Bill was too young and too seldom with him to make fathering a particularly fulfilling role. Nor is it clear how good a father Fred was to the boy, who did spend long stretches at Rosedale Heights. He told fairly imaginative bedtime stories about the adventures of the "little nigger," a rootless, restless outsider who wandered over the face of the globe. But he found the routine of parenting a little boy irksome, complaining in his diary that Bill was spoiled or willful. He expected a lot from his son and, like many strong fathers, would probably have striven too hard to make the child live up to expectations. He wanted Bill to be tough and hard, not a soft city boy. One way of getting the boy used to reality was to bring him into the lab to help decapitate mice, sort of like killing the chickens in the old days on the farm.

Fred still wanted a wife and more children – a real home and family. Some of his friends thought he had a well-developed sense of guilt about his marriage and his treatment of Marion. He occasionally told them he wished it had turned out differently. He must have thought back to Edith, too, and wondered how that would have worked out. His oldest friends all thought she was the real love of his life, the girl he should have married.

They did not know that Fred was having a new romance in his late forties. Henrietta Ball was a native of Stanstead, Quebec, born in 1912, who had taken a B.A. in science at Mount Allison University in New Brunswick, worked for three years in the tuberculosis laboratory in Saint John, New Brunswick, then come to the University of Toronto in the 1936-37 academic year to begin studies for an M.A. degree. She got a part-time job in the Department of Medical Research, then did her M.A. research there. She was not a brilliant researcher; Hugh Lawford, for whom she worked in the department, remembered that the only remarkable thing Miss Ball ever did was drop a jar of live tubercule bacilli at his feet and then run. The men in the lab looked on her as another sweet kid, an attractive little girl. Fred was attracted to her, and in the fall of 1937 they began to see each other outside the lab. They kept their relationship a secret from almost everyone. Only the Hipwells were in on it from the beginning; Lillian nicknamed Henrietta "Henrie," so if her name was mentioned casually no one would make a connection.

Not much is known about Fred and Henrietta's relationship, partly because their correspondence was destroyed. The courtship was a model of clandestine romance, but had its tempestuous elements. Henrietta seems to have dated other men and, judging by one confused midnight meditation of Banting's, resisted giving herself completely to him outside of marriage. Banting was envious and possessive. "For eleven months I have, by planning, been able to see this young and beautiful creature at will," he wrote to himself in the summer of 1938. "We had had our fights. At times I have been bitterly disappointed in her conduct. She had not been one whom one could rely upon. She has had very much time to herself for I have been very busy and had to go out a great deal. I always told her before so she could know what nights she would be free in advance. And she has often taken advantage of this fact."[20]

In the fall of 1938 Henrietta went to England to see friends and do further studies. After much agonizing, Fred followed her over, determined to reach some kind of understanding. He was terribly afraid of the relationship – worried about Henrie's youth and apparent fickleness, afraid he was heading for a repetition of his first marriage. Sadie Gairns, who knew of the affair, thought he was, and told Fred it wouldn't work. Her patience with her boss exhausted, Miss Gairns was threatening to leave the lab. Another close friend, Bill Franks, was advising him not to marry Henrietta, but just to set her up as his mistress. During the crossing to England, Fred agonized about the situation, writing out his loneliness and turmoil in long letters never sent:

I did love that girl. With me it was true and I wanted a home and house full of children. But I must have honesty, truth, and one hundred percent. I think she has the makings of a 2nd Marion. Why do I pick that sort? I am so unhappy and so lonely and here I am nearly fifty and have not got a home. . . .

. . . I love her, and have loved her and am not ashamed to admit it. I love her because I see in her a female with a splendid body that would have strong babies. I am not interested in social life or position. I am only interested in my research and my home – and I want a family – and a large family – I want the baby daughters . . . I have so many dreams that have not come true – so many things to do yet in life. I got to look after this family right away or it will be too late.

Fred and Henrie reached an understanding in England, consummated by several days in London registered as man and wife. They were married the next June in a private ceremony by the Reverend Peter Addison, Fred's old minister from Alliston. Only the Hipwells, Mrs. Ball and an uncle were present. Dr. and Mrs. Banting – actually Sir Frederick and Henrietta, Lady Banting – spent a short honeymoon in Penetang on the shores of Georgian Bay before returning to Toronto to 205 Rosedale Heights Drive. The boys in the lab were astounded when they heard that Fred had married. Ed Hall had been kept so much in the dark that he didn't know who the bride was.

Banting had stopped talking about Russia; his leftist sympathies did not lead to any contribution to the efforts to support the Republicans in the Spanish Civil War other than a single letter of support for a committee organizing aid. Political events only interested him insofar as they got in the way of his support for medical research or pointed to the coming of another war in Europe. During the Czechoslovakian crisis in the autumn of 1938, when war seemed imminent, Banting called his department together to discuss the situation. It was agreed to offer the whole services of the Department of Medical Research to the National Research Council. Banting wrote Andrew McNaughton to convey the offer, adding that useful work could be done organizing Canadian supplies of vaccines, studying the effect of gases on the lungs and looking into "the whole subject of medical warfare."[21] Banting was disgusted with Canada's enthusiasm for Neville Chamberlain's policy of appeasing Hitler. His former associates do not agree on Banting's exact reaction to the news that war had been averted by the Munich agreement, more or less giving Hitler his way: some think he said "Balls!"; others remember "Bullshit!"

General McNaughton responded to Banting's offer of help by inquiring about the state of British work on bacteriological warfare, particularly the stockpiling of vaccines. As the urgency of the Czech crisis faded, so did the interest. But another set of problems came to McNaughton's and Banting's attention when Major A.A. James of the Canadian army's medical corps, assigned to Air Training Command, approached Banting in December 1938 hoping to interest him in problems involving aviation medicine.

As men flew higher and faster, it had become gradually clear that a new area of medical research was being opened up. What were the physiological effects of flying at high altitudes, with little oxygen and low air pressure? What happened to the body in high-speed turns and dives when it was subjected to centrifugal forces several times that of gravity? Could the body adjust easily to rapidly ascending or descending through many thousands of feet? What psychological qualities were most desirable in pilots? As war approached, questions like these were becoming increasingly important to medical men interested in aviation. Little research was being done to answer them anywhere, none in Canada.

Banting was at first skeptical, but after several meetings with James that winter, gradually became interested in some of the problems he described. He persuaded several other members of his department to begin thinking about research in the area. He thought there should be a broader, national organization to support aviation medicine research and began discussing it with McNaughton at the NRC and some of the senior officers of the Royal Canadian Air Force. He was able to arrange the establishment of a small inter-departmental committee, the Aviation Medical Research Committee, involving the departments of Defence and Transport and the NRC. It held its first meeting on June 27, 1939, and resolved that the two priorities in the field were work on the body's response to low pressure (which would require the construction of a decompression chamber) and psychological investigations of candidates for flying. The committee drew up a tentative budget of $14,000; in mid-August its request was not just approved, but exceeded, when the Department of National Defence agreed to allot $16,000 from RCAF funds.[22]

In the meantime Banting had ventured a last fling into political expression. In the winter and spring of 1939 a young mining millionaire who owned the Toronto *Globe and Mail*, George McCullagh, tried to create a mass movement of ordinary Canadians disenchanted with politics – with the failure of national politicians to rally to Britain's side, strengthen the country's defences and balance the budget. The Leadership League, as McCullagh called his organization, was dedicated to pressuring the politicians into stopping their pointless bickering; the thing to do was to get on with the job of giving Canada real national leadership.

Banting was impressed with a series of radio talks McCullagh gave on the need for leadership, thinking he had "hit from the shoulder at the vitals of the weakness in Canada." He agreed to appear prominently on the platform with McCullagh and the League's chairman, Herbert Bruce, at a mass rally in Toronto's Maple Leaf Gardens on March 15, 1939. It was reported that Banting had become vice-chairman of the League. But in fact the Leadership League was already fizzling, a nine-days' wonder, and Banting announced that he was too busy to take a permanent post; the vice-chairmanship had been for that one meeting only.[23] Fred's interest in the League had stemmed from his impatience at the lack of preparedness and the general shilly-shallying in international relations of Mackenzie King's Liberal government.

Another quasi-political issue in the last years of peace was the desire of refugee scientists to emigrate to Canada. Banting had gradually shed his anti-semitism, and had no truck whatever with the racist ideas of the Nazis. He allowed his name to be used by a Canadian committee to aid Jewish refugees and gave at least one speech encouraging a liberal policy toward the immigration of Jews. He found it remarkable to total up the number of great scientists produced by central European Jewry.

In specific cases, however, Banting went along with the prevailing policy of admitting only those refugees whose skills could be of use to Canada. When F.C. Blair, Director of the Immigration Branch of the Canadian government, asked him to comment on an application to come to Canada by a former associate of Sigmund Freud, Banting replied that "there are very few doctors in Canada who subscribe to Freud's theories," that there was already a surplus of doctors in Canada, and a man in his sixties was not likely to be useful. An Albanian Jew, a highly recommended surgeon, did not seem to Banting to have the research qualifications he claimed, and therefore "is not the type of immigrant who would benefit Canada by his admission." Banting had visited the lab of yet another supplicant back in 1925 on his Nobel trip, and had been unimpressed with the man's scientific ability or integrity. Canada didn't need him either. It cannot be said that Banting, willing as he was to take in Bruno Mendel and other qualified Jewish scientists, went very far out of his way to help open the doors to Jewish refugees. Not many of his generation of Canadian scientists did, at least at the University of Toronto. When Charles Best was looking for an organic chemist for the Connaught Laboratories early in 1939, he wrote H.H. Dale that "There are presumably expatriate Jews available but we would wish to be very sure of the personality and ability of a candidate. These matters are easier to arrange in the University when there is not too high a proportion of Jewish blood."[24]

Fred and Henrie and the Hipwells had a particularly happy

ten-day holiday in the early summer of 1939 at Billy Ross's former cottage on an island near the mouth of the French River on Georgian Bay. It was now Banting's cottage, for Ross had given the property to him. It came with a loud complement of frogs, who kept the humans awake the first night. Never again: Fred rigged up a lure for frogs and served up a fine dinner of frogs' legs.

For years Banting had been talking, and writing, about retiring from the department, and told several people that he would make the break when he turned fifty, in 1941. He had groomed Ed Hall, who had a flair for administration, to take over. Perhaps he would retire altogether and just paint. Or, more likely, he would abandon his headship and stay on as a Professor of Medical Research, tinkering away to his heart's content at cancer or some other problem. In August 1939, he was reading about dementia praecox and wondering whether enough attention had been paid to a toxic approach to insanity. Perhaps some neuro-toxin in the blood caused mental disorders. Would transfusions, or just drinking large quantities of water, help a manic depressive? "Brain-extracts might conceivably contain enzymes derived from brain-cells which might affect abnormal metabolism of brain." Nothing happened to the mice he injected with blood from a manic depressive human.[25]

When it became clear that war between the British Empire and Hitler's Germany would soon begin, Banting called a departmental meeting and told everyone not to join the armed forces. They would be needed in the lab to work on military research. When war became more imminent, Fred became one of the first Torontonians to re-enlist in the army. Until his new uniform came, Captain Banting wore an old First World War outfit that Fred Hipwell had kept in storage.

CHAPTER TWELVE

Warrior Scientist

"I join with mixed feelings – I hate war . . . I have all the fears of shells and bombs that anyone, no matter how cowardly, ever had. I am upset by the noise of the drop of water from a leaking tap. I have as deep a sense of inward fear in the presence of danger as any man ever felt. I suffer just as severe a reaction after I have passed thro' danger to safety as ever experienced by anyone. Yet my country is at war . . ."[1]

It was a time for even frightened men to prepare to go to war. Banting had rejoined his old unit in the Royal Canadian Army Medical Corps, No. 15 General Hospital, agreeing to serve as pathologist. Despite all the talk to his department about serving as researchers on the home front, his first instinct was to get into a unit that would get him abroad, near the fighting. Of course it was quixotic, not just because Banting was forty-eight years old, but in view of all the responsibilities he had for medical research, including aviation medicine, in Canada. Banting was too valuable to be allowed to become just another medical officer. He was promoted to major and told to carry on with his research and NRC work. He ought to have been promoted to a considerably higher rank, but was not interested, wanting to be an ordinary medical officer like any of the boys.

Banting toyed with a compromise scheme that would make him a kind of research director in the field. He and Hall and some of the others in the department worked up a plan for a special medical research unit which would serve as an adjunct to the RCAMC. It would be located in a university town behind the lines and delve into all the problems of chemical and biological warfare, neurophysiology, chemotherapy, and so on, that the fighting posed. In mid-September Banting was in Ottawa, meeting with anyone who would listen to him, to urge quick approval of this project and other plans that A.A. James and some of the lab people were drawing up for aviation medical research.

In the chaotic early weeks of the war all sorts of well-meaning people were proposing a host of enthusiastic schemes to overworked military authorities and civil servants. When Banting and Hall's memorandum finally got to a senior officer of the RCAMC, he dissected it clause by clause, and after finding out what the British were doing concluded that most medical research was better done at home in Canada. Banting had already cabled both the Medical Research Council in London and the British aviation medicine experts offering Canada's help. It gradually dawned on both British and Canadians that some kind of personal liaison would be necessary to plan a coordinated research effort.

The researchers were thinking up ideas faster than an organization could be put in place. The most eager of Banting's team was Bill Franks, who for several months had been thinking about the problem of flyers blacking out when subjected to high gravity forces in dives and turns. Franks had often used a centrifuge in his cancer research. When his spinning test tubes were sometimes smashed by the high centrifugal force, Franks had found that he could counter the pressure by suspending them in water. He wondered whether there might not be some way of applying the principle to humans. When the war started, he decided to find out. His first step was to test mice in the centrifuge: Franks would put a mouse into a rubber condom, tie it in firmly (the cords looked like little bow ties, one of the observers remembered), suspend the condom in a container of water, and give it a whirl. The hydrostatic pressure of the water seemed to protect the mice from the centrifugal forces, enabling them to endure many times the strength of gravity, forces that normally would have killed them.

Franks needed money to keep on developing his idea. Learning that Harry McLean, a wealthy, eccentric businessman might be persuaded to support the work, Franks and Banting went to see McLean in his mansion in Merrickville, Ontario, where, according to Banting, he was "the big toad of the ville." The scientists arrived early one morning in mid-October. McLean was drunk, Banting wrote in his diary. "He insisted that we have a John [Tom?] Collins. We then had breakfast. I was all for getting out. However after

255

breakfast he assumed a business-like manner & wanted to know what we wanted. When Franks was half through McLean said – How much will it cost? – $5,000 – I will give it to you – and nothing more was said about it. Conversation turned to the Holy Bulls in the Bank in Calcutta and the Holy Cow that blocked traffic."[3]

Early in the war they had a visit to the lab from a refugee German chemist who wanted to turn over a formula he possessed for an antidote to mustard gas, a commonly used poison in the First World War that burns and blisters the skin. Hall and Lucas made up the preparation according to the secret formula. They tested it on animals and then several members of the department, including Banting, tested it on themselves. The antidote seemed to work fairly well against small mustard gas burns on the arm, so perhaps the pain Banting suffered for a week from the untreated control burn was worth it. Banting passed the prescription for anti-mustard gas to the NRC, which forwarded it to the Medical Research Council in Britain.[4]

As head of the NRC's Associate Committee on Medical Research, Banting was the logical Canadian to go to England to study the situation there and determine how Canada could best contribute. An old acquaintance from diabetes work, Israel Rabinowitch of Montreal, was also chosen to go. Rabinowitch had been studying gas toxicology for many years, and had volunteered his services to the NRC as an expert on poison gas. Although McNaughton already had some work under way at the NRC, mostly on anti-gas respirators, he thought it would be useful if Rabinowitch scouted developments in Britain with a view to organizing a research program back in Canada.[5]

Another Canadian researcher who wanted to go to Britain was Charles Best. As a result of his graduate work with Dale in England, Best had many friends in high places in British medical research who thought very highly of his ability. When Best received a letter from A.V. Hill, the secretary of the Royal Society, describing the urgent need for liaison, he asked Banting if he might go over. Neither Hill nor Best knew of the plans for a Banting-Rabinowitch trip. Banting obligingly suggested that Best come with them. But neither McNaughton, who was leaving the NRC to take command of the Canadian division en route to Britain, nor his successor, C.J. Mackenzie from the University of Saskatchewan, was very enthusiastic about Best making the trip. Not only was there no good reason for Best going along in addition to Banting, but he had done something to annoy the NRC people in Ottawa. "I got letters from Mackenzie which showed that Charley was trying to doublecross the Associate Committee of Medical Research," Banting wrote in his diary in October. The reference is probably to some act of Best's which was interpreted as an attempt to bypass the NRC, for Mackenzie was extremely anxious that the organization maintain its position as coordinator of all Canadian research. The NRC decided that Best would not join Banting and Rabinowitch on their mission.[6]

Before leaving Canada Banting held endless meetings with Hall, Franks and the other researchers to discuss possible war work. Several members of the lab went to U.S. medical schools to see what was being done there in the aviation medicine field. Hall, who had followed Banting's example and enlisted, was convinced that the RCAMC was hopelessly unable to cope with aviation medical problems and was working with James to press for the creation of a separate RCAF medical service. Banting had his own delicate NRC problem in having to keep aviation medical research within its aegis. As he beat the long path by train from Ottawa to his lab and back again, Banting decided he did not like the Ottawa life – "too many small men in big positions" – and particularly did not like the circle of Ottawa politicians. He was now keeping very detailed diaries, writing down all his opinions, hopes and fears. For example:

October 20: 2.00 A.M. and I am alone in the study – have just been thinking for two hours – mostly about the war being one of brains and scientific ingenuity rather than man power, mass infantry and massacre.

Our job is to lick the Germans under Hitler – and those boys have courage and brains. He is a fool who does underrate the enemy. Our people at Ottawa are peace time rulers who have one eye on the French Canadian vote which keeps them in power & the other eye on the rest of Canada and how they can remain in office. There is no eye left for Canada itself. . . .

McKenzie King – senility, vain glory, poetry, – a Rasputin without even the semblance of a Czarena to seduce – a foxy politician without a constructive idea. . . .

God Help Canada. . .

November 3: Tonight I do not feel that I can settle down to anything. And that feeling reminds me that it has been a long time since I have been able to settle down. The world is all upset and it is impossible to be composed and quiet when everything is upset. In contrast one thinks back to the peaceful days on the farm. There was work and each day there was something of the labour of ones hands to be seen at the end of the day. There was a sense of security – and a peace of mind. One was always content to sleep each night, and one was rested and strong in the mornings.

How different life is now. Tension. One smokes all day and continuously in the evenings. There is always the dry throat, stiff sore tongue & tight tickling cough. One is widest awake at bedtime and therefore requires the assistance of two or three drinks to get to sleep. One never sleeps longer than five or six hours at a stretch. One never is able to sleep in of a morning. One has to have twenty minutes to an hour in the middle of the day, otherwise one can hardly keep the eyes open in the afternoon. Thus the old body and mind drag themselves through strenuous days. . . .

On his forty-eighth birthday Henrie cooked a chicken dinner and Fred blew out all the candles on his cake with one breath. They had a quiet evening together. Three days later, on November 17, he and Rabinowitch sailed from Montreal for England.

The wartime crossing was nerve-wracking. Their blacked-out ship, one of the Duchess liners, sailed without an escort of any kind ("I had thought that there would be a convoy of fifty or sixty freighters with destroyers & cruisers but here we are all alone with not a thing in sight"), away from all the traditional sea-lanes, changing its course every little while to confuse a watching or waiting enemy. The passengers wore their life-belts at all times, never knew where they were, heard no news bulletins. The steward tried to reassure Banting that enemy submarines were not the problem: they were more worried about mines and pocket battle-ships. Banting was not comforted. Rabinowitch, who had a mathematical mind, calculated that it was 185 times more dangerous to be on the ship than to be at home, and that the Germans had a 1 in 200 chance of getting them. Banting slept a lot, read, and worried through page after page in his diary about the danger they were in:

Each morning when one wakens one sort of congratulates oneself for being still safe and still alive and coupled with this pleasurable sensation is the question – will I be alive and well by this time tomorrow. Each meal ends with the mental querie – will this be my last? . . .

Deep inside everyone feels fear. External evidence takes various forms of expression. Some drink, some talk, some keep emotion entirely under control & say nothing. On the whole they are a well disciplined and very intelligent lot. There will be no stampede if the ship were torpedoed or were to hit a mine. . . .

One looks about the cabin & checks the various things that he must wear for warmth. I pick up my boots and loosen the laces so that I can get into them in a hurray. I look to trousers, coat, overcoat and all, before I go to bed. I know well where everything in the Cabin is. I could do it in a minute & in the dark. I have it fixed in my memory – socks, pants, boots, shirt, coat, overcoat. In the pockets I have the urgent things I need. I know where all these things are. Rab in the next room is ready too. He cannot swim but I have promised to tow him if he needs propulsion & he says "Let's talk to each other" if anything happens, and "Keep on talking to each other."

When we are back in Canada – seasoned war time travellers – we'll laugh at all this nonsense. But now it is no mere joke. It is serious.

Banting thought that if the worst came he would give a good account of himself. "The will to do has a great deal to do with everything. I have the will to do in everything except stopping to smoke cigarettes – and on occasions – too much rye." On this sleepless night his mind turned to writing a story about their ship, but the only plots he could think of involved their being torpedoed or captured.

They arrived in London on November 25, and registered in the Victoria Hotel where Fred and Henrie had stayed the year before. The blacked-out city seemed deserted compared to the blazing metropolis, thronged with soldiers and their girls, that Banting had seen in the last war. The fear, of course, was that massive bombing, unlike anything seen in the Great War, could begin at any time. Science and technology had made it possible. Banting had come over to learn all he could about that kind of science and its implications:

Whether we like it or not similar and more diabolical inventions must be made by our scientists. Traditions and sportsmanship must be put on the shelf while we are dealing with Mr. Hitler and his crew. After the war virtues may be restored. There is no one who believes more firmly than I do that Science was meant for the benefit of mankind, but our enemy has used science for the invention of most destructive weapons of warfare. Therefore we must do likewise. Hitler will win this war if we do not. No amount of bravery, no amount of human flesh will win against scientific weapons of destruction. Self-preservation demands that we use the same weapons.

Banting had bet "Rab" they would hear an air-raid siren within 24 hours of reaching London. Nothing in fact was happening during these months of the "phoney war" between the fall of Poland and the German blitzkrieg in the spring of 1940. On their first night in London, Banting and Rabinowitch took in the first British war movie, *The Lion Has Wings*. When the air-raid siren in the movie went off, Banting ordered Rab to pay up.

Not much was happening on the medical warfare front either, for the British were not interested in sharing their secrets with visiting Canadians until many more letters of introduction had been written. "The old boy struck me as being a proper old English ass," Banting wrote after his first day's interview with Air Marshal Richardson. "Arrangements will undoubtedly be made ultimately – but it will take time and energy to penetrate senile inertia & red tape."

In fact the letters were quickly written at Canada House and the red tape dissolved. Banting and Rabinowitch were given complete access to everything the British were doing. Banting spent a strenuous three weeks touring research laboratories, universities, military bases and, most impressive of all, the extensive gas warfare research facility at Porton Downs, near Salisbury. British scientists gave their time generously ("Dale was never so nice") to talk over what they were doing and speculate with Banting about the future course of war research and the role Canada might play. The doctors often talked shock, worried about trench nephritis, speculated on how many vitamins could be packed into chocolate bars or cheese snacks for the soldiers. These were still the pioneer days of military medicine, before there was any hint of the most important British wartime medical achievement, the development of penicillin. Consequently, a fairly typical conversation Banting had on the trip was this discussion with a bacteriologist of the problem of streptococcal infection of wounds:

> He discussed the new form of one treatment that was developed in Spain during the revolution. This form of treatment consists of the immediate surgical removal of all tag ends of tissue in the wound, followed by the filling of the wound with plastic plaster of paris, followed by the application of a plaster cast, which rendered immovable the area of the wound. The plaster cast is left on in position for many days. A high degree of odour may develop, but this is not to be taken as an indication that the cast should be removed. The temperature often rises to 102 degrees. If, however, the temperature should go higher, or be accompanied with throbbing pain, the plaster cast is removed and irrigation or hot water treatment is administered. Col. Colbrook is anxious to know if the plaster cast treatment delays or prevents the streptococcic infection. He also desires to know at what time this infection gains entrance to the wound.[7]

Banting spent much of his time investigating British research in aviation medicine. He visited air bases, talking to aircrew and their medical officers, "and found out more about Spitfires and Wellington bombers than about research," he wrote Ed Hall. Mainly he found out that the pilots were fed up with irregular hours, lack of action and the limitations of their aircraft. The pilots of Blenheims doing night patrol told the Canadian that they wouldn't be able to see a German plane even if there was one in the sky. "The whole nosecap of their particular type of aeroplane is of glass which frosts over, and in order to see ahead of him, the pilot must open a window to the left of him."[8]

The British were only just beginning their program of serious aviation medical research. Their laboratories at the RAF's Farnborough complex were still housed in a lean-to; it was hard to schedule experimental flights because of bad weather and tight controls on military airspace. One aviation researcher Banting talked with had thought of trying to protect pilots with a water-jacket, the same idea Franks was working on back in Canada, but had not as yet gotten around to doing anything. The Britishers seemed eager to have the Canadians go ahead in this and other areas of aviation medicine, and Banting wrote Hall urging that "the work of Franks and your own group be carried on as rapidly as possible. In regard to Air Medical Research I feel that we are as far on in Canada as they are here."[9]

Medical men, especially psychologists, were deeply involved in research to develop reliable intelligence, personality and physical tests for pilots. One of Banting's University of Toronto colleagues, E.A. Bott of the Psychology Department, had been active from the beginning developing tests for Canadian airmen. On this trip Banting visited the Cambridge lab of the leading British researcher in that area, Frederic C. Bartlett. Bartlett had room after room full of elaborate testing apparatus, was too busy to give Banting more than a short interview, and told him his technicians were too busy to duplicate any of the apparatus to send back to Canada. In his formal report to the NRC, Banting concluded that "The whole visit to Professor Bartlett's laboratory gave me an impression of hyper-mechanization. As far as I could see, very little attention was paid to the pilot under examination as to his character, personality, courage or intestinal fortitude."[10] In his diary he was more pungent:

> I do not know if anyone else ever felt as I do about Cambridge, but I feel that they think they are God's annointed – they know every-thing worth knowing – no one else could possibly know anything more. God gives all ideas to Cambridge and they take the pick of them to work on but know of all the answers to all the questions. The whole visit to Bartlett's lab gave me the impression that there was a hypertrophy of mechanization – a hellofalotof Louie – a heavy swing of the pendulum off into astronomical space. A new instrument is invented every week but damned little done in the way of working out the problems of how to choose a man for piloting a war machine. . . .

In the last years of peace Banting had worried that another war would feature the use of diabolical chemicals and bacteria. His visits to the Ministry of Supply's Chemical Defence Experimental Station at Porton, where any one of the ten buildings contained more facilities than his whole department, reassured him that Britain was fully prepared for gas warfare. They had a superb team of well-equipped specialists at work, were being kept informed of enemy activity in gas warfare by military intelligence, and were constantly testing gas, antidotes and new equipment. The Toronto anti-mustard gas solution had been tested at Porton and Banting was shown the findings: it was not a bad cleansing fluid, but was not nearly as effective as the British ointment that was already standard equipment.

Banting realized that Canada need not try to duplicate Porton. The experts there advised him that Canada should contribute by sending over scientists to work at the station. Banting agreed, and cabled the suggestion home to the NRC as a recommendation. He specifically suggested that Charles Best should come over to work at Porton.[11] In the meantime, Rabinowitch, who had come over for the purpose, immersed himself in gases and the work at Porton, taking special training courses and then instructing the officers of the newly arrived First Canadian Division in the principles of gas warfare.

Banting also found out the prevailing British opinion on biological warfare. They were obviously taking chemical warfare very seriously, but, as they had felt before the war, the British were skeptical of most suggestions about ways of waging germ warfare. Banting saw and copied a Medical Research Council set of notes on the subject. Its conclusions included the following:

> . . . the aeroplane is, for most purposes, a very clumsy and inefficient bacteriological instrument, because it cannot usually fulfil the essential condition of depositing the selected infecting agent in the right place at the right time. . . . We need not be greatly disturbed by the prospect of the release of any possible number of plague-infected rats from aeroplanes. . . . We have strong reasons for believing that, even if a certain number of primary anthrax infections could be produced, the disease would not spread. . . . The dropping of infected lice [with typhus] seems no more likely to be effective than the dropping of the infecting organism. The louse does not survive for long apart from a man on whom it can feed and very few of the lice dropped from an aeroplane would be likely to land in a situation convenient to themselves. . . . It has been suggested that the enemy intends to release from aeroplanes mosquitoes infected with yellow fever. This suggestion, like so many others, ignores our knowledge of the complex biological factors concerned in the spread of infectious disease. . . .[12]

During his British visit Banting saw only one small experiment being done relating to bacterial warfare, a project on the sterilization of air. The Cambridge researchers, whose attitude so offended Banting, told him England had nothing to worry about from biological warfare. Any attempts at infecting the population or the livestock could be controlled. Sir Edward Mellanby, secretary of the Medical Research Council, told him the MRC had no interest in taking up the subject; neither England nor Germany would use bacteria in warfare, and if they did there would be no epidemics. Mellanby echoed expert British opinion that dropping high explosives on people was far more effective than dropping bacteria.

But Banting talked to other Englishmen, including the Chief Pathologist of the Royal Army Medical Corps, who believed the menace of German-induced bacteria was worth taking seriously. Privately they fed his lurid suspicions that Germany was planning something, and encouraged his view that more work should be undertaken. On December 22 Banting met McNaughton, and told him of the British medical research situation. "And finally I told him about the greatest of my worries – namely what to do about research on Bacterial Warfare. We discussed the problem for some time and in a characteristic manner he decided what I should do – I should write a memorandum for the National Research Council." McNaughton would make sure the memorandum was presented to the British authorities. "If the British Army & Research Council expressed the desire that research should be done on the matter – then I would be fully armed with the necessary credentials to approach the subjects and ask the support of the National Research Council of Canada and of the Canadian Government."

He had expected to head back to Canada before the New Year, but Banting interpreted McNaughton's request as virtually an order to stay in Britain until his memorandum had been written and dealt with. He spent the Christmas season steeping himself in the subject of bacteriological warfare. On Christmas Day he took time to have dinner with some friends of Henrietta's, one of whom, Eileen Parton, he employed as a stenographer. Before dinner they played every nursery card game Fred could remember. After dinner he showed them how he could crack walnuts with his bare hands. On the evening of Boxing Day he got nicely started on the memorandum:

Tonight as usual I undressed early and have been working in pyjamas all evening. I have a nice fire going. I got some good ideas concerning Bacterial Warfare during the day. My imagination is working and I feel it is my own fault if I cannot cause the whole damned British war council to change their minds – and then I will have to win over these stoggy British Bacteriologists – and then I can go home and meet Mr. Mackenzie King and talk nicely for the hundred thousand dollars that I want immediately for urgent and necessary work. I still do not understand why a scientist should have to spend his time and energy on the means rather than the ends. It should be evident to anyone. But these things sent to try us, help to build up what is in us. Life is a battle . . .

Banting's nineteen-page "Memorandum on the Present Situation Regarding Bacterial Warfare" was rather alarmist in tone; he tended simply to disregard the difficulties the British experts saw in the way of spreading bacteria by shells or aeroplanes. But he also made a certain amount of sense in arguing that even the British believed secret agents could infect water supplies and other facilities in a damaging way, and they had not taken account of all other possible ways of transmitting bacteria and viruses. Banting himself had many ideas for spreading bacteria, ranging from infected propaganda leaflets to creating artificial insect bites from bacterial-impregnated silica particles. As well, he argued, research on how to take the biological offensive was necessary if the threat to retaliate was to be a credible deterrent. He could not see why there was not a parallel between biological warfare and chemical warfare – both were outlawed by various international conventions, but the British were only taking the latter seriously. Banting concluded his memorandum by recommending that an organization similar to the Porton anti-gas establishment be created "to protect both man and animals against bacteriological warfare." It would engage in extensive research in methods of both offensive and defensive biological warfare. The National Research Council of Canada, Banting suggested, would be pleased to take on the responsibility if a properly channelled request came from the British government.[13]

Canada's High Commissioner to Great Britain (and Banting's old Arts and Letters Club friend), Vincent Massey, arranged for Banting to see the British minister who had responsibility for chemical and biological warfare, Lord Hankey. Banting described their interview:

The good Lord set forth all that had been done and evidently wanted a little praise which I gave him but shot the research right at him. He stood the shock very well. I tried to make only one point – the necessity for immediate research into Bacterial warfare. Mr. Massey supported the arguments, as he had read the memo. Lord Hankie asked for a copy – and said it certainly should be presented to the committee [probably the Microbiological Warfare Research Committee].

He said it was the first thing that had come their way that had definite proposals or that was backed by a scientist of standing. He wanted to know if I had talked with scientific men about the project – I said I had a little. He asked me if I would be available to meet the committee, and I said I was at his service.

As he listened to the conversation, Vincent Massey reflected to himself that Canada had rarely produced anyone who combined as many distinguished qualities as Banting, "including the rarest of all – modesty."[14]

Banting waited around London for several weeks wondering about the fate of his memo. If a big biological warfare program was approved, would he have a role to play in it? Would that role be on the spot in England or back in Canada? If nothing developed in that line, perhaps he should now join up with his unit, No. 15 General Hospital, which was about to arrive in England. He also had a job offer at Canadian Military Headquarters in London, and he had shown an interest in heading up some research facilities being constructed as part of a Canadian Red Cross establishment at Taplow.

While he waited, Banting filled some of his time writing about the discovery of insulin. He had told Rabinowitch the whole story on the way over, and Rab had urged him to get it down on paper. After all, neither of them might survive the war. Banting noted in his diary that his "objection" to the story was the "many sordid things connected with the discovery." Then, one night early in his London stay, Banting wandered into a newsreel theatre and, to his surprise, saw a film about the discovery. He didn't much care for the film ("extremely artificial . . . smacked of Hollywood . . . not convincing to me and I watched it entirely unmoved"), but a few days later started writing out his history, "The Story of Insulin." He wrote compulsively, page after page, reliving the past until his arm and fingers hurt. By the time he put the history aside, unfinished, never to be revised, he had written about 30,000 words in longhand. Another way of killing time was to drop in to the cinema, an ideal program being a combination of the latest newsreel with Donald Duck cartoons.

Banting did not meet the Microbiological Warfare Research Committee. He learned indirectly that the British specialists who saw his memorandum were highly critical of it and did not support his recommendations. Apparently they saw no reason to discuss it further with him. He had been talking to many people in England about other "far-out" ideas for diabolical weapons of war, or research that should be done – the kind of far-fetched idea talk that scientists, inventors and tinkerers glory in, and Lord Hankey was impressed enough to have him meet with a secret committee on "mad ideas" chaired by the distinguished physicist, Edward Appleton. Banting passed on to the British what he recorded in Holmesian fashion as the "ideas concerning poison by catalytic agent", "the silica cloud platinum black", "the idea of the hard metal overhead shrapnel & the poisoning of the fish idea." After the interview he wondered "if these birds were taking me for a ride or if they were sincere. They knew or seemed to know a devil of a lot about all aspects of war. They flattered me and said that all these ideas were new and that they seldom had three new ideas in one day."

The group in the department back in Toronto began to wonder if Fred was ever going to come home. It would be just like him to take an army posting and stay there for the rest of the war. To most of his friends, who felt he was the sparkplug of Canadian medical research, the prospect was alarming. Velyien Henderson finally cabled Banting urging a return to his duties in Canada. Ed Hall, however, who was making great progress organizing the aviation medicine work, was in no hurry for Banting to return, assuring him that both the Red Cross research and the biological warfare project were great opportunities. Hall could hold the fort "until your return, whether it be next week or three years hence."[15]

On January 28, 1940, McNaughton told Banting he could take the next boat home. Banting left Britain three days later, having apparently failed to get approval for his ambitious BW project.

Banting never knew that Lord Hankey, who had been interested in chemical-bacteriological warfare for years, did mention his paper to the British cabinet later that month, arguing that although Banting "took a somewhat alarmist view" of the situation, Hankey might ask for authority for a further program in Britain. Banting's memorandum seems to have been used as a talking-point in the internal British debate about whether to engage in BW research. By 1941 those who shared Banting's view, or some more sophisticated variation of it, had won their case, and an extensive Microbiological Research Establishment was developed at Porton.[16]

The trip home was the roughest crossing Banting had ever experienced. One night in his cabin a sudden roll pitched him head-first into a bulkhead, knocking him out. Although the German propagandist, Lord Haw-Haw, had announced the departure of their ship on what he said would be its last voyage, the submarine menace was in temporary recession. Banting spent his time writing (he listed the books he wanted to write as soon as there was time after the war: his autobiography, a history of the Alliston area, Indian medicine, medical research, the story of aviation medicine) and thinking, concentrating on ideas for making war. Two that he thought worth putting down on paper were for a harpoon gun to remove barbed wire from no man's land, and the concept of the "splat shell," a projectile full of wet cement which could splat onto pillboxes and other enemy fortifications, harden, and seal them shut. Probably trench mortar splat shells could be made for use against machine gun emplacements. "The only means of defence is by the use of 'pushers' while the wet cement is fresh – before it has time to harden."[17]

C.J. Mackenzie was in his ninety-third year, living quietly in his retirement in Ottawa, when he described to me how Banting brought these and thirteen other ideas to him directly on arriving in Canada. Mackenzie listened patiently and told Banting they were all impractical. Banting thanked Mackenzie and said, "Now I'm relieved. I can go home and have a drink with my wife."

Not many of the ideas Banting had picked up in the British visit had amounted to much. Bacterial warfare seemed lost in the maze of British bureaucracy. The idea he had cabled home of having Canadian scientists sent to work at Porton got lost in the undergrowth of Canadian wartime planning; no one seemed to know how to authorize and finance such a scheme. In any case, the one scientist Banting had named as a possible worker at Porton, Best, had no desire to go there and was relieved that the proposal was impractical.[18] Banting did not bring back many ideas for Canadian work in the several areas of relevant medical research, and in fact had not formed particularly close ties with the medical research establishment in Britain, headed by Mellanby at the Medical Research Council, H.H. Dale, and A.V. Hill of the Royal Society. Dale wrote Best of his disappointment that Banting had spent so much time at Porton. When Banting did spend time with Dale and the other physiologists, however, they had mixed feelings, for they found him so out of his depth in serious discussions of medical research that it was something of a problem to know what to do with him. Dale and the other leading Britishers would have much preferred to have Best as the Canadian working with them.[19]

The one area in which Banting had a green light from the British was aviation medicine, partly because his department was off and running anyway. While Banting in England was learning that the British had not done much in the field, and had not previously told the Canadians the details of what they had done for fear of it leaking to the neutral United States, Ed Hall and others in the department had gone off to the United States and become fully briefed on the state of the art by top-notch American aviation experts. Hall had surveyed the field, decided what problems needed looking into, bought samples of U.S. oxygen equipment that was better than anything available in Britain or Canada, and even placed an order for a decompression chamber to be installed in the department. As Hall had found through taking his own test "flights" in a chamber at the Mayo Clinic, it was a marvellous tool for researching the effect of high altitude and the impact of rapid pressure changes during ascent and descent. The British had only one chamber themselves, a Great War relic at Oxford.[20]

Bill Franks had been taking real flights that winter, the first airplane flights of his life, testing the liquid flying suit he had built. It seemed to work, but had a lot of wrinkles to be ironed out. For one thing, Franks discovered, only certain parts of the body needed the counter-pressure of the water in the suit; his tests of the first, uncompartmentalized water suit were very painful, especially in areas where men are sensitive. Airborne testing was expensive and somewhat hazardous. It seemed sensible to build some kind of centrifuge or accelerator on terra firma that would be big enough to whirl around a human being for the ongoing experiments. Franks spent the winter hard at work on his suit and on plans for the human centrifuge/accelerator.

Banting was surprised and delighted by the progress the aviation medicine research team had made while he was gone. His first priority became to do all he could to further the work. Much more money was needed, as well as clearer coordination with and from Ottawa. The only government funding had been the $16,000 granted to the interdepartmental Aviation Medical Research Committee set up in the summer of 1939. Banting and Hall had spent another $30,000 from their departmental funds and located other private "angels" to support Franks' fight against the forces of gravity.

Banting decided that the Aviation Medical Research Committee should be reorganized under the umbrella of the NRC, becoming a body parallel to the Associate Committee on Medical Research. He spent many hours, a lot of them on the train to and from Ottawa, planning the future of the work. An Associate Committee on Aviation Medical Research would be formed, and projects would go forward requiring $109,000 in new money. These would include construction of the accelerator for Franks as well as a new decompression chamber in a cold room to simulate the low temperature in addition to the low pressure of high altitudes. Banting got the proposal accepted in principle by all the key people and departments involved, then cooled his heels waiting for final government approval while the politicians fought and recovered from a general election.[21]

He wanted to get aviation medicine on a firm foundation and then get back to England to work with the army. "I have been down at Ottawa so often and have met so many of *the powers that be*, and talked with them that I am greatly afraid that I am becoming a slippery slimy politician." His other semi-political work in Ottawa involved discussions on gas warfare generated by his visit and Israel Rabinowitch's detailed recommendations. The NRC already had begun research on gases and respirators through the secret activities of its innocent-sounding Committee on Container Proofing. Banting was instrumental in having its powers greatly enlarged.[22]

He was still waiting for his aviation proposals to be acted on in April 1940 when serious fighting resumed with the German attack on Denmark and Norway. Now all his responsibilities weighed more heavily under the added burden of worry about the war. Part of his diary entry for April 17 is a good sample of his daily routine, as well as the state of Canadian medical research that spring:

This afternoon's mail brought letters from McGill – psychologists of the Penfield group that apparently are not working in nor do they know anything of the activities of Prof's Tate & Morgan of psychology at McGill let alone Bott and the Queen's group or Humphrey's & Co. I believe we will have to have an Associate Committee on Psychology in the NRC.

Another letter from McGill's prof. of Anatomy concerning Selye's work on shock is startling in that it states that a specific for surgical shock has been discovoured. They desire to publish.

Best wants to go to England & have his way paid by the Dept of Defence or by the National Research Council.

Franks gave a demonstration at 5.20 p.m. of the anatomy of the Eustacian Tube, & ear trouble in Flying personnel.

I had a talk with Lt. Col. James on the phone & discussed among other things the "Jacket pressure Chamber". It is an idea as far as I know, originating with James, & modified by me – of impregnating Franks cloth with rubber and encasing a man under pressure at high altitude – supplying O_2, absorbing CO_2 w soda lime. – having a valve for safety. This thing is theoretically sound & should be economical to produce – lucite windows – a door rubber sealed by pressure, cylindrical in shape, with the joy stick inside & allowing freedom of movement for the pilot. I think that the whole thing could be made at a cost of a few hundred dollars for trial – step by step. . . .

I am so tired that I cannot sleep nor do I want to go to bed. I feel that I want time alone to think what is best to do. If I could only get sleep and be rested & fit for my work I would be happy. On top of all these things I have to draft a memorandum on the Medical equipment required for our troops when they go to Greenland. Diet, high fat, vitamines, infectious diseases, clothing, frost bites, lice, drugs, etc etc are circulating through my head. The protection of the native against infectious diseases is important. T.B. veneral disease, psychology of troops going on such a mission, are added problems.

It is hardly possible for one small brain to accomplish the various tasks that I set myself. But it is war. My greatest worry is that I make mistakes, & because of my negligence that our troops may suffer, or even that men may lose their lives. – Despite everything life is sweet. I would hate to lose my own life – I hate to think of the sacrifice of life in war.

Banting experienced some of the hardships of the fighting men vicariously when he took "flights" in the American-made decompression chamber Hall had procured for the department. Fred was often a human guinea pig in the tests of this or that drug to help clear the aural passages during descent, some new piece of oxygen apparatus, some experiment to observe the development of air embolism or "the bends," when gas bubbles form in the blood at high altitude. He also became a guinea pig again in the department's ongoing mustard gas research project. A long series of experiments was carried out treating mustard gas wounds in the eyes of rabbits. (Wartime research was particularly hard on animals; to test treatments intended for soldiers, scientists had to mutilate the animals the same way the gas and bombs mutilated humans.) In this case, the tests led to the conclusion that cold water was as good a preventative of lesions as could be found. Would treatment with ice-packs prevent mustard gas burns developing on human skin?

Most medical researchers of Banting's generation tested their discoveries on themselves; Fred was by no means the only mustard gas volunteer. But he did have a tendency to want to fly higher than anyone else, and to try more mustard gas. Early in May, after tests on his left arm and left leg, he allowed 100 milligrams of mustard gas to be spread on a 6½ by 1½ inch area of his lower right leg. It was left on for five minutes, then blotted off, and five minutes later ice was applied. The situation looked good until the next afternoon when he was working in his garden and a grass fire broke out. While he was fighting it, the ice on his wound melted. His leg got very hot and began to blister. It became a very nasty mustard gas wound, "one holy terror," which kept him in pain and sometimes immobilized for much of the next two months. Some of his friends worried that he might lose the leg. Despite the distressing results of the test, the Toronto ice-cube treatment for mustard gas seemed successful enough to forward by secret cipher to Sir Edward Mellanby at the Medical Research Council.[23]

The British cannot have been impressed by this latest message from Banting's department. Although their aviation medicine people were very supportive of the Canadian effort, the medical research heads kept puzzling over the Banting-Best situation. A.V. Hill, who visited Canada early in May, contrasted the "very big" aviation medicine program in Banting's department with the under-utilization of Best's Physiology Department. He could not understand why Best's desire to come to England was being frustrated. Hill spoke to Mackenzie of the NRC about this, Banting noted, "But

Mackenzie told Hill what had been done and the manner in which Best had acted." The British now realized that Best was not in the best graces of the Canadian research establishment. It was all exasperating to Dale, who had such little regard for Banting's capacity to do his job: "Frankly I am afraid that the Canadian Banting complex is at the moment detrimental. He is sent over here, and spends nearly all his time & interest at Porton, goes back to Canada, and apparently tries to push Best off to Porton, and loses interest in him when he does not go; and has now been given leading authority over another field of researches, namely aviation, for which he has no obvious qualifications."[24]

Banting himself had few illusions about his abilities, and no real desire to carry on this political-administrative work. He thought back to the relatively easy life of the last war. "I was at all times under orders. There was no great responsibility. In this war all is different. I never feel free of responsibility. If I take time off I feel as though I were stealing. I miss the contact with soldiers. Effects of work are so remote that it is sometimes difficult to see any connection with the army." He often remarked to friends and correspondents that he would sooner be a battalion medical officer than do any other job in the army.

Nursing his mustard gas wound, using work as an ointment, he was more or less resigned to his Canadian duties when the German invasion of France and the Low Countries rekindled his desire to be back near the front: "I have an all consuming desire to be in England or Belgium – closer to the sight of action." On the afternoon of May 11, 1940, he received an order to report to Ottawa. He took the night train in a fairly gloomy mood about his role in Canada: "There has been so much inertia this last 3 months that I am disgusted with any hope of accomplishment. The aviation selection is progressing under Hall & the black out suit is progressing under Franks. But I feel personally that I am of no value. Irwin & Lucas have something in the cold (ice cube) applications for mustard gas. But more & more I am becoming an administrator and a politician for the obtaining of funds."

To his delight, Banting found that there had been a request for his services from Canadian Military Headquarters in London. McNaughton and the Canadian medical people on the spot wanted him to come over to coordinate Canadian medical research in Britain. He spent a long day talking over the proposition with

Mackenzie, and apparently making plans to leave. Back in Toronto the next day he ran into a snag when Sadie Gairns told him bluntly she would leave the department if he went overseas. Then Mackenzie phoned from Ottawa to say he had talked with Banting's army superior and they had decided to keep him in Canada until the beginning of July. Mackenzie believed Banting was indispensable to the smooth progress of wartime medical research in Canada. A few weeks later he laid down the law: Banting would not go overseas in July either. There was more research work to be done in Canada than could possibly be done in England under current conditions. "I know that there will be a certain amount of disappointment on your part, but I do feel that your duty is here," Mackenzie wrote.[25]

CHAPTER THIRTEEN

"A Dark Sense of Duty"

I
t was hard to think about anything but the war in the dark summer of 1940. Every night the radio told of Nazi advances, Allied retreats, the collapse of Holland, Leopold's surrender in Belgium, Dunkirk, the fall of France, England alone, the beginning of the Battle of Britain. Himself a casualty of gas warfare in his own lab, Banting wrote thousands of words in his diary that spring and summer about the war, the Germans, Britain and politics. Private life, private thoughts, faded as the fate of the world seemed to be hanging in the balance. And there was so damned little a Canadian could do about it. Here are samples from Banting's diary in late May:

May 20:

It is impossible to concentrate on anything. I have not been able to read a book or do any quiet thinking. Even dear old England may be invaded at any time. This massive Brute Force of the German is rampant and threatens the destruction of Civilization. It is all too horrible for words.

May 25:

With Germany at the Channel ports, and Italy on the eve of war, and France & England with their backs to the wall, and King still Prime Minister; and Canada doing very little, a Canadian cannot help but feel low. One sees it in ones friends – particularly those who served in the last war and are too old for this war. . . .

The curse of it all is that Germany itself remains free from destruction, while her neighbouring neutrals are layed low by bombs & shells & fire. I hope that every city in Germany may be levelled to the ground, and that these brutal people may know what war is.

May 27:

Earlier in the day I told Miss Gairns that there was only one man who could bring Canada to its maximum of usefulness – and that was McNaughton. That man has everything. He is the most honest man I have ever met. He combines professional knowledge with executive capacity. He is a human dynamo. He is non political. He has the confidence of every Canadian high & low. I have been turning over and over in my mind all day how it could be brought about that McNaughton could be brought back to Canada, and given the post of Supreme Command. Leave King as Prime Minister to speech, to strut, to glorify himself, and leave members of Cabinet to carry on, yet with McNaughton in Supreme Command – to conscript money & man power.

I have wondered what my duty is. . . .

On the night of June 3, after nine hours of meetings at the NRC, Banting looked out of his window at the Chateau Laurier and saw the lighted beacon on the Peace Tower indicating that Parliament was in session. Although his leg was very sore, he decided to go over to see the Government of Canada in action. There was no security to screen visitors, and hardly anything for them to see: a handful of members of Parliament in the House of Commons chamber listened to a member of the Opposition talking about a grant to beautify Ottawa; a government member drew attention to the costs of the cement sidewalks of Ottawa. The $100,000 being debated for Ottawa municipal improvements was more than the NRC had available to spend on non-military medical research all across Canada. Banting reflected that his party might have been members of the German-American Bund carrying bombs – "but scarcely likely, for our government is Hitler's finest weapon. By their inertia and senile somulance Hitler marches on. . . . It is another world!"

No one in Canada was more determined to pull his weight in the war effort than Fred Banting. He listens to one of J.B. Priestley's moving radio broadcasts from England and writes in his diary: "My life I consecrate to my Country, to my King, to the British Empire. I hold back nothing – because I believe in the cause that is Britain's."

He refuses to take a holiday. All the money he can find goes to the War Loan. He goes to see a war movie, and on the way home feels guilty about not having done anything useful for his King, Empire, or country that day. Banting and Duncan Graham take in an escapist film, Clark Gable and Myrna Loy in a light-hearted romp, and forget the war for an hour or two – "but as we walked home I could not help but think of the millions in Europe that cannot go to a movie or enjoy an hour free from fear. The war was upon us again."

The nearest that peace came to Banting was on summer weekends when he found an hour or two to go back to the land – to dig in his garden, to feed the roses he was nurturing. July 21: "It was quiet in the back garden this afternoon. The roses have never bloomed in such perfusion – in white – red – climbers – yellow & red in the lower bed. I watched a pair of wrens gathering their supper. The train whistle in the distance sounded like rain. The song of birds filled the air. For a few minutes I forgot about the war. Then it came back to me and I felt a little guilty that I had been unfaithful."

Banting's chief service to the war was in fostering the aviation medicine program. It seemed to take forever to design and install the human centrifuge and the cold decompression chamber that had been approved as aids to research in Toronto. There was no room at the Banting Institute, which already had the original decompression chamber, for such major facilities, so both were built at the rapidly growing RCAF No. 1 Initial Training School, built on land bought from the Eglinton Hunt Club at Eglinton Avenue and Avenue Road, several miles north of the University. There were endless snafus in the installations, ranging from complex engineering problems through roadblocks tossed up by air force people who thought the doctors were planning impractical, unneeded research, especially with the accelerator.[1] The cold decompression chamber was finally completed in January 1941. The human centrifuge, the first to be used in the British Commonwealth and for many years the most advanced in the world, was completed in the autumn of 1941.

Banting's personal involvement in aviation medicine after his return from England led to difficulties with Ed Hall, who had made so much early progress with the program in Banting's absence. In the spring of 1940 Hall arranged to have RCAF recruits brought into the Department of Medical Research for trial flights in the decompression chamber to introduce them to anoxia and other physiological effects of flight. The experiences were useful for the airmen, but did little to advance the cause of research, especially when the rapid expansion of air training in Canada meant that the chamber was being used for nothing but the RCAF training flights. Banting became impatient with this situation. On June 5 he had a confrontation with Hall, accusing him of putting the needs of the air force ahead of those of the department. Characteristically, he gave Hall 24 hours to decide whether he was going to give himself to the air force or research. Hall replied by writing a long, pained and ambiguous letter: "If my enthusiasm for the work and my youthful exuberance have given you the impression that I am trying to play a lone hand or to assume responsibility for all those projects or that I fail to collaborate with you I am exceedingly sorry for such was neither my intention nor desire." This annoyed Banting still further.[2]

On June 7, after another meeting with Hall, Banting decided to place Colin Lucas in charge of administering the department. Banting expected complete personal loyalty from his associates; he was no longer sure of Hall. A few weeks later he wrote a long, revealing diary entry about the Hall problem:

> It worries me when Hall rebels & seeks to double cross me. He has been with me for some 12 years during which time he has written some large number of papers. I have promoted him in every possible way. I have loaned him money to buy his house. I have backed his notes. I have provided him with workers, and with facilities for his research. At the beginning he needed me much more than I needed him & now he thinks that I need him & that I cannot get along without him. I fear that he is very ambitious. That he is selfish and that he seeks to undermine me and the department. I fear that I have given him responsibilities that he could not take and that I gave him a position in the scientific world that he could not wholly fill. He is like MacLeod & Best. He is clever. He talks well. He writes well. He impresses the superficial. He, like his audience, lacks depth.

Suffering from too much work and worry, Hall was not well during the summer. Banting, who was working very hard, was not happy with the way the aviation medicine program was going. The air force men were still taking up most of the decompression chamber's time. Franks, who went his own way, seemed to be making slow progress with his flying suit. "The war will be over before he finishes fiddling with the suit," Banting wrote grumpily. Banting thought Hall was "dissipating his energy in worry & coniving". He had heard one rumour that Hall wanted to head an aviation medicine program at McGill. In fact Hall had decided to leave the department, but was choosing to go with the RCAF. The movement he had helped organize to have an RCAF medical unit created separate from the RCAMC had finally succeeded. On September 24, Banting suddenly got a telegram from Hall, who was in Ottawa, saying he had been appointed Director of Aviation Medicine Research for the RCAF, would be taking leave of absence, and wanted to discuss cooperation with the NRC's Associate Committee on Aviation Medicine, as well as with the department.

Banting was furious at what seemed to him both a personal betrayal and an RCAF manoeuvre to bypass the NRC in research matters. He dashed to Ottawa, where he confronted Hall, and the new head of RCAF medicine, Group Captain R.W. Ryan. "It's a vicious cur that bites the hand that feeds him," he began his diary entry that night, and then described the meeting:

About 3:00 p.m. in the library of H.Q., Ryan, [Major J.W.] Tice, Hall came down where I waited. I congratulated Ryan. There was a long pause. We sat down. Ryan outlined the set up for Air Medicine. I told him that [Hall's] telegram was disconcerting. I showed him the telegram. . . . Ryan said that he had not seen the telegram before it was sent.

A number of points were discussed. I explained to Ryan that the NRC was the official scientific body of the Canadian Government & that I desired to have a definition of "Director of Aviation Medical Research," because if he was setting up a director that it was against the policy of all the other Departments of Government.

He then asked if I would cooperate & I said that my idea of cooperation was not doing a thing such as making a research appointment & then discussing it, but discussing it first & coming to an agreement.

Ryan said that he wanted a Research "Senior Officer" & had chosen Hall.

It was three against one.

I said that I had not had cooperation from Hall during the past four or five months. Hall said that he cooperated & I said that he was a liar if he said he had cooperated. And I pointed out that he had not voluntarily come to my office since before June 6 to discuss matters pertaining to Aviation Medical Research . . .

They worked out a modus vivendi. Hall would supervise only clinical research on RCAF personnel. All other aviation medicine research would continue to be channelled through the NRC's Associate Committee. Banting decided he was well rid of Hall: "a double-crosser – a exploiter – a foreflusher – an advertizer – one of unbalanced judgement." Before leaving Ottawa he made it clear to the Deputy Minister that he would not accept a plan of Ryan's to send Hall to England as a representative of Canadian medical research. Banting's name and his evident integrity made his influence with Ottawa bureaucrats decisive. It was decided that Hall should not go to England. "I dislike all such interviews," Banting wrote, "for I hate to say ill of any man."

The loss of Hall did not seriously cripple Banting's aviation medicine program. In fact it was expanding and becoming more sophisticated as it attracted attention in the United States. The leading figure in American and international aviation medicine, for example, Dr. Harry G. Armstrong, came to the department in the summer of 1940 to begin a research project on the physiology of high altitude flying. H.C. Bazett from the University of Pennsylvania, a pioneer in aviation medicine research with the RAF during the Great War, was recruited more or less as Hall's replacement. As the United States inclined towards siding with the British Empire against Germany, these American contacts were becoming more common and valuable. In November Banting and a party from the NRC visited Washington to find out what the Americans were doing in the field. A group of leading American aviation medicine people visited Toronto later in the month. All the discussions went well, and Banting was well pleased with the work – as he deserved to be; except for silicosis, this was the first time since insulin that he was on the real leading edge of important medical developments, helping to turn Toronto and his department into a world leader in aviation medicine.

He took a hand in the research himself, supervising a series of experiments on rabbits in a small decompression chamber. It had been hard to create experimental "bends" in small animals, who did not seem susceptible to the high altitude problem. Banting came up with the idea of subjecting them to extra-high pressure, two or three atmospheres, before sending them up in the chamber. He was delighted when they developed all the symptoms of aero-embolism, for now it seemed possible to study the problem without risking human lives.[3] These were Banting's last experiments on animals.

The mustard gas fiasco had not cured his eagerness to take the risks of experimenting on himself. He spent many hours in the decompression chamber, sometimes by himself, sometimes with a visitor or colleague. He seemed pleased when he was able to handle the pressure changes better than George Manning, or C.B. Stewart, or some RCAF flyer. When the cold chamber opened at Eglinton, he was the first to fly in it, "climbing" to 25,000 feet and –59F. He was wearing an oxygen mask and signalled that he wanted to go still higher. Fortunately the operator realized that the oxygen mask had frozen in the cold, and Banting was confused by the intoxicating effects of anoxia. He brought him down.[4] Stewart recalled to me how worrying it was to have to operate the decompression chamber while Banting took one of his flights. What would happen to the operator if something went wrong, as it easily could have, and the world-famous Dr. Banting killed himself during one of those sessions in the frigid, airless rooms?

Some of Banting's diary entries suggest that his flights were sometimes more than routinely experimental. On the last day of 1940, after a bad morning in the lab, Banting stayed away from a funeral he was supposed to attend and instead flew by himself in the department's decompression chamber for more than three hours. He may have been trying to recapture a breath of the euphoria he had felt a few days before when he had been visiting an RCAF base and was taken up in a Harvard trainer and shown the sensations of aerobatics: "Below were planes, people, mud, dull brown fields where people toiled wearily, above was sunshine, solitude, a primaeval dream world. The plane looped, banked, dove, rolled. There seemed nothing to stop us or limit movement.... It was a grand and glorious experience. On dull grey days I shall always remember that the sun shines up above the clouds. Sunshine is not very far away." There was a kind of sunshine, a kind of peace or release, even in the decompression chamber. A good, manly kind of peace, for you were proving yourself again, all the while you were experiencing it.

Being tough, hard, showing you were made of the right stuff, something like the boys on active duty.

This research was a kind of active duty. "In this war," Banting wrote, "the research man must be prepared to sacrifice his surface to mustard gas, his interior to anoxia, his ear drums to rupture in rapid descent, and his consciousness to nitrogen bubbles if he desires to have the privilege of the name of a research man."

The darkest side of this war's research requirements was never far from his consciousness in 1940. In June, as soon as Banting realized he would be staying in Canada, his mind turned back to biological warfare. The British had done nothing with his memo, it seemed. How could he start the ball rolling in Canada? It was easy. Banting convinced Colonel R.M. Gorssline, the Director General of Medical Services, as well as Mackenzie of the NRC, that some investigation of the subject would be wise. On July 9, the Minister of National Defence, Colonel J.L. Ralston, gave his approval for a secret project. Money was starting to flow easily for war projects now, and Banting was assured of at least $50,000.[5] Then he met with a group of bacteriologists and virologists at the University, including the Connaught Laboratories' experts in vaccines and antitoxins.

There was some confusion about what might be done and who could do it, for everyone was fairly busy by now on war work of his own. There seemed to be a consensus that tropical or insect-borne diseases were not worth investigating, that viruses offered the greatest threat, and that the key problem in aerial germ warfare would be to determine the "sinker," i.e., the material which would be impregnated with bacteria or a virus and then dispersed into the atmosphere. Banting kept particularly good notes of a meeting of the BW group in his department on September 17:

Defries, Hare, Fraser, Irwin, Greey came for meeting. Hare said – "Before making virus it is necessary to know how to disperse them – because the way you make the material depends on its dispersal." Dry dust, dilute dust, wet spray, etc. Greey thought that we should make a list of problems & then see who could be responsible for each. Defries thought that there should be extra workers who could give their full time to the problem.

Fraser suggested fluorescent dyes, for tests on dispersion.

There was much talk.

After which it all boiled down to:

(1) sinkers – dispersion – rate of fall – varying altitude 500 to 25,000. Destruction by sunshine & moisture.

(2) Combination of Bacteria & Sinker – viability, virulence & Protective colloid.

(3) Selection of organism & mass production.[6]

Banting decided to proceed directly with the first stage of his mandate by having some sinker material tested. Colin Lucas had suggested they try sawdust. Through his Ottawa contacts Banting arranged to have an airplane made available for dispersion experiments.

The first experiment in Canada aimed at spreading deadly diseases by air was conducted over Balsam Lake, fifty miles northeast of Toronto, on October 9, 10, and 16, 1940. Balsam Lake was chosen because it was the site of Colin Lucas's summer cottage. A week or so earlier, Lucas and Philip Greey, a bacteriologist working in the department, had done the preliminary work assembling sawdust. They had more than a ton of it, in various grades of size, stored in the boathouse. The RCAF provided a float plane equipped with a hopper, from which the sawdust could be released. Banting, Lucas, Irwin, Greey and several RCAF officers were on hand to witness the tests.

The methodology was outlined in semi-scientific language in the group's official report to Mackenzie of the NRC. The aim of the experiment was "to study the dispersibility of particulate materials from aeroplanes:

Observation of Distribution: The sawdust was released over a calm lake. The distribution was observed by noting the area upon the surface of which the sawdust could be found floating. Measurements were made only of the lateral spread since obviously the length of the strip contaminated by sawdust depends upon the duration of release from the plane.

Observers, in motor boats, were able to note both the total area involved and the uniformity of distribution within the area by diverging from a central point under the line of flight. The distance between the boats when the outer limits were reached was measured by means of a range-finder.

Variable Factors Studied:
(1) The size of the particle.

(2) Altitude of plane.

(3) Direction of flight of plane in respect to wind.

(4) Rate of delivery of sawdust from hopper.

During three days of experiments the plane made at least fourteen passes over Balsam Lake. It flew at 125 miles per hour. Winds were light. Sawdust delivery times – about 18 to 25 seconds for 25 pounds through hopper openings varying from 2 x 8″ to 4 x 8″ – were only approximate because manual aid had to be applied to evacuate the hopper. Opening the windows of the plane was counter-productive, for it caused backdraughts which not only retarded delivery but blew the sawdust around the cabin. On the 16th the plane had an improved hopper.

Measurements were made of the dispersion of three grades of sawdust, released at several different altitudes, with the plane running across and against the wind. The principal conclusion of the experiment was that "sawdust was found to be remarkably evenly distributed over a wide area when released from an aeroplane." Coarse sawdust, about 10 mesh, gave the most accurate coverage of a specific area.[7] Banting either appreciated the lighter side of the experiment, or had drunk a lot, or both, when he wrote in his diary the night of the 9th that "Never before in the history of the Universe has mere sawdust assumed to command such a degree of importance."

When the first two days' experiments were finished, about noon on the 10th, Banting flew back to Ottawa on the plane. He got in touch with the Deputy Minister of National Defence for Air, James Duncan, who arranged for him to see the Minister of National Defence, Ralston, at ten o'clock that evening. "We had a most unhurried, informal & chatty interview," Banting recorded: "I placed the matter squarely & fairly before him – as I saw it. We were beyond the purely experimental stage – it was a matter of production on the pilot plant plan. – Not for protection but for obtaining the means by which we could retaliate 100 fold *if* the Germans used bacterial warfare." He went on in his diary with his own thoughts: "To me the whole thing is – whether or not we should proceed with the investigation of the methods of production on the large scale of bacteria. We have diddled around the bush enough now. It is time that the old school tie was ironed free of wrinkles & folded up & put in a box until this show is over. Our job lies clearly before us. We

284

have to kill 3 or 4 million young huns – without mercy – without feeling. The job of self-preservation is uttermost. It has to be done by whatever means seems best under the circumstances."

James Duncan phoned Banting from Ottawa on November 19 and told him the green light was on for an absolutely secret BW project.[8] Banting immediately got his team together to discuss suitable microbes – now that they had a proven sinker in sawdust – and methods of mass production. They decided to consult the head of the Ontario Research Foundation, Dr. Horace Speakman, who knew a lot about biochemistry and had been complaining that his establishment did not have much war work to do. The gentle Speakman was interested in doing work on problems of livestock disease in Europe. He must have been surprised when a zealous Banting, according to Banting's notes, posed the problem to him this way: "Give me a mill or a plant where I can produce a hundred tons of virulent organisms with safety to the workmen, economy, & speed." Speakman gamely agreed to do what he could, and was soon coming up with ideas of his own, such as substituting sugar for sawdust. One of its advantages would be that it would dissolve in moisture, leaving no trace.[9]

A lot of preliminary research would have to be done to see how well virulent microbes would adhere to the sinker, be it sawdust or sugar. On reconsideration, the group agreed that a room in the Banting Institute might do for the pilot BW mill. Philip Greey was to be in charge of the project in the first stage. Fred MacCallum, who had worked in Banting's department anesthetizing chickens before going off to Britain and becoming a skilled virologist, was to be invited back to Canada to handle the virus side of the work. At the same time, the group decided to contact experts at other universities for their opinion of the agents most likely to be used by the enemy. Banting had already had some discussions with Dr. C.A. Mitchell, an animal pathologist in the Department of Agriculture, who believed it was possible to cause serious outbreaks of rinderpest and other animal diseases.

Word came back from Britain that MacCallum's job producing yellow fever vaccine for the government was too important for him to be released to Canada. But some of the bacteriologists at other Canadian universities, including E.G.D. Murray of McGill and G.B. Reed of Queen's, expressed their interest in the work. Banting invited Murray and Reed, as well as a Department of Agriculture representative, to a meeting at his home on the evening of December 17, 1940. The scientists sat in the front room at 205 Rosedale Heights, overlooking Fred's roses and the city of Toronto, discussing how to spread plague, rabies, cholera, anthrax, typhus and several other diseases. They made a list of agents they should study and divided up the work. Banting said he could provide any funds needed for their projects. It was to be ultra-secret research (which was coming to be known as Project M-1000), disclosed only to the Minister of Defence and perhaps the Prime Minister. Banting explained to the group that after laboratory experiments, the establishment of plants for mass production would have to be discussed. "If the enemy knew that we were well prepared, BW would probably never be used."[10]

While he was working on these special interests, Banting had a hand in a wide variety of other military research projects through his membership on the NRC and his chairmanship of the Associate Committee on Medical Research. The NRC's financial under-nourishment ended abruptly in the summer of 1940 when the government decided to funnel its way several large private donations in aid of war work. Suddenly there was almost an embarrassment of riches, a "Santa Claus fund," as the T. Eaton Company, the CPR, the Bronfman brothers and Inco contributed more than a million dollars to support new research. Banting was a member of the special NRC – Department of National Defence Technical and Scientific Development Committee set up to administer the fund.

Part of the impetus for the fund and the committee had come from the enthusiasm for research generated by recent British visits to Canada, particularly the time spent in Ottawa by Sir Henry Tizard, one of the fathers of radar, during a North American mission. Banting, Collip, Mackenzie and Tizard had most of Monday, August 19, together, with Tizard urging the Canadians to go full speed ahead in research of all kinds. Banting was suitably though not uncritically impressed by Tizard – "He has a fine record for Science & for Daring & Initiative. But he does not know very much more about details than I do" – and was unreserved in the support he gave Mackenzie and the NRC for launching total scientific war on Germany.

Banting was involved in planning a raft of NRC projects, ranging from work with radar and asdic to experiments in the design of wooden aircraft. Toward the end of August 1940, his diary contains references to alpha, beta and gamma rays, uranium 235, Gilbert LaBine and his Port Hope uranium refinery, and the mystifications caused by physicists: "I do not know why physicists always seek to complicate a simple truth by explaining it by means of complex formulae with signs, equations, greek letters and always a smug conclusion." The "simple truth" Banting was trying to understand was the theory of atomic energy, and its possible application to the war. Dr. George C. Laurence of the NRC was beginning work in the council's labs on a pile of crude uranium ore, trying to see if the right kind of bombardment might cause some kind of sustained or chain reaction. It was the primitive beginning of Canada's contribution to the development of atomic energy. Banting boned up on the physics, wondering about radiation and cancer as he went, and enthusiastically supported Laurence's request for funding. The poles of his interest that summer of 1940 are encapsulated in one diary entry on August 26: "I talked with Lawrence [sic] this afternoon on U 235. He is off to Port Hope & Toronto for *Uranium*. I urged Mackenzie to take a strong and progressive stand on the research aspect of the whole Uranium project but where in hell does all this get one? I still maintain that I would sooner be a Medical officer of a battalion in the line than any other job in the Medical service."[11]

Banting was also on hand to expedite the development of Canada's involvement in a project that had long interested him – gas warfare. It still seemed likely that gas would be used in battle, the British did not have the open space at Porton to carry out large-scale experiments, and an Allied gas research facility in the Sahara desert had been lost with the defeat of France. Over in England General McNaughton was anxious enough to have gas experts on his staff that he had Israel Rabinowitch plucked back out of private life and brought over again. Banting helped arrange Rab's return to Britain, and then engineered the funding of several research projects in his department and elsewhere on gas problems that Rabinowitch passed back to Canada. As a result of one of these projects, he wrote to McNaughton, "the smell of geraniums and goats float about the top floor of the Institute."

At the same time, in the autumn of 1940, a British expert from Porton visited Canada to firm up a plan, possibly first suggested by Rabinowitch, to found a major gas research facility in the Canadian West. The NRC, Banting, and the other pioneers of Canadian gas warfare all cooperated as the British and Canadian military authorities and governments moved quickly to create the Chemical Warfare Experimental Station on semi-Saharan grazing land at Suffield, Alberta. It became Canada's major wartime and postwar centre of chemical warfare research.[12]

Canadian medical research was becoming increasingly oriented toward the war, as other investigators followed Toronto's lead in turning to military problems. By the summer of 1940 the Associate Committee on Medical Research was supporting an extensive project at McGill on shock; a multi-university project on infections, especially gas gangrene; a McGill-Toronto project on blood storage; fatigue studies; nutritional research; and other investigations. Banting spent many hours discussing them, an increasing amount of that time with Collip, who had become vice-chairman of the Associate Committee in September 1939, and directed it while Banting had been in England. Collip had moved from Alberta to McGill in 1928 and through the 1930s had been the creative centre of endocrinological research in Canada, possibly the most creative and productive medical researcher in the country.

Reorienting medical research for war was not an easy job. Some of the scientists were particularly distressed at the way the passion for secrecy limited the free publication of scientific information. The American-born Wilder Penfield, for example, argued during one of the early wartime committee meetings that basic research findings should be made openly available, even to the Germans. Banting replied angrily, Penfield recorded, "that he would not tell the ____ ____ Germans a word of what we were doing."[13] Another immigrant scientist in Montreal, Hans Selye, was also deemed unreliable when he began publishing some of his conclusions on shock without authorization from the Associate Committee or mention of his NRC support. He was struck off the committee's list for further grants. Selye had no friend at court in his former supervisor, Collip, who had broken with him some time before in a bitter disagreement about Selye's research methods.[14]

For his part, Banting was finding it increasingly difficult to understand how to accommodate the ambitions and talents of his former assistant, Charles Best. Best had been an energetic researcher, doing important work on choline and the anti-coagulant heparin. He was very well connected in Britain, reasonably influential at the

University of Toronto, but not highly placed in Canadian medical research circles, where his ambition was often interpreted as self-interest – not least by Banting, who wrote one day in July 1940, for example: "I also saw Best. He is rather a sorry figure. He thinks so much of Best that it is difficult to know how to use him. . . . He has sent further memos to England."

The Best problem was compounded that autumn by infighting at the University over Best's future. J.G. Fitzgerald's death opened up several important positions, including the headship of the School of Hygiene and the Connaught Laboratories. When President Cody decided to replace Fitzgerald with R.D. Defries in both positions, he found it politic to suggest to Best, who was talking about leaving the University, that it was time to found an Institute of Physiology. Best would head the institution. Best was immediately enthusiastic, spoke to Banting about it, and got what he interpreted as enthusiastic support from Banting. He missed the cynicism: "Charlie has drawn the idea of a Physiological Institute as a red herring across the trail. Cody said yesterday that it was Best's idea & Best said it was Cody's idea that there should be a Physiological Institute to commemorate the name of Best. I even suggested that it be built next to the Banting Institute."

In his exuberance Best asked the Banting Research Foundation, "as the co-discoverer of insulin . . . to make money available to me in the same way as it has for many years to Sir Frederick Banting."[15] Velyien Henderson, who had served as secretary of the Foundation since its inception, was furious, and complained to Banting. "One thing that Henderson emphasized," Banting wrote, "was that Best wanted to take over Biochemistry, Pharmacology & now Histology. He also wanted to take over the Research of the Connaught Laboratories – I told Henderson that as far as I was concerned that Best could take over the Department of Medical Research with the others."

Best's opponents tried to enlist Banting in their resistance to a Physiological Institute. Banting and Best had one discussion of a grant for it from the Banting Research Foundation. "He says he is going to have an Institute – and that he does not know where but he hopes it will be in Toronto. I repeatedly told him that all the Faculty would be with him provided he did not interfere with existing Departments and existing Financial Arrangements. But that if he took money that would more properly go to others of the Faculty that everyone would be against him. Best is naive in his abject selfishness."

Banting was still involved in discussions of an overseas trip for Best. He and some of the other Canadian researchers were beginning to wonder whether the almost total non-communication that existed between Canadian medical workers and the British Medical Research Council may not have stemmed from British determination to work with Best and no one else. To an extent it did, for whenever Hill, Dale or Mellanby were urged to communicate with Canada they again asked that Best be sent over. But they felt that only "the jealousy of Banting" stood in Best's way. "I think Mellanby and Dale and the High and Mighties over there are sore at me because their darling Best has not been sent over," Banting wrote in December. "I have been doing my best to have him sent. . . ."[16]

There were several other reasons for the lack of liaison. In general medical research the British still tended to assume that Canada had little or nothing to contribute. In aviation medicine the RAF saw little reason for exploratory work on the frontiers of high-altitude and high G-force flying, for these seemed beyond the experiences of fighting airmen. There was little British enthusiasm about Franks' flying suit at first, for example, because British flyers had found out that a crouching position enabled them to withstand up to 7 or 8 G's without blacking-out. This, the RAF aviation medicine expert wrote Banting, was "all that is wanted under modern war Fighter conditions . . . quite enough stress on the air craft as constructed at present."[17]

This British conservatism often infuriated a North American son of pioneers, who correctly assumed that much of the point of research was to prepare the frontier for the time when pilots came to it. Through 1940 Banting often complained about British smugness, British arrogance, British resistance to innovation. He did not like American materialism, but thought that Canada's future was linked with the United States because the two peoples had so much in common.

Early in December 1940, the NRC agreed to contribute $1,000 toward the cost of a British trip for Best. By then the ambitious physiologist was at work on a major dried blood serum project with support from the Red Cross and the International Health Board. He thought it possible to make a trip that would serve his several research interests.[18]

Banting wanted to go to England as much as any man in Canada. All the while he had been organizing research, reorganizing his department, negotiating grants, arranging trips for others, riding overnight trains to Ottawa and back to Toronto and back and back again, he had longed to be closer to the front, closer to the reality of war he had known the last time:

July 22:

. . . I thought how nice it would be to be a battalion medical officer again. I shall always remember that experience for it was one of those rare times in ones life when one could honestly feel proud of the fact that medical knowledge & skill was the means by which men had a chance to live – to be present when wounded men who gave their lives for their country, needed a medical officer was a privilege.

July 26:

I am not pleased to be kept at home while others are in peril. . . . I am not brave. There is no one who has more abject terror of shells, bombs, bullets and death or destruction in any form than I have. But surpassing this fear is the privilege of service to the wounded, to those that fight, to the forces in the field – to comrades in arms.

Comrade has a meaning to those who have served which is all its own. There was a comradeship in the army – among those who served our country dangerously which is not understood by those who have not experienced enemy fire. Men were drawn together in common danger. There was a companionship which would never have existed apart from war. There was sacrifice, there was unselfishness, there was devotion to duty, there was heroism, bravery, and Strength of Character, which would never have existed or never have been known were it not brought out by mutual reciprocal and common danger. Men showed their metal in this melting pot of war.

August 26:

I know that there is a greater service to be rendered to the

291

country by means of the stimulation of Scientific research than in any other field, but there is the primitive urge to be doing something for the troops.

August 27:
I'll be damned if the system will get me down. God forbid that I will ever assume the defeatist attitude.

September 11:
I feel that I should get into something more active – where I would have something to show for my work.

Poor old England is being given a terrible amount of punishment and she is giving just about as much. I would like to be doing something more to help.

October 28:
It was a privilege and an inspiration to meet men who had distinguished themselves on land & in the air in this war.

It is difficult to come down to the ordinary business of sleeping after such an experience. Men who had bombed the Scharnhorst, men who had been thro' the evacuation of Dunkirk, men who had sweat blood over scientific developments. . . . It makes one wish to have some small part in the whole show.

On November 10, knowing he would not get over during 1940, Banting went to a local radio station and cut a record, sending Christmas greetings to Cec Rae and the boys in No. 15 Canadian General Hospital. It is the only surviving record of his voice.

Fred's mother, now eighty-six, had been declining for several years and had gradually become bed-ridden and semi-coherent. All his life Fred had written to her on Sunday afternoons when he was away from home. When he visited her in Alliston on December 1, 1940, she looked very bad. He thought she recognized him and that she muttered "My sweetheart." The next day Thompson Banting phoned to say that their mother, Margaret, had passed on. Fred went back up for her funeral on a dark, snowy day. "My dear old mother looked well in her coffin, but I want to blot from my memory these very last years and think of her as the bright & happy mother of thirty or even ten years ago. Her love for fun, her enjoyment of good books, her memory, her poetry, her kindness and her love. Her

292

Sunday letters to me and how I will miss writing to her. Mother had a great sense of appreciation for anything one ever did for her. . . ."

His family life with Henrietta does not emerge clearly from his diaries, partly because he tended to write only about their occasional quarrels. He was often away, of course, often fatigued, and a little worried about his sexuality. One night when she was out without him he worried that she was changing toward him, that Sadie Gairns' dark prediction, "two years," might be coming true. Perhaps, he thought, the problem was that Henrietta had not had a baby. He drank as he wrote, and knew he was using liquor almost like sex, as a stimulant/relaxant: "When one reaches the age of 50 and sex and female attraction wains it is a grand provision of nature that alcohol is readily available as a replacement to those subtle attractions of youth." During another quarrel he convinced himself that with his mother gone and his wife cold to him, there was nothing to do but go overseas and die in the war. Men think these things in alcoholic stupor; then, as Banting did, feel numb and a bit silly the next morning. Henrie brought him his coffee as though nothing had happened. A few days later he remarked on how "My dear Henrie, who sees me only when I am washed out, forgave, as usual, my indisposition."

The New Year, 1941, brought a lull in Banting's duties. All his projects, all the NRC programs, were well under way, with none presenting serious problems. In January Banting began to extend his activities. Taking Henrietta with him, he spent a week in Halifax and Quebec City, discussing local public health problems, research and the needs of the navy. The main medical issues in Nova Scotia were, in about equal measure, a diphtheria epidemic in Halifax and local resentment that imported orange juice rather than Nova Scotia apple juice was required in menus in military hospitals. Banting drafted a memorandum on seasickness, a serious, debilitating problem in the navy, akin to the airsickness that interested aviation medicine workers. He recommended that several seasickness research projects be started. On the other hand, an inspection of tanks and tank personnel at Camp Borden, Ontario, later in the month did not reveal any special medical problems. The most interesting discovery Banting felt he brought back from these trips was the new French-Canadian interest in English Canada's medical schools now that Paris was closed to them. Banting saw "a great opportunity to unite the Medical Profession of Canada by

293

making special efforts to provide our young French Canadian medical men with facilities for their post-graduate training."[19] This quest for national medical unity nicely balanced extremely unflattering comments about French-Canadians in some of Banting's more violent tirades a few months earlier.*

Banting still wanted to get overseas. A good case could be made for his going: it was a year and a totally different war since his last trip; transatlantic medical communication had not been good, and the channels needed clearing up and straightening out. Things were well under control in Canada. Other key Canadians, many of them his friends, were there, ranging from Rabinowitch and Mc-Naughton to A.A. James in aviation medicine and all the Canadian doctors serving with 15 General Hospital. As Rabinowitch argued to McNaughton, and the Canadian general agreed, they – the fellows in England – also thought Fred should come over to see for himself what was happening, what needed to be done, what Canada should do.[20]

But Best, easily as competent as Banting, had been approved for a trip by the NRC and the Associate Committee. Banting could not have hoped to get over early in 1941 had not Best begun to question the wisdom of going. Professionally he was deeply into his blood serum project. Then his father suffered two heart attacks while visiting the Bests in Toronto over Christmas. So Best decided to defer his British trip for several months.[21]

Seeing his opening, Banting started pressing his case for a trip. Neither C.J. Mackenzie nor Banting's military superior, Colonel R.M. Gorssline, had good reason to reject Banting's arguments. Mackenzie, however, who had come to rely on Banting as a kind of senior workhorse in scientific Ottawa, did not want him away for long. "If he could fly, and stay there three weeks, it would be alright," Mackenzie wrote in his war diary. Among Banting's associates only Sadie Gairns was strongly opposed to a trip, partly

---

*E.g., Banting's diary, August 9: "They are Priest ridden. They rule in our democracy because of their numbers. They delight in being prolific. They speak a different language. They think in terms of selfish attainment at the expense of other Canadians. They have the balance of power because of their numberical votes. Many of them are good fellows but many are petty politicians & grafters. In science they are far behind for they have always followed old lame selfish France. More imposters of science have appeared in France than in most countries. They have prostituted Pasteur. They have sought by pseudo science to snare the unsuspecting. They are charming, they have the veneer of culture. They ensnare the unscientific in verbiage. It is impossible for the layman to distinguish between the charlatan & the saint in the personnel of French science of the past quarter of a century."

because she was afraid he would find a way not to come back.

Banting kept arguing his case, making tactical use of the claim that he *had* to go since Best was not going.[22] Privately, and to some of his friends, he presented the idea of a trip as a kind of test of manhood, one that Best had just failed. He wrote in his diary on June 28, viciously and with no discernable justification, "I must say privately that I am inwardly disappointed in Charlie Best. He has no guts. He has the opportunity for which he has long been belly-aching to go to England & he has passed it up. I think it has worried him and he blames his family and the conditions at home but essentially it is a matter of guts. He has not the required number."

At the end of a hectically busy two days in Ottawa on January 30-31, Banting spoke to a senior naval officer who assured him there would be no difficulty getting a passage to England by way of a destroyer or a corvette. Just before he checked out of his hotel that Friday evening, Mackenzie phoned and invited him to a farewell reception for James Duncan, an influential Toronto businessman who was leaving Ottawa after a short term as Deputy Minister of Air. Banting found the cocktails, the hors d'oeuvres, the brilliant socializing, all "peculiar" in wartime Ottawa. "The war was upper-most in my mind."

While he was chatting with Air Marshal A.A.L. Cuffe, Banting mentioned his interest in finding quick transportation across the Atlantic. Cuffe said it might be possible for him to fly the ocean in nine hours, aboard one of the Hudson bombers being ferried through Montreal to Great Britain. Banting's spirits leaped at the suggestion, "the ray of hope."

He boarded the late train for Toronto. It was about midnight on January 31 and he had nothing on hand to drink when he wrote this remarkable meditation on the coming month, the coming trip:

What will this month bring forth? German invasion of England? Gas warfare? What will Hitler do? I want to be in it all; and when it happens I want to be in the thick of it.

Never was there a time in my life when I had so much to live for – and so much to die for. I curse Hitler with all my heart for his Lust takes me from the only home I have ever had.

Yet it is for this same home for this same privilege of living that I give myself if chance and need be call that my time is up.

– I want to be there when there is action.

– I have lived my life for almost fifty years. Every day of these years have been filled with action. Work has been my motto & my salvation thro' life. Of relaxation & of rest I have had so little that it is not worth the mention.

Over there, there are my dearest Friends in all the world. They have survived. They are in the Front line and we at home cannot make too great a sacrifice for their sakes.

When I get there if I ever do I feel that I will not want to come back. I will not want to leave. My heart is there where Democracy with all its faults stands, where brave men defend the Empire.

But if it should be that I can serve my day & age – my country & my King to best advantage here at home then I am content to stay.

But only this far. I only want to know where I may best serve – and service without thought of selfishness – no ribbons, no honours, no trumpet calls of publicity.

– but in the quiet solitude of a trench or behind some straggling line where men suffer may I serve – may I because of my medical knowledge be of use to those whose life is endangered by our ruthless foe.

May I lay down my life that I live in those whose life I try to save? Our armies are filled with youth – they have time before them to live. For me I have lived & it is better that I die in glory serving our youth than to live long and wain & fade and be disliked, then hated, then cursed, then blamed & then have people pleased when I should die.

Is life so selfishly pleasant as all this? Can one as I am on the borderline of youth & age – decline to offer what he has and face our youth and ask them to place their all upon the throne of sacrifice? . . .

It is but human nature to be proud of honours won yet our real heros are not decorated. I think & wish that I might have the courage to decline the thing that I most wish for – further honour, because I do not think that I would with the courage that I have ever really be worthy of honour.

When his train pulled into Toronto that Saturday morning, Banting had a haircut at Union Station, two cups of coffee, and went to the lab for a morning's work. After a university luncheon, Henrietta picked him up. There is another remarkable, sad entry in his diary: "[She] told me of the Air Crewman O.T. who had dated her for tonight. I went cold. She wept & kept on weeping throughout the day. I'm licked. I go overseas. I'll not come back. Life to me is not so finite or glorious that I want to take second place to a reject."*

Banting went back to Ottawa at the end of the next week. On the train he wrote a letter to Henrietta which he tore up the next day. Authorization for a trip to England, and passage on a Hudson, came through. "I am excited & thrilled with the prospect of flying the Atlantic." He began attending to the scores of details to be tidied up before he left Canada to go to the war.

*We know nothing more about this incident. It was probably an enormous misunderstanding, hinging on a fairly innocent desire by Henrietta to be sociable to men in uniform. After the disaster of his first marriage, and with his fear that this one might go wrong too, Fred was programmed to suspect the worst.

CHAPTER FOURTEEN

At a Post of Duty

H e never asked himself, "Why me?" That was a question others asked later about his mission. Why Banting? Was he carrying details of some secret weapon, possibly a method of nullifying a German poison gas attack? Was he rushing the latest Canadian medical discoveries to Britain? Was he taking over the Franks flying suit to help the RAF win the final round of the Battle of Britain? Was he on a secret mission for "Intrepid," the Canadian spy-master, William Stephenson? Afterwards, the Prime Minister himself told the House of Commons that it was "a mission of high national and scientific importance."

There is no truth in any of the speculations. Banting was on his way to England officially to find out what was up in the field of wartime medical research. He might learn some secrets, and he certainly would bring back ideas about how Canadian science could help the war effort, but he was not taking across anything of much use to the British. The Franks flying suit, for example, which was still very much in the experimental stage, was in any case about to cross the Atlantic with Franks himself. There was nothing as significant in Banting's mission as there would be about, say, Andrew Goderich's flight to Britain in a Hudson ten months later.[1]

Unofficially, Banting was an old soldier going back to the front, back to his comrades and the fellowship of men facing a common foe. As he had done for years, he was travelling to escape the stress and loneliness of being Banting in Toronto, the famous scientist turned figurehead and administrator, from whom everyone took so much. He always wanted to get away from Toronto, to get away from being Banting. He hoped and feared that this trip would be the final break – hoped that he could stay with his friends near the front

298

until the war was over; feared that something might go wrong and he would die. Insignificant as it was for the war, or for any greater cause, the mission told a lot about Fred Banting.

He was in his office in the lab when the call finally came at noon on Saturday, February 15, ordering him to report to Montreal the next morning. Sadie Gairns had been almost alone in opposing the trip. To the end she was tempted to go and see Duncan Graham, the one person in Toronto who might be able to talk Banting out of it. "Miss Gairns' good-bye was deep and yet I think she was proud," Banting wrote that night. "She did her best to hold in. When I told her that I wanted to be as useful as possible she said 'That is the trouble – you may be so useful over there that they may not let you come back.'"

Later that afternoon he asked Bill, now eleven years old, to come up to his study. He told the boy that he was going overseas. "I thought you were dad on account of the revolver and the Sam Browne belt," Bill replied (a friend had told Fred that everyone in London wore a Sam Browne and a revolver). Bill was excited to hear that his father was flying over in a bomber, and then suddenly serious when Fred mentioned the danger involved in doing this, his duty. Apparently thinking of what would happen if the plane crashed, Bill told his father that he could live as long in cold water as any person – a thought that had been on Banting's mind too. The father told the son he would do his best to give a good account of himself. Bill asked his dad to bring him back a bomb fragment.

Henrietta drove him to the train station. Fred and Lillian Hipwell came along to see him off. Fred Hipwell had taken some snapshots of Fred just before the departure. Banting had been too honest to hide his anxiety about the trip. He had told the Hipwells, Sadie and his old friend and self-appointed biographer, Dr. Billy Ross, that he was frightened.

Sunday morning in Montreal, Banting was taken to a supply depot and outfitted for winter flying. The only item unavailable was a pair of warm gloves. He met one of the officers of the civilian company that was ferrying the twin-engined Hudsons over to England. They had been bought in the United States and were now being delivered to the RAF. It was a relatively new idea to fly them across rather than ship them. Banting would be only the second passenger to cross on the ferry operation.

Delays were likely in the crossing, for the airports being used in

Newfoundland and New Brunswick were shut in by weather about half the time. "Today I will rest – and try to get a pair of mitts," Banting wrote at noon. "Research has left my mind for the present. All I ask is weather. If one comes thro' such experiences it is fine but grey hairs are the result. One learns to depend on alcohol if kept in its place."

He had a nap that afternoon and then a long talk in his hotel room with Bert Collip, who would handle his NRC duties while he was gone. They began reminiscing about the insulin days, from which they had both mellowed. Collip apparently told Banting that in his view the credit for the discovery of insulin should be apportioned 80 per cent to Banting, 10 per cent to Best, and 5 per cent each to Collip and J.J.R. Macleod.[2] We do not know what Banting said. Judging by comments he was making to other friends about the same time, he probably said, "You know damn well we couldn't have done a damn thing without you." As they parted, Collip gave Banting a pair of sheepskin gloves to wear on the flight. Collip was the last of Banting's friends and colleagues to see him alive.

Fred wrote letters to Bill and Henrietta, and made yet another entry in his diary, breaking into his odd doggerel:

. . . one wishes time to pass rapidly. A disagreeable job is to be done and the sooner it is over the better. Time please fly,
Be fast in speeding past.
Bring tomorrow soon.
For Tomorrow holds fate.
– Life, experience, or doom.
risk is high
but duty must be done.
Life & honor or blackout
Where all ceases.
Whatever comes
I can take it.
All I have is but little
compared with the cause for which we fight.

The two-engine Lockheed Hudson bomber, T-9449, left from St. Hubert's field outside Montreal at 9.50 a.m. on Monday. It carried a pilot, a navigator and a wireless operator, plus Major Sir Frederick Banting. A peacetime antecedent of the Hudson, the Lockheed 18 was in service as Trans-Canada Airline's standard passenger plane, but this Hudson was a skeleton craft, fresh off the assembly line, with none of the amenities civilian passengers would enjoy. They had a smooth flight to the newly enlarged base at Gander, Newfoundland, covering the eight hundred miles in just under five hours. The cold was not nearly as bad as Banting had feared. But his bladder bothered him, and he found it embarrassing to make so many trips back to the little toilet in the tail, for the change in the Hudson's weight distribution required making an adjustment to the trim each time.

They had hoped to take off that evening from Gander, but were grounded by reports of bad weather over Britain. So they joined the crews of five other Hudsons piled up in Gander waiting to cross. Banting had had no idea how difficult the weather made flying the Atlantic, and was shocked to hear that only one Hudson had been able to cross so far in 1941. For all his worrying about the danger, he may not have realized exactly how pioneering this ferrying business was. When the first flight of Hudsons had left from Gander on November 10, 1940, they were tackling the north Atlantic later in the year than anyone had ever flown it. Only four flights, totalling about twenty-five Hudsons, had crossed so far. One Hudson had crashed on take-off, another had had to return to Gander.[3] The planes had to be grossly over-loaded with fuel for an extraordinarily long flight in difficult atmospheric conditions. The civilian crews who had just been hired to do the ferrying (by a subsidiary of the just-formed Canadian Pacific Airlines) had virtually no experience at long-distance, midwinter flying on unfamiliar, twin-engined planes. There was a madcap, seat-of-the-pants aspect about the whole operation, something like the way Banting had always approached medical research. To the south the Americans were flying the Atlantic commercially and safely via the Azores and neutral countries. Banting would have been far better off on an American flight. But here he was in Newfoundland, about to become one of the first handful of people ever to fly the north Atlantic in February.

His presence was not particularly welcome to his pilot, Joseph C. Mackey, a sky-writer and barnstormer from Kansas City making his second ferrying flight. In the evening of their arrival in Gander, a radio officer on another Hudson, C.M. Tripp, heard Mackey talking about how "the Old Gent should consider himself lucky he had got as far as he did with such a bum pilot and pick some one else to fly the ocean with." Mackey would have known the risks of the flight, and knew he was crazy enough to take them, but why the hell make him carry a passenger?

Radioman Tripp didn't know who the "Old Gent" was, except that he was a major and an army medical officer. Thinking he should help make the stranger feel at home in Gander—a raw, primitive airstrip in the middle of nowhere, fringed by a few makeshift huts and railway cars—Tripp asked him if he'd like to meet some of the locals, and shepherded him over to the officers' mess of the local unit of the Royal Rifles of Canada. Tripp introduced the visitor to the local commanding officer, and for the first time heard the guest introduce himself, "Banting, Major Banting." The C.O. came slowly to attention. "Not the Banting?" Then, "Gentlemen!" and every officer in the room snapped to attention. Even then it was only later in the evening when Tripp was introducing Banting to the medical officers at Gander that he finally realized this was the Banting of insulin fame. What would the discoverer of insulin be doing flying the ocean in a Lockheed Hudson in the middle of winter?[4]

The medical officers filled Banting in on life in Newfoundland, not yet a province of Canada, telling him there were only two classes on the island, the very rich and the very poor. "Few of the poor can read or write," Banting recorded. "They are inbred. T.B. is prevalent. Diet of poor is mostly bread & fish. The man in charge of this hotel asked my name & as I spelled the letters one by one he wrote 'fgbanting' on the card."

The next day, Tuesday the 18th, the weather was still bad to the east. Some of the stranded flyers staying at the "Eastbound Inn" had minor colds. Dr. Banting wouldn't hear of the M.O. being called, but went out himself to get hot water bottles and medicine. Having always believed in the medicinal use of alcohol, he probably brought back some fairly strong stuff. He had lunch with the colonel of the Royal Rifles, visited the Gander hospital, and then, as a blizzard settled in around the base, spent another evening with the medical officers.

A big party was held at the base that night, with a train load of women brought in for the occasion. Pilot Mackey was well loaded when Banting ran into him late in the evening. Now Mackey warmed to the gent. He said he had sworn never to take a passenger across the Atlantic, but he would take Banting. "I take him to be a hard drinker, hard flyer & if in a box a hard fighter," Banting wrote. "He should be in the movies, for he has dash, poise, nerve & nothing phases him."*

The blizzard continued through the morning of the 19th. There wasn't much to do at Gander except drink, play poker and talk. Not being able to find a single magazine or book, Banting sat around drinking coffee with the Newfoundlander kitchen help and talking with the airmen about weather, winds and the performance of their machines. Icing and engine over-heating were the most common mechanical problems they had to worry about at high altitude in cold weather. Fred must have mentioned his pissing problem on the flight from Montreal, for he triggered a flood of urination stories. The best was from a pilot who waited until an obnoxious passenger had gone to the lavatory, then whipped the tail up and down violently, simulating turbulence and causing a satisfying number of wet spots on the passenger's beautiful light-coloured suit. Another airman told Banting he never hesitated to relieve himself during flight, using the floor if necessary, for he didn't want to share the fate of the old darkey who held it in so well on a motor trip that he ruptured his bladder and died. Banting could reply with his own store of peeing stories, picked up a few weeks earlier from his American colleague, Dr. Harry Armstrong. Some planes had tubes through which pilots could urinate; one of the first flyers to try the tube found his ground crew had upped the suction; he became intimately attached to the tube.†

Radioman Tripp solved the bladder problem by offering to supply Banting with some of the pint-sized sanitary cups he had filched from Trans-Canada Airlines in Montreal. All of the flyers liked

*A plausible story, which unfortunately cannot be confirmed from the written record, is that Banting had been scheduled to fly with a different pilot, had been switched to T-9449 in Montreal when temporary engine trouble developed in his original plane, and now refused to leave Mackey for fear that it would be interpreted as a snub to the pilot and his crew.

†Experienced aviators point out that Armstrong was evidently stretching the truth, for there would be no suction in these relief tubes. It is true that extreme cold can cause adherence to the tube.

Banting's interest in bodily functions aboard aircraft was not unusual. When Lindberg had his audience with King George V after his 1927 flight, the king began by saying, "Now tell me, Captain Lindbergh. There is one thing I long to know. How did you pee?"

Banting, and they reassured him about the Hudson's safety. After you got it up you could fly the Atlantic on a single engine. Piece of cake. Climbs like a homesick angel.

They still couldn't get out on the 19th. Fred and Flying Officer Clifford Wilson took in the afternoon movie, "Stardust" with Linda Darnell and Roland Young. Wilson lent Banting a book, *How to Fly a Plane*. On the morning of Thursday the 20th, Banting sent a wire to Henrietta; afterwards he talked with Wilson about his life in Toronto, his home and his family. "I have never been happier in my life," he told Wilson. He said that he was looking forward to retiring to a home somewhere in the country. He had told several of his friends that the prospect of this flight scared him, and repeated these fears in conversations at the base with Wilson and with the chief meteorologist, Patrick McTaggart-Cowan.[5]

Banting was keeping not one, but two diaries. He had with him the plain stenographers' notebooks he normally wrote in, and also a 1941 day-book he had been given for Christmas. The last entry in his normal diary was made on the evening of the 19th. After describing the events of the day, Banting concluded with these reflections:

> Since coming here I have gained more & more confidence in both the machines and the men. One cannot however entirely eliminate sabotage from one's immagination. This would be a grand place for it. An agent could certainly play the devil with the final checking. The Hanger is overcrowded & planes have to be left outside & there is continual moving of planes for reconditioning. Several new hangers are being built, but at present the conjestion is acute.

At 5:30 p.m. on Thursday the 20th he filled in his day-book entry:

> It looks as tho tonight was the night. The boys are packing. Coffee in thermos flasks has been ordered. Three Hudson flying pals were killed yesterday [taking off from St. Hubert in Montreal]. It makes the third crash. This afternoon I walked around the airdrome. I feel tired so I hope that I'll be able to sleep tonight. It will be cold. My difficulty is that my hands and feet perspire and become damp when they get cold. When Pilots get killed the other pilots blame the way he handled the situation. Few accidents appear to be due to the mechanism of the plane.

Flying Officer Wilson helped Banting into his "teddy bear" flying suit. Banting had to remind Tripp of the offer of the sanitary cups. Tripp ran over to his plane to get them. Banting seemed happy to be finally getting away, Tripp thought, and didn't seem nearly as nervous about the flight as Tripp was himself. Mackey and his crew had T-9449 revved up and ready to go. Banting shook hands with Wilson who wished him happy landings. "Oh, we'll have those!" Banting said. He ran out to the Hudson and Tripp helped him aboard.

Five of the six Hudsons took off at 1958 hours. One remained on the ground with engine trouble. Not long after take-off, the radio operators on four of the Hudsons heard Bill Snailham of T-9449 asking Gander for bearings back to the airport. They never saw T-9449 again. Neither did the personnel at Gander, who responded to Snailham's request with directions for the plane's return.

Stories that T-9449 had been sabotaged may have started because of that last entry in Banting's diary. Then they persisted because flyers, like most of the rest of us, resist the thought of being the victims of random accidents. The Banting sabotage story was in print again as late as 1983.[6] In 1984 Joseph Mackey's widow told me that two members of the ground crew at Gander had put sand in the Hudson's oil and had later confessed to the crime and been executed. An old airman added that the culprit(s) had been buried in an unmarked grave in Newfoundland. The plot seemed to thicken because my extensive searches of archives in Ottawa, London, Newfoundland, and Montreal had failed to uncover any of the four copies that were made of the report of the official inquiry into the crash. Documents seldom go accidently missing from so many archives.

The sabotage story is in fact wildly implausible, utterly undocumented, and unnecessary to explain the crash. No one who was at Gander in 1941 believes it, nor does any historian of Canadian aviation or the Canadian military. The real problem, described to me vividly and authoritatively by Patrick McTaggart-Cowan, who was on the spot, was in the new oil cooling systems being installed on the Hudson that winter. Rectangularly-constructed grids that produced faster cooling were turning out to be weaker in cold weather starts than the old circularly-gridded coolers. In extreme cold the new oil coolers had a tendency to rupture on starting. The problem would show up shortly after take-off.

T-9449 was about fifty miles northeast of Gander, over the Atlantic, when the failure of an oil cooler forced Mackey to shut down his starboard engine and head back. He could have made it easily on one engine. But then the oil supply to the port engine failed. The dead Hudson would not even glide smoothly, for one of the propellers had not been feathered and was windmilling, creating tremendous drag and vibrations.[7]

Mackey jettisoned his excess fuel and ordered the others to throw out everything they could to reduce weight. Then he realized he would not get back to Gander. The Hudson was going to crash in the dark. When he was certain they were back over land, and were still at about 2,500 feet, Mackey told Snailham, the radio operator, sitting beside him to order the others – Banting and Flying Officer William Bird, the navigator – to bail out. Feeling a lightening of the plane, he thought they had.[8]

Mackey could not or would not bail out himself. A gutsy pilot took his plane down, even to certain death. It flashed through Mackey's mind that he had a chance of hitting a smooth surface, for Newfoundland was supposed to be 50 per cent lakes. He almost made it, coming in just at the shore of a pond about twelve miles southwest of Musgrave Harbour, on Newfoundland's east coast. The bomber sheared off some small trees, hit a bigger tree with one wing, and lost a wheel. Hudson T-9449 hit hard and stopped. It did not break up or burn. Still at the controls, Mackey was knocked out.

Banting had not jumped. Neither had Snailham or Bird. Perhaps they had not heard the order. In another version, Banting's not having a parachute suggests he had decided not to jump. The prospect of jumping into snow and cold and black wilderness, maybe the ocean, would daunt anyone, let alone a man who had never had anything to do with parachutes. Banting was never sure whether his courage was fear. Either courage or fear or some mixture of both, and perhaps a sense of resignation, caused him to stay with the Hudson as Mackey took it down.

Banting's mistake was not to have braced himself, his back against the cabin bulkhead, for a crash.[9] Mackey, who was braced, and perhaps belted, sustained only minor head injuries when the plane hit. He came to a few minutes later. He found Snailham and Bird both dead. Banting was lying unconscious on the floor of the main cabin. He had evidently been thrown forward, crashing into the frame of the aircraft. He had smashed the left side of his head, broken his left arm, and had other injuries, but was still alive.

Banting and the whole cabin were bathed in a ghostly, silvery glow, having been covered with aluminum powder from flasks of sea markers which had burst on impact. Mackey was able to get Banting back to semi-consciousness and move him onto the bunk in the cabin. He made bandages and blankets from parachute silk. During periods of confused consciousness that night, Banting ordered Mackey to take dictation. He did not know where he was and did not recognize Mackey as a pilot. But, Mackey wrote, "he seemed to feel he was carrying on at a post of duty." Banting talked and talked, would rest, then sit up and talk again. To Mackey it sounded like an endless stream of highly technical memoranda and formulae. Occasionally Mackey would go through the motions of writing down the words in order to quiet Banting.

By noon the next day, February 21, Banting had fallen into deep unconsciousness. It was later learned that a fractured rib had punctured his left lung. Thinking he had to find help, none too clear-headed himself, Mackey made crude snowshoes and stumbled away from the plane. While he was gone, Banting somehow got off the bunk, found his way outside the plane, and staggered a few feet in the deep snow. He fell face down in the snow and died. Had he been conscious, Banting surely would have been almost content to face death while doing his duty, in the northern wilderness, far from the cities and the people who had wanted so much from him.

The weather was so bad that Gander could not get planes up searching for the Hudson until 2:00 p.m. on Friday, just about the time Banting was dying in the snow. The rescue aircraft could not find T-9449. Late in the day the RCAF began informing Banting's colleagues at the University and the NRC that the plane was missing and presumed lost. Duncan Graham broke the news to Henrietta. They all hoped against hope that the flyers and their passenger would be found alive. The searchers were still looking late on Sunday when it was decided to inform the public that Sir Frederick Banting was missing on a flight to England.

Mackey had come back to the plane and stayed with it, trying to light signal fires as the search planes passed over him. On Monday morning he was about to give up and try to trek to the railway, when the crash was finally seen by a searching Hudson – apparently because of the aluminum powder Mackey had scattered outside.

Mackey stamped out a message in the snow, THREE DEAD – JOE. The Hudson dropped rations for Mackey and a message to some Newfoundlanders who were hunting rabbits in the vicinity.

The first news about the location of the plane mentioned one survivor. Everyone in Canada hoped the survivor was Banting. His friends all thought that if anyone could survive a plane crash it would be Fred. He was so vital, so determined. Then they found the survivor was the pilot. The public announcement of Banting's death was made in the House of Commons, by the politicians whose activities he so despised.

The Newfoundlanders found the plane and the pilot and took Mackey into Musgrave Harbour. A party from that outport went to the crash and retrieved the three bodies. They were sewn into white sheets and kept for several days in the local Orange Lodge. Finally the weather cleared enough to allow ski-equipped planes to land and bring them back. There was a brief service in Musgrave Harbour, and almost the whole community turned out to see the planes depart. The Salvation Army band played a parting hymn and "God Save the King." All of Banting's personal papers, including his diaries, were retrieved from the crash. The military posted a guard on the plane. The first reporter to visit it, an employee of the Toronto *Star*, was kept away.

Bird and Snailham were buried in Halifax. Captain Mackey was taken to Montreal. For a substantial sum of money, which he gave to Snailham's three parentless children, Mackey sold the exclusive story of Banting's last flight to the Toronto *Star*.

Reverend Peter Addison, who had known Fred all his life, conducted a private service for family and close friends in a Toronto funeral home on Monday, March 3. Then the body was moved to the University's Convocation Hall, to lie in state the next morning while thousands of visitors paid their respects. Canon Cody, the president of the University, conducted the state funeral service that afternoon. Banting's friend from the Arts and Letters Club, Healey Willan, played the organ. One of the prominent mourners who helped comfort Henrietta was ninety-seven-year-old Sir William Mulock.

After the service the flag-draped casket was placed on a gun carriage, and a two-hundred-man military escort accompanied the procession through mid-Toronto. An RCAF pipe band played the funeral march. Dressed in the uniform of a major in the Canadian

Army, his Great War medals on his chest, Banting was lowered into his grave in Mount Pleasant Cemetery. Three volleys were fired over his grave, four trumpeters played "The Last Post," then "Reveille," and his fellow officers gave Fred a last salute.

The newspapers paid the usual tributes to Banting. Henrietta received hundreds of personal notes of condolence. She and Bill were only modestly provided for: Fred's estate totalled only $72,000, including life insurance. Henrietta enrolled in medicine at the University of Toronto that autumn, graduating in 1945. She was a very private person who never remarried, and died in 1976 after many years of quiet and effective service at the Woman's College Hospital in Toronto. Bill Banting, who was artistically inclined, made his career with the Canadian Broadcasting Corporation. His mother, Marion, died of cancer in 1946.

The men sat silent, none able to bring himself to speak, when the NRC's Associate Committee on Medical Research convened for the first time after Banting's death. J.B. Collip particularly mourned Fred Banting. Collip became his successor as senior administrator of medical research in Canada and the leading figure in Canadian medical research. After the war, Collip moved from McGill to Western, attracted there by Ed Hall, who became Dean of Medicine and then the university's president. Collip died in 1965.

The research projects Banting had initiated or supported were carried on by his colleagues in the department and by Ed Hall's team in the RCAF. Franks' flying suit was used in combat, and is recognized as having been the world's first anti-gravity suit for aviators. Canadian research in aviation medicine during the war is thought to have been of extremely high quality, one of the finest collaborative achievements of Canadian scientists. Even the biological warfare research was eventually taken up, largely by animal pathologists, and experiments at the old quarantine station on Grosse Isle in the St. Lawrence River produced a useful vaccine for rinderpest.

The University of Toronto had not done a particularly good job in the way it had handled the personnel problems created by the discovery of insulin in 1921-23. Now it made the appointment Banting would have least favoured, in giving the headship of the Banting and Best Department of Medical Research to Charles H. Best. Perhaps it was the only way a difficult situation could be resolved in the interests of future research at the University, but those closest to Banting were the most opposed to the appointment. Sadie Gairns was one of the first of several staff members to leave the department. In 1950 the University of Toronto opened the Best Institute, next door to the Banting Institute. It currently houses the Department of Medical Research. Best died in 1978.

In 1941 there was a proliferation of Banting medals and Banting lectureships to honour the fallen research man. Since then, several Canadian high schools, a United States Liberty ship, and a crater on the moon, have all been named after him. So has the house he owned that year in London, Ontario, which is now Banting House, headquarters of the Ontario branch of the Canadian Diabetes Association, and a local tourist attraction. Similarly, the Banting farm at Alliston has been recognized as a Canadian historic site.

As the men and women who had worked with Fred Banting and grown to love him came to the end of their lives in the 1980s, there was a danger that he would only be remembered and known as a desiccated symbol. It is better to remember him as an ordinary man who dreamed of and was touched by greatness, many times fell woefully short of his goals, but kept on trying to do his duty.

Notes

Foreword (pp. 7-13)

1. C.J. Mackenzie to A.G. McNaughton, April 17, 1941, in Mel Thistle, ed., *The Mackenzie-McNaughton Wartime Letters* (Toronto: University of Toronto Press, 1975), p. 74; also, National Research Council Archives, Ottawa, War Diary of C.J. Mackenzie.
2. Banting Papers, Fisher Rare Books Library, University of Toronto, Box 38, Miscellaneous note, March 13, 1938.
3. F. Scott Fitzgerald, *The Great Gatsby* (New York: Scribner's, 1925), p. 6.
4. Leonard Mosley, *Lindbergh: A Biography* (New York: Doubleday, 1976), p. 320.
5. Joan Didion, *The White Album* (New York: Simon and Schuster, 1979), p. 53.
6. Justin Kaplan, *Walt Whitman, A Life* (New York: Simon and Schuster, 1980), p. 196.

Chapter One: "A White Boy, a Right Boy" (pp. 15-27)

1. This incident and most of the others described in this chapter are drawn from the autobiographical writings contained in the Banting Papers, Box 38.
2. BP, Box 62, Isabel Knight to Henrietta Banting, c. 1968; interview with Ella Knight Graham, 1981.
3. Toronto *Star*, Jan. 2, 1924.
4. Banting's junior matriculation results are in BP, Box 1; for the interview with the principal see BP, 47, clipping from the Toronto *Evening Telegram*, Jan. 18, 1923.
5. BP, 33, undated small notebook.
6. Saskatoon *Star-Phoenix*, Feb. 28, 1941.

Chapter Two: Becoming a Man (pp. 29-43)

1. Canadian Diabetes Association Archives, Rev. Harding Vowles to Thora Mills, June 11, 1981; Addison in undated obituary clipping; interview with Marion Walwyn.
2. Interview with Mr. and Mrs. S.H. Graham.
3. For the modernization of the University, see Michael Bliss, *A Canadian Millionaire: The Life and Business Times of Sir Joseph Flavelle, 1858-1939* (Toronto: Macmillan, 1978). The quality of Toronto's medical facility is confirmed in the Flexner Report of 1910.
4. Interviews with Spencer Clark and S.H. Graham.
5. BP, 22, "Psychiatry" notebook, "Mollie" story.
6. BP, 40, "The Story of Insulin."
7. Ibid.
8. Ibid.
9. Ibid.; BP, 1, FGB to Isabel Knight, May 6, 1917.
10. BP, 1, FGB to Isabel Knight, Jan. 17, 1918.
11. Ibid., March 30, 1918.

12. Interviews. There may be an echo of this story in the reference to Banting's extravagant purchases of china in Lloyd Stevenson, *Sir Frederick Banting* (Toronto: Ryerson, 1946), p. 41. See also, Chapter Six, p. 132.
13. "The Story of Insulin."
14. BP, 39, "Captain Grant" file, "Just Murder" file.
15. "The Story of Insulin."
16. BP, 38, "The Horse."
17. Quoted in Stevenson, p. 51.
18. BP, 47, p. 179 contains the letters to his mother; Gallie's visit is mentioned in Stevenson, p. 53.
19. See Stevenson, pp. 51-53.
20. BP, 1, FGB to Isabel Knight, Dec. 13, 1918; "The Story of Insulin"; BP, 38, miscellaneous notes, "Christmas in Edinburgh."

Chapter Three: Getting out of Town (pp. 44-60)

1. "The Story of Insulin."
2. Ibid. Robertson's work is described in Max Braithwaite, *Sick Kids* (Toronto, 1974).
3. "The Story of Insulin"; diary of Rowland Hill, privately held; interview with S.H. Graham.
4. "The Story of Insulin."
5. Rowland Hill diary, Sept. 20, 1920.
6. "The Story of Insulin."
7. In the first edition of *The Discovery of Insulin* (Toronto: McClelland and Stewart, 1982), I interpreted this change slightly differently, as a post-midnight correction. My own correlation of days and dates was inaccurate. October 31 was Sunday, not Monday. It is possible, of course, that Banting got the idea late on the Saturday night, October 30.
   For more details concerning all aspects of the discovery of insulin, as well as more complete documentation, refer to *The Discovery of Insulin*.
8. Rowland Hill diary, Nov. 6, 1920.
9. The discussion of Banting's and Macleod's meetings is developed from three sources. Banting's versions are in "The Story of Insulin," and in his September 1922 account of events, published in "Banting's, Best's, and Collip's Accounts of the Discovery of Insulin," *Bulletin of the History of Medicine*, 56 (1982), pp. 554-68. Macleod's September 1922 account of events is "History of the Researches Leading to the Discovery of Insulin," *Bulletin of the History of Medicine*, 52 (1978), pp. 295-312.
10. BP, 1, C.L. Starr to FGB, Dec. 14, 1920.
11. Academy of Medicine, Toronto, FGB Notebook, FGB to C.S. Sherrington, March 8, 1921.
12. Letters appended to Macleod, "History . . . ."
13. "The Story of Insulin."
14. Letters appended to Macleod, "History . . . ."

Chapter Four: The Discovery of Insulin (pp. 61-86)

1. Academy of Medicine, FGB Notebook is the principal source of the recreation of the experiments until July 6.

2. "The Story of Insulin."
3. BP, 1, Best to Macleod, Aug. 9, 1921.
4. Ibid.; the principal source for the re-creation of the balance of the experiments is the series of Banting and Best insulin notebooks contained in the Banting Papers.
5. Banting and Best, "The Internal Secretion of the Pancreas," *Journal of Laboratory and Clinical Medicine*, VII, 5 (Feb. 1922), 256-71.
6. BP, 1, FGB to Macleod, Aug. 9, 1921.
7. Banting and Best, "The Internal Secretion of the Pancreas."
8. BP, 1, Macleod to Banting, Aug. 23, 1921.
9. "The Story of Insulin"; FGB 1922 in "Banting's, Best's, and Collip's Accounts . . ."; Macleod, "History of the Researches . . ."; University of Toronto, W.R. Feasby Papers, National Film Board file, Best dictation, March 20, 1956.
10. Interview with Maynard Grange, then the departmental librarian.
11. BP, 22, index cards; I. Pavel, *The Priority of N.C. Paulesco in the Discovery of Insulin* (Bucharest, 1976).
12. BP, 1, FGB to C.L. Starr, Oct. 19, 1921; BP, 39, typed diary entry, Nov. 14, 1921.
13. FGB 1922 in "Banting's, Best's, and Collip's Accounts . . ."; memoir of Professor Noble Sharp, University of Toronto *Graduate* (Spring 1983).
14. Macleod Papers, Fisher Library, University of Toronto, folder 342, Joslin to Macleod, Nov. 19, 1921; reply Nov. 21.
15. Collip, "History of the Discovery of Insulin," *Northwest Medicine*, 22, (1923), 267-73; also in "Banting's, Best's, and Collip's Accounts . . . ."
16. BP, 22, index cards; Banting and Best notebooks.
17. Joslin, "A Personal Impression," *Diabetes*, 5, I (1956), 67-68.
18. Banting 1922 in "Banting's, Best's, and Collip's Accounts . . ."; "The Story of Insulin."
19. Macleod, "History of the Researches . . . ."
20. "The Story of Insulin."
21. Banting, Best, Collip, Campbell, and A.A. Fletcher, "Pancreatic Extracts in the Treatment of Diabetes Mellitus. Preliminary Report," *Canadian Medical Association Journal*, 2, 141 (March 1922), 141-46.
22. Macleod, "History of the Researches . . ."
23. "The Story of Insulin."
24. Collip Papers, Weldon Library, University of Western Ontario, Collip to Dr. C.F. Martin, Nov. 23, 1949.
25. "The Story of Insulin"; Feasby Papers, Best to H.H. Dale, Feb. 22, 1954.
26. The agreement is in BP, 48, p. 61.
27. Banting and Best, "Pancreatic Extracts," *Journal of Laboratory and Clinical Medicine*, VII, 8 (May 1922), 3-11.
28. BP, 18, Notes re Cancer Research file.
29. "The Story of Insulin."
30. Banting, Best, Collip, Campbell, Fletcher, Macleod and Noble, "The Effect Produced on Diabetes by Extracts of Pancreas", *Transactions of the Association of American Physicians* (1922), 1-11. The Toronto group did not know of earlier suggestions, by de Meyer (1909) and Schafer (1916), that the hypothetical internal secretion should be named "insuline."

Chapter Five: Banting Triumphant (pp. 87-108)

1. Memoir of Professor Noble Sharp, University of Toronto *Graduate* (Spring 1983).
2. Toronto *Star*, Nov. 7, 1923.
3. See Joseph H. Pratt, "A Reappraisal of Researches leading to the Discovery of Insulin", *Journal of the History of Medicine*, 9 (1954), 281-89.
4. "The Story of Insulin."
5. FGB 1922 in "Banting's, Best's, and Collip's Accounts."
6. "The Story of Insulin."
7. Havens family papers, privately held, James Havens to Joslin, Nov. 22, 1957.
8. E.C. Noble Papers, Fisher Library, University of Toronto, manuscript account by Noble.
9. Falconer Papers, 76, Falconer to C.S. Blackwell, June 19, 1922.
10. BP, 1, memorandum dated "About June 1922"; Havens papers for correspondence about Eastman.
11. "The Story of Insulin."
12. Best family papers, privately held, M.M. Best scrapbook, Banting to Best, July 15, 1922.
13. "The Story of Insulin."
14. Eli Lilly and Company archives, Indianapolis, J.K. Lilly to Eli Lilly, July 26, 1922.
15. "The Story of Insulin."
16. BP, 47, p. 10, Detroit *Free Press*, Aug. 26, 1922. For his fees see BP, 1, FGB to Graham, Oct. 27, 1922; also desk calendar, Aug. 3, 1922.
17. Stevenson, *Banting*, pp. 159-60; interview with Helen Best Crisp, Banting's former secretary.
18. BP, 1, Clowes to FGB, Aug. 11, 1922.
19. Feasby Papers, Toronto, C.H. Best dictation, November 24, 1961.
20. "The Story of Insulin."
21. FGB. "Insulin," *Journal of the Michigan State Medical Society* (March 1923).
22. "The Story of Insulin."
23. Ibid.
24. Ibid.
25. Elizabeth Hughes Gossett Papers, privately held, Elizabeth Hughes to Antoinette Hughes, Oct. 17, 1922.
26. Ibid., Oct. 21, 1922.
27. Ibid., Nov. 26, 1922.
28. BP, 9, Ruth Blenchly to FGB, July 19, 1923; Blaustein file, patients' records, Lewis Blaustein to FGB, Nov. 27, 1922; Richards file, Gladys Richards to FGB, Aug. 19, 1923; Stickelberger files; BP, 1, J.T. Clarke to FGB, Dec. 11, 1922; letters from patients files, Bonnie Powers to FGB, Dec. 13, 1922.
29. Insulin Committee Papers, University of Toronto archives, clippings file, New York *Tribune*, Dec. 22, 1922.
30. BP 47, scrapbooks.
31. Segall diary, privately held.

Chapter Six: The Hero of Insulin (pp. 109-35)

1. Macleod Papers, folder 342, Macleod to Collip, Feb. 28, 1923.

2.	Toronto *Telegram*, Jan. 18, 1923.
3.	W.L.M. King Papers, Public Archives of Canada, *Diary*, Feb. 13, 1923.
4.	BP, 26, desk calendar, Feb. 14, 1923.
5.	FGB to C_____, Oct. 1, 1936, as quoted in Stevenson, *Banting*, p. 154; Seale Harris, "Banting: Benefactor of Mankind," *Journal of the Florida Medical Association*, XXVIII, 1 (July 1941).
6.	Kevin F. Quinn, "Banting and His Biographers: Maker of Miracles, Maker of Myth," *Queen's Quarterly*, 89, 2 (Summer 1982), 243; Mary Vipond, "A Canadian Hero of the 1920s: Dr. Frederick G. Banting," *Canadian Historical Review*, LXIII, 4 (1982), 482.
7.	BP, 49, p. 22, unidentified clipping.
8.	Stephen Leacock, *Arcadian Adventures with the Idle Rich*, 1914; (Toronto: New Canadian Library edition), p. 24.
9.	Toronto *Star*, Feb. 24, 1923.
10.	FGB 1922 in "Banting's, Best's, and Collip's Accounts"; Macleod, "History...."; Macleod Papers, folder 342, Macleod to A.B. Macallum, Sept. 14, 1922.
11.	Toronto *Globe*, Sept. 9, 1922.
12.	Collip Papers, privately held, Macleod to Collip, Sept. 18, 1922; Macleod Papers, folder 342, Macleod to A.B. Macallum, Sept. 14, 1922.
13.	FGB 1922 in "Banting's, Best's, and Collip's Accounts."
14.	BP, 1, FGB to Macleod, Sept. 27, 1922; FGB to J.G. Fitzgerald, Oct. 5, 1922.
15.	BP, 7, Insulin Notebook, Nov. 4, 1922; unless otherwise noted all accounts of Banting's research activities are compiled from the original notebooks in the Banting Papers.
16.	BP, 34, draft paper, "Cause of Diabetes Mellitus."
17.	BP, 7, FGB memorandum in "Notes on Diabetes" file. Nobel Committee Archives, Caroline Institute, Stockholm, Nomination for the 1923 prize by August Krogh. I did not notice Banting's memorandum until after publication of *The Discovery of Insulin*.
18.	BP, 1, Ross to FGB, July 10, 1923.
19.	BP, 26, desk calendar, Feb. 26, 1923.
20.	King Papers, JI, 77025-30, Mulock to King, March 23, 1923.
21.	BP, 1, March 1923 file, letters of Joslin and Allen.
22.	King Papers, JI, 74205-9, Hughes to King, March 16, 1923.
23.	Ibid., 72677-78, Falconer to King, June 2, 1923.
24.	Macleod Papers, Macleod to H.H. Dale, May 15, 1923.
25.	BP, 26, desk calendar, May 26, 1923.
26.	Ibid., April 15, 1923.
27.	BP, 1, Mulock to Ross, undated in July 1923 file.
28.	BP, 1, July 1923 file; Best Papers, privately held, M.M. Best scrapbooks, Banting to Best, July 15, 1923.
29.	Ibid.
30.	BP, 26, desk calendar, June 14, 1923.
31.	BP, 1, FGB to Hipwell in July 1923 file.
32.	BP, 26, desk calendar, July 14, 1923.
33.	"The Story of Insulin."
34.	BP, 47, p. 44, clippings; "The Story of Insulin."
35.	BP, 26, desk calendar; *British Medical Journal* (Sept. 15, 1923.).
36.	BP, 47, p. 44, clippings.
37.	BP, 26, desk calendar, Aug. 10, 1923.
38.	BP, 1, FGB to Geyelin, Nov. 10, 1923; *Star*, Aug. 18, 1923.

39. BP, 47, CNE clippings.
40. "The Story of Insulin."
41. BP, 1, Banting to Geyelin, Nov. 10, 1923; interview with Robert L. Noble, whose father was president of the Academy that year.
42. See *Nobel, The Man and His Prizes*, issued by the Nobel Foundation (Stockholm, 1950; third edition, New York 1972).
43. Stevenson, *Banting*, p. 170. In the first edition of *The Discovery of Insulin* I was probably mistaken in accepting Banting's 1940 memory that the money came to $24,000. A telegram in his papers is the basis of the revised estimate. The papers also contain his correspondence with his financial advisers.

Chapter Seven: The Elixir of Life (136-56)

1. BP, 7, Insulin Notebook, Nov. 23, 1922, *et seq*.
2. Ibid; F.G. Banting and S. Gairns, "Factors influencing production of insulin," *American Journal of Physiology*, 68 (March 1924), 24-30.
3. BP, 21, Diphtheria Notebook.
4. BP, 47, clipping, Oct. 11, 1922.
5. BP, 9, Clowes to FGB, Oct. 11, 1922.
6. *Star*, Oct. 19, 1922; BP, 47, pp. 55, 73, clippings.
7. See Graeme Gibson, *Perpetual Motion* (Toronto: McClelland & Stewart, 1982).
8. BP, 1, FGB to Geyelin, Nov. 10, 1922; J.H. McPhedran Diary, March 11, 1929.
9. FGB, "Medical Research and the Discovery of Insulin"; *Hygeia*, 2 (1924), 288-292.
10. Harris, *Banting's Miracle*, p. 130.
11. BP, 39, "The Revolt" file.
12. BP, 26, Diary 1924.
13. Stevenson, *Banting*, p. 199; Bailey K. Ashford, *A Soldier in Science* (New York, 1934), p. 345.
14. BP, 14, Cancer Notebook, 1924; Stevenson, *Banting*, pp. 208-9; FGB, "The History of Insulin," *Edinburgh Medical Journal* (Jan. 1929), 1-18.
15. BP, 33.
16. Harris, *Banting's Miracle*, pp. 138-40; Stevenson, *Banting*, p. 204; Ashford, *A Soldier in Science*, p. 350.
17. Harris, *Banting's Miracle*, p. 136.
18. BP, 26, Diary 1924.
19. BP, 14, Cancer Notebook, 1924.
20. BP, Suprarenal Notebook, Dec. 2, 1924.
21. "The Story of Insulin."
22. PAC, RG 10, Box 374, University of Toronto file, J.J.R. Macleod to J.W.S. McCullough, Oct. 19, 1922, and enclosures.
23. BP, 1, Cornell to Banting, undated file.
24. University of Toronto Archives, Banting Research Foundation papers; see also the BRF files in the Falconer Papers; *Globe*, March 16, 1925; Toronto *Mail and Empire*, June 27, 1925; *Star*, June 9, 1925.
25. FGB, "Medical Research," *Annals of Clinical Medicine*, 3 (March 1925), 565-72.
26. BP, 47, p. 108, clipping.

1. BP, 1, FGB to Best, April 16, 1926; 21, Pregnant Rabbits Notebook.
2. BP, 1, FGB to Collip, June 30, 1925; reply, July 7.
3. "The Story of Insulin." p. 65.
4. Interviews; Records of the Supreme Court of Ontario, Banting *versus* Banting, 1932, intervention by W.R. Robertson.
5. BP, 39, "The Revolt" file.
6. *Arrowsmith*, Signet Classic edition, pp. 398, 397.
7. BP, 39, "Si" file, including Vernon McKenzie to FGB, July 15, 1927.
8. BP, 25, Notebook.
9. Interview with Helen Best Crisp.
10. *Star*, Nov. 10, 1923; Stevenson, *Banting*, p. 233; A.Y. Jackson, "Memories of a Fellow Artist, Frederick Grant Banting," *Canadian Medical Association Journal*, 92 (May 15, 1965), 1077-84. Jackson described Banting's paintings as "mostly awful potboilers. When I first knew him I laughed at these purchases."
11. *Star Weekly*, Jan. 24, 31, 1925.
12. Jackson's accounts of his friendship with Banting are in "Memories of a Fellow Artist," his 1943 booklet, *Banting As an Artist* (Toronto, Ryerson Press), and his autobiography, *A Painter's Country* (Toronto: Clarke Irwin, 1958). Jackson mentions his relation with Macleod in the tape of an address from which "Memories of a Fellow Artist" was compiled; the transcript omitted the Macleod story. The tape is in the Banting Papers. Hunter Bishop, archivist and fellow member of the Arts and Letters Club, kindly searched club records for me to ascertain membership details. Jackson remembered his first meeting with Banting as 1927, but it must have been earlier.
13. Jackson, "Memories of a Fellow Artist."
14. *Arrowsmith*, pp. 308, 410.
15. For Banting's relations and correspondence with the Department of the Interior regarding this trip, see PAC, RG 85, vol. 778, file 5713; Royal Society of London, Sir Henry Dale Papers, Best to Dale, July 25, 1927.
16. Jackson's two diary accounts of this trip have been published in A.Y. Jackson, *The Arctic, 1927* (Moonbeam, Ont.: Penumbra Press, 1982); Banting's travel diary is in the Banting Papers, 28, and has been published in *Northward Journal*, Number 14/15, 1979.
17. Jackson diaries, Aug. 13.
18. *Star*, Sept. 7, 8, 1927; Department of the Interior records (see note 15); Roy Greenaway, *The News Game* (Toronto: Clarke Irwin, 1966).
19. Archives of the Hudson's Bay Company, Public Archives of Manitoba, *Minutes*, March 13, 1928; Jackson, "Memories of a Fellow Artist."
20. Ibid.; Banting's diary of this trip is in the Banting Papers, 28.
21. Falconer Papers, 118, Physiology file, H.S. Roper to Duncan Graham, May 10, 1928; ibid., 115, Macleod to Falconer, Dec. 10, 1928.
22. BP, 2, Mulock to Banting, May 26, 1928.
23. Ibid., Banting, Mulock, Best correspondence, Jan. 27 – Feb. 20, 1930.
24. BP, 1, Joslin to FGB, Jan. 12, 1926; Abel to FGB, Jan. 30, 1926.
25. "The Story of Insulin"; also Claude T. Bissell, *The Young Vincent Massey* (Toronto: University of Toronto Press, 1981), p. 257.
26. "The Story of Insulin," p. 76.

27. Falconer Papers, 119, Falconer to FGB, Sept. 13, 1929; FGB to Falconer, Oct. 11, 1929.

28. "The Story of Insulin"; Stevenson, *Banting*, p. 288.

Chapter Nine: Banting *versus* Banting (pp. 184-205)

1. BP, 18, Notes in Calgary, July 13, 1926.
2. BP, 18, Cancer Notebooks, Aug. 12, Sept. 3, May 10, 1926; March 21, 1928.
3. BP, 18, Notebook, June 8, 1929.
4. BP, 34, Research, miscellaneous notes, draft speech at Albany, N.Y., 1931.
5. Ibid.; BP, 21, Notes re diarrhoea in infants.
6. C.C. Lucas, "Chemical Examination of Royal Jelly," *Canadian Medical Association Journal* (Nov. 1942).
7. George Dana Porter, "Notes of a Trip to Washington With Sir Frederick Banting," *Saturday Night*, May 13, 1944; BP, 2, FGB to Sherwood Fox, Sept. 18, 1930; FGB to W.L. Grant, Sept. 18, 1930.
8. BP, 19, FGB ms. account of work on silicosis; D. Irwin, "The Contribution of Sir Frederick Banting to Silicosis Research", *Canadian Medical Association Journal* (Nov. 1942).
9. Records of the Supreme Court of Ontario, Banting *versus* Banting, 1932, FGB application for divorce; W.R. Robertson intervention.
10. BP, 28, 1930 travel diary, March 8.
11. Ibid., March 8, 11, April 1.
12. Ibid., 1931 travel diary, March 12.
13. Ibid., 1930, March 11; Jackson quote in Anne McDougall, *Anne Savage: The Story of a Canadian Painter* (Montreal: Harvest House, 1977), p. 98.
14. BP, 28, 1930 travel diary, March 12.
15. Ibid., March 16.
16. Jackson, *Banting As an Artist*, p. 30; BP, 28, 1930 travel diary, March 23.
17. BP, 38, Notes, Nov. 14, 1931.
18. Ibid., Sept. 2, Feb. 10, 1930.
19. Ibid., Sept. 2, 1930.
20. Banting *versus* Banting, W.R. Robertson affidavit.
21. BP, 62, Blodwen Davies to FGB, "Thursday."
22. BP, 25, poem, Jan. 2, 1932.
23. The primary source of detail regarding the raid and the relations in this triangle is the affidavit by D.M. LeBourdais in the records of Banting *versus* Banting. See also the affidavits by FGB, W.R. Robertson and Wm. Blatz. Some of the comings and goings, including the meetings with Mulock, are recorded in BP, 27, Banting's 1932 pocket diary. The Toronto newspapers were used, and these documents were supplemented by interviews.
24. Gordon Sinclair to the author, May 17, 1983.
25. Interview with Mrs. Fannie Lawrence.
26. Interview with Isabel (Mrs. D.M.) LeBourdais.
27. D.M. LeBourdais was the kind of person who told the truth about episodes like this to Isabel, the girl he later married (after they both had arranged divorces). She told it to me, and would have had no hesitation admitting the truth if an affair had taken place.

Chapter Ten: Banting *versus* Capitalism (pp. 206-30)

1. BP, 27, Sketchbook 1932.
2. BP, 62, Blodwen Davies to FGB, "Tuesday."
3. Ibid. Priscilla White file; interview with Priscilla White.
4. BP, 62, Blodwen Davies file.
5. There does not appear to be any foundation for the statement in Clara Thomas and John Lennox, *William Arthur Deacon: A Canadian Literary Life* (Toronto: University of Toronto Press, 1982), p. 12, implying that Banting was a member of the Toronto Theosophical Society.
6. BP, 27, Sketchbook, July 22, 1933; 27, Calendar, Jan. 17, 1935; Sketchbook, April 27, 1935. See also Banting's publications on cancer, 1934.
7. BP, 2, Gye to Banting, Dec. 7, 1933.
8. BP, 2, J.S. Haldane to Banting, Nov. 8, 1934; also D. Irwin, "The Contribution of Sir Frederick Banting to Silicosis Research."
9. BP, 2, Cody to FGB, Nov. 8, 1934; Wellcome Library for the History of Medicine, London, H.H. Dale statement on the insulin controversy, Oct. 1959, in documents relating to the insulin controversy; BP, 30, 1935 Diary, June 5.
10. BP, 48, p. 92, clipping June 4, 1934; ibid., p. 88; BP, 3, R.A. Stapells to FGB, June 4, 1934.
11. Harold Perkin memorandum to the author, June 1983.
12. BP, 27, Sketchbook, Jan. 12, 1935.
13. The account of the European trip and all quotations come from FGB's travel diary, contained in BP, 30.
14. BP, 48, p. 96, clippings re June 1934 CMA meeting.
15. BP, 38, miscellaneous reflections.
16. The account of the trip to the USSR and all quotations come from FGB's travel diary, contained in BP, 30.
17. *Globe*, Sept. 9, 1935.
18. BP, 35, miscellaneous notes; also "Science and the Soviet Union" file; interview by V. Shatzker, University of Toronto oral historian, with Mrs. Herbert Bruce.
19. BP, 35, "Trend of Civilization" speech; also miscellaneous notes.
20. Roderick Stewart, *Bethune* (Toronto: New Press, 1973), p. 73.
21. Ibid., p. 74. See also Ted Allan and Sydney Gordon, *The Scalpel, The Sword: The Story of Dr. Norman Bethune* (Boston: Little Brown, 1952).

Chapter Eleven: Maturity (pp. 231-53)

1. John Swettenham, *McNaughton* (Toronto: Ryerson, 1968) I, p. 331; G.H. Ettinger, *History of the Associate Committee on Medical Research* (Ottawa: National Research Council, 1946).
2. National Research Council Archives, File 36-5-0-4, FGB Confidental Memorandum for Major General McNaughton, received Sept. 18, 1937.
3. Swettenham, *McNaughton*, I, p. 328; NRC Archives, File 36-5-0-2, vol. I, Captain K.A. Hunter, "A Review of the Possibilities of Bacterial Warfare"; File 36-5-0-6, vol. I, Committee of Imperial Defence, Bacteriological Warfare Memorandum from the Medical Research Council, April 13, 1934;

Report of the Sub-Committee on Bacteriological Warfare, March 17, 1937.
4. Edward Banting Papers, Public Archives of Ontario, FGB to Margaret Banting, Dec. 4, 1938, Oct. 30, 1938.
5. National Research Council, Banting Papers, FGB to Thorlakson, May 18, 1939, reply August 12.
6. C.B. Stewart to the author, March 15, 1983; NRC BP, Stewart to FGB, Jan. 30, 1939.
7. G.W. Manning, *Banting. Insulin and Medical Research* (limited edition, privately printed, June 1980).
8. BP, 3, FGB to the editor of *Life and Health*, June 1939; BP, 50, Vancouver *Sun*, Dec. 6, 1938.
9. Irwin, "The Contribution of Sir Frederick Banting to Silicosis Research"; "Report of the Task Force on Aluminum Inhalation Therapy to the Minister of Labour," Jan. 11, 1980, published in Government of Ontario, Advisory Council on Occupational Health and Occupational Safety, *Second Annual Report*, 1980.
10. The overview of the activities of the Department of Medical Research is derived largely from the detailed departmental reports contained in the annual University of Toronto *President's Report*.
11. BP, 48, p. 116, *Telegram*, July 16, 1938, and other clippings; interview with B. Leibel.
12. BP, FGB War Diary, Oct. 2, 1940.
13. Manning, *Banting*, pp. 32-3; Harold Perkin to the author, June 1983.
14. BP, 27, Notes made July 29, 1938.
15. BP, 25, Miscellaneous views; Literary Efforts file.
16. BP, 25, Literary Efforts file.
17. BP, 38, Notes March 13, 1938.
18. Rebecca Sisler, *The Girls* (Toronto: Clarke Irwin, 1972).
19. BP, 28.
20. BP, 62, FGB Personal Note on _____
21. BP, 3, FGB to McNaughton, Sept. 16, 1938.
22. NRC BP, Aviation Medical Research Committee Minutes, June 27, 1938; P.C. 2207, Aug. 17, 1939; National Research Council, *History of the Associate Committee on Aviation Medical Resesarch, 1939-1945* (Ottawa, June 1946).
23. BP, 49, clippings re Leadership League; Ottawa *Journal*, April 19, 1939.
24. NRC BP, FGB to F.C. Blair, March 1, 1939; FGB to Blair, April 13, 1939; FGB to J.L. Malcolm, Aug. 5, 1940; H.H. Dale Papers, Royal Society of London, Best to Dale, Feb. 24, 1939.
25. BP, 22, "Psychiatry" Notebook.

Chapter Twelve: Warrior Scientist (pp. 254-74)

1. BP, 3, handwritten memorandum, Sept. 3, 1939.
2. NRC BP, Hall and Banting, Memorandum on a Proposed Medical Research Unit, 1939; Memorandum by Col. J.A. Linton, Sept. 20, 1939.
3. FGB War Diary; the best history of the Franks flying suit is Peter Allen, "The Remotest of Mistresses: The Story of Canada's Unsung Tactical Weapon: The Franks Flying Suit," *Canadian Aviation Historical Society Journal*, 21, 4, Winter 1983; other material on Franks and his suit derives from an interview with Franks, as well as conversations with Peter Allen.

4. NRC Archives, File 32-1-12, vol. 1, FGB to Mellanby, Oct. 21, 1939, inc. Memorandum on Mustard Gas Antidote.
5. Ibid., Memorandum re Visit of Dr. I.M. Rabinowitch, Sept. 30, 1939; Rabinowitch to McNaughton, Oct. 2, 1939.
6. NRC BP, A.V. Hill to C.H. Best, Sept. 23, 25, 1939; C.B. Stewart to FGB, Oct. 24.
7. NRC BP, FGB to C.B. Stewart, Dec. 4, 1939.
8. NRC BP, Memorandum of Chairman's Visit to England.
9. Ibid.; also FGB to Hall, Dec. 23, 1939.
10. Ibid., FGB to C.B. Stewart, Dec. 23, 1939; FGB to A.E. Bott, Dec. 23.
11. Ibid., FGB to C.B. Stewart, Memo #2, Dec. 11, 1939; FGB to C.J. Mackenzie, Dec. 12; NRC Archives, File 32-1-29, vol. 1, Mackenzie to J.B. Collip, Dec. 27, 1939.
12. NRC Archives, File 36-5-0-6, vol. 1, "Some Notes on Defence Against Bacteriological Warfare," Medical Research Council, Oct. 24, 1939.
13. Ibid., File 36-5-0-3, vol. 1, "Memorandum on the Present Situation Regarding Bacterial Warfare", Jan. 9, 1940.
14. Vincent Massey, *What's Past is Prologue* (New York: St. Martin's Press, 1964), p. 328.
15. Hall-Manning Papers, University of Western Ontario, Weldon Library, Hall to FGB, Jan. 25, 4, 1940.
16. Stephen Raskill, *Hankey. Man of Secrets* (London: Collins, 1974), III, 321-24, 432.
17. FGB War Diary, and NRC BP, Box 4, Misc. Correspondence, Memo on Splat Projectile.
18. NRC Archives, File 32-1-29, C.J. Mackenzie to Hon. W.D. Euler, Dec. 27, 1939; Mackenzie memorandum, Dec. 29, on scientists for service in war research in England; Collip to Mackenzie, Jan. 16, 1940; Mackenzie to Collip, Jan. 18.
19. Dale Papers, Dale to Best, March 8, 1940.
20. NRC BP, Hall to C.B. Stewart, Jan. 29, 1940, enclosing four memoranda on aviation medicine. Mellanby of the MRC was also head of the Flying Personnel Research Committee, charged with responsibility for aviation medicine research. Banting's liaison in this field, however, was with Air Vice-Marshal H.E. Whittingham, who was much more enthusiastic than Mellanby about the Canadian team's potential contribution.
21. Ibid., FGB Memorandum re Committee on Aviation Medical Research, March 12, 1940; FGB to Col. R. Linton, April 10, 1940; Proceedings of the Third Meeting of the Committee on Aviation Medical Research, March 9, 1940; C.J. Mackenzie to A.G.L. McNaughton, March 12, 1940, in Thistle, *The Mackenzie—McNaughton Wartime Letters*, pp. 24-25.
22. Mackenzie to McNaughton, March 1, 1940, in ibid., pp. 20-21.
23. FGB War Diary, and BP, 20, Mustard Gas notes.
24. FGB War Diary, May 20, 1940; Dale Papers, Dale to Mellanby, June 10, 1940.
25. NRC BP, Mackenzie to FGB, June 22, 1940.

Chapter Thirteen: "A Dark Sense of Duty" (pp. 275-97)

The chapter title is a phrase applied to the lost pilot, who cannot land, in Antoine Saint-Exupery's *Night Flight*, published in 1932.
1. NRC BP, Memorandum re Aircraft Acceleration, June 19, 1940, by J.J.

Green, J.L. Orr, G.S. Levy, and enclosed rebuttals.

2.   Hall-Manning Papers, UWO, Hall to Banting, June 6, 1940.

3.   NRC, C.J. Mackenzie War Diary, Nov. 13, 1940; a copy of the notebook recording these experiments is in the BP.

4.   Manning, *Banting*, p. 50.

5.   FGB War Diary; NRC Archives, File 36-5-0-0, vol. 1, FGB to Mackenzie, June 24, 1940; NRC BP, FGB to McNaughton, July 12. The official letter to the secretary of the NRC initiating the project was from the Acting Deputy Minister (Militia) on July 12, and asked for research "along the following lines:
(a) The possibility of the distribution of infectious agents by bomb, shell or aeroplane;
(b) The determination of the infectious agents which might be used;
(c) The determination of suitable methods for the protection of personnel against infectious agents distributed by such means, including large scale production, etc.;
(d) Investigation of any other matters pertaining to or arising from any aspect of Bacteriological Warfare which may be considered important."
NRC Archives, File 36-5-0-0, vol. 1.

6.   FGB War Diary, Sept. 17, 1940; for these plans see also NRC Archives, File 36-5-0-1, vol. 1, Extracts from notes made by Dr. Banting of meetings held by various people in connection with B.W. from July 11-Dec. 2, 1940.

7.   NRC Archives, File 36-5-0-4, vol. 1, Memorandum re Project M-1000.

8.   Ibid., File 36-5-0-1, Extracts from notes . . .

9.   Ibid.

10.   Ibid., File 36-5-0-5, Notes of a meeting held . . . Dec. 17, 1941.

11.   For Laurence's work see Wilfrid Eggleston, *National Research in Canada, The National Research Council 1916-1966* (Toronto: Clarke Irwin, 1978), pp. 158-60.

12.   BP NRC, McNaughton to FGB, Aug. 13, 1940; FGB to McNaughton, Dec. 9, 1940; Swettenham, *McNaughton*, II, 134-35; D.J. Goodspeed, *A History of the Defence Research Board of Canada* (Ottawa: Queen's Printer, 1958), pp. 144-46.

13.   Jefferson Lewis, *Something Hidden: A Biography of Wilder Penfield* (Toronto: Doubleday, 1981), p. 176.

14.   FGB War Diary, Aug. 19, Nov. 22, 1940.

15.   Cody Papers, University of Toronto Archives, Best to Cody, Sept. 25, 1940, enclosing Best to C.S. Macdonald, same date; Best to C.E. Higginbottam, Nov. 7, 1940.

16.   Dale Papers, Hill file, Hill to Mellanby, Nov. 15, 1940; NRC BP, A.A. James to FGB, Oct. 10, 1940; BP, 3, FGB to James, Dec. 8, 1940.

17.   NRC BP, H.E. Whittingham to FGB, June 17, 1940.

18.   NRC, Mackenzie War Diary, Dec. 13, 1940; FGB War Diary, Dec. 12, 16.

19.   FGB War Diary, Jan. 11, 1941; Mackenzie War Diary, Jan. 17.

20.   NRC BP, McNaughton to FGB, Jan. 9, 1941, enclosing Rabinowitch to McNaughton, Jan. 8.

21.   Dale Papers, Best to Dale, Jan. 17, 1941; FGB daybook, 1941, Jan. 17.

22.   The view that Banting was undertaking the mission because Best had decided not to go was published in Thistle, ed., *The Mackenzie–McNaughton Wartime Letters*, p. 62, Mackenzie to McNaughton, Feb. 11, 1941: "Dr. Best has been wanting to go and we finally made arrangements but he then decided he had other work to do so Banting is going." It

cannot be said, however, that Banting was on the plane Best would have taken, for Best would undoubtedly have crossed by a more orthodox air or sea route.

Chapter Fourteen: At a Post of Duty (pp. 298-310)

1. See Hugh Hood, *Black and White Keys* (Toronto: ECW Press, 1982).
2. NRC, Mackenzie War Diary, March 4, 1941. I did not discover this surprising allocation of credit until after publication of *The Discovery of Insulin*. I do not believe it is accurate, despite Collip's obvious credentials. In addition to discounting it for the bonhomie of the Collip-Banting meeting, there is also the possibility that the grief-stricken Collip garbled the 'story in telling it to Mackenzie after Banting's death.
3. Geoffrey P. Jones, *Attacker: The Hudson and its Flyers* (London: Kimber, 1980), Chapter V.
4. BP, 45, file 1, CM Tripp account of Banting's visit to Gander.
5. Clifford Wilson's notes, quoted in Stevenson, *Banting*, chapter 25.
6. Richard S. Malone, *A Portrait of War* (Toronto: Collins, 1983), pp. 48-49.
7. NRC, Mackenzie War Diary, April 2, 1941; interview with P.D. McTaggart-Cowan, Jan. 1984.
8. Joseph Mackey's account of the crash was published in the Toronto *Star*, March 13, 14, 16, 1941.
9. This point is made by both McTaggart-Cowan and those who remember the conclusions of the commission of inquiry. The uncertainty about the parachute situation in the preceding paragraph is caused by slight discrepancies between Mackey's account and McTaggart-Cowan's memory. Another version of the cause of the crash, which may have influenced the commission of inquiry, blames engine icing. According to McTaggart-Cowan, icing was often used to cover up the details of mechanical failure. Maintenance crews at Gander began automatically changing the Hudson's oil coolers until the manufacturer corrected the defect.

Sources and Acknowledgements

By far the most important sources for this biography were the contents of the sixty-two boxes of Frederick G. Banting Papers housed in the Thomas Fisher Rare Book Library at the University of Toronto and owned by the University. These were fully opened to qualified scholars when I began my research in 1980; although there are still minor restrictions to protect living people, they are now fully accessible. The papers contain all of Banting's research notebooks, extensive scrapbooks of newspaper clippings, all of the correspondence that he kept (he was not a prodigious letter writer), copies of his speeches and articles, his attempts at creative writing and, most important, the diaries that he compiled from time to time. His diaries include travel journals for most of his major trips; occasional fragments in notebooks or on desk calendars; and long, detailed daily entries from September 1939 until his death. Banting appears to have kept almost all the private writing he ever did. There are a few signs, however, that he or his widow occasionally destroyed particularly sensitive writings or letters. His University correspondence as Head of the Department of Medical Research has apparently also been destroyed.

A second collection of Banting Papers is held at the Library of the National Research Council of Canada in Ottawa. It consists of several boxes of correspondence and printed documents relating to Banting's work as a member of NRC and its committees after 1937. These papers, plus the diaries in Toronto, plus a number of files in the NRC archives relating to chemical and biological warfare, are the principal sources for Banting's war-related research.

Many other collections of papers, published primary and secondary sources, and interviews were used to flesh out the documents Banting kept. A complete list of the sources used to recreate the discovery of insulin is contained in *The Discovery of Insulin* (Toronto, Chicago, Edinburgh, 1982). Many of those same sources, such as the Best, Collip, Falconer, and W.L.M. King Papers, contributed additional information used in this book. Other collections and sources were searched as necessary for material pertinent to Banting's career after insulin; these are cited in the notes as they are drawn upon.

Interviews with everyone I could find who had known Banting, or had known those close to Banting, were a vital part of my research for this book, as they were for *The Discovery of Insulin*. Many interviewees asked that I not attribute material directly to them. This explains some unattributed quotes in the text. The notes from the interviews (I seldom use a tape recorder), as well as my correspondence with people who knew Banting, will be deposited at the University of Toronto.

This book concludes a two-volume excursion into a fascinating and wonderful series of events in Toronto, centring on the enlargement of the possibilities of our human condition that occurred when insulin was discovered. These books could not have been written without the help of many people and institutions. With two exceptions – one individual and the Canada Council – I have received invaluable encouragement, help and advice, from medical scientists old and young, librarians and archivists, fellow scholars, and an extraordinary array of men and women who knew Banting or who have been interested in his life or who are simply interested in helping history come alive. The following list is an acknowledgement, in alphabetical order, of those who contributed to this book in addition to the help given me for *The Discovery of Insulin* and acknowledged there. Many who contributed to my research will not agree with my conclusions, which they will read here for the first time. As author, I alone am responsible for my selections of facts and interpretations, and for my errors.

Thanks for interviews, help with sources, comments and criticisms to: Peter Allen, Harold Averill, Edward Banting, William R. Banting, Edward Bensley, Henry Best, Margaret Mahon, (Mrs. C.H.) Best, L.W. Billingsley, Hunter Bishop, Helen Brown, Spencer Clark, Elizabeth Cleghorn, Robert Cleghorn, Stella Clutton, Bruce Collier, Helen Best Crisp, T.A. Crowther, Harold Ettinger, K.M. Fells, Gladys Fidlar, W.R. Franks, Sadie Gairns, Elizabeth Hughes Gossett, Ella Knight Graham, Jean Graham, T.S.H. Graham, J.L. Granatstein, Maynard Grange, Reginald Haist, Eleanor Hamilton, Yvonne McKauge Hausser, Barbara Hazlett, Michael Henderson, Karen Hendricks, Clarence Hill, Sir Harold Himsworth, Hudson's Bay Company Archives, Henry Janes, Phyllis Hipwell Janes, Robert Kerr, Richard Landon, Hugh Lawford, Fannie Lawrence, Isabel LeBourdais, Cecilia Long, Frederick MacCallum, Ian Macdonald, F.C. MacIntosh, Ross MacKay, Mrs. Joseph C. Mackey, C.J. Mackenzie, Patricia McLennan, P.D. McTaggart-Cowan, Linda Mahon, George Manning, Katharine Martyn, C.G. Matthews,

Clara Mills, Thora Mills, Robert Noble, Jean Orr, G.R. Paterson, Harold J. Perkin, J.M. Peterson, Burns Plewes, I.M. Rabinowitch, Allison Roach, Royal Society of London, David Rudkin, Mildred Ryder, Theodore Ryder, Valerie Schatzker, John W. Scott, Harold Segall, Gordon Sinclair, O.M. Solandt, Norman Stephenson, C.B. Stewart, Sheila Swanson, A.W. Tickner, Lady Todd, Toronto *Star* Library, Carl Vincent, Helen Findlay Waldon, Alan Walters, Marion Walwyn, LeRoy Wardner, Priscilla White, Gordon Whitfield, Hilton Wilkes, Victoria Wilkes, Barbara Wilson, Glenn Wright, Barbara Collip Wyatt, C. Jackson Wyatt, Sir Frank Young, Suzanne Zeller. Apologies to anyone who has been inadvertently omitted from this list.

Special thanks to my editor, Diane Mew, to McClelland and Stewart, to ace proof-readers James, Laura, and Sara Bliss, and to Liz.

This book was begun during a year as a Connaught Senior Fellow in the Humanities at the University of Toronto. A small grant from the Jason Hannah Institute for the History of Medicine helped with some of the research costs.

Michael Bliss
Toronto, December 4, 1983.

Bibliography of Frederick Grant Banting

F.R. Miller and F.G. Banting, "Observations on Cerebellar Stimulations," *Brain*, 45 (1922), 104-112.

F.G. Banting, C.H. Best, and J.J.R. MacLeod, "The Internal Secretion of the Pancreas," *American Journal of Physiology* (Proceedings of the American Physiological Society), 59 (1922), p. 479.

———, and Best, "The Internal Secretion of the Pancreas," *Journal of Laboratory and Clinical Medicine*, VII (1922), 256-71.

———, and Best, "The internal secretion of the pancreas," delivered to the Academy of Medicine, Toronto, Feb. 7, 1922, printed by the Academy.

———, and Best, "Pancreatic Extracts," *Journal of Laboratory and Clinical Medicine*, VII (1922), 464-72.

———, Best, J.B. Collip, W.R. Campbell, and A.A. Fletcher, "Pancreatic Extracts in the Treatment of Diabetes Mellitus," *Canadian Medical Association Journal*, 12 (1922), 141-46.

———, Best, Collip, Campbell, Fletcher, Macleod, and E.C. Noble, "The Effect Produced on Diabetes by Extracts of Pancreas," *Transactions of the Association of American Physicians*, 37 (1922), 337-47.

———, Best, Collip, Macleod, and Noble, "The Effect of Pancreatic Extract (Insulin) on Normal Rabbits," *American Journal of Physiology*, 62 (1922), 559-80.

———, Best, Collip, Macleod, and Noble, "The Effects of Insulin on Experimental Hyperglycaemia in Rabbits," *American Journal of Physiology*, 62 (1922), 559-80.

———, Best, Collip, and Macleod, "The Preparation of Pancreatic Extracts Containing Insulin," *Transactions of the Royal Society of Canada*, 16, Section V (1922), 27-29.

———, Best, Collip, Macleod, and Noble, "The Effect of Insulin on Normal Rabbits and on Rabbits Rendered Hyperglycaemic in Various Ways," *Transactions of the Royal Society of Canada*, 16, Section V (1922), 31-33.

———, Best, Collip, J. Hepburn, and Macleod, "The Effect Produced on the Respiratory Quotient by Injections of Insulin," *Transactions of the Royal Society of Canada*, 16, Section V (1922), 35-37.

———, Best, Collip, Macleod, and Noble, "The Effect of Insulin on the Percentage Amount of Fat and Glycogen in the Liver and other Organs of Diabetic Animals," *Transactions of the Royal Society of Canada*, 16, Section V (1922), 39-42.

———, Best, Collip, and Macleod, "The Effect of Insulin on the Excretion of Ketone Bodies by the Diabetic Dog," *Transactions of the Royal Society of Canada*, 16, Section V (1922), 43-44.

———, Campbell, and Fletcher, "Insulin in the Treatment of Diabetes Mellitus," *Journal of Metabolic Research*, 2 (1922), 547-604.

———, "The Value of Insulin in the Treatment of Diabetes," *Proceedings of the Institute of Medicine of Chicago*, 4 (1923), 144-57.

———, Campbell, and Fletcher, "Further Clinical Experiences with Insulin (Pancreatic Extracts) in the Treatment of Diabetes Mellitus," *British Medical Journal* (January 1923), 8-12.

———, Best, G.M. Dobbin, and J.A. Gilchrist, "Quantitative Parallelism of the Effect of Insulin in Man, Dog, and Rabbit," *American Journal of Physiology* (Proceedings of the American Physiological Society), 63 (1923), 391.

————, "Diabetes and Insulin," Opening Address to the British Medical Association, *British Medical Journal* (1923), 446.

A. McPhedran and Banting, "Insulin in the Treatment of Severe Diabetes," *International Clinics*, Series 33, 2 (1923), 1-5; *Transactions of the Association of American Physicians*, 38 (1923), 370-73, 405-10.

Banting, Best, and D.A. Scott, "Insulin in Blood," *Transactions of the Royal Society of Canada*, 17, Section V (1923), 81-85.

Gilchrist, Best, and Banting, "Observations with Insulin on Department of Soldiers' Civil Re-Establishment Diabetics," *Canadian Medical Association Journal*, 13 (1923), 565-72.

Banting, "Insulin," *Journal of the Michigan Medical Society*, 22 (1923), 113-24.

————, "The Use of Insulin in the Treatment of Diabetes Mellitus," the Nathan Lewis Hatfield Lecture, *Transactions of the College of Physicians of Philadelphia*, 45 (1923), 153-64.

————, "Insulin," *International Clinics*, Series 34, 4 (1924), 109-116.

————, "Experimental Work Upon Insulin. Its Use in Diabetes," Beaumont Lecture, in *Anti-diabetic Functions of the Pancreas*, Series II, C.V. Mosby Company, St. Louis (1924).

————, and S. Gairns, "Factors Influencing the Production of Insulin," *American Journal of Physiology*, 68 (1924), 24-27.

————, "Medical Research and the Discovery of Insulin," *Hygeia*, 2 (1924), 288-92.

————, and Best, "The Discovery and Preparation of Insulin," *University of Toronto Medical Journal*, I (1924), 24-28.

————, "Glandular Therapy: Pharmacologic Action of Insulin," *Journal of the American Medical Association*, 83 (1924), 1078.

————, "Medical Research," *Institute Quarterly*, Springfield, Ill., 15 (1924), 11-18.

————, "Insulin," *Proceedings of the International Conference on Health Problems in Tropical America*, 1924, I, 728-43.

————, "Canada's Record in Research," *Maclean's Magazine*, Nov. 15, 1924.

————, "Medical Research," *Annals of Clinical Medicine*, 3 (1925), 565-72.

————, "Diabetes and Insulin," Nobel Prize Lecture, Stockholm, 1925; *Canadian Medical Association Journal*, 16 (1926), 221-32.

————, and Gairns, "Suprarenal Insufficiency," *American Journal of Physiology*, 77 (1926), 100-13.

————, "Medical Research," *Canadian Medical Association Journal*, 16 (1926), 877-81.

————, "The History of Insulin," Cameron Prize Lecture, *Edinburgh Medical Journal*, 36 (1929), 1-18.

————and Gairns, "The Antitryptic Properties of Blood Serum," *American Journal of Physiology*, 94 (1930), 241-46.

————, Gairns, J.M. Lang, and J.R. Ross, "A Study of the Enzymes of Stools in Intestinal Intoxication," *Canadian Medical Association Journal*, 25 (1931), 393-99.

————, "With the Arctic Patrol," *Canadian Geographical Journal*, May 1930.

————, "Medical Research," *New York State Journal of Medicine*, 32 (1932), 311-15.

————, and Gairns, "Resistance to Rous Sarcoma," *Canadian Medical Association Journal*, 30 (1934), 615-19.

————, and Gairns, "Study of Serum of Chickens Resistant to Rous Sarcoma," *American Journal of Cancer*, 22 (1934), 611-14.

D.A. Irwin, Gairns, and Banting, "Study of Rous Sarcoma Tissue Grafts in Susceptible and Resistant Chickens," *American Journal of Cancer*, 22 (1934), 615-19.

Banting, "Silicosis," *Journal of the Indiana Medical Association*, 28 (1935), 9-12.

A.R. Armstrong, and Banting, "The Site of Formation of the Phosphatase of Serum," *Canadian Medical Association Journal*, 33 (1935), 243-46.

J.T. Fallon, and Banting, "The Cellular Reaction to Silica," *Canadian Medical Association Journal*, 33 (1935), 404-407.

———, and Banting, "Tissue Reaction to Sericite," *Canadian Medical Association Journal*, 33 (1935), 407-11.

G.E. Hall, G.H. Ettinger, and Banting, "Experimental Production of Coronary Thrombosis and Myocardial Failure," *Canadian Medical Association Journal*, 34 (1936), 9-15.

Banting, "Ivan Petrovitch Pavlov (1849-1936)," *American Journal of Psychiatry*, 92 (1936), 1481-84.

———, "Science and the Soviet Union," *Canadian Business*, Feb. 1936.

Ettinger, Hall, and Banting, "Effect of Repeated and Prolonged Stimulation of Vagus Nerve in Dog," *Canadian Medical Association Journal*, 35 (1936), 27-31.

Banting, "Silicosis Research," *Canadian Medical Association Journal*, 35, (1936), 289-93.

———, "Early Work on Insulin," *Science*, 85 (1937), 594-96.

———, and Hall, "Experimental Production of Myocardial and Coronary Artery Lesions," *Transactions of the Association of American Physicians*, 52, (1937), 204-209.

Manning, Hall, and Banting, "Vagus Stimulation and Production of Myocardial Damage," *Canadian Medical Association Journal*, 37 (1937), 314-18.

Banting, Hall, J.M. Janes, B. Leibel, and D.W. Lougheed, "Physiological Studies in Experimental Drowning (Preliminary Report)," *Canadian Medical Association Journal*, 39 (1938), 226-28.

———, "Resistance to Experimental Cancer," Walter Ernest Dixon Memorial Lecture, *Proceedings of the Royal Society of Medicine*, 32 (1939), 245-54.

Index